Faubus

Faubus
THE LIFE AND TIMES
OF AN AMERICAN PRODIGAL

by ROY REED

The University of Arkansas Press
Fayetteville   1997

01   00   99   98   97   5   4   3   2

Designed by Alice Gail Carter

☺ The paper used in this publication meets the
minimum requirements of the American National
Standard for Permanence of Paper for Printed
Library Materials   Z39.48-1984.

Library of Congress Cataloging-in-Publication Data
Reed, Roy, 1930–
    Faubus : the life and times of an American
prodigal / Roy Reed.
        p.   cm.
    Includes bibliographical references and index.
    ISBN 1-55728-457-1 (cloth : alk. paper). —
ISBN 1-55728-467-9 (paper : alk. paper)
        1. Faubus, Orval Eugene, 1910–   .
    2. Governors—Arkansas—Biography.
    3. Arkansas—Politics and government—1951–
    4. Segregation in education—Arkansas—Little
    Rock.   I. Title.
    F415.3.F37R43   1997
    976.7'053'092—dc21   96-53868
    [B]   CIP

For

Norma, Cindy, and John

ACKNOWLEDGMENTS

Orval Faubus and I became acquainted in the late 1950s when I first began to cover his activities as a reporter for the *Arkansas Gazette*. I started research on this book in 1988. During the next six years, he and I had seventy-seven formal interviews and numerous informal conversations. He was unfailingly civil, friendly, and, within the constraints we both understood, helpful.

My most important advisor throughout was my wife, Norma Pendleton Reed. In many ways, this is her book as well as mine. She transcribed more than two hundred tape-recorded interviews. She advised me on the writing. She helped me find lost books, documents, and scraps of paper. She accompanied me on some of my research travels. Most of all, she encouraged me, and, when she thought it necessary, she goaded.

Paula Thompson, writer, actress, director, farmer, and businesswoman, spent hundreds of hours in Mullins Library as my research assistant examining documents and microfilm.

A number of institutions provided financial help. The Fred Darragh Foundation was especially generous. The board and the staff of the Arkansas Humanities Council expressed their belief in the Faubus project through repeated annual grants. Smaller but no less appreciated grants came from the Fulbright College of Arts and Sciences, the Gannett Foundation, and the National Endowment for the Humanities.

There were a few whose help was singular. Alta Haskins Faubus and Janice Hines Wittenberg Faubus, the two wives who survived Orval Faubus and who knew him better than anyone else, spent many hours—sometimes at great emotional cost—trying to help me understand him. Faubus's sisters Bonnie Salcido and Connie Tucker and his brother Doyle Faubus were especially helpful.

Thanks to Fred Darragh not only for money at a critical time but also for hospitality and good company. Harry Ashmore, my old boss at the *Arkansas Gazette,* encouraged me early and often. Bob Douglas, another friend from the *Gazette* and the University of Arkansas, read the manuscript and made valuable suggestions. Willard Gatewood, a distinguished historian on the University faculty, read the manuscript and served as counsel and advisor in my various efforts at obtaining grants. Bill Harrison offered good advice on the organization of the book from the perspective of a novelist and screen writer. Patsy Watkins, the chair, and the rest of my colleagues on the faculty of the Department of Journalism at the University were considerate and forgiving. Don L. Stevens Jr., my friend and neighbor, kept my computer running. My son, John Reed, helped with research in the labyrinth of Arkansas's government.

Special thanks to Michael Dabrishus and his staff of patient assistants in the Special Collections Division of Mullins Library at the University. I also received generous help at three other libraries, the University of Arkansas at Little Rock, the Eisenhower Library at Abilene, Kansas, and the Reuther Library at Wayne State University, Detroit. Walter L. Brown, secretary-treasurer of the Arkansas Historical Association, and his successor, Jeannie M. Whayne, along with their assistants, provided organizational support in the arcane business of grants sponsorship and bookkeeping.

Cindy Reed Buck, my daughter, read the manuscript with the eye of the skilled editor that she is and, by correcting dozens of shortcomings, kept me from making a fool of myself in front of my old colleagues and students in the proud craft of journalism.

Ernest Dumas, whose knowledge of recent Arkansas political history is unsurpassed, provided vital information. He and his wife, Elaine, supplied room and board and good talk.

Among others who helped were Bob Besom, Diane Blair, Roy Bosson, Sam Boyce, David Chappell, Bill Cobb, Will Counts, Travis Doster, Rodney Dungan, John Egerton, Gretchen Gearhart, David W. Hacker, W. Q. Hall, Donald Harington, Peggy Harris, Bill Higgins, Kenneth Howell, Lorraine Howell, Elizabeth Jacoway, Denyse Killgore, Charlotte and Raymond Koch, Ginger Shiras, Steve Smith, Jim Turner, and Mamie Ruth Williams.

Finally, I wish to thank Debbie Self, my editor at the University of Arkansas Press. She spotted gaps in the story that needed filling and repetitions that needed removing. She also caused me to revise my estimate of my skill at punctuation.

INTRODUCTION

It is difficult for young Americans of the late twentieth century to believe that it was once against the law for blacks and whites to drink from the same water fountain, use the same restrooms, or even sit in the same waiting room at the bus station. Everywhere south of the Mason-Dixon line, except for a handful of localities, segregation was the law and, more importantly, the custom. Few whites understood the resentment that was steadily building in the black community, especially among young people. Equally ominous was the reactive resentment among southern whites when they began to see the full outline of the black revolution that threatened their position. What developed in response to the black movement was nothing less than a revival of southern nationalism. That is not to say that anyone of consequence thought of attempting secession a second time. But the political movement that erupted to fight the black advance was of a kind, emotionally, with the one that formed the Confederacy. It was nationalism in its rawest, narrowest, and potentially most murderous form.

Even now, it is impossible to guess with any assurance what would have happened if the resentments of young black southerners had not finally been addressed by the federal government. One thinks of the seemingly permanent divisions in the Balkans, the Middle East, and Northern Ireland, with their endless cycles of hatred and slaughter. As easy as it is now to speculate on such matters, in the 1950s it would have taken a rare political leader in any southern state to be able to predict the coming explosion, and an even rarer one to summon the courage to lead the Dixie nationalists in another, more accommodating direction. There were a few: Gov. James E. Folsom in Alabama, Gov. LeRoy Collins in Florida, Sen. Estes Kefauver in Tennessee—they and a few others tried to warn their fellow white southerners of the folly of continuing the resistance to common sense and decency. But the white masses still believed they could preserve their way of life, and the more unyielding of them cried for leaders to fight for them.

There were plenty to answer the call: Strom Thurmond of South Carolina, Lester Maddox of Georgia, Leander Perez of

Louisiana, Jim Johnson of Arkansas, and many others—all gifted men who understood how to stir the primitive desires and fears. Any of them would have been at home in the tumult of Ulster or the Middle East.

Then there was Orval E. Faubus.

America had progressed reluctantly toward racial equality throughout the 1940s and early 1950s. The federal courts had begun to dismantle the more blatant legal affronts. Pres. Harry S. Truman had begun the attack on segregation in the military and the workplace. America had ended World War II in a flourish of egalitarian rhetoric, and for a brief time it seemed that, despite the grudging pace, the promise of full citizenship for African Americans was on the verge of fulfillment.

Then came the reaction. Segregationist sentiment started to jell when the Supreme Court took its most sweeping action against racial inequality with its school desegregation decision, *Brown v. Board of Education,* in 1954. Segregationists immediately looked for a place to make a stand. There were skirmishes in several towns across the South. Then came Little Rock, with no appreciable recent history of racial conflict, and Governor Faubus, the least likely leader of a southern resistance.

Led by a man thought until then to be a liberal—a man who had been reared in a Socialist family—Arkansas's government opposed the burgeoning civil rights movement and its federal protectors in every way that the segregationist mind could contrive. Most dramatically, the governor called out the National Guard and blocked the entrance of nine black students to all-white Central High School. Pres. Dwight D. Eisenhower sent army troops to enforce the federal court orders, but the army could not fight on every front. Mobs were encouraged to bully black students and demonstrate for the television cameras. Law enforcement agents harassed black leaders and their white sympathizers. Laws were passed to "interpose" the state's authority between the national government and Arkansas's citizens, to reassign pupils and close schools to evade desegregation orders, to investigate and shut down lawful organizations, to expose and intimidate teachers and college professors who dared oppose the white supremacist movement.

Lawsuits by the National Association for the Advancement of Colored People challenged every obstructionist state action. But before the cases could percolate through the federal courts, the resistance ignited at Little Rock spread across the South. Violent opposition erupted in New Orleans and other cities. Pres. John F. Kennedy had to send army troops and federal agents to enroll black students at the state universities of Mississippi and Alabama. Blood was shed and lives were lost. Millions of white southerners were misled into believing that if they mounted a large enough show of defiance—a truly massive resistance—the "southern way of life" could be preserved.

Then the court decisions began to drop. Every challenge thrown up by Faubus and the segregationists in Arkansas and across the South—interposition, pupil reassignment, school closing, harassment of organizations, loyalty oaths for teachers, gubernatorial meddling with federal powers—was swept away.

The constitutional crisis provoked by Orval Faubus in 1957 was a watershed in civil rights history, not because of its success on behalf of "massive resistance" but precisely because of its failure. Faubus became not only the first bold symbol of the resistance. He also, as it turned out, set in motion the beginning of its end. The hard-line segregationists had always been suspicious of him. One went so far as to write a book suggesting that Faubus was part of a Communist plot to subvert segregation. That is a most unlikely interpretation of his motives. But whatever his intentions—honest peace keeping, cynical opportunism, bumbling demagoguery, crafty subversion, states' rights idealism—there is no doubt about the result. He forced an unenthusiastic federal administration to act, and thereby hastened the doom of the very resistance he was thrust up to lead.

Faubus himself flourished in Arkansas until 1967. He was touted as presidential material by certain right-wing enthusiasts. More significantly, he amassed enormous political power in his state, perhaps more than any other American governor except that which Huey P. Long had acquired in neighboring Louisiana a generation earlier. Until the election of Bill Clinton as president in 1992, Faubus's action in 1957 was the most important political event in Arkansas since Reconstruction.

In spite of his extraordinary notoriety, the man was never well known beyond certain superficial qualities. For example, it was not publicly revealed until years after he left the governor's office that he had been reared in a Socialist household. Long after George C. Wallace's famous conversion to integration and after his own decades-long effort to reconstruct his reputation, Faubus still was unable or unwilling to admit that he might have made a mistake in 1957.

A biographer ought to be able to say with some conviction that he has found out what makes his subject run. This biographer spent hundreds of hours listening to his subject and looking him in the eye and is forced to admit that Orval Eugene Faubus is more mysterious now than when the process began. For starters, I don't know whether his eyes were hazel or brown, and I studied them from a distance of three feet over a period of six years. It is not just that he was opaque. He appears still in my mind, even after his death, as an insoluble mixture of cynicism and compassion, of guile and grace, of wickedness and goodness. I have observed his life off and on for forty years, and I don't know whether he was good or evil, or even whether those are the choices. There was a time when I knew. But that was long ago and I was young.

One thing can be said with some certainty. He was the last proud and pleading cry of the rural voice in his state before the urbanites took over. As a country man, his attitude toward his life's vocation was from another time. He was one of the last to play politics for the pure, driven, impulsive pleasure of the game, as another might play chess or golf. The men and women who have come after him have played it with a variety of motives: for the advancement of issues and causes, for the fulfillment of some serious purpose, for the furthering of their own careers. But Orval Faubus, who was taught as a child to make his own entertainment, was one of the last Americans to perceive politics as a grand game. He was always a little surprised that other people did not understand that.

Faubus

CHAPTER 1

Snow was falling on the darkened hills. Neighbors tiptoed through the cabin, whispering. The old midwife muttered about his size, barely two and a half pounds. The doctor declared—out of the mother's hearing, we assume—"This baby will never live 'til morning." But they got him breathing, then cleaned and wrapped him and sat down to wait.

It enrages common sense to suggest that anyone there might have thought, much less uttered aloud, that this wretched infant not only would survive but would someday become known throughout the world, would be remembered among other things as probably the last public figure in America to have been born in a log cabin. These were not Kennedys. There was no fortune waiting to finance the ambitions of genius. And genius itself was not much in evidence. Of all the children, who eventually would number almost as many as their contemporaries the Kennedys, only this one would go much beyond the ordinary. No burning siblings would be watching from the wings.

On that first night, January 7, 1910, it is probable that the only one in the cabin who believed in the baby's chances with any shred of conviction was the seventeen-year-old girl. Her motherly longing and belief must have been absorbed by the child, and in a few days he had grown large enough that the girl could no longer display him like a kitten cupped in one palm. In later years, she would tell people that her newborn son could have fit into a quart jar with the lid on.

So how could he not have been afraid, not just at the beginning but on down? The claw of fear was in him as he tested the wildness of first the rocky hillside yard and then, slowly, the extending forest of Stanley Mountain and Ritchie Branch, and then the outer world that seemed enormous to a frail, quiet boy: Greasy Creek winding down to the White River, the town of Combs, the railroad disappearing into the mystery.

Much later he would come to think of nature as his friend. But in the beginning, nature was his monster. It was nature's deep spring of sweet water that he fell into when he was just old enough to say a few words, reaching to retrieve his only toy, a tin cup—and

Orval as a baby. He weighed two and
a half pounds at birth but, as Sam put it,
"growed off like a spring chicken."

somehow did not drown but clambered out in time to meet his frantic mother racing down the path.

It was nature that killed his two playmates when he was seven, one felled by diphtheria and the other by a sawn tree. He learned early that if you move slowly, the woods will crush you, and that if you attract the wrong germ, you will slowly suffocate.

For years, he feared that he would choke to death. He had the croup one night when he was a year old. His father snatched him from his bed, ran out into the cold air, and plunged a finger into his throat to clear his trachea and make him breathe again. Many years later, as an old man, he would walk a visitor through the Combs cemetery and point out the shortened grave depressions all over the yard, the tombstone inscriptions saying, "Infant of . . ." One plot had four short graves in a row bearing cousins of his, each tomb-stone labeled, "Infant of Mr. and Mrs. John E. Faubus."

Flux swept the community when Orval was a boy and killed two children in a neighboring family, a three-year-old girl and her seventeen-month-old brother. They died thirty minutes apart. "I never will forget. I went to the funeral, and you could hear men crying half a mile away as they came walking up through the field there to the cemetery where they were buried."

Death was everywhere. Farm animals died. Dogs were executed for killing sheep. Hawks were shot for killing chickens. Crippled chicks were not pampered; they were killed. His mother handed him an unfortunate chick one day and told him to get rid of it. "It was a cold day. And I cupped it in my hands, and it began to cheep, you know, like it had found a friend. And I had to take it out there and kill it."

Old people did not die in hospital rooms. They died where they stopped breathing. His grandmother Joslin died of a heart attack while she was holding Orval's baby sister Bonnie. The boy watched as his father caught the falling infant. The family's friend Will Hunt died working in a field.

> The ants were crawling over his face and in and out of his mouth. Those things make an impression on a rather timid youngster like I was. There were a lot of hardships and things that the modernists today say would cause trauma. Hell, we

never heard the word then. We got over it all right without all the counseling that you have to do now.

Then there was the fear within the boy's own dreams. For he was burdened with great pride. He saw the scorn of the neighbors when his father preached his radical opinions. The boy would do almost anything to avoid scorn or looking like a fool.

I once heard a story of a drunken stag party at a hunting camp at which he, by then the occupant of the state's highest office, by then a man of chilling gravity, deliberately made himself ridiculous by riding a donkey backward through the crowd. I do not believe that it happened, not unless, against all odds, he was so drunk that he managed for a brief hour to escape the terrible confines of his mind and become ordinary.

Even as a boy, he knew that he was not ordinary. Pride and self-knowledge set him on an early course for what was in the beginning merely escape from that place and circumstance. He could not claw his way out through brute strength, as some had done. He remained frail almost until manhood. But he also knew his advantages. He had a good mind and an extraordinary memory, so that he was able to store all that he read and heard.

He could read before he entered first grade at the Greenwood School. He had a gift for language, and he learned that language bestows power.

Through it all, the dread and fear remained. And of all the fears the boy acquired and cultivated, one was more persevering than all the others. He would eventually conquer his fear of nature's monstrosities, of illness and accident, of war, finally even of death itself. But there was one apparition that he never outran. The dreadful shadow that haunted him all his life was the fear of failure—the fear, in its everyday, ordinary form, of looking like a fool.

Orval Eugene Faubus was born in a rented log cabin on the slope of Stanley Mountain a few hundred yards above Ritchie Branch in Madison County, Arkansas. Ritchie Branch waters the Gulf of Mexico by way of Greasy Creek and the White River. The White flows impertinently north through the Arkansas Ozarks into southern Missouri, then back south across hills and delta into the Arkansas River and thence into the Mississippi and on into the world.

Where the parents got the name Orval is uncertain. There is no uncertainty about the middle name. Sam Faubus's hero was Eugene V. Debs, the Socialist leader and labor organizer who, in less than ten years, would be in federal prison for his beliefs. Sam and nine other men of the Combs community chartered their own chapter of the Socialist party in May when the baby Orval was four months old. John Samuel Faubus was twenty-two years old when he became a father and a Socialist.

The farming community of Greasy Creek, a mile and a half north of Combs, was no more prosperous than any other rural habitat of the Ozarks. The residents scraped by and felt lucky to do so. Food came from the soil, cultivated by both parents and all the children old enough to handle a hoe, and from the meat of animals, wild and domesticated. Money came from selling one's spare labor in the woods—cutting and hauling logs, barrel staves, and railroad ties. Quiet cash could be picked up in the distilling and sale of whiskey. Women and children often had a little egg money.

Combs throve. The dirt streets were always busy with wagons drawn by horses or mules. When Orval was a boy, the town had three hotels, two physicians, two blacksmith and barber shops, and enough general stores to provide a brisk competition. The Black Mountain and Eastern Railroad built tracks through the town to transport the crossties and other wood products to the manufacturing centers. There was a sawmill and its lumber yard next to the railroad. As a boy, Orval dreaded going to Combs because the steam engines frightened him.

> Think about that vast isolated region where the loudest sound you ever heard was the sound of the chopping axe and the voice. And then that big hissing steam locomotive would scare the mules to death. You had to get out and get them by the bits and hold them. So I was always afraid we'd come to the railroad the time the train was coming through, and I was always scared the mules would run away.

Nearly every family kept a milk cow, even in town. Cattle, sheep, and horses ran loose on the streets, as they do today in many of the cities and towns of Asia and Africa. One Halloween, some boys of Combs built a high pen of crossties around one man's cow. It might have been the same bunch who disassembled a farmer's wagon and put it back together on top of Barron's Store.

The dappled and improbable history of the South that has engaged scholars for generations is mainly that of the plantation country. Black and white whirled together there, tolerating and rubbing each other raw, joined like carelessly attached Siamese twins in something more than a dance and something less, usually, than mortal combat. For better and often for worse, they stole each other's manners, speech, style, music, and tastes. These became the southerners of popular romance fiction.

Up on the rim of the South beyond the fertile cotton land, an entirely different history teased itself out. The upland southerners were, except for the steadily displaced Cherokees and the other indigenous tribes, predominantly Anglo-Saxons and Celts from the British Isles. Many were Scotch-Irish, a convenient label for those Scots who had paused in Ireland for two centuries without ever becoming Irish and had then paused again, just briefly, on the Atlantic seaboard of North America before pushing into the wilderness, taking the frontier with them, living always on what Frederick Jackson Turner called the meeting place between savagery and civilization. The upland southerners evolved into something quite different from the lowlanders. These were Orval Faubus's people.

By the late sixteenth and early seventeenth centuries, the Scotch-Irish had shoved up the Shenandoah Valley of Virginia and into the piedmont of North Carolina. They crossed the Alleghanies into Kentucky and Tennessee during the time of the American Revolution. From there, they drifted south and west along the ridges and valleys, settling the higher altitudes of Georgia and Alabama, and finally—just before reaching what would become the barrier border of the Indian Territory—Arkansas.

Thousands of Scotch-Irish arrived in the Ozark Mountains of Arkansas during the middle of the nineteenth century. They huddled in the hardwood hills, isolated except for the adjacent Germans and French of the Missouri Ozarks and the Cherokees who, prodded by the Europeans, had drifted west and settled uneasily in the same Arkansas hills and hollows.

The French and Spanish had moved into the lowlands of eastern Arkansas late in the seventeenth century. The Ozark highlands were virtually innocent of Europeans until early in the nineteenth century. Fayetteville had become just a village by 1828. It was connected to the more populous eastern precincts by a single path known as the Carrollton Road. By 1829, much of eastern and central Arkansas was served by postal routes; west of Batesville, the Ozarks were untouched by this hint of civilization. Settlers followed the numerous rivers in other parts of the state. Ozark streams were as unnavigable as the wooded slopes were impenetrable. Only those Europeans who were foolhardy or desperate or hardheaded or visionary saw any reason to venture in.

There were some advantages. While the soil of the slopes was thin, that of the creek bottoms and the northwestern prairie was reasonably fertile. Wheat and corn did well there. Madison County, where the Faubuses settled, was among the top-ten corn-producing counties of Arkansas by 1860. But for cotton—that is to say, for real money—settlers chose the malarial delta, and brought slaves. Migrants into the lowlands tended to come from the lowlands of Mississippi, Alabama, Georgia, and South Carolina. The stubborn Scots sought the infertile highlands, as if enslaved by a genetic disposition against wealth.

There was another difference. The uplanders were never quite southern in the demonic sense of the word. Lacking large numbers of slaves, or indeed any neighbors who did not look like themselves except for a few Indians, their race prejudice was not the same as that of the lowlanders. On the one hand, they were largely free of the virulent fear and hatred of black people that lowlanders were capable of. On the other, they lacked the sympathy for blacks that the lowlanders were also capable of. Bereft of proximity, the uplanders had no deep feelings toward black people other than a strong and atavistic distaste for strangers.

The Faubuses were not among the first settlers in the Ozarks. Those first arrived in some numbers during the 1830s. Orval's ancestors the Thornberrys and Salyers were settled in Madison County before the Civil War—some perhaps as early as 1840—after the savage edge of the frontier had been dulled a little. They were known, in fact, as prosperous farmers. One of the Salyers became a leading merchant of the town of St. Paul after the Civil War.

The first American Faubus known to the family was one William. He spelled it Faubous. The name has had many spellings. It is believed to be derived from the Scottish Forbes. In America it has been Forbis, Forbush, Furbush, Forbus, Fawbush, Faubush, Faubous, and Faubus. Members of the family remember being addressed as Fawbush as recently as 1954.

William was a Scot who migrated to New York about 1750, without benefit of hiatus in Ireland. He fought under George Washington in the French and Indian Wars and perhaps later in the Revolution. A military size roll of 1758 or 1759 describes him as a planter living in Virginia. It says he was 5 feet 7½ inches tall, of fair complexion and red hair, and lusty (stout, robust) with good limbs. He would have been about twenty-five years old.

Orval's family records show no direct connection with William Faubous. However, Orval's great-great-great-grandfather John Faubus was born August 25, 1759, in Frederick County, in the hills of western Virginia, about the time and place that the immigrant William would have produced children.

The Faubuses were hill people from the beginning. Before the Revolution, John's family moved on down the Appalachians to Burke County, North Carolina. Family lore has it that young John fought the British in the Revolution, and that he was wounded in one eye by a bayonet at the Battle of Eutaw Springs. About 1786, he moved his family to Washington County, Tennessee, still clinging to the hills.

Further family lore says that Orval's great-great-grandfather Thomas Faubus enlisted in the War of 1812 and fought under Andrew Jackson at the Battle of New Orleans. Afterward, Thomas pursued the traditional family occupation of farming and added a new venture, distilling whiskey. Thomas's son, Ellis, Orval's great-grandfather, was born in 1827 in eastern Tennessee. The family moved again when the boy was sixteen, this time to Laurel County, Kentucky, less than fifty miles northwest of the Cumberland Gap. If the Faubuses ever owned slaves during any of their hill-country migrations, it would have been in meager numbers.

In 1868, when he was forty-one years old, Ellis made the longest family move since William's voyage from Scotland to New York. Gathering up his family, including a babe-in-arms, Ellis migrated six hundred miles from eastern Kentucky to northwestern Arkansas. The family legend is that they made most of the trip by boat and disembarked on the Arkansas River at the town of Ozark, thence overland to Madison County. By 1889, Goodspeed's *History of Northwest Arkansas* reported that he had left his original homestead, nine miles away, and was "now the owner of 200 acres of excellent land, it being in the White River Valley." It was there in the White River valley of Madison County that a core of the Faubus clan would remain, in various numbers, on through the twentieth century.

There are indications that the new country in Arkansas was not uniformly generous, even with the "excellent land." Ellis wrote to a nephew in Kentucky in July 1892. It appears that the nephew had been left in charge of selling some Kentucky land in which Ellis had an interest. "If there is any thing for me," he wrote, "I will Expect it as soon as posible to make all things rite." In the same letter, Ellis reported that crops in the White River valley were favorable in spite of a "terrible wet and backward spring" that had delayed planting. Then he added a dark note: "Times is hard in this country."

Hard times or not, the Faubuses reproduced in abundance. William Henry, the baby when Ellis brought the family from Kentucky, grew up and married Malinda Sparks. The Faubuses probably considered it a good marriage for young Henry. Malinda's mother was from the prosperous Salyer family, which owned much of the town of St. Paul. A distant relative in the Sparks family became governor of Alabama. The Sparkses also provided the northern sentiment when the Civil War was remembered; Malinda's father, Eli, had been a Union soldier.

Henry and Malinda produced seven children. The oldest, John Samuel, was born October 24, 1887, on Mill Creek a little south of Combs. Sam Faubus was destined to enter history as the father of a famous man. If history had been more logical, a little less given to luck and caprice, it might well have come about that the first Faubus to be governor of a state would have been not Orval but his father.

<table>
<tr><td>

CHAPTER

2

</td><td>

Sam Faubus could not stand dishonesty. He was not merely impatient with it; his system would not tolerate it. We are not talking about common lies, although he had no stomach for those, either. What Sam could not abide was intellectual

</td></tr>
</table>

dishonesty, corrupt thought, the fraud that cunning people perpetrate on the innocent. He spent all his adult years trying to make people see that they were being systematically deceived by greedy, powerful forces. This prejudice caused him trouble during his seventy-eight years. He earned a reputation for disputation and contrariness that went well beyond ordinary standards of rural eccentricity. Where he got his taste for going against the herd is not known. The odds are that he got it from his mother.

Malinda (Lindy) Sparks Faubus was independent, outspoken, and hard-headed. So was Sam. But in one important way, the two were different. Lindy's scruples, by some accounts, were less robust than her instinct for survival. The mild-mannered woman who eventually married Sam came to know her mother-in-law well enough to dislike her intensely. Addie Joslin Faubus told her own children, some of whom never saw their grandmother until they were half-grown, that Lindy was mean and dishonest and that she had tried to teach Sam and his siblings to be dishonest. It is true that one of her sons grew up to be a small-time thief and that another was shot to death by a neighbor with what seemed to be good reason.

For his part, Sam was honest to a fault. His register of lies, frauds, and intellectual confidence games would eventually include everything from simple country superstitions to organized religion. The world's greatest con, as he saw it, was capitalism, and he devoted considerable energy to trying to overthrow the American economic system. That his taste for radical expression put him at odds with most of the people of his time and place, including large numbers of his own family, did not bother him.

Sam and Addie Faubus at about the
time of their wedding December 24, 1908.

Lindy undoubtedly liked that in her son. She herself was unconcerned about what other people thought. She had found herself
widowed with seven children during the winter of 1900. Her husband, the son of the Kentucky migrant, had moved his family to 160
acres on Greasy Creek, north of Combs, a few days after Christmas
of 1898. Just over a year after that, he died of pneumonia. A young
widow with a house full of children could not afford either self-pity
or a long, delicate mourning. Ignoring public opinion, she quickly
found a new husband, and in so doing doubled the population of
her household.

Sam, her oldest, discovered at age thirteen that his easiest years
were behind him. The new stepfather, John Nelson, was friendly
and jovial, but not one to stand up to his domineering new wife.
The pair between them had fifteen children. The house on Greasy
Creek was filled with noise, tumult, and tension. And there was
more: Some of the young men in the family "drank a lot and fought
a lot and womanized a lot," as one relative put it.

Young Sam was never fully at ease with the arrangement. He
soon quit school and went to work. By the time he ended his formal education at age seventeen or eighteen, he had had no more
than four complete years of schooling. He confessed late in life that
he had gone to school a total of three or four months by the time
he was eleven years old, and that he did not learn to write until he
was twenty. But he learned to work.

Even the poor Ozarks had a pecking order in those days, and
the lowest place in the order was the tie hacker. The hacker used a
chopping axe and a broad axe to hew railroad crossties. Sam's main
income as a young man, and for years after he was married, was
from hewing crossties. The railroads paid thirty cents to forty cents
a tie, depending on the size.

Hundreds of men in the Madison County hills earned money as
hackers to supplement the poor living from their farms. Not much
money, though. In one typical year, after his seven children were
born, Sam's total earnings away from the farm were $360.

At age twenty-one, the journeyman hacker apparently felt that
he had enough reputation as a worker and enough promise as a
provider to justify taking a wife. Nothing is known of the courtship
beyond a few lines of poetry that he wrote years later. One poem

referred to "one of the sweetest girls in all the world." Another contained these verses:

> It was there on a beautiful night in May
> As the whippir-will called to his mate
> We left the porch and the old wooden bench
> And walked down to the gate
>
> There I took you in my arms
> And pressed you to my heart
> I held you close and kissed your lips
> And then we had to part.

It is not clear that those lines describe the girl he married. Young Sam was known as a ladies' man. His friends called him Brigham, apparently after the Mormon polygamist Brigham Young. In any event, he married Addie Joslin on Christmas Eve, 1908, at her parents' home on east Greasy Creek. The ceremony was conducted by Sam's stepfather, who was a justice of the peace. Sam on his wedding day had been old enough to vote for exactly two months. His bride was sixteen.

Addie's people, the Thornberrys and Cornetts, had been in Madison County since well before the Civil War. They had made their way west along the southern highlands in much the same way that the Faubuses had.

Addie's mother, Sarah Thornberry, married an outsider. Tom Joslin's origins were as mysterious as his fate. Tom and Sarah and their four children lived at the head of west Greasy Creek. This alien grandfather of Orval's was considered better educated than most people in the community. He kept books and read a great deal.

Then one day when Addie was four years old, and her youngest sibling was barely old enough to retain a few fleeting memories, Tom Joslin left and never came back. Some said he went into the Indian Territory to sell books, and disappeared. Whether he fell victim to foul play or simply abandoned his family was never known. Unlike Sam, who came of age surrounded by exuberant tumult, Addie and her siblings grew up in the hush of loss and uncertainty.

In more ways than their upbringing, Sam and Addie were opposites. Addie was quiet, shy, sweet-natured, and given to no strong opinions except as regarded the welfare of her family. Sam was outgoing, outspoken, and argumentative. All his opinions were strong. Crowds pleased him. He liked being with people, especially if they were inclined to argue politics or religion.

Finding time for those pastimes was a problem. Sam's farm was typical of the time and place. There were no tractors. Horses pulled the plow, the hay mower, and the rake. But hay had to be stacked in the meadow or muscled into the barn, and that required people. The corn had to be harvested and thrown into the crib by people, then shucked and shelled by human hands. Every farm had an assortment of hoes, axes, and other hand tools that had to be kept sharpened and repaired in the family blacksmith shop. When the work animals got sick, Sam became an amateur veterinarian.

He had homesteaded 160 acres on a slope above Greasy Creek in 1910. He had worked hard clearing it and turning it into a farm, so he never considered leaving the land. But many times he had to leave home to earn money. He worked temporary jobs on the railroad as a section hand. He followed the wheat harvest through the Midwest starting in June in Oklahoma and moving north through Kansas and Nebraska to Canada. He worked a couple of years in the lead mines at Pilcher, Oklahoma, doing piece work, paid by the bucket.

For all the seemingly endless labor, Sam's family found time for fun. They made their own entertainment, as did everyone else in rural America. The Faubus house was one of the liveliest in the community. There were Saturday night dances and musicals. Card games, considered Satan's work in many households, were frequent and competitive. Sam's favorite card game was pitch, a country cousin of bridge, and that was the first card game that young Orval learned.

Sam also liked outdoors fun, especially baseball and hunting. Orval was allowed to join his father in the woods when he was six or seven years old. In the winter, they hunted raccoons for their pelts, which could be sold for as much as ten dollars each. The boy learned quickly that having a good time could be strenuous and a little shocking. One night after a heavy rain, the dog treed a coon across flooded Greasy Creek. Sam chopped a tree with his axe and felled it across the creek for a footlog. Then he climbed the tree with the coon and shook it out. The dog killed it.

The boy entered into the jollity and excitement, but sometime during his growing years he felt the first twinge of doubt—and the first hint of filial rebellion. Once, during another late-night hunt, he saw the face of a raccoon as it tried to push through a hole in a hollow log to escape the baying hounds. The dogs won, as usual. Years later, he wrote that he had never forgotten the coon's desperation and its very pretty face. "After seeing its face I had the passing thought then that I would like to see it escape." One evening, Orval's eleven-year-old sister Bonnie, always soft-hearted, was being ridiculed by the rest of the family for killing a trapped and dying rabbit and then crying over it. Orval was the only one who sympathized. He told her, "That's all right, Bonnie. You had true courage."

For other entertainment, there were community gatherings such as singing schools. An itinerant singer from a neighboring town or county would hold classes in the evenings, and adults and children for miles around would attend. The teacher usually got twenty dollars for ten nights or, more often, the proceeds of a pie supper on the last festive night. Addie Faubus, normally so shy that she dreaded being seen on the streets of the county seat, opened up at the singing schools. Unlike her oldest son, she had a good voice. Her youngest son, Doyle, inherited her voice and love of music. He would become a writer and singer of ballads and earn a local reputation as a singer.

Sam learned to sing tenor, but not very well. He was somewhat better at playing the banjo and liked performing for parties and dances. Mainly, he was known as a good-humored fellow who liked any social gathering—a game of cards, a little drinking, a gathering at the country store, a chance meeting at the crossroads—any occasion that gave him an opportunity to swap ideas.

Community affairs provided one outlet for his restless mind and social impulses. He served on the school board several years. He circulated petitions to have electricity brought in by the Rural Electrification Administration during the 1940s. He supervised the census enumeration in the community.

But for Sam, no entertainment beat a good, heated argument. And of all the subjects he loved to argue, nothing topped religion.

Greenwood School on the bank of Greasy Creek was used for Sunday church services whenever a preacher was available. A few people, such as the Baptists, were numerous enough to support a

Five of the Faubus children in 1922 at the family home on Greasy Creek. From left, they are Elvin, Cressye, Connie, Orval, and Bonnie.

monthly visit by one of their own preachers. Other times a visiting clergyman from one denomination or another would drop by and preach, and word got around. Sam was reasonably ecumenical, and besides he loved a crowd, so the Faubuses turned out for many of these preachings. He went so far as to take in an occasional bout of the Holy Rollers in nearby Combs. Those services were adorned by shouting, talking in tongues, ecstatic seizures, and general delirium, all of which provided ammunition for Greasy Creek's most skeptical citizen.

Sam's father had been a strict believer. Henry Faubus's religious beliefs were so hide-bound that he would not allow his family to play cards. Sam was decidedly more intellectually adventurous. He studied the Bible and found it filled with contradictions. He concluded that a person could not believe in both the Bible and science. He told his children, for example, that a just God would not punish innocent people by drowning them in a flood.

In spite of his skepticism, he and Addie joined the Church of Christ, a fundamentalist group, and attended with some regularity. It is clear that the chief value of church attendance for Sam was the chance to visit and gather more material for provoking his friends. All the while, he followed the various national debates over religion and sided enthusiastically with the unbelievers. When Clarence Darrow defended John T. Scopes in Tennessee's "monkey" trial, Sam rooted for the evolutionists. He named his last son Darrow Doyle.

He was openly contemptuous of preachers. Many, he thought, were ignorant. He once confided to his diary, "Went to Huntsville with Arch, Ira, Sam, Ben H. and Orval. We drank several bottles of wine & peach brandy coming back. Went to church. George Glen was the preacher. He may be a good man but is very unlearned." A fifteen-verse poem that he wrote attacking conventional belief contained these lines:

> You can prate about your churches,
> Your dogmas, sects and creeds,
> You can mumble prayers and praises,
> As you count your blessed beads.
>   • • •

You cannot measure religion,
By the glory songs you sing,
Nor by pretense that you hope,
To someday spread a wing.

. . .

Joy and peace and happiness,
Can all be had right here,
A heaven you cannot have on earth,
Is not worth having anywhere.

For years, he maintained a lively correspondence with others who called themselves freethinkers and rationalists. They exchanged thoughts about books, including one titled *Why I Quit Going to Church*. He and his pen pals had little use for well-known ecclesiastical leaders, including the Pope. In one letter toward the end of his life, Sam noted that "the big Papa" had issued a statement saying the Catholic Church no longer held all Jews to be murderers for killing Jesus. "The Church keeps advancing a step at a time," he wrote, "but it is always about a century behind." In another letter to the same man, he noted the large number of new churches he had recently seen during a drive through Oklahoma. "Well," he said, "if the number of church houses had anything to do with it the people of Oklahoma should be very good. They had 15 in the little town of Tahlequah when I left there but I found a long time ago that you couldn't judge the people by the number of churches they build. Tahlequah has more gambling and bootleg joints than any town its size in the country."

If he was impatient with religion, he had no tolerance at all for traditional folk superstitions. A neighbor once asked Sam to fill one of his shoes with water to cure the neighbor's child of trench mouth. The water would be used to rinse the baby's mouth. Sam refused and told the man to use his own shoe if he believed in such.

Unlike his neighbors and even his own parents, Sam put no stock in planting by the phases of the moon or in dowsing or "witching" for water. He taught his children not to believe anything that could not be proved scientifically.

He enjoyed telling ghost stories, as did many mountain people. But he was disgusted with people who believed in spirits. If he encountered a puzzling phenomenon, he investigated. One night he heard a moan as he walked past a decaying empty house. Instead of hurrying on, and recounting later how he had heard a ghost, Sam went into the house with a flashlight. Finding nothing inside, he crawled under the floor and found a dying sheep.

Late in life, Sam summed up his feelings about humbug in an essay titled "Man." He signed it "Jimmie Higgins," one of his pen names. Noting that man is the only animal with the gift of reason, he added that man too often discards his gift and relies on superstition.

> Of all the animals on earth, man has shown himself to be the most cruel and brutal. He is the only animal that will create instruments of death for his own destruction.
>
> Man is the only animal on all the earth that has ever been known to burn its young as a sacrifice to appease the wrath of some imaginary deity. He is the only one that will build homes, towns and cities at such a cost in sacrifice and suffering, and turn around and destroy them in war.
>
> He is the only animal that will gather his fellows together in creeds, clans, and nations, line them up in companies, regiments, armies, and get glory out of their slaughter. Just because some king or politician told him to.
>
> Man is the only creature in all existence that is not satisfied with the punishment he can inflict on his fellows while here, but had to invent a hell of fire and brimstone in which to burn them after they are dead.
>
> Where he came from, or when, or how, or where he is going after death he does not know, but he hopes to live again in ease and idleness where he can worship his gods and enjoy himself, watching his fellow creatures wriggle and writhe in eternal flames down in hell.

Orval believed that his father became more respectful of religion in his advanced years, even as he remained skeptical of such dogma as the virgin birth and the resurrection. "But he came to realize that if our society is to hold together, there are certain principles which must be inculcated and which must be followed in order to have an orderly society where we could all live together."

Sam could be abrasive in an argument, and he had a temper. After some neighbor boys stole watermelons from his patch, he accosted the father of one of them. The man replied that Sam's sons had stolen a barrel of his from the woods. As the quarrel escalated, Sam struck the neighbor full in the face. The ensuing fight was one of the bloodiest ever seen in downtown Combs. The neighbor, who was larger and stronger, later complimented Sam in a backhanded way. He told him he was "a pretty good fighter for a little man."

There was no doubt about Sam's courage. He once risked being shot to face down another neighbor. He had briefly moved most of his family to Huntsville where he sold Rawleigh products as a peddler, using a wagon drawn by mules. Addie was never comfortable in the town. And the younger children, who by then were approaching their teens, suffered the indignities of being country cousins. So Sam moved his family back to Greasy Creek.

On the way home, the wagons had to follow a road that crossed a neighbor's land. The man, already upset over a squabble with someone living temporarily on Sam's place, blocked the road. One of the teamsters driving Sam's other wagon suddenly found himself attacked by an axe. The blow knocked him down. Sam ordered the neighbor out of the way. The man called to his wife to bring his shotgun, and she was about to hand it to him when Sam grabbed his own shotgun and told her, "Don't hand him that gun. If you do, I'll kill him!" At the same time, he frantically whispered to his son Elvin to hand him a shell. Only later was it learned that Sam had been bluffing with an empty gun.

Sam's social instinct was strong, but he also valued solitude. He read voraciously, even sometimes when the hoes needed sharpening or tools needed repairing. From the age of twenty, he had devoured all the books he could find. He saw to it after he married that his house had books, even when money was scarce. Orval recalled one Christmas when he was a boy. The family had come into a little extra money, so Sam and Addie ordered two books. One was H. G. Wells's *History of the World,* the other *Tarzan and the Apes* by Edgar Rice Burroughs. Young Orval especially liked Tarzan. Addie read it to the children at night. "I remember sitting there enthralled," Orval said.

Sam also liked writing and developed considerable skill at it. He became the Greasy Creek correspondent for two weekly newspapers. A taste for language was not rare among the mountain people. There were always a few who seemed to search for some hint of elegance in the rawness of their lives. Sam's poetry could not be called polished, but he took it seriously.

Sam yearned to teach. Any time he found himself with children, he began to talk about the world around them. Whether the children were his own, a neighbor's, nephews and nieces, or, later, his grandchildren, his response was automatic: Tell these youngsters about the trees, the flowers, the birds, and the animals. He loved it when little Orval, toddling at his heels in the woods, asked the name of this flower or that tree.

He did not believe in killing birds or animals except for food or income. He did kill poisonous snakes, but pointedly protected the king snake, which preyed on rodents. Orval once fought two other boys who were trying to kill a king snake.

Sam also taught the children about the larger world—the troubles in Europe, changing geographical lines, America's economic problems, social injustice. Orval thought his own interest in geography might have come from conversations with his father. "We'd be working, and I'd ask my father, 'What's Germany going to do if France does so and so?'"

Sam's impulse to teach extended to adult neighbors as well, and he frequently lost patience when they proved unresponsive. As he grew older, he gained some balance in his attitude and developed enough tolerance to remain friendly with someone he thought mistaken in his politics. He apparently learned that if he was to enjoy drinking and playing cards with his friends, he had to cut them a little slack in their retrograde opinions. But tolerance did not mean keeping his mouth shut.

Greasy Creek people did not cultivate diplomacy or "put-on." Without fumbling for euphemism, a man was quick to tell another that he was lying. "Even family members, we were so candid with each other that, looking back now, it seemed almost brutal," Orval recalled. Affection and sentiment were likewise meager. Orval's youngest sister Bonnie did not remember ever being hugged or kissed by either parent. She never doubted that her mother loved her, but she missed the affection. Sam and Addie were not alone in that regard. Hill people have always shunned public displays of emotion. Even funerals in the Ozarks tend to be less demonstrative than in other regions.

Sam, in particular, could be cool toward his family. Conversation with his children was one-sided. "He'd be telling us world problems," Bonnie recalled. "Not to lie, steal, or get into trouble in the neighborhood. Be a good citizen. Preachers were no good; all they wanted was a little money and a chicken dinner. My mother thought he worried more about world conditions than our home or us, and she was right."

Sam could be stunningly unkind. On a walk in the woods, he once became impatient with little Bonnie and yelled, "Come on, you little slut!"

Addie remonstrated with him for that. She herself had felt his insensitivity. One Christmas Eve, their wedding anniversary, he was reading in the living room. Addie came into the room and said to the children, "Do you kids know what day this is? It's the day we married." The children had never heard the anniversary mentioned. Bonnie recalled what happened next.

"She went and sat on his lap and put her arms around his neck. He never said one word nor stopped reading. Just kept moving the paper as she got into his way. I'll never forget how her face fell—the humiliation and sadness. She got up and left the room."

It became apparent that this was a one-sided romance, that Addie was the only partner in love. Sam seemed to be one of those rational persons who never succumb to romantic love. Some thought that he married not because he was in love but because he decided he ought to have a wife. More than fifty years after her mother's death, Bonnie remembered her as "very sad." Nevertheless, Addie loved him as long as she lived.

Bonnie softened her feelings toward her father in later years. She once wrote an open letter to him that was published in the *Madison County Record*. She called him a wonderful father, good-looking, and scholarly. "The books you preached for us to read seemed boring to us but now I find that *The Age of Reason* and the other books you read are highly recommended by all the great educators. No wonder you burned what you called 'trash.' At every opportunity you burned our Western stories and True Romances, which made us furious."

Sam was more romantic than his children knew. The impulse had nothing to do with women.

<table>
<tr><td>CHAPTER

3</td><td>One night during the winter of 1917–18, seven-year-old Orval was sleeping in the living room of the house high on the slope of Faubus Mountain. A sound woke him. He saw two figures, warmly dressed, going out the door with cloth</td></tr>
</table>

satchels slung over their shoulders. He recognized his father and Arch Cornett.

The men walked five miles on a dark path across Wolf Pen Mountain and some of the roughest woods in the Ozarks. They arrived at St. Paul late at night and spent the next hours hanging packets on every business and doorway in the town. The satchels the boy had seen on their backs contained Socialist leaflets and writings condemning America's participation in the First World War.

The night's expedition caused a stir in the little town and in the countryside around. For months, no one in authority knew the identity of the midnight protesters. But everyone understood that whoever it was could be in trouble. In the eyes of the government, this act of defiance violated the Alien and Sedition Act. Sam and Arch knew the risk. They had seen their national heroes pilloried by the government. But they were ready for defiance. These two had become the angriest men in their community.

How did a hillbilly tie hacker with a fragment of education and only a glimmer of contact with the outside world become a committed, dedicated Socialist? This was before television. Talk shows and instant coast-to-coast communication were far in the future. Even newspapers could be had by mail subscription only, and not many country people could afford more than their local weeklies.

Socialism's invasion of Greasy Creek is a mystery, even though it had been an accepted political phenomenon in other parts of the region from the turn of the century. Nearby Oklahoma, particularly the eastern agricultural section, was a hotbed of socialism during the first years of the 1900s. In 1912, when Eugene V. Debs got only 6 percent of the vote for president nationwide, he took 16 percent in Oklahoma. Two years later, the Socialist party's candidate for governor took 21 percent of the vote. The party elected five state representatives and a state senator in addition to numerous lesser officers at the local level.

The Oklahoma Socialists had one striking thing in common with those of Madison County, Arkansas. They were largely country people. The party in Oklahoma went against its national history and decided that an industrial base was not necessary for the advancement of socialism. The party leaders there understood a simple truth: angry farmers could be as vociferously anticapitalist as organized union workers in a factory.

In Marshall County, Oklahoma, barely eighty miles north of Dallas, Texas, farmers turned out for the Socialists in astonishing numbers. The crossroads community of Lark, where farmers were furious over falling cotton prices, price gouging from merchants, and the perceived evils of Wall Street, gave almost 68 percent of its votes to the Socialist candidate for governor in 1914.

In Arkansas, the Socialist party developed into a considerable political force during the same period. The origins of socialism in Arkansas are vague, but apparently were rooted partly in the populist discontent of rural areas during and after Reconstruction. A radical farmers' organization called the Brothers of Freedom claimed forty thousand members, mainly in northwest Arkansas, during the early 1880s. The members were mostly yeoman farmers descended from hill people who had owned few or no slaves before the Civil War. The glue that bound the organization was a fierce resentment of privilege and aristocracy. The Brothers proclaimed themselves as being for the laboring class and against capitalist oppression.

After the decline of the Populist party and its various progenitors such as the Agricultural Wheel (with which the Brothers of Freedom merged in 1885), some of the still-discontented farmers of the Arkansas hills began to look sympathetically toward the Socialist party. Socialism had already made inroads among the coal miners of western Arkansas and trade unionists in the Little Rock area.

The Socialists during this period enjoyed a measure of respectability that might be puzzling to later generations of Americans who witnessed the Cold War and who developed an apprehensive distaste for any form of political collectivism. During the early years of the twentieth century, the party published 14 periodicals in Arkansas. The party local that Sam Faubus served as secretary was one of 121 that were active in the state in 1910. National leaders like Debs and Mother Jones visited Arkansas regularly and touched the lives of thousands of people. By the election of 1912, the party was strong enough in the American Southwest that Debs received eighty thousand votes in just four states—Oklahoma, Texas, Louisiana, and Arkansas.

Just how radical the rural Socialists were is debatable. They certainly were more radical than the Populists who preceded them. The Populists, angry as they were at Wall Street, the bankers, and the merchants, were not essentially anticapitalist. They took the view that, with a little luck and a level playing field, they could prosper as mightily as their more fortunate neighbors. The Socialists, on the other hand, believed that the basic system had to be changed to put the means of production in the hands of "the people." But, while clearly more radical than the Populists, the country Socialists of the Southwest were not preponderantly the doctrinaire Marxists found in the Northeast. They were not by and large revolutionary zealots. They were more likely to exhibit the zeal of the natural optimist, or, as George Gregory Kiser put it, they were "naive in their dream of a world in which economic inequality had no place."

Kiser's description might have been written personally about Sam Faubus. His approach was that of the vocal protester. He wrote letters to the editor—angry, impassioned letters. He preached the gospel in public debates, a favorite entertainment in the Ozarks. He once told Orval, "If you could get 51 per cent of the people educated, Socialism would be accepted."

Sam was not content to speak and write. He circulated petitions calling for such Socialist-backed proposals as woman suffrage, old-age pensions, and abolition of the poll tax. After the economic collapse during the Hoover administration (the only vote Sam ever regretted was the one he cast for Herbert Hoover for president in 1928), Sam was so agitated over the condition of the nation's farmers that he rode a freight train to Chicago, in a blizzard, to attend a conference called to address farmers' problems.

Sam's children could not be sure how their father became a Socialist. He had told them of his first awareness of politics. His maternal grandfather, Eli Sparks, the old Union soldier, had talked to the boy about public affairs. Grandfather Sparks was also a kind of dissident; like many mountain people, he was a Republican. His party held its own in the Ozarks, but in the larger region political affairs were dominated by Democrats. When Sam and his friends started a local chapter of the Socialist party, one of the charter members was his grandfather Sparks.

Sam's family had always known of his reputation as a "well-posted man." Somehow he developed a taste for left-wing publications. He brought them into the house from the early days of his marriage. He subscribed to the leftist *Guardian* published by the E. Haldeman-Julius Company and saw to it that the publication was mailed to several other families in the community. He read the periodical *Appeal to Reason* published by the same company. E. Haldeman-Julius also published the inexpensive Little Blue Books, some of them condensed versions of the classics, others works of left-wing authors. The *E. Haldeman-Julius Weekly* magazine was a fixture in the Faubus house.

For a while he subscribed to the *Daily Worker,* the newspaper of the American Communist party. Unlike many Socialists of the time, he was not rigidly opposed to communism; he thought it was not all that bad. In later life, though, he was offended by what he saw as its extremism.

The only conventional daily newspaper that Sam subscribed to when Orval was a boy was the Oklahoma City *Daily Oklahoman.* The *Oklahoman* in later years became one of the more conservative organs in the Southwest. For much of his life, Sam was a devoted reader of the *Arkansas Gazette,* the state's newspaper of record and, in its last generation, a pillar of liberal opinion. Through the years, he also read the *New York Times* with some regularity.

Orval believed that Sam began to get literature on the Socialist party through the mail soon after he and Addie were married. He apparently was persuaded by the party's arguments that big corporations controlled the American economy and that people like himself had little power.

There is a strong likelihood that Sam's socialism was imported from the North. Sometime around the turn of the century, a middle-aged bachelor named O. T. Green moved into the community. He was believed to be from Illinois. He was known as a Socialist. Green lived for a time in Mrs. Ida Bevins Brashears's boardinghouse at Combs. He was a gentlemanly, educated sort, but his political views caused embarrassing political arguments from time to time. After a while, he moved to a small farm at Greasy Creek and raised goats and peacocks. He maintained contact with his Socialist comrades beyond Madison County. He became a friend of Sam Faubus and found the young man to be interested not only in politics but also in poetry and language. Green was fond of the poetry of James Whitcomb Riley and Edgar Allan Poe and often recited it for young people willing to listen. Sam was a good listener. There seems little doubt that he developed a taste for more than poetry from his friend. The older man was a frequent visitor in the Faubus household during Orval's boyhood.

When Green grew old and sick, Sam looked in on him. "It sure is hell to be old, sick and homeless under this system," he wrote in his diary after one visit. "I sometime think it would be better to have the Russians system." His mentor died three weeks later, and Sam helped dig his grave. He noted in his diary that a community leader had preached his funeral. "O.T. didn't believe in superstition but he has spent the most of his life trying to make this a better place in which to live."

One of the party's more effective organizers and public speakers in Arkansas was J. C. Thompson of Little Rock. He traveled the state well into the 1930s whipping up support among farmers and others who were gripped by hard times.

Orval's father took him to hear Thompson when the organizer was trying to rebuild the Socialist party after World War I. Years later, Orval remembered the speaker's message: Now, you raise potatoes and you raise corn, and you trap fur from the forest, and you cut timber from your land and you haul it in and you sell—whose price do you take? You take their price. All right, you go to buy some food, some flour, some salt, some sugar, some cloth, some shoes, clothing for your family—whose price do you pay? Their price. Now, he said, under that kind of a system, there's not a thing in the world to keep them from skinning you alive except the conscience. And a corporation doesn't have a conscience.

Thompson and the Socialists described Sam's condition perfectly, as Sam saw it. The teens and twenties were rough years on Greasy Creek. Now and then a lucky farmer would supplement his cash income from crossties with a few days' work on the railroad, repairing track. Sam had a friend who had the enviable job of conductor for one of the railroads. Just before his retirement, the company found a technicality that permitted it to fire him, so he never drew a pension. Two or three relatives of Sam's were railroad workers, and they were fiercely pro-union. They had to fight a primitive mentality in the companies. For example, when a small motor was invented to run the handcars that the workers rode to their repair jobs on the tracks, the workers had to buy the motors. The company deducted the cost from their paychecks.

Sam's economic theories came not just from his reading. His own family, as he saw it, was a victim of the monster of capitalism. Every spring, the food harvested the preceding fall began to run out. First the meat was gone from the smokehouse, then the potatoes were all eaten, then the jars of canned vegetables were emptied.

One late spring day, young Orval shot a squirrel to put a little meat on the table. But the family dogs, themselves thin from hunger, pounced on the creature and ran into the woods to eat it. Orval realized for the first time that the dogs were almost starving. His reaction was embarrassment that the family had not provided food for them.

Sam saw things differently. He understood from his reading and thinking that the family's poverty was part of a larger problem. People would not have been hungry if they had had dependable income. Selling hardwood a wagonload at a time was not a satisfactory solution. And the hardwood was running out.

Even in the rural fastnesses, anticorporation resentment began to build during the years after the turn of the century. At Greasy Creek, Sam Faubus and his friend Arch Cornett, a teacher and a relative of Addie's, signed up large numbers of their neighbors as members of the Socialist local. The charter from the state committee identifies the group as the Mill Creek Local and is addressed to "the comrades of Combs." It is dated May 1910 and carries the names of ten men, four of them named Faubus. All the names were written on the charter by the same hand. The second name, after that of one J. H. Ford, is S. J. Faubus—almost certainly a mistaken copying of J. S. (Sam) Faubus. The post of secretary, carrying with it the responsibility of chief organizer, went to Sam.

Sam and Addie reared their seven children in this house a few yards above Greasy Creek in Madison County, Arkansas.

Another on the list was elderly James Simmons, who had been Sam's teacher at Greenwood School. Sam went to Simmons as a young man when he needed advice or help solving mathematics problems. Another charter member was Arch Brandenburg, the husband of Arch Cornett's sister. He was a rough, whiskey-drinking, hard-working man who, years later, accompanied Sam and Orval to the Pacific Northwest to work in the timber.

Three years later, Sam persuaded his wife to join the party. A Socialist card dated October 1913 from Greenwood (Greasy Creek), Arkansas, is made out to Addie Faubus. In those days, a wife did whatever her husband wanted in such matters.

As many as thirty people, including some from neighboring communities, might have been members of the Mill Creek Local at one time. The party had a majority of the residents of Greasy Creek. Madison County had at least two other thriving Socialist locals, one at Witter fifteen miles south of Huntsville and the other at Kingston in the eastern part of the county. Both enrolled considerable memberships.

Altogether, the Socialist party members and their extended families were numerous enough to constitute an important swing vote between the Democrats and Republicans in local and county elections. The election of 1912 demonstrated the Socialist influence. In 1908, Madison County had divided its presidential vote pretty much as usual: 1,441 for the Democrats, 1,541 for the Republicans, and 83 for the catch-all category of "Other." Then came the Socialist surge during the next few years. In 1912, the Democrats got only 932 votes and the Republicans only 786. Support for "Other" ballooned to 309. It is a fair guess that most of those votes for "Other" were cast for the Socialist Debs, thanks to the impact of Sam Faubus and his friends.

A map of Socialist party locals in 1910 shows that they were numerous all across Arkansas, especially in the western counties. The Ozarks boasted chapters at Sulphur Springs, Garfield, Eureka Springs, Berryville, Harrison, Decatur, Rogers, Fayetteville, Winslow, Flippin, Yellville, St. Joe, Leslie, Hardy, Mulberry, Ozark, Van Buren, Clarksville, and Atkins.

The success of socialism at Greasy Creek was without doubt due to the persuasiveness of Sam Faubus and Arch Cornett. Cornett, who never married, shared Sam's love of the language. He wrote lengthy essays on socialism for the *Madison County Record*. A two-and-a-half-column article of March 16, 1933, argued with an eloquence that might have been seen in a learned Eastern journal.

"The great propounders of democracy," Cornett wrote, "have learned that socialism is the only true democracy and that our boasted freedom is a farce so long as the mines, mills, shops, store-houses, transportation lines, steam ship lines, electric light and water systems, etc., are owned by the few for the enrichment and private profit of the few, and for the unemployment, poverty, and degradation of the many."

Sam's letters to the editor tended to be shorter and blunter. In a typical comment, after Franklin D. Roosevelt became president, Sam wrote, "This country is owned and controlled by a few bankers and other capitalists and the quicker Mr. Roosevelt takes over all industry the better it will be for the country." He signed it "Jimmie Higgins." That was a common nom de plume for Socialists and one that Sam used most of his life to sign letters to the editor and other writings. A Jimmie Higgins was a party member willing to do the menial work, one who would sweep the floors and hand out leaflets.

The platform of the Arkansas Socialist party contained the usual polemics against capitalism. But it also carried a number of reform ideas that in time would be considered middle-of-the-road. Socialists opposed the death penalty and corruption in elections. They favored the initiative and referendum, woman suffrage, and the graduated income tax. The Arkansas party attracted considerable public sympathy. In 1910, some two thousand people turned out for a Socialist rally in Fort Smith to hear Debs speak.

But socialism, for all the exertions of the Sam Faubuses and Jimmie Higginses, did not enjoy much influence beyond the early years of the century. Its undoing came just before and during World War I and coincided with a period of national prosperity, zealous persecution of antiwar activities, and a series of byzantine party squabbles.

Internal party friction had already taken a toll before the United States intervened in the war. Some of the more radical believers had split and gone with the Industrial Workers of the World. The Socialists had been in a continuing debate over admitting Negroes as members, with a majority resisting the idea. In spite of the claims of some that the party in Arkansas was integrated, especially among the tenant farmers of eastern Arkansas, there is evidence that it remained lily-white and that that caused resentment. Some University of Arkansas people and their intellectual friends had established a chapter of Fabian Socialists at Fayetteville in 1909. Those idealists were most likely seen as dilettantes by the coal miners and farmers of the party's mainstream. Many religious leaders who had been attracted to socialism became alarmed at a growing strain of atheism (Sam, while perhaps not an atheist, could certainly be called an agnostic), so that what might have been a natural alliance of church people and Socialists disintegrated.

Then came the war and the Red-baiting that erupted with it. Inflamed by what passed for patriotism, the nation plunged into a spasm of intolerance. Socialists, many of them outspoken pacifists, were a ready target for opportunist prosecutors and bellicose supporters of U.S. intervention in the war. Even so strong a politician as Sen. James K. Vardaman, the Mississippi white supremacist, was hounded into political impotence because he dared speak against intervention.

In Arkansas and Oklahoma, there were several cases of "patriots" acting against people suspected of being less than enthusiastic in support of the war effort. The president of the World Peace League went to Elk City, Oklahoma, in the spring of 1918 and had the bad judgment to criticize the Liberty Loan scheme to a group of friendly Socialists. Non-Socialists heard of it and tarred and feathered him. Liberty Bond vigilantes physically intimidated nonsubscribers at Collinsville, Oklahoma. That state saw scores, perhaps hundreds, of such acts of terrorism.

Similar outrages occurred in Arkansas. In West Helena, a person who had uttered derogatory remarks about the government was publicly flogged. A Fort Smith man was charged with espionage after speaking disrespectfully of the army and the president. An umbrella peddler was whipped, tarred, and feathered in Malvern for "disloyal" utterances. In Springdale, a man of German ancestry saw his home raided by a mob led by the city marshal. They confiscated pictures of German leaders and replaced them with pictures of Pres. Woodrow Wilson. A one-armed farmer at Paragould, known to be "peculiar," was fined for disloyal remarks. A Corning man was rescued from a lynch mob, only to be charged with abusing the government. And at Hot Springs, just weeks before the end of the war, a farmer was murdered for his pro-German sympathies.

Around the nation, the war fever occasionally became ludicrous. A newspaper item on May 31, 1918, read as follows: "Sauer kraut may be eaten without disloyalty. The Food Administration today said that the dish is of Dutch rather than German origin."

Increasingly, the Socialist party became a target of official and unofficial enforcers in the Southwest and across the nation. Federal agents raided the party headquarters in Chicago. Victor Berger, the Milwaukee Socialist, was elected to Congress but denied his seat. He and other party leaders were indicted under the Espionage Act for interfering with the war effort. Debs himself finally faced charges of sedition. In September 1918, after deliberately provoking arrest with a critical speech at Canton, Ohio, the party's perennial candidate for president was tried and sentenced to ten years in federal prison. He ran his 1920 presidential campaign from his prison cell. Sam Faubus got a button saying, "Vote for Convict Number 9653 for President."

Arkansas Socialists began to be harassed more severely during the winter of 1917–18. Party members who opposed the war were arrested in Hoxie and Bauxite. One John Beston, described in print as a "rank Socialist," was arrested on a charge of espionage at Fort Smith during the summer of 1918.

When the "seditious" literature appeared in St. Paul, the weekly newspaper there, the *Mountain Air*, ran a story about the anonymous pamphleteers and their exploit. Sam and Arch chuckled when they read it. But, as Orval said when he told the story for the first time seventy-six years later, their stunt had been "marvelously naive." On September 20—just six weeks before the armistice—the two men were arrested.

The *Arkansas Gazette* reported the arrests on an inside page.

> HUNTSVILLE, SEPT. 20.—Arch Cornett and Sam Faubus of Combs have been arrested by a government agent on a charge of distributing seditious literature and uttering numerous disloyal remarks concerning the conduct of the war. Cornett was a teacher in the public schools and is said

to have refused to support any patriotic undertaking. Under the guise of internationalism he openly attacked his own country, it is charged. Faubus was long the Socialist party leader in Madison County and is alleged to have championed the cause of the I.W.W. and the anarchist elements in his party.

There is some evidence that Sam had joined the Industrial Workers of the World, the radical "Wobblies." Bonnie Faubus Salcido, Sam's youngest daughter, remembered that, some years after World War I, he carried an I.W.W. card. Whether he was a member or not, some in the community believed that he was, and that did his reputation no good. "That was about the same as being a horse thief back then," said Carl Vanlandingham of Pinnacle, a pupil of Orval's who also knew Sam.

Sam undoubtedly was attracted to the satisfying notion that the working people should simply rise up and seize the railways, mines, and mills, as the I.W.W. advocated. His brother-in-law Jess Johnson, who married Addie's sister Minnie, was rumored to have joined the Wobblies while working as a lumberback in the West. There was speculation that two of Jess's brothers, Tom and Anderson Johnson, also came under the influence of the dreaded I.W.W. during their time in the log woods of the Northwest. Sam worked alongside them, and he still leaned left in his politics during those years. During one stay in Washington State, he wrote an angry letter to the editor of the *Wenatchie Daily World* denouncing a Republican leader for "trying to start a campaign of red-baiting."

Sam probably had not wanted his protest to go so far as arrest. He had registered for the draft and was deferred because he had dependents. He probably would have gone if his deferment had expired and he had been called. Orval, who became a postmaster after the next world war, speculated that government agents found the midnight visitors to St. Paul by tracing the delivery of Socialist literature from one of the local post offices. Sam and Arch had innocently assumed that the U.S. mail protected a citizen's privacy.

Somehow, Sam arranged for the right legal representation. His lawyer was Claude Fuller, one of the most prominent in the Ozarks, a member of the political establishment, later a congressman. With Fuller running interference, Sam made a couple of court appearances during which he made no attempt to deny distributing antiwar literature. Then, before any action was taken, the war ended, and the charges against both men were quietly forgotten. No doubt, Fuller's influence had something to do with that.

By 1920, socialism was effectively finished as a mass movement in the United States. But along Greasy Creek, near the remote headwaters of the White River, the party did not die without a fight. Sam and Arch and their friends went on studying, pushing literature into receptive hands, writing letters to publications and to like-minded freethinkers around the United States, and, above all, talking. Sam took every opportunity to promote socialism in public once the war hysteria had subsided. On at least one occasion, he had the help of his eldest son.

A favorite entertainment among Ozark mountaineers was debating, and southern Madison County had a lively debating group during the early years of the century. Like the baseball teams, the local debating groups traveled to neighboring communities for competition. The St. Paul School caused a small stir sometime in the fall of 1932 with a debate on socialism versus the two major political parties. Speaking for the major parties would be two teachers. Speaking for the Socialists would be Sam Faubus and his twenty-two-year-old son Orval.

Curtis R. Swaim, one of the teachers—a conservative Republican who would become Orval's friend and political associate years later—described the scene toward the end of his life: "The people had been stirred up a few weeks before the debate by a Socialist leader [probably J. C. Thompson] who had come to the community and had lambasted the two old parties unmercifully—much to the delight of Sam Faubus (and to be honest about it, the Socialist speaker pleased a lot more people than just a few). The prospect of the backwoodsman and his son taking on two local teachers added to the interest present in the up-coming debate."

Sam had prepared by asking for help from an acquaintance at Commonwealth College. Sam Sandberg was a student there and state secretary of the Socialist party. In a letter with the salutation, "Dear Comrade," Sam instructed Sandberg, "Paint capitalism as black as hell and make the socialist system look like a flowery bed of ease for me if you can." He added in a postscript, "Send all the information on Russia that you can."

People came from miles around. The schoolhouse was over-flowing. Swaim and the other teacher, Clyde Mix, knew better than to take the debate for granted. Sam was a poorly educated farmer, but he was known to be articulate and well read. Young Orval, shy as he was, had even in the early grades recited long poems in front of audiences, and he had won at least one interschool declamation contest.

Recalling the debate a generation later, Swaim said that the Faubuses bore down on the greed of the major parties and the power-lessness of the public. Land was falling into the hands of the wealthy few. Men were jobless, and homes were being lost through mort-gage foreclosures. People were standing in bread lines. They avoided mentioning the linchpin of socialism, nationalization of industry and business, but it was known in the community that they believed in that.

The Socialist party never regained its earlier strength during the years between the world wars, in spite of the exertions of Sam and people like him. The Greasy Creek chapter finally faded into history. Sam remained a committed Socialist, however, until Orval was grown and had embarked on his own political career.

In the early 1930s, Sam Faubus made one more effort to revive the local in the Combs area. His friend J. C. Thompson was trav-eling from village to village speaking on socialism, lodging with friends in the party, supporting himself from the meager contribu-tions at meetings and from the sale of literature. He spoke at Combs on a spring night in 1932, and that same day the Greasy Creek chapter was reorganized. During that same season, the traveler made his way to Commonwealth College where a group calling them-selves Militant Socialists had obtained a charter from the national party. Thompson and the Commoners joined forces and resolved to turn the depression into an opportunity for converting the jobless into Socialists. They called a state convention on the shore of Lake Hamilton near Hot Springs. For two days, they thrashed out orga-nizational problems and platform planks and at the end announced that a slate of candidates including one for governor would be fielded in that year's election. Two months later, the Mill Creek Local had been joined by twenty others around the state.

Not much came of it all. Clay Fulks, the gubernatorial candidate, ran poorly. Only a few hundred active members resulted from all the effort statewide. Thompson made several other appearances around Madison County, but only ten members joined Sam's revived local. It was eventually disbanded.

Impressed by the New Deal's depression-fighting efforts, many who might have joined the Socialists became Democrats. Sam himself finally became a New Dealer, but not before getting in a few tough punches. Six weeks into the Roosevelt administration (Sam, like many in the out-country, pronounced it Ruesevelt), he was railing against it in his Combs column of the *Record*. "Well," he wrote, "Roosevelt began his 'new deal' by closing all the banks in the United States. Eggs went down to five cents here and chickens to two cents a pound, the lowest that has ever been known here. Mr. Roosevelt may save the bankers and keep us on the 'gold standard' but us farmers and wage workers will catch hell while he is doing it."

As late as 1941, Sam still showed an interest in left-wing politics. He noted in his diary that he had just received a copy of *The Soviet Power* by Hewlett Johnson, the "red" dean of Canterbury. Six weeks later, Germany invaded the Soviet Union, and Sam hoped that meant the beginning of the war that would end the capitalist system.

The fervor that colored Sam's politics seemed to be more than idealism. He was driven by some outsized passion that came from his grandmother Lindy or his friend O. T. Green or some source he probably could not have named. Whatever its origins, it gave him a reputation for impracticality in his everyday life. An ordinary farmer sharpened hoes or mended harness on rainy days. Sam sat in the house and read. Feeding his brain—and his anger—was more important than weeding the crops.

Only a man whose idealism, passion, and anger had overwhelmed his sense of the practical would sow Marxism on the stony ground of Madison County. Only a man with more fight than judgment would risk imprisonment for opposing a war that a disproportionate majority supported in a blind and dangerous flood of patriotism.

Orval would say later that his father's politics had not seemed to hurt Sam's relations with those in the community who did not agree with him. Others disputed that assessment. Some of his neighbors, convinced that he was a "Wobbly," whispered about his politics behind his back. Orval, in his first political race, encountered hostility that could easily be traced to his father's radical reputation.

Sam, like his mother, was stubbornly unconcerned with what the neighbors thought. He wore his intellectual defiance like a private flag, emblem of a one-man nation. He had appendicitis in 1928, a period when that affliction was a threat to life. They rushed him to the hospital for the dangerous operation. The last words he uttered to his wife and the bedside attendants as the ether took hold and his mind wandered toward oblivion were, "Some of them recanted, but I didn't."

CHAPTER 4

Orval told a pen pal about his dog Mack, a cur he had bought for forty-five cents and converted from a sorry lay-about to a useful, loyal friend. The pen pal, without Orval's knowledge, sent the story to a boys' magazine. The story was published, and Orval got a check for one dollar.

His parents praised him extravagantly. Sam speculated that his son might one day become a successful writer. He was shocked to hear the boy erupt in anger. Examining his reaction many years later, Orval said that he had never been able to accept praise from his family when he was a boy and that, for some reason, his father's attitude about the dog story had angered him. "He seemed to infer too much," he said.

Unlike his gregarious father, Orval disliked sharing himself even as a boy. He resented intrusion into his private thoughts and yearnings. A protective dignity was already forming around his soul, like shell around a mussel.

The boy became a bookworm, further feeding his sense of privacy and self-absorption. He especially liked the western fiction of Zane Grey. But he also developed a taste for history. An old neighbor, a foreigner, gave the boy a book of Greek history and mythology. He became interested in Alexander the Great and other famous figures of the past. In time, he was reading history books the way other boys read westerns.

The Faubus family in 1932, left to right:
Cressye, Addie, Bonnie, Sam, June, Elvin,
Doyle, Connie, and Orval.

His interest in books probably sprang from his physical frailty. His sinuses troubled him, costing him energy and making him appear to be lazy. He had to push himself to get things done. He forced himself to walk the round of the neighbors' houses to sell Cloverine salve. Most of the children in the area did the same thing, so the market was quickly saturated. Being rebuffed on a sale hurt, but he learned to hide it.

The boy's pride was tested frequently. He was smaller and weaker than the other boys, and they put him through the usual indignities: dunking him at the swimming hole, rubbing sand in his hair. Ninety percent of them could lick him. He took it quietly, absorbing the pain. He also learned to stay in the creek eddies, out of the mainstream where the bullies played.

He was not a loner shrinking from competition. What he learned to do, perhaps by instinct, was to seek the competition where his slight build (his wrists, even as a man, were not much larger than a woman's) was no obstacle. For example, he was fast on his feet, and in the school-ground games of wolf and sheep he was often the last child to be caught. The same quickness and agility made him at least an average basketball player, and he enjoyed the game.

The other boys nicknamed him "Sourbush," a play on the family name, which at that time was commonly pronounced "Fawbush." But if they ever considered him a sissy, they kept it to themselves. Sissies did not work in the timber and the fields, and sissies did not hunt game.

He learned to avoid physical confrontation as he grew older. After the minor scrapes of boyhood, he was twenty or twenty-one before he had his first serious fisticuffs. That was over a dispute during a basketball game. He and a fellow from Combs had to be separated by the other players after Orval took up for his brother Elvin in a spat.

Unlike Elvin and many other young men in the community, Orval had little interest in cars or mechanics. His strong suit, finally, was the mind. He could read before he started to school. He could read a three-stanza poem twice and commit it to memory. He absorbed books and magazines as enthusiastically as his father. He became a model student from the earliest years. His first teacher was his aunt Minnie, and under her prompting he completed the first three grades during his first year at Greenwood School. Somehow, he failed to learn handwriting. He taught it to himself later, but all his life his handwriting was awkward.

Beyond his mental ability, the boy had a talent for getting along with people in authority. He seldom caused trouble or earned a teacher's punishment. In fact, he seemed to be rule-bound—a trait probably inherited from Addie, who, unlike Sam, feared breaking the rules and being talked about by the neighbors. Whatever the source, he seemed to understand early that observing the rules protected a person from making a fool of himself.

Orval grew up with much of Sam's intellectual curiosity, but oddly enough he was never as close to his father as one of his younger brothers. Elvin had no taste for academics; he dropped out before graduating from high school. He was not interested in history, geography, politics, or other matters that engaged Orval from early years. But somehow Sam was more relaxed with his second son. They could talk about drinking with the boys as they labored together in the woods. Elvin developed a spiritual kinship with his father that Orval perhaps envied.

Sam might also have admired Elvin's macho attitude. Elvin was known as a ladies' man and, perhaps to the chagrin of his shy older brother, always seemed to have a pretty girl on his arm at the neighborhood dances. Orval was not lucky with girls. He was once sweet on a certain girl for a long time and never had the nerve to ask her out.

Sam and his oldest son developed a kind of intellectual rivalry as the youth grew toward manhood. As the boy formed his own opinions, he tested them frequently against his father's. Tempers flared sometimes. The dinner table finally became such an argumentative battleground that the older girls refused to sit with them. One day, during an argument over politics or religion, Sam got so angry that he threw a jar of jelly at Orval. The youth ducked, and the jar splattered against the wall. During their arguments, Orval slowly and instinctively found that the most effective rebuttal of extremism was moderation. He agreed with Sam's main themes. But by the time he was grown, he increasingly argued for a flexible, middle-of-the-road course, to his father's consternation.

Orval's closest sibling, and probably his favorite, was his sister

Connie, who was less than two years younger than he. He gathered flowers and roamed the meadows and woods with her. He did not want to go to first grade without Connie, so they let her tag along for a few days. Once a few years later, both Faubus children were disciplined on the same day for a minor infraction of the teacher's rules—laughing out loud or some such. They knew they would be scolded when they got home. On the somber walk to the house, Orval finally said, "I won't tell if you won't."

It is painful to consider the tension that must have been growing inside the youngster during the years after he started to school. On the one hand, he was being pushed by his parents, his teachers, and his own pride and sense of self-worth to enter the larger world of educated, cultivated people, a world that he saw, even at a tender age, as one of possibilities and rewards. On the other hand, the boy was so burdened with shyness that he was reluctant to take any step that would jeopardize his fragile dignity. The word shy has been devalued in the age of psychology. But when Orval Faubus was a boy, it still had a definite meaning, and it was not applied lightly. No coyness was intended when people said that young Orval was shy. His contemporary Richard M. Nixon, growing up half a continent away in somewhat similar circumstances, would one day be scrutinized for the origins of his single-minded ambition, and some would suggest that he owed it to his sense of insecurity. Orval Faubus grew up with the same burden.

It took his parents a while to understand the depth of the problem. When he was seven, they sent him to school two miles away in Combs. The family finally realized that something was wrong. His aunt Minnie, Addie's still-single sister who lived with them, walked him to school each day and noticed that the boy trailed behind, lifeless, uninterested even in the flowers beside the path. His grandmother Sarah Thornberry Joslin, who earned money working as a domestic at the Meadors Hotel in Combs, bought him a new pair of shoes to lift his spirits. Nothing helped. They finally understood that he could not bear the strangeness of the town school, and let him quit.

> It's hard for anybody to imagine nowadays with all our
> communication and association how shy country boys and

Orval and his sister Connie, the sibling to whom he was closest in age and affection.

girls could be, who are raised in isolated areas like that. I was so bashful I'd go off behind the house to keep from being introduced when a stranger would come.

Even at eighteen, when he first went away to civil military camp in Kansas, he suffered miserably from homesickness and discomfort among strangers. But he had come to understand by then that at least one thing was worse than the fear of strangers. "I knew if I came back home, they'd all make fun of me and laugh at me. So I just bowed my neck, as the saying goes, and toughed it out."

Hill people have habitually felt that they might be inferior to outsiders. Orval suspected that he had an additional source of shyness, a genetic one inherited from his mother. Addie's face became a mask when she had to walk to the store in Huntsville.

Orval slowly overcame the handicap, and along the way he began to develop an authority that might have seemed unusual in one so young. For example, he gradually took over the task of disciplining the younger children. Earlier, the parents had shared that job. Sam was the one they feared if a serious breach had been committed, although he apparently enforced discipline more with the threat of whipping than with actual punishment. Addie kept a peach-tree limb handy and would offer an occasional swat.

Then Orval inherited the responsibility. "I got to be the boss in the family. My younger sisters and brothers, in later years, one of them would be doing something they didn't think he should, they'd say, 'I'll tell Orval on you.'" He was not sure how he developed this authority except that he had "some very definite ideas about conduct."

As a disciplinarian, Orval set rules for the others and expected them to be followed. The younger siblings alternated between staying out of his path and yearning for his approval. He had discovered that an adult's approval was more effective than a switch. Almost a lifetime later, his sister Bonnie remembered the feeling. "If he looked at me with disgust, I was killed."

Orval worked to make his own spending money from age fourteen. He not only bought his own clothes but also helped his father, who was continuously in debt. Sam once borrowed money from an elderly man in the neighborhood and was unable to repay it. Orval helped pay the debt. Financially, Sam always lived on the verge of disaster. Old Dr. Ellis of Combs operated on Addie to remove a tumor. Sam offered him a mortgage on the farm until he could pay the bill; the physician refused it.

During one period as a youngster, Orval thought it would be wonderful if he did not have to work. Then after his first year of high school, he had nothing to do for two months. "And I'd get up and go downtown and fool around, go back home, get bored, go back to town again. That was the most miserable period I believe in my life." He finally went to work cutting wood for an old man for one dollar a day until school started.

His siblings learned early that their older brother was different from them. The thing that separated him was an uncommon seriousness. He was determined to amount to something. While the others listened to music, danced, and read lightweight magazines, Orval studied. Sam encouraged his children to read Tom Paine's *The Age of Reason*. Orval was the only one who showed any interest. Before he was grown, he ordered a typewriter from Montgomery Ward and taught himself to type. Combs had no Boy Scout troop, so the boy wrote away and joined the Lone Scouts. He wore the uniform and hat around the farm. At age fifteen, he became president of the reorganized 4-H Club at Combs. He had little time for frivolity. He never learned "round dancing" until his younger sisters taught him after he was grown. Unlike other young men in the community, he did not care for strong drink.

Orval was not a risk taker. When the older boys swung onto the coaches on the outskirts of Combs and rode the Frisco trains into the station, Orval looked on with envy but never tried it. He had neither wildness nor any taste for mischief. He was appalled one day when two of his friends, killing time on a rainy day, went out to the barn on one of their farms and tied together the tails of two cows. The cows panicked and jerked off the end of one of the tails. Young Orval would never have done such a thing, just as he would not have joined the group who assembled a wagon on top of Barron's Store.

Beyond Orval's own inclinations, there were the twin models of Addie, the quiet Christian, and Sam, the idealist. Sam's instruction extended past his moral and political ideals. Even though Sam railed against the political system, he had an almost exaggerated respect for the law. For example, he enjoyed whiskey and distilled and sold it from time to time. His children learned that their father operated a still in the woods when they were small. He made good money for a while, but left the illicit business after a neighbor was sent to the penitentiary for bootlegging.

During Prohibition, Sam once found himself in a crisis of conscience. Like almost everyone else in the community, he kept a bottle on hand. Then some neighbors began stealing hogs from the woods where everybody, by common consent, let their animals roam free. Sam and many others knew the culprits. But they also knew that if they had them arrested, the thieves would probably bring charges against their accusers of keeping and drinking illicit whiskey.

"So Dad swore off. He wouldn't touch it, and he counted the days until the statutes of limitations run and he could be what he called a good citizen again by reporting on robbers."

During that same period, Orval himself was once called on to decide between loyalty and civic duty. His cousin Zember Cornett got drunk on illegal whiskey at a party. Orval was there. Word reached the Faubuses that the county grand jury planned to call Orval to testify against his cousin, who had been one of his closest pals since they were toddlers. Sam persuaded his sister, Zember's mother, to have the boy plead guilty and pay a fine. Orval had made his mind up, in any event. "I was not going before the grand jury and lie for him."

Orval finished the eighth grade at Combs School, then, because no other school was at hand, took it over again the next year. He was eighteen when he finished it the second time. His teacher, Arthur Johnson, told Sam and Addie that Orval was intelligent enough to be a teacher and that he should take the examination to get a certificate. No college training was required of a teacher in those days.

Sam and Addie were a little surprised to hear that their shy son might be able to run a classroom. He took a similar view of his abilities. They had to push him out of the house. One day in March, 1928, he set off to Huntsville on foot to take the teachers' examination. He walked most of the twenty-five miles until he got a ride in a Model-T Ford the last five or six miles.

"When I got to Huntsville, I was tired. And there was a bench outside a store on the north side of the square, and I sat there on that bench. And I sat there and I never spoke to anyone. Finally, a man in the store came out and they saw me sitting there for a long time, and they finally induced me to come inside." The man who took pity on him turned out to be another teacher, one Newt Reynolds, who guided the young man to the town's boardinghouse. There he kept to himself until the next day. Then he took the examination and started home.

He returned by a different route, and, finding himself wandering in the mud and cold late at night, he stopped at a house to borrow a lantern. The owner happened to be an acquaintance, T. D. "Tod" Parker. The man urged the youth to spend the night, but Orval said he had to get on home. Parker responded that Orval would never make it as a teacher. When Orval asked why, Parker said, "A fellow that ain't got no more sense than to go on home on a night like this rather than stay all night ain't got sense enough to teach school."

The neighbor was probably as surprised as the young man's parents when shortly afterward he received a teacher's certificate in the mail. Once more, Sam and Addie pushed him out of the house. He left reluctantly.

"I started back through the hills walking. I knew there was a school district every few miles, and by chance I wound up on top of the mountain in the Pinnacle School District." His trek had taken him twelve miles northwest of his father's farm, following a succession of mountainous paths. The Ozarks then had few roads through the higher elevations.

The bashful youngster arrived at the home of the Rev. Alonzo Ledford, who was sick in bed. Anxious as he was, the youth had the wit to go in and introduce himself. The minister's wife fixed a meal for him. As he ate, she told him that their youngest son had died a few months earlier. She seemed to take to the young stranger.

"He was commonly fixed," she told a reporter years later. "One of his soles was flapping off one of his old brogans, so he had to lift one foot higher than the other. I tacked the sole back on. He was wearing an old pair of pants with a patch on the seat."

He returned to the Ledfords later, and the minister took him to see the other school board members. He was hired. His first class at Pinnacle would have seventy-four students.

Then came the day when he had to stand in front of a room full of people and speak.

> I dreaded that first day of school worse than I did going to war. Because I had to get up before all the students and some of the school board members who were there, and a few of the patrons had come in. I didn't know you could have fever without being sick, but you can. For two weeks, I had a rather high fever.

Orval stuck it out. During the next eleven years, he taught at five schools in southern Madison County. Among his pupils at one school were three of his siblings and his young wife.

He had paid the girls little attention until he was eighteen and earning his own living. Even then, he did not bother with a girl unless it was "someone that I was sweet on." At parties and other social gatherings, he seldom had female company. He had a crush on Elva Collins, but she did not care for him, and in any event she moved away. Then he met Alta Haskins.

Alta lived on an eighty-acre farm at Ball Creek, five miles from the Faubus farm. Her father, J. C. Haskins, was a Baptist preacher who walked miles every Sunday to hold services in various small churches. He raised apples, read the Bible, called himself a Republican, and voted Independent.

A woman teacher took the girl to a teachers' institute at the University of Arkansas one day, and when Alta got home she announced that she had met the man she intended to marry. That was strange, because her first impression of handsome young Orval Faubus was not favorable. "Maybe I thought he was just a little too forward or something. I don't recall just what it was, but I had that feeling that I didn't like him."

Not long afterward, though, Orval took Alta on a date to a spelling bee at a neighbor's house. Their transportation was Orval's saddle mare, Queen.

"We rode that horse a lot on dates," she said as she called up memories from more than half a century. "Later, he bought an old Model-T car."

She was convinced as she looked back that he had selected her because he thought she would make a good wife for a politician. Even at age twenty-one, it was clear that he had ambitions. So did she. "I wanted better things. I always felt like I wanted to do something special." She continued taking classes at Greenwood School after they married, with Orval as her teacher. Alta never forgot her ambition. She finished high school, then took the teachers' examination and taught at several rural schools.

Sam slowly got ahead. He managed to double the size of the original homestead and became the owner of 320 acres of land. Twenty-six difficult years after first moving to the house on Greasy Creek as a boy, after struggling into early middle age, Sam bought the house for himself and moved back there with his own family. Orval, then fifteen, would remember the house fondly the rest of his life. It was somewhat grander than many other houses of the neighborhood. The logs had been covered with painted siding. The house had two floors with fireplaces on both levels. The family slept in two bedrooms upstairs and one downstairs next to the kitchen. The children could look out the front windows and watch wagons passing on the road a few yards away, just up the slope from the swift-running creek. Behind the house Sam built a log barn. There was a smokehouse for storing meat and potatoes.

Improved as it was, life was still hard for the Faubuses. The cured pork ran low at the end of every winter, and by planting time only the bacon and less desirable cuts were left. Money seemed to disappear at the same time, which meant there was no flour in the house. Corn bread instead of biscuits for breakfast signaled visitors that the family was on hard times. Every spring, Sam and the older boys had to go to the woods and cut timber for money to provide necessities until the crops came in. "Dad used to call it a hand-to-mouth existence. He knew what was happening to us, but he never could think out down the road how to cure it."

Modern conveniences were still far in the future. The Rural Electrification Administration would not reach Greasy Creek with its lines until the 1940s. When it finally arrived, it was after Sam had walked the countryside signing up potential customers. Before electricity, one of the family's few items of luxury was a battery radio. They bought it during the early 1930s. The girls liked to listen to Bob Wills and the Texas Playboys at noon, but if Orval was home they had to change the dial to get the news. One thing the family all agreed on was prize fights. Those were the glory days of the great heavyweight champion Joe Louis. The Faubuses were the only family on Greasy Creek who rooted for the black man.

Meanwhile, Addie still cooked on a wood stove and cleaned up after the evening meal by the light of a kerosene lamp. The lamps were smelly. The globes grew dark with smoke after a few days, and one of the children was assigned to clean them regularly.

Laundry was drudgery. Clothes were boiled in a kettle over an open fire, with one of the children punching them occasionally to work the dirt out. Each item was then lathered with lye soap and knuckled up and down a rub board. The sturdiest available child was required to hold one end of a pair of overalls while Addie twisted the garment to wring out the water. Washing was usually done on the bank of Greasy Creek. One washday, Addie found that the kettle had been washed away by high water after a heavy rain.

Lye soap is made by combining the extract of leached wood ashes with grease. To get the grease, Addie boiled the fat guts of hogs at butchering time. The children were required to take the raw cut-up guts to the creek and wash them. Hogs were butchered in cold weather to prevent spoiling, so washing the guts was a cold, miserable job.

Before electricity, clothes were ironed with flat irons heated on the cookstove. To keep from heating the kitchen unnecessarily, the women tried to iron during the morning while breakfast and the midday meal were being cooked.

The family made do with cold leftovers on summer nights to avoid firing up the stove and spreading heat through the house in the afternoon. Even so, the whole family sometimes slept on pallets in the yard during the early hours of the night to escape the hot bedrooms.

Added to the toil, fatigue, and discomfort were the periodic episodes of hard luck. One weekend, Orval came home from his classes at Pinnacle and learned that his younger brother had care-lessly let the hogs get into the cornfield. Their father arrived home a little later from his Rawleigh peddling. They surveyed the field and found that the marauders had destroyed a third of the crop. In an afternoon, one-third of the labor that had gone into the plowing and planting was gone, along with one-third of the food from that field. Sam was angry for days. Anger and worry were becoming constant companions of the hill people during those days.

Orval Faubus lived his youth during the last years of the pioneer idyll. In every respect except for the paradox of the calendar, his was entirely a nineteenth-century boyhood. The wooded slopes of the Ozarks still produced game for the table—not nearly as much as in earlier years, because some wildlife, such as deer, had been hunted out. The clear-running creeks and rivers still gave up plenty of fish, unpoisoned. The river bottom land was rich if limited, and the level benches on the hillsides had enough topsoil to grow corn, hay, vegetables, and fruit. People had to work hard, contrary to the myth of the shiftless hillbilly, but the fruit of their labor was a good living. In 1910, Greasy Creek was still a good place to be a child. There was little to indicate that the idyll was doomed.

The boundary of young Orval's world was the mountain across the valley from his uncle's field. He watched the snow and rain cross the mountain headed for his father's fields. He listened every day for the whistle of the train going into Combs behind the mountain, a reminder that a larger world lay out there, mysterious and a little threatening.

> In the autumn when the wind was from the south, we were hurrying in the fields to get the fodder all in before it rained. And the wind was damp with the clouds and mois-ture from the south, down Mill Creek. That's where the BM and E Railroad came up the valley from Cass. I'd see that train go out there in the morning with that white steam.

The railroad and the world beyond held no fear for the boy as long as he had the meadows and trees of home close by. In spite of the poor farming practices that would soon be its undoing, the farm produced almost all the food the family needed during Orval's boyhood—potatoes, corn, cane for sorghum molasses, fresh vegetables for canning, pork, chicken. The soil in the "new ground," the newly cleared fields, was still fertile. Sam cleared additional land beside one impoverished old field and planted it in giant red clover. "That clover grew so high that it lapped over the backs of the mules as they were pulling the mowing machine. And you had to keep them in a half run to keep the mower cutting the hay, it was so thick."

The slowly encroaching poverty was obscured in other ways. The woods, for example, contributed not only wild game for meat, but also wild fruit and nuts, along with blackberries and huckleberries for jam, jelly, and pies. Retrieving the largesse could be a problem.

> The chiggers would nearly run me nuts. They've always bothered me, still do. They'd just cover you. And you always had to watch for the snakes in the blackberry patch. Then you'd go pick huckleberries; those are the little short vines in the woods. And never did we ever go get huckleberries but what sometime during the period of picking we'd find a rattlesnake under the bushes.

Many of the people who settled the Ozarks after the Indians were pushed out were poor keepers of the bounty. The settlers (Scots, English, Scotch-Irish, a few Germans, a spattering of denationalized Africans tossed up from the plantation country) seemed to believe that the continent and its resources were limitless.

The soil was the first to go. The mountaineers knew little of conservation. Contour plowing to reduce erosion was seldom considered. Then there was corn, an infamous depleter of soil. Corn was the staple for both humans and livestock. Like most hill people, the Faubuses ate corn bread twice a day. When one field was used up, its nitrogen leached out by the corn plant, another was cleared of forest and plowed. The new fields produced lavishly for a while.

He lapsed into the accents of his youth as he talked about it years later.

When it was first clurred, if it was virgin soil, they were very productive. But this is a sandy loam. It erodes easily. And by the time we could get the rocks and roots out of it so we could plow it with some ease, it was becoming sterile. So the old farmers settled here, and they labored to get their fields in better shape. And by the time they got 'em in better shape, they were unproductive. Kind of a losing game. But they didn't know it. That was the only life they knew.

Government men who had studied the soil made some meager headway in Madison County, preaching conservation and fertilization, before Orval was grown. Orval remembered one year when an uncle tried the new way and fertilized part of a field. "From our house across the valley, you could tell to the row where the fertilizer was." But most of the fields were eventually abandoned and taken over first by blackberry vines and sassafras bushes, then by the resurging forest.

The forest—that was the next to go.

Orval's father was uncommonly perceptive. "I can remember him saying so many times over and over again, 'This timber is going to be gone pretty soon, and what are we going to do when the timber is gone?'"

Sam and Orval were working in their upper field one summer day. They stopped at the spring for a drink and sat talking for a while in the shade of a large white oak. The tree stood far enough into the field that it interfered with crops, and Orval asked his father why he had never cut it. He replied, "I thought one of you kids would need a place to settle some time and build a house. And we left this big tree for a shade tree, and a spring."

Orval knew that he would never live under the white oak.

The settlers' era ended just as he came to manhood. The Ozarks entered their second economic crisis at that time. The first had been caused by the Civil War when the countryside had been heavily depopulated. The settlers who had come in large numbers during the late 1840s and 1850s fled to escape the warring troops and the bushwhackers. After the war the railroad was built, and people came back to cut and ship the timber. The region boomed. One day, Orval counted thirty-two wagonloads of timber on the Greasy Creek road headed for the buyer at Combs. But by the 1920s, the timber was largely gone after years of thoughtless exploitation, and the once-fertile fields had lost their soil and their life. Combs was in decline. Stores and hotels closed.

Then came the Great Depression. For the Faubus children, nothing was left on Greasy Creek. Land itself had become one of the least valuable commodities. For a time, a good mule might be swapped for more than twenty acres. Like most of the others in the countryside around, the Faubus children scattered to find work as soon as they were old enough. Most of them headed west where the nation's few remaining jobs seemed to be. Not one of them built a house next to the spring.

> Here were all their ancestral connections, their history. Everything that appeals to people above an ordinary material existence was there. But they had to forsake them. They poured out of here. They like to have wore out Highway 66 going to California.

Sam, in middle age, joined the young and began to travel to other states to earn money. He went to Washington State to work in the timber in 1936. Orval and several of his siblings became migrant food harvesters and labored in the big timber woods of the Northwest. The Madison County schools kept classes only a few months of the year. He had to leave home to earn money during the rest of the year.

> I read a book, *The Path to Power,* about Lyndon Johnson, [by Robert Caro] and it tells about how his people were trapped in the hill country. And he had a big chapter, the title of it was "The Trap." Very similar to this. We were trapped in the hills. Now, the only way to get out of that grinding work and toil—and a mere existence was about all you got out of it—was to become a school teacher or run for county office or leave the country. Go away and find employment some- where. So when the virgin timber was cut out, and the rail- road was going downhill, and all the villages, too, the people started streaming out of here. Madison County at the turn of the century had about 20,000 people. And it got down to less than 7,000.

Finally, the depression faded. Many moved to southern California when World War II began, and there they found their first real prosperity working in defense industries. Wichita, Kansas, and Tulsa, Oklahoma, much closer to home, also attracted Ozarks people during the war, drawn there to work for big aircraft companies.

They kept their old loyalties. At election time, they voted absentee for their Madison County favorites. At one time, the village of Alabam had more voters living in Wichita than in the home township.

The trees and soil were not alone in their exhaustion. Sometimes it seemed as if the people themselves were wearing away inside, scoured of hope. There was a violence that seemed to rise from the surrounding wildness, not always willful but constant, as if some greater predator was systematically at work on the more vulnerable of the human community, like a hawk preying on the abject mouse.

This was the era of the dust bowl when the climate cooperated with the economy to drive farmers into ruin—and sometimes into crime. This was the time of Charles Arthur "Pretty Boy" Floyd, the Oklahoma farmer-turned-bandit who became a public demon or folk hero, depending on which side of the teller's window you occupied. Some of the Faubus family migrated to harsh Oklahoma, and at least two of them died violently. One was Sam's brother, shot to death when he took up a no-account relative's cause in a neighborhood quarrel. Sam himself once wanted to move to Oklahoma, and Orval was relieved when the sensible Addie vetoed it. "If I'd been out there, I might have got into something like that and might have gotten killed or might have got in jail."

Greasy Creek had its own outbreaks caused by acts of God, bad luck, and plain meanness. Their neighbor Bob Lemaster came to the Faubus house one day selling knives. The telephone rang, and Addie ran to the porch shouting, "Bob Lee, your house is on fire!" Orval watched the visitor and his father race down the road, then waited for his father to come home and report that the house had burned down.

There was the endless skein of death. Orval was seven when little Sherman Thornberry, a distant cousin, went squirrel hunting one day with an older brother. The brother cut a hollow den tree to flush a squirrel. A nearby tree, weakened by the falling den tree, collapsed on Sherman and killed him. About six months later, Orval's stepcousin Howard Nelson died of diphtheria. Both boys were playmates of Orval's. For quite a while, he had no other young friends who were so close.

Then came the global epidemic of influenza in 1918–19. About twenty million people worldwide, including five hundred thousand Americans, died in that outbreak. Southern Madison County was hit hard. Many families lost children or old people. The Socialist O. T. Green braved the risk and went from house to house with a nurse, caring for the sick and dying. The Faubuses were spared, but once again young Orval was quietened and made to wonder.

"You come to an early realization that life is not all roses. It's not all one great adventure, even though in fairy stories we used to read where you lived happily ever after."

The creatures of the woods and fields were not immune. The deer had been virtually hunted to extinction for food by the time of the depression, but there was a violence toward wildlife that had nothing to do with human need. The weekly paper once reported that the last known panther in Madison County had been spotted near Ball Creek. The men of the neighborhood turned out and killed it for sport. A large egret, uncommon to the area, turned up at Greasy Creek. The children admired it as it flew around the neighborhood. It lasted less than three days. Someone shot it and hung it from a post by the road.

The old-timers had not even slipped the grasp of that most violent of events, the Civil War. The boy heard the talk. His mother's family, the Thornberrys, were Confederates and his father's were Unionists. Their common memory was of the killing and the savagery.

The war divided many families in the Ozarks, far from the slave country of the delta. In some ways the war hurt the mountains more than the plantation areas. Explosive sentiment washed back and forth through the hills bringing dominance by first one side, then the other. Many tried to stay aloof, but found that the only way to do that was to get out. Northern sympathizers fled north, southern sympathizers south. After the war, the Unionists returned to Madison County as avid Republicans, and the Confederates returned as enthusiastic Democrats.

Orval's great-grandfather Owen Thornberry was a Confederate soldier. He survived the war unscathed. But one of Owen's brothers was killed as he was fleeing south to escape the violence. He made it as far as the Mulberry River, was caught in a skirmish, and died. Another Thornberry relative was killed by Unionist sympathizers only a few miles from home, near St. Paul.

Orval's great-grandfather Eli Sparks, Sam's maternal grandfather, was a Union soldier. With that division in the family, Orval learned early not to talk about the war too much. His great-grandmother Minerva Thornberry, Owen's widow, had no such reticence. She carried her bitterness to the grave. Minerva told young Orval of saving potatoes for seed during a drought year, and of having to hide them from northern raiders. Another raider ripped the cloth from her spinning wheel, and she ran to his horse and grabbed it back. The boy heard of a group of Confederate sympathizers being shot and killed at a local blacksmith shop. An eighteen-year-old boy hid in a barn, only to be found and executed by a Union officer— a man of Minerva's acquaintance. "She couldn't speak that man's name without hate being in her voice." This great-grandmother was the one who died of a stroke in the Faubus house while holding a baby when Orval was about fifteen.

At about that same age, from reading history at school, Orval had developed a sympathy for the Union, in spite of his great-grandmother's stories. One day in class he expressed some anti-southern sentiment. His teacher, Robert M. Reed, explained how good citizens of the county—Confederates—had been red-lined and disqualified from voting to allow the Carpetbaggers and Republicans to control elections. Orval's sentiments drifted back toward level—that is, undecided.

The deracinated Africans who had crouched for four years in the eye of the hurricane were confined mainly to the rich lowlands of the South. In Arkansas, those lowlands lay east of the Ozarks and south of the Arkansas River. But a few thousand had been brought into the hills as slaves to work the narrow river bottoms and to serve in the hotels and houses of the towns. They stayed on after the war, huddled together in small communities through the hills.

One such community occupied a speck of Madison County about ten miles southeast of Huntsville on Wharton Creek. The community had its own all-black school until economics dictated that it be merged with a nearby white school. That was years before the Supreme Court's *Brown v. Board* decision of 1954, and was clearly against Arkansas's school segregation laws. The illegal accommodation was made quietly, and no one complained.

The Wharton Creek people were not the first African Americans young Orval had seen. As a small boy, he saw black men loading crossties on the railroad cars at Combs. The men were a traveling crew who lived in a rail car and moved every few days to a new job. Occasionally, a black baseball team from south of the Arkansas River came to play one of the local teams.

Legend has it that some Ozarks towns had signs at the railroad stations saying, "Nigger, don't let the sun go down on you here." Orval heard of those towns, but he never saw such a sign anywhere in Madison County. As far as he knew, coming up in the house of a liberal and a Socialist, the white people of his county were tolerant toward black people.

Railroad crews came to eat at Mrs. Ida Bevins Brashears's boardinghouse when their work cars had no cook. One day a black railroad worker showed up for dinner, and a white worker refused to sit at the same table with him. Mrs. Brashears told the black man to stay put and said to the white man, "You can eat in the kitchen." He left in a huff.

Sam sympathized with the blacks, of course, regarding them as fellow sufferers under the lash of capitalism. He and other Ozarks mountaineers had heard how the plantations in the South treated black workers; a few had gone to the delta to pick cotton and had come back with stories. "Dad, he was on the side of the blacks. He felt they were mistreated. They were wage slaves just like the rest of us."

Not surprisingly, the Wharton Creek Negroes voted for Orval when he first ran for office in 1936. Then, like the rest whose hope had eroded with the hillside soil, they quietly moved away, gnawing at survival.

<table>
<tr><td>

CHAPTER

6

</td><td>

Orval came to understand that the hills of home could not support him. The shyness and caution that he inherited from Addie kept him close to the hearth for a time. Then another quality inherited from somewhere—from Sam, from

</td></tr>
</table>

the mysterious Tom Joslin, maybe from the wild Ozarks themselves —began to agitate him and finally impelled him out into the world.

The two accepted forms of travel at that time among millions of young men, many of them collapsed suddenly from the middle class into desperation, were hitchhiking and riding freight trains. Orval hitchhiked when he made his first trip to Missouri to pick strawberries. He was nineteen. He never considered spending precious pennies for bus or train fare. When he traveled to Michigan in 1935 to pick berries, he rode the freight trains. A train crossing Missouri one night stopped at a small town, and a railroad detective threw all the illicit riders off. For good measure, he boxed Orval's jaws and threw away his flashlight.

The youth met an old man on that trip, a one-time radical farm organizer from White County, Arkansas. They arrived in Chicago during the World's Fair, and from the park benches they could see the sky-ride in the distance. Many users of the park, like Orval and his companion, could not afford admission to the fair. More prosperous residents read their newspapers in the park and left them on the benches for the homeless men, who would use them for cover when they slept in the parks at night. "I never knew there was so much protection from a newspaper before if you handle them carefully." About 4 P.M. each day, a policeman chased everybody off the benches. The moneyless men hid behind the hedges until it was safe to gather the newspapers and make ready for the night.

Orval and the old man scraped up sixty-five cents each and rode a steamboat across the lake to Michigan City, Indiana, and from there they rode fruit trucks to the orchards and berry fields at Baroda, Michigan. They learned that the strawberry harvest had failed because of dry weather, but that raspberries would be ready in about a week. Orval spent the days reading books from a lending library. He and the old man slept on a slatted platform beside the railroad track. A couple with three or four children slept near them, all hoping for work. When the raspberries got ripe, Orval moved to a berry farm and slept in a barn. His old companion had gone elsewhere, taking with him the forks and spoons that he had shared with Orval. Orval asked the farmer for a spoon. "He wouldn't let me have one. I got a bad impression of Yankees right there."

Orval earned enough to buy a change of clothes when he went back through Chicago. He also splurged and spent one dollar to see the World's Fair. On the streets, he had never seen so many black people. White people warned him away from black neighborhoods at night. He was happy to hop a freight for home.

He had learned the hazards of riding the trains. During his late teens, he joined the Civil Military Training Camp, a federal program to allow young men to earn a little money and avoid idleness during summers. He had to make his way to Fort Leavenworth, Kansas, for his first encampment. He rode the freights. A railroad detective caught him on his first stop, in Monette, Missouri.

"He said, 'If I turn you loose, will you go on out of town and not come back to the railroad yard?' I said, 'Yes, I will.'"

Orval hitchhiked west to Pittsburg, Kansas, then hopped another freight. He rode to Leavenworth in the coal car and emerged black with coal dust.

A few weeks later, he caught another freight for the trip home. Somewhere during the middle of the first night, he and two other men ran to catch a moving train in a rail yard. Orval managed to grab a stirrup on the side of the baggage car.

> I knew I had to hang on 'til the next stop. I couldn't get tired. So I hooked my arms through there and took as restful a position as I could.
>
> And then I saw someone looking from the rear of the car, and then very shortly the door opened and he had me get inside. We sat down, and he said, "It looks like you young fellows are going to get killed in spite of everything I can do." I remember the phrase "sweating blood" as he wiped his brow. It was a mail car where they had the railway mail, and they were putting up mail in the boxes. At that time, my knee was hurting real bad and I was kind of sick, so I laid down.

I said, "I'd have made it all right. I could have hung on to the next next stop."

He said, "You just think you could. Listen."

And we passed through one of those bridges with the framework on the side. I never would have known what hit me. 'Cause I was leaning out, see, hanging on.

You know, that didn't hardly faze me. But years afterwards, sometimes I'd wake up in the middle of the night in a cold sweat thinking about it.

Back in Madison County, the young man continued his teaching career spending a year at a time at Ball Creek, Greenwood, Pinnacle. There was a term at Good Hope, also known as Yellerhammer. In 1931, the year he and Alta were married, he kept school at a community called Accident. The newlyweds boarded with the Ledford family for a while, then moved in with his parents at Greasy Creek.

Rural Arkansas schools were simple when Orval was a teacher. Boys and girls sat on opposite sides of the room. Many country schools had no toilets until the Works Progress Administration of the Roosevelt administration built them. One of the teacher's first tasks at the beginning of a term was to assign the boys to use the woods on one side of the building and the girls on the other. Curriculum was usually limited to reading, arithmetic, writing, spelling, geography, and history. The teacher sat on a stage, and the seating next to the stage was the recitation bench. Orval called the pupils to recite by grade, just as he had been called as a pupil by his aunt Minnie: "First grade!" The first graders got ready. "Rise!" They stood. "Pass!" They marched to the front and sat on the bench. At the end of the lesson, they marched back to their seats, and the second grade was called. The system had a built-in discipline that made it easier for the teacher to deal with as many as eight grades in a single room.

Orval taught as he had been taught. He set rules and expected the students to follow them. Sometimes they were rigid, but that's the way school was run in those days. He tried to maintain discipline by force of personality. When that failed, he did not shrink from the switch. Most whippings were administered for fighting, lying, or using vulgar language, but not always. He once switched his own wife, to the amusement of the other students. Alta, then a pupil of his at Greenwood, and a small band of teenaged girls—one of them Orval's sister Bonnie—annoyed the teacher one day by continuously ringing the school bell. Orval sent word that he would whip the girls if they did not stop. It was only after the girls presented themselves for punishment that he realized that Alta was one of the miscreants.

Orval already was developing what would become a quite formidable gravity, a quality that would make him not merely respected but sometimes feared. His friends in the timber woods of Washington State began to notice it when he was in his mid-twenties. He did not tell bawdy stories or get drunk with the others. Even his father enjoyed jokes and drinking, but not Orval.

His sister Bonnie, ten years younger than he but a full generation removed in her mind, was one of the first to feel his growing sense of weight and power. It was not just that she knew not to go into her brother's well-ordered room where he kept his magazines, Boy Scout paraphernalia, arrowheads, and other treasures. There was something more. At some point in her childhood, Orval replaced their father as the dominant authority in her life. If Sam told her to be quiet, she might or might not take it seriously. But a mere look from Orval was enough to wilt her. One day when she was a teenager, she was teaching their sister June a new dance step in a room where Orval was typing. June was slow to get it, and Bonnie kept repeating the instructions: "It's a little half-step. It's like half-time, you know, when you sing half-time." Orval said nothing at all. "All at once, he just turned around from what he was doing and he looked at us. That's all he had to do. We got out of there." Bonnie learned to stay out of his way, as did many others in the years ahead.

Orval enjoyed the dances at the family house, but not with abandon. He was the one who arranged everything. He organized the sets and made sure everyone pitched in the few cents required to pay the musicians. He enforced behavior in the youngsters. He once caught June gaping at a well-dressed woman who had come up from Combs and ordered the child to move on. Later, when he went into politics, he learned to take a drink. Back then his dignity did not permit it. He could not risk making a fool of himself.

The depression was in full force. Orval's salary from teaching had dropped from sixty and seventy dollars a month to forty dollars, and that income was available only during the three or four months a year that the impoverished districts could afford to keep the schools open. Around the nation, a fourth of the work force was unemployed. Drought struck. The wind carried the dust clouds eastward, darkening the sky over Greasy Creek and thousands of other communities and reminding them that they were not alone in their hardship.

Sam's family was as hard up as always. The children never went hungry, thanks to the garden and the hogs, but all other possessions were meager. Nice clothes for the girls were a luxury. Addie made many of their dresses from flour sacks, and as the girls got older they were dressed so poorly that they were ashamed to be seen in public. Bonnie once wore a flour-sack dress to a community reunion and was snubbed by a little friend in a yellow organdy dress and white slippers. She was eight years old.

Occasionally, the poverty was edged with a sadness that made it even harder to bear. Orval and his young wife needed a bed. They rode horseback one day to an auction and went into debt twenty dollars for a bed and some other household goods. When Orval went back two or three days later to get the goods, he found that the departed owner had abandoned a small dog. The day was cold and wet, and the sight of the helpless creature was more than Orval could stand. All his life, he loved dogs. Indeed, he often showed more affection toward dogs than toward members of his family. He took the dog home with him. But when his school term ended and he had to leave home to find work, no one else was willing to look after the pet. He made the decision that was customary at the time. He shot it.

The people who left the Ozarks looking for work in those days almost always traveled west or north. Going south would have offered nothing more productive than they could have found at home. Going east went against some instinct. Just as weather moves west to east on this continent, people move in the opposite direction. Going east is considered effete. Artists, intellectuals, and journalists go east, but those in the more manly pursuits migrate west or, in a pinch, north.

The Northwest drew large numbers of Madison County residents during the 1930s. Orval spent some of the long seasons between school terms with his father and several neighbors working in the big timber of Washington State. He worked for the Biles-Coleman Lumber Company of Omak most of 1937—April to November—and part of the spring of 1938. He had a contract to pile brush after the logging crews cut the trees. The job paid 47½ cents an hour. That beat working in the canning factory back home for 10 or 15 cents an hour. Orval bought a pickup one summer, installed a canvas top over the bed and benches on the sides, and, for a few dollars a head, hauled eleven men to the timber woods. The trip out took several days. They slept in haystacks by the roadside and fed on cheese and crackers.

In central Washington, near Omak, the men spent part of the season piling brush and the rest picking apples in nearby orchards. It was in the timber woods that Orval first encountered a labor union and with it a political decision. Before the Arkansawyers arrived, there had been a bitter, violent strike by union workers against the large timber company that Orval and his friends contracted to work for. The company had beaten the strikers, then had formed a sweetheart union to thwart any new organizing. Orval and his friends learned this background and made up their minds. One day, representatives of the company union approached and asked them to join. Orval was the spokesman for the Arkansawyers. He told them no. "If we have to go down the road, we'll go," he told them. "So you can tell us now or you can bring us back word from the boss." They kept their jobs and never heard any more from it.

The migrants encountered another problem that was more complex. To their surprise, they were looked down on by many residents of the region. They were treated with some of the same contempt that the Anglos expressed for Mexican immigrants in later years. There was a jarring similarity at the root of the problem: The Arkansawyers talked different.

At that time, Ozarks people still spoke a dialect that had not changed appreciably during the many generations their people had inhabited North America. Unlike residents of the Deep South, Ozarkers believed in the letter R and used it with the same firmness that their ancestors had picked up in Scotland and Ulster. They expressed themselves in ways that would have puzzled outsiders. A Madison County man offering a ride to a stranger might say, "I'll carry ye to town." In response to a surprising statement, an Ozarker might exclaim, "Well, I swan." Asking a favor, he might say, "I'd be obleeged to ye iffen you would do that." Acknowledging error, he would say, "I thought he were somebody else." Asked to do something, he would say, "I'll get to it dreckly [directly]." Instead of "you all," the Ozarker would address himself to "youins."

Then there were the peculiar pronunciations of common words: thar for there, jist for just, git for get, cheer for chair, flar for flower, whup for whip, heared for heard, shore for sure. Natives of the Northwest could not be expected to appreciate the history of the Ozarks language nor to understand that it carried an integrity no longer found in much of the evolving language used by other Americans. Away from home, any Ozarker could expect contempt as soon as he opened his mouth. Add to that the fact that the Arkies were desperate for work and it is understandable that they were the Mexicans of that time.

But at least two of the Madison County men puzzled the Washington residents. Sam was enigma enough, what with his articulate monologues on politics, socialism, union labor, and war. "Me and the boys are laying around talking about fascism and other weighty subjects," he confided to his diary one summer day. He did mission work for the Socialist party by passing out copies of the *Guardian*. He amazed them further by writing poetry to send to his home county newspaper.

The real mystery was his son. While Sam was talkative, Orval was reticent and studious. He spent the evenings after work sitting on the porch reading. Some of the resident loggers thought that was unusual, but when the word got around that he was reading law books and studying to be a lawyer, they were flabbergasted. Here was an Arkie who put cardboard in the soles of his shoes and laced them with haywire, and he presumed to think he would become a lawyer. He never bothered to let them know that he was reasonably well read, or that he had taught school several years, or that he was not reading for the law.

Back home during the winters, Sam continued to dabble in local politics. He was elected to the school board at Greasy Creek several times. He was appointed road overseer. Once he consented to stand for justice of the peace on the Republican ticket. He won, but never took office. His brother Eli was a sheriff's deputy, which gave the family added political clout in local affairs.

Orval had first become aware of the attractiveness of politics as a boy when he had listened to his father and the other men talk about public issues and elections. At age eight or nine, he was already listening silently as the men expressed their excitement over the victory of their candidates. He also noticed that they went into something like despair when their candidates lost. He was a clever boy, and he understood that the appeal of politics was its competitiveness. It was a game.

Sam understood the game at another level: That it could be played with gusto without any hope of winning. As a Socialist, he and his friends might provide the swing vote to win a local or county election. But in national elections, his vote was merely an act of defiance. As a young man, before he entered the game as a candidate, Orval felt the same way as his father. "We weren't trying to be for a winner. We picked the candidate we wanted, and we supported him even if he wasn't going to get but 10 percent of the vote, because that was true when Dad was voting for Norman Thomas [the perennial presidential candidate of the Socialist party during the years after Debs]."

Sometime during the late 1920s or early 1930s, Orval began to study the game more seriously. His study led him to a fateful decision. He refused to join his father's political party. Sam and his friend J. C. Thompson, the Socialist organizer, tried to persuade the young man to run for office on the Socialist ticket. Thompson offered to return to Madison County and campaign for him if he would run for the legislature as a Socialist.

But Orval already was developing the political instinct for which he would later become famous. He sensed—or deduced from observation and logic—that a Socialist had no future in Arkansas politics. "I knew even then that membership in the Socialist local, being openly identified, would not do me any good as a public figure, as a school teacher." He also understood that the depressed and turbulent times that had partly revived the parties of the left after the stock-market crash of 1929 would not last.

So Orval parted with his father. While he was at it, he turned his back on the Republican party, too, even though the Republicans had been strong in the mountain counties since the Civil War. In 1930 he might have had a job as census taker if he had been willing to become a Republican. Even at an early age, he calculated that a Republican had little greater future in Arkansas politics than a Socialist.

> I determined that you couldn't get anything done by losing. And so I deliberately chose a course to be a Democrat, because that was the dominant party in Arkansas. And then I was glad of it from the standpoint of opinion and conviction when Roosevelt came along and began doing all the good that he did nationwide.

That was a shrewd decision. It was also his first political compromise.

There remained the problem of guilt by association. Some called Sam a Red and a radical behind his back. Whether that hindered his son's career is a matter of speculation. Orval recalled one man who advised him not to run for county clerk because he thought, mistakenly, that Orval had written Socialist essays for the *Madison County Record*. The man had confused Orval with Arch Cornett, Sam's Socialist comrade. In Orval's later race for circuit clerk, his opponent, Howard Garrett, dug up something Orval had written speaking favorably of Socialist theory. Garrett ran the excerpt in an advertisement. One of Garrett's associates was heard to refer to Orval as "a Socialist and a little old farmer." There was little evidence that any of this hurt Orval very much. But even after he returned from combat in World War II, Orval was suspect in some quarters. One prominent politician in nearby Fayetteville referred to him in anger as "that com-MUNE-ist over there in Madison County."

Through it all, Orval tried not to blame his father for whatever damage was done to his political fortunes.

I felt that he was a good man. I had nothing there to be ashamed of. I knew he was unorthodox in a way and a sort of political maverick. And I didn't inherit any great political strength from him to help me in my endeavors when I started out. But that was just a circumstance which I recognized. He was recognized as an honest person, a man who was a good neighbor.

Orval in later years was careful to distance himself from his father's social theories. But he liked to say that Sam's socialism had good points. "There was some merit to the ideals which he had of government ownership of property. Because the Post Office Department, that was government-owned, and that was the poor man's agency then, you know—a postcard for one penny, two cents to mail a letter."

Addie Faubus came to weigh about 230 pounds, which apparently aggravated a problem with high blood pressure. She took medicine to control it, but periodically ran out and failed to replace it until the next trip to town.

One weekend in January 1936, Orval came to his parents' house from his teaching job at Ball Creek School, across the mountain from Greasy Creek. Several young people came to visit on Saturday night. After supper, all except Addie went into the living room to sing and listen to one of the young men play the guitar. Addie washed the dishes before joining the crowd. The youngsters called out, "Hi, Addie," and she said, "What's going on here? Sounds like a party." She danced a little jig, to the delight of the crowd, then went upstairs to bed.

Sometime during the early hours of January 26, after everyone had gone to bed, Addie went back downstairs. She called, "Sam! Sam!" He and Orval awoke and rushed into the room in time to see her fall to the floor. They got her onto her feet and discovered she could not speak. Orval hugged her and said, "Oh, Mama, can you talk to me? Can you tell me anything?" She fought for breath, then stiffened and stopped breathing. They stretched her out on the floor, and Orval tried, with no success, to revive her with artificial respiration. She was dead at the age of forty-three.

The typical country person became a member of a church at age ten or twelve. It often happened during a summer revival when the young people were hungry for diversion. At the end of a frightening sermon about the perils of hell, while the congregation sang "Why Not Tonight?", one or two or half a dozen youngsters would respond to the preacher's altar call, confess their sins, and affirm their faith in Christ. They would be declared saved from eternal damnation, and at the next opportunity all the new Christians would be baptized. For some denominations, this meant being escorted to a hole of water in a nearby creek and held briefly under water by the preacher as he said the appropriate words: "In the name of the Father and the Son and the Holy Ghost . . ." That pretty well solved the question of religion for most country people, and they never gave it much more thought.

Whether because of his father's insistent skepticism or his own independent turn, Orval did not follow the usual route. He heard the fire and brimstone sermons, but somehow was not made afraid. Instead, he developed the habit of wondering as he walked and worked in the woods and fields. Observing nature, he came to believe that some omnipotent power was behind it all. He also observed the hardships of his family and neighbors and concluded that there must be some hope beyond the present life, else why put up with the misery?

His mother had wanted him to join the Church of Christ. So had Alta, a member of the same group. For three years after his mother died, he shopped around, much the same way he had shopped for a political party. He listened to the arguments of first one denomination, then another. He finally determined that denomination was unimportant to one's soul. That settled, he opted to become a Baptist. It may or may not have been significant that the Baptists were the largest voting group in Arkansas.

He then calculated the best way to make his conversion official. Not wanting to be accused of joining the church for political gain —he was already in county office—he asked a Baptist minister whose views he liked to baptize him. The preacher with his wife and one other couple met Orval at a deep hole on Holborn Creek west of Huntsville. The convert, aged twenty-nine, was immersed. No one from his family was there.

Orval Faubus and Alta Haskins were married in 1931, and the union threatened to unravel in less than three years. The wedding itself, an inelegant affair befitting an inelegant time in American history, might have been an indicator.

Orval had been to Huntsville that day on business. To save another trip to the county seat, he had acquired the marriage license; they had already agreed to marry, but had not set a date. That afternoon, the couple decided they might as well use the license without further delay. They slipped off that evening to the neighboring home of a Church of Christ minister, the Rev. S. P. Edens. One of Alta's cousins was a witness. The bride was dark-eyed, brunette, and pretty but not dazzling. She liked to think that they had eloped. Maybe so. Orval could be romantic, wandering in the flowering woods, musing over beauty. But chances are he just caved in to common sense. The day was November 21, 1931. He was twenty-one; she was nineteen.

Orval was teaching that year at Accident for forty dollars a month. The newlyweds boarded with the Ledford family at nearby Pinnacle in quarters so cramped that intimacy was a challenge. Nevertheless, the bride got pregnant, and a baby boy came the following September. Both Orval and Alta had grown up with large numbers of brothers and sisters. They wanted lots of children of their own. To their sorrow, their baby boy was born dead. That was the first blow to the marriage.

Orval found work nearer home. He taught at Greenwood School on Greasy Creek in 1932–33. The pay was better—fifty dollars a month. But the economy grew steadily worse, and the next year he returned to Pinnacle where the patrons were able to raise only forty dollars a month for a six-month term. The couple remained there a second year, boarding with the bustling Ledford family.

The young marriage began to show strains. A troubling dual nature in Orval began to keep Alta off-balance. He could be kind and even gentle. Working in the field, he would pick wildflowers and pretty leaves for her. But he had also become preoccupied and thoughtless. He came and went as he pleased and rarely bothered to explain. She believed, with some resentment, that he was "the freest man that was ever married." He showed increasing disregard for his wife, sometimes ignoring her and other times belittling her.

Perhaps Alta in her hurt could not fully appreciate an unease that was growing in Orval, one that went beyond the normal problems of marriage. The ambition that had ignited in him when he was a schoolboy was burning hotter with each passing year. And alongside the ambition was fear. How could he ever amount to anything? The nation's economy had collapsed, joining south Madison County's in obliterating opportunity. There seemed to be no way to advance or even to escape, unless you counted riding the freight trains and living as a hobo as escape. Simply keeping food on their table and clothes on their backs was daunting, even frightening.

Coupled with that was the knowledge that a teacher with only an eighth-grade education would never prosper and in time would be forced out of a job. To forestall that prospect, he needed to make sure that he would keep his teaching certificate. He made a move that, incredibly enough in hindsight, was bold. He started to high school.

His first classes were at St. Paul High School, a five-mile walk over a mountain from Greasy Creek. He could not attend year-round. He had to enroll after his own term of teaching ended each year. The high-school classes added to the couple's financial burden. He borrowed money to live on each spring until his salary resumed in August. Borrowing was to become a habit that would plague him like drink all his life. But it paid off in those early years.

His best subject was history. His worst was algebra. Failing to pass the state test on algebra would eventually keep him from obtaining the highest certificate to teach. Because he was able to go to high school only three or four months a year while he was teaching, it took six years to graduate. He transferred to the Huntsville State Vocational School and graduated there in the spring of 1934. He got his diploma just before his second child was conceived.

He was happier with the diploma than the pregnancy. Both he and Alta had wanted a large family, but Orval, after their failed beginning, was not ready to try again. He was worried about advancing his education. During the worst of their emotional stress, when Alta was eight months pregnant, he made one of the larger decisions of his life. He left home on an adventure that would haunt him the rest of his life. Alta told him that if he went, she would leave him. They spoke the dreaded word, divorce. Alta asked, "What about the baby?" Orval said, "If it's a boy, I want it. If it's a girl, you can have it." He went, and she thought he had left for good.

Alta needed the comfort of family. She moved in with her parents fifty miles away at Lincoln, near the Oklahoma border. There she fell into lassitude and depression. There was little to do at her parents' house. Her father went off each day to do farm work for neighbors. She had no transportation, no way to get away from the place, no friends to visit, no stimulation. All she did was sit and read.

Her time for delivery grew near. She sent for Orval, not knowing whether he would come. But whatever peril the marriage was in, he rushed to be present for the birth of his second child. On March 27, 1935, the couple went to a medical clinic at nearby Prairie Grove. It was another difficult delivery. The clinic's experienced doctor was away. The young man attending her did not know how to perform a Cesarean section, which might have saved the child.

The second baby, like the first, was a boy—Orval's boy. Like the first, it was born dead. The picture was vivid in his memory for the rest of his life.

> That infant was the most beautiful creature I have ever seen. I remember, Dad and some of the neighbors went and dug a small grave there in the cemetery. The casket was fixed very nicely. We didn't have any service. There's three or four old mountaineers. So I wanted to open the box and look at it one more time. And they looked at it, and they were struck speechless. I never saw anything affect people like that. Its hair was long enough that it looked like it needed a haircut. Black as a raven's wing. And it was so beautifully shaped, its face. And because of that, they never did show it to Alta. They were afraid it would affect her too much, so she never did see it. But that's one of the images that's stayed in my mind—well, forever. That little baby was so beautiful.

He stayed home long enough to bury the baby, then left again, chasing his dream. Years later, that youthful dream would return to alter his life in a way that he could not have imagined in 1935.

CHAPTER
7

Tuckerman is a farming town of a few hundred black and white citizens in fertile northeastern Arkansas. It sits athwart the Missouri Pacific Railroad and the Little Rock to St. Louis highway. Here, on the unusually warm morning of July 31, 1954, the candidate got up to make his first speech of the day, the first of the runoff campaign for the Democratic nomination for governor. The preceding weeks had been exhausting as he had traveled the state trolling for votes with his message: End utility rate gouging, don't raise property taxes, and, above all, show more respect for the old folks on welfare. It was going well. He could tell that the message was getting through. He could also guess that Gov. Francis A. Cherry had figured out that his once-obscure opponent was gaining on him. He knew what to expect. At Tuckerman, he got the first indication that history was hot on his own heels.

As Faubus spoke from a flat-bed truck, he noticed men quietly drifting through the crowd passing out what appeared to be copies of a newspaper. It was the latest issue of the weekly *Arkansas Recorder* published in Little Rock by John F. Wells, a veteran journalist and political activist. Wells was a Cherry partisan. The paper being circulated that sultry morning in Tuckerman revealed what until then had been known for years in Faubus's home community but by a mere handful of confidants elsewhere: that as a twenty-five-year-old schoolteacher, almost two decades in the past, he had attended Commonwealth College—a "Communist" school. The implication was hardly subtle. The man threatening to unseat Francis Cherry after his first term as governor was a subversive—maybe an outright Communist.

Most Americans had forgotten the Communist threat during World War II. After all, it was Uncle Joe Stalin and his Communists in the Soviet Union who helped us whip the Nazis. But when the chimera revived after the war, it came back like a wind from hell. Alger Hiss, driven to ground by Whittaker Chambers and Richard Nixon, was accused in 1948 of passing secrets to the Russians from his high State Department position. He was imprisoned five years for perjury. In 1949, eleven leaders of the U.S. Communist party were convicted of advocating the overthrow of the government and sent

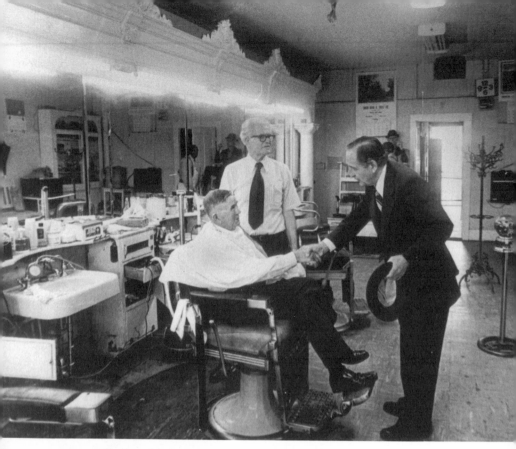

Faubus on the campaign trail,
probably in 1954.

to prison. The nation went to war in Korea a year after that to stop Communist aggression in Asia. Sen. Joseph R. McCarthy's Communist hunt went into full howl at home, aided immeasurably by the espionage convictions of Julius and Ethel Rosenberg. In the spring of 1954, just as the Arkansas governor's race got under way, the Red menace was thrust into the nation's living rooms via television as McCarthy and the army squared off, he accusing the army of harboring Communists and the army accusing him of unethically obtaining favors for a young serviceman. Less than a month later, on May 17, the Supreme Court ruled that school segregation was unconstitutional—an event that the more alert white supremacists saw as part of that same Communist plot to take control of America. It was not a good time to be a left-winger in the United States.

The Commonwealth issue might have been less troubling to Faubus if he had not gone to such lengths to put it behind him. It was not as if he had forgotten it. He never forgot anything that had a bearing on his ambition—any favor, slight, misstep, or small triumph. But for almost twenty years he had walked the narrow path of patriotic public service and had given no one cause to question his loyalty to the United States. He had, in fact, risked his life in war to prove his loyalty.

His career in public office had itself been a model of small-town American politics. It began, as often happens, with a setback. In 1936, at the age of twenty-six, he made his first run for public office. The Madison County seat in the state House of Representatives came open, and he felt the pull. It was an urge that certain people feel at an early age: the desire to match wits against others of like mind. He was also feeling the first signs of the politician's ego —the need for the goodwill and favor of a majority of the people.

Orval was one of five candidates. He ran second—four votes behind the winner, a friend, a son of the Ledford family with whom he had boarded for years. There was murmuring about election fraud, and some of his friends urged him to challenge the result. He declined. It was one of the shrewdest decisions of his political life. What he already knew by observation and instinct was that contesting a close election causes bitterness and that a grudge is a political liability. Laying aside his grievance over his first defeat earned him the enthusiastic support of the Democratic party elders in the next election two years later. He was rewarded with the office of circuit clerk and recorder. Throughout his long life, he continued to cultivate his enemies. There is no way to know the harm he suffered from swallowing so much bile, but he was repaid handsomely in the coin of political gain.

Public office was not the only reward of those years. Just months into his first term, on April 5, 1939, Alta gave birth to a healthy son. Farrell was delivered by Caesarean section. She and the baby spent a month in a Fayetteville hospital while she recuperated. Orval lavished attention on the boy, and the youngster, even as a toddler, went everywhere with him.

Moving to Huntsville was as good for Alta as it was for Orval. The town had the bustle of any count seat, but was small enough that she gradually came to know practically everyone. She grew comfortable. As the wife of a county official, she quietly took her place as one of the town's respected citizens. She slowly regained some of the confidence that had been shaken out of her by her husband's outbursts of disregard and by the shock of moving from the farm to town. She was not shy, but neither was she assertive. Huntsville suited her fine.

Orval won a second term as clerk and recorder in 1940. He was clearly on his way as a man of standing in Madison County politics. He fleshed out his formal education during those years by taking six hours of night courses through the the University of Arkansas's Extension Service at Huntsville. That was his closest brush with a normal college education. In 1942, he was nominated without opposition for county judge, probably the most important political job in the county. Before he could nail down the office in the general election, he went to war. His son was just three years old.

The aging officer (he was thirty-two when he volunteered as a private and quickly won a commission) was much more aware than most of his comrades of the historical importance of their enterprise. He understood the full enormity of the Nazi menace, that it threatened not just Europe but all of Western humanity. (His father perceived the war in a different way. Shortly after the United States entered it, Sam, who had made no secret of his belief that Soviet communism was preferable to American capitalism, wrote in his diary, "I hope this is the beginning of the war that ends the capitalist system.")

World War II might have been simply an interruption for Orval. It was that for other ambitious young men. But for Faubus, as for other journeyman politicians—Lyndon Johnson comes to mind— it was an opportunity. It was also frightening, miserable, and dangerous. Unlike the up-and-comer from Texas, who spent most of the war in safe places, Faubus was in harm's way for months during some of the heaviest fighting in Europe. One of his best friends died in Normandy. As an intelligence officer in Gen. George S. Patton's Third Army, Faubus was in acute danger many times. Day after day during the Battle of the Bulge, he and his driver had to thread their way between exploding German shells. In addition to interrogating prisoners of war and crawling the front for intelligence on enemy positions, he dodged bullets, shells, and shrapnel. He was the last person to speak to a guard outside a command post in northern France moments before a German shell blew the man to bits.

The war changed him. It hardened him and made him aware of the preciousness of life. It also broadened his view of the world. Like many GIs he discovered cognac, fine wines, and exotic foods. Then there were the exotic people. He stayed in Europe a year after the war ended, helping in American demobilization. During that time, he further explored the pleasures of the flesh and expanded his knowledge of peoples who had been merely inhabitants of textbooks before the war. Between the broadening and the hardening, he left his innocence in Europe. What Alta saw when he finally came home was a husband who had drifted away from her and a father who had lost interest in his child.

The war did one other thing to him: it sharpened his appetite for a richer life. His father had taught him the small joys of dabbling in politics as a game. Now he saw the game as something more, as a route not just to power—that vision would come later—but to the good life. Each day's survival not only made life more precious; it also made him more determined to escape the ordinariness of the farm and the classroom when he got home. His ambition for public office became a kind of greed. And with the swelling ambition, he found that he had inherited, in some genetic throwback, the deviousness of old Lindy, his paternal grandmother. He learned to mask and manipulate.

Perhaps to avoid the risk of more loss, he withdrew from his son.

He had carried one of Farrell's little shirts all through the war so as to remember. But once the war was over, he had little time for the boy. He would not pay him any real attention again until years later when it was too late.

But he knew that he had to have a family to show to the public if he was to succeed in politics. He shaded the truth. He pretended, put up a front, covered his feelings. Few people knew the pain that Alta suffered as her husband set about planning his future.

All through the war, Orval never lost sight of the local political implications of what he was doing. He sent twenty-nine lengthy letters to the county seat paper, the *Madison County Record,* during his two years of training at various bases in the States. He managed another ten from Europe during the remaining year of the war. Each dispatch, written in letter form, was filled with praise for Madison County soldiers he encountered or merely heard about in other parts of the world. His writing was also generously spiced with the kind of scolding that would touch a chord with the home voters. He had no use for civilian slackers and big-union bosses who threatened strikes in vital industries.

All of this kept his name before the voters. He returned as something of a local hero. He clearly expected the voters to reward him. Instead, Major Faubus was put rudely in his place.

Leading a ticket of Democratic war veterans, he ran again for county judge. A Republican who had stayed home during the war beat him by 105 votes. All the Democratic veterans were defeated. Disappointed, bitter, worried, and still exhausted from the war, Faubus was grateful when his old friend Rep. J. W. Trimble had him appointed postmaster of Huntsville.

The postmastership might well have been the end of the line if his disappointment and fatigue had overwhelmed his ambition. He had tasted financial security in the army and in minor public office. He knew that his meager education would not propel him far. It did not help to know that the lack of higher education was his own fault. Others equally hard-pressed had worked their way through the state university or one of the small public colleges. Why he had not done so is not easily explained by his own argument that he had had to earn a living instead. Many others had faced the same need and had found a way. After the war, government-financed education was available to veterans through the GI Bill. Indeed, he flirted with the notion of going to Law School using that popular subsidy. The university at nearby Fayetteville offered returning veterans a truncated program that would provide a limited law degree without the usual pre-law requirements. Faubus and several acquaintances went together to investigate. But before he could enroll, the postmastership was offered and he chose that.

Faubus seems always to have been more interested in succeeding by his wits rather than through intellectual labor. He had little taste for learning simply for love of learning. His father's natural curiosity rubbed off on him in small ways; he prided himself on an amateur's knowledge of flora and fauna, for example. But his study was not serious in the academic sense. He read fairly widely but without depth or discipline. Some of the Faubus children resented Sam's obsession with reading. Orval never admitted to such resentment, but it is revealing that he, probably the most intellectually gifted of them all, chose to avoid the rigors of formal education. He preferred the country man's traditional mental exercise of outwitting an opponent through craft, cunning, deception, and manipulation. Those of course are invaluable weapons in sports, business, law, and politics. It was to politics, his father's other gift to him, that Orval turned once again after recovering from his electoral defeat and resting from the long years in the military.

Elsewhere in Arkansas, the returning GIs were enjoying considerable success. A marine hero named Sidney McMath returned home to Garland County, cleaned out its corrupt political machine, and was on his way to the governor's office. Faubus, who bought the *Madison County Record* in 1947, watched with interest. He published numerous articles about the charismatic McMath, helping to spread his fame beyond Garland County. He also shored up his own support, involving himself in every public enterprise. He editorialized on local and state affairs. The arrogant leaders of the Arkansas Power and Light Company, who had had their way in state government for a generation, were among his targets, although it is not likely that they were damaged much by this hillbilly advocate of public power.

Orval had not fully escaped from his father's reputation. In his early races, he had had to fight the charge that he himself was a

*Alta, Farrell, and Orval in 1942. Lieutenant
Faubus was so proud of his three-year-old son
that he dressed him in a soldier's uniform.*

PERSONAL COLLECTION OF ALTA FAUBUS.

radical and a Socialist. Through it all, though, he remained fascinated by politics as a great game. There were fellows who, like the
best athletes, would go to almost any lengths to win the game.
Sometimes a man would spend more to win a county office than
the job paid, all for the unbeatable satisfaction on election night of
walking the courthouse square as the winner, the recipient of the
people's approval. And, beyond that, something a little perverse, a
muted but open acknowledgment that here walks a master of
intrigue, the shrewdest strategist, the cleverest maneuverer, the best
gamesman. And even beyond that a sweet and secret knowledge
that by winning the grand game he has been set apart and elevated
above the common level.

Faubus talked about this many times toward the end of his life.
One day, his eyes glistening with the memory of it all, the old man
recalled a race long ago in Newton County and a fellow he knew
who had spoken admiringly of the winner. "He said, 'Yeah, he just
out-slickered them.'"

Faubus knew the feeling. He began his first race for governor
by slickering the Little Rock political establishment. He relished
the memory as long as he lived.

He had quietly studied Governor Cherry's second-term chances
and had come to believe that, contrary to public perceptions, the
incumbent was vulnerable. He had ascertained that others with
greater name recognition were not interested in making the race.
He decided to run. Even if he lost, which was likely, he would gain
statewide recognition and become a favorite to win in 1956.

On April 2, 1954, Faubus went to Little Rock to scout the
terrain. To his dismay, he quickly ran into an obstacle. Men whose
business depended on the goodwill of the governor's office urged
him not to oppose Cherry. One was especially blunt. W. R. "Witt"
Stephens, the Grant County farm boy who had made a fortune in
bonds and natural gas, was considered one of the most important
kingmakers in state politics. He walked into Faubus's hotel room
and demanded, "Who is putting you up to this?" Faubus replied,
"Did it ever occur to you that it is my own idea?"

"You wait two years and we'll be for you," Stephens said. "You
run this time and we'll beat your ass."

Later the same day word came that "they" would find an opponent for his friend Representative Trimble if he persisted.

Faubus hatched his plan. The next day, he issued a statement to the press saying, "I will not be a candidate at this time." Then he went home and disappeared, presumably back into the obscurity from which he had come.

However, his was an obscurity with a difference. He was virtually unknown among the ordinary population, but he was on good terms with scores of the most influential local leaders in the state. He had Sid McMath to thank for that.

Faubus had campaigned hard for McMath in the 1948 governor's race and had seen Madison County go for the Hot Springs man by two to one. McMath rewarded him with an appointment to the prestigious and powerful highway commission. Representing a district that stretched well beyond Madison County meant that he suddenly had far greater political clout. No issue was more urgent than better roads in the late 1940s. The hill counties were especially desperate. Faubus's own county had no more than twelve miles of paved highways when he joined the highway commission. His public stature expanded exponentially with every mile of asphalt that was laid.

After eighteen months, Faubus left the commission to join the governor's staff as administrative assistant. There he added to his network of statewide contacts. Every local leader who needed to see the governor spoke first to one of his assistants, and that frequently was Faubus. This was the man who as a child could read a poem twice and memorize it. He quickly committed to memory the names of all the important people of the state along with their problems and desires. He left the governor's office and returned briefly to the highway department as its director, and there he renewed old contacts in the all-important world of contractors and road building.

When McMath ran for a third term, Faubus took to the stump for him and made still further contacts around the state. It did not escape his attention that Francis Cherry, the man who defeated his boss, was a political unknown. Cherry, a Jonesboro chancery judge, vaulted out of his own obscurity using a radio show known as a talkathon in which he answered questions from callers for twenty-four hours nonstop. Faubus's device was to be more traditional. He would simply talk to more people, make more speeches, shake more hands, and persuade more voters than anyone else. He calculated that the plan could work because he would be building on a base of political professionals that he had already established.

For three weeks in April, after Stephens's rebuff, Faubus bided his time in Huntsville. He quietly raised fifteen hundred dollars to pay the filing fee for the Democratic primary. Then on April 26, the day before the deadline, he drove to Little Rock with two friends, O. J. Hobson, who owned a small telephone company at Huntsville, and Rolla Fitch, a former member of the legislature. They got a room in the Sam Peck Hotel, well away from the political nerve center, the Marion Hotel.

A little after 11 A.M., less than an hour before the filing deadline, they slipped out of the Sam Peck and drove to the Marion. Faubus entered through a side door and rode the freight elevator to a room above the mezzanine where the filing table was set up. No one but a few trusted friends knew he was there. Fearing that the party officials would not accept his check, he sent one of the friends to cash a fifteen-hundred-dollar check so that he could pay the filing fee in cash.

About twenty minutes before noon, the candidate shouldered his way through the crowd, filled out the forms, and paid the fee. There was no time for his opponents to field a candidate against his friend Trimble. He pointed out to the surprised reporters at the Marion that his withdrawal statement had included the words "at this time." That was not the last time he would play games with his public words.

In a memoir written after he left office, Faubus said that he had encountered two friends shortly after the filing deadline and that both were angry because, he learned later, they had been promised thirty thousand dollars for keeping him out of the race. He never identified them publicly.

The primary race that drew the most initial attention that summer was former governor McMath's challenge of Sen. John L. McClellan, a liberal versus conservative battle that would cause bitterness for years. But acute observers might have speculated about the explosive power of certain issues waiting to be exploited in the governor's race.

There was, for example, an event in late May, well before the campaign season heated up. The state public service commission approved a $3.9 million increase in electricity rates for the Arkansas Power and Light Company, one of Governor Cherry's main corporate supporters. This was the same band of corporate high-binders who only a few years earlier had torn down the billboards of Clyde Ellis, a well-known advocate of public power, when he had run unsuccessfully for the Senate. Customers were already nettled by increases in telephone and natural-gas rates. In Little Rock, even the water rates had gone up. All those increases would be used to advantage by the Madison County slicker, who had grown up as a grateful beneficiary of cheap public power when the Rural Electrification Administration brought electric lights to the hills. In the opening speech of his campaign, he lambasted the utility raises and blamed them on Cherry.

He would also find the governor vulnerable on other economic issues. In his campaign against McMath in 1952, Cherry had criticized as unfair a sales tax on seed, feed, and fertilizer. That had endeared him to poultry growers, who deeply resented the tax. Then when the legislature passed a bill repealing it, Cherry vetoed it. Faubus would make sure the poultry growers knew that. He also would remind the voters that the governor had pushed through the legislature a proposed constitutional amendment requiring the assessment of all property at 100 percent of true market value. Such a requirement probably would have been smart policy. For generations, small property owners had paid a disproportionate share of the tax load because many large owners had the political clout to manipulate assessments. But in the deft hands of Cherry's challenger, 100 percent assessment would be made to look like a huge tax increase. Predictably, the proposal went down to defeat in the 1954 election.

Probably the most emotional and effective issue for Faubus was welfare. This was long before the time when welfare would be equated with race. In Arkansas, many recipients were poor rural whites. As the campaign heated up, Faubus reminded the old people with a few laying hens and a garden that Cherry's welfare department had tried to deprive them of a few dollars a month because they had those meager means of support.

Cherry had, in fact, boasted that he had cut ten thousand people from the welfare rolls. He had also made the mistake of referring to certain aged recipients as "old dead heads." Faubus told his audience who those dead heads were. One was an old man in Little Rock who earned a few extra dollars selling newspapers, thus accumulating a "surplus" that reduced his welfare benefit. Another was an old country man who sold a few broilers and, when his benefits were cut off, had to take his wife and go live with relatives in California. "The youngest daughter came in and loaded those two old people in a car and drove them away from that house forever and took them away, and they died in a foreign place and were buried there. That old man cried as they went down that valley. They said you could have heard him a quarter of a mile." Then there was the old woman who admitted to a welfare investigator that she had two hundred dollars in the bank. The investigator said her grant would be reduced until she used up her savings. The old woman then explained what the money was for. "I've got that money saved to put me away nice when I die."

The candidate knew how to read his audiences. He watched the undemonstrative old mountain men in overalls as he told these stories. They nodded silently and punched their friends with their elbows. He guessed that he was getting through to them.

The first primary vote was a shocking confirmation of that guess. Governor Cherry got only 48 percent. Two of the three challengers drew a total of 18 percent. Faubus, the third, who had begun so far back that his early campaign stories never made page one of the capital newspapers, got an astounding 34 percent. Since custom dictated that all the opponents joined against the incumbent in a runoff, it was clear that Cherry was in trouble.

The two candidates eliminated in the first primary were Gus McMillan of Sheridan, who was never given much chance—he had in fact been put into the race by Governor Cherry as a stalking horse to divide the opposition's votes—and state senator Guy "Mutt" Jones of Conway, a colorful little man with an oratorical gift that compelled people to take him seriously.

Both quickly lined up behind Faubus—temporarily, as it turned out, in McMillan's case. Faubus brought Jones around by agreeing to pay his campaign debt and certain "expenses" and by promising to make him a chief administration spokesman in the Senate should Faubus win. Unknown to Faubus, he was helped by Governor Cherry's wife. William J. Smith, an influential lawyer and Cherry supporter, had Jones lined up for Cherry in the runoff. But when he took him to the governor's mansion to talk it over, Margaret Cherry stormed into the room complaining that Francis was turning her home into a political den. Jones drove straight to Faubus headquarters. In the U.S. Senate race, McClellan defeated McMath and the other challengers by a clear majority. Thus the decks were cleared for one main event in the runoff: a two-man fight to the finish between the stiff, genteel judge from Jonesboro and the crafty country boy from Greasy Creek.

Faubus's first obstacle in the runoff would be his own history, the most troubling part of his past. Once again, though, he came up with a plan that worked.

He lied.

Francis Cherry was worldly enough. He had manners, taste, and intelligence. He was at home in the country clubs of the state. He also enjoyed high moral standards and had no stomach for dishonesty. Much of his work as governor was aimed at making it harder to corrupt government with bribes and skulduggery. He established a fiscal code that regularized state finances and record keeping. He created a model purchasing law.

But there was in him a naivete that is often seen in those who come late to politics. He himself was straightforward, and he expected the same quality in others. He refused to play the game. It seems strange that a man of so little tolerance for the shadowy artistry of politics should have craved public office.

Soon after he defeated McMath in 1952, Cherry received a visit from two prominent political figures from east Arkansas. One was James H. Crain of Mississippi County, a ruthless, powerful planter who controlled large numbers of votes by one method or another. He was vice chairman of the highway commission; he had first

Francis Cherry, Faubus's first statewide victim, addressing the 1954 Arkansas Democratic Party Convention.

been appointed to the commission in 1941 by Gov. Homer M. Adkins. The other was Charles Adams of St. Francis County, also a planter and a highway commissioner. He had been a central figure in a scandal that had led to constitutional reform of the state's highway-building system. Both had supported McMath. Now, they told Cherry, they wanted to show there were no hard feelings. They understood that the victor had a large campaign debt. They wanted to help pay it.

Cherry told them that he was accepting no more than five hundred dollars from any contributor. Then he added that he did not want the support of the likes of them and practically ordered them out of his office.

Adams was a personable but bumbling sort whose support the governor could do without. Crain was a different matter. He carried weight, and he never forgot a slight. There was a story—impossible to confirm, but believed in certain circles—that Crain once entrusted a small-time operator with a large amount of money to bet on a certain candidate in an election. The man crossed him, bet the money on the other candidate, lost it, and had to leave the state for several years to escape Crain's wrath. When Francis Cherry crossed Jim Crain, he made an important enemy.

The governor had little instinct for the ordinary niceties of politics. Across the state in the hills of Yell County, Sheriff Earl Ladd was the main political power. Like all sheriffs, he had to visit the governor's office regularly to discuss law enforcement, prisoners, parolees, et cetera. Sheriff Ladd was dignified and proud. He was educated, witty, and sharp-spoken, the kind of man accustomed to being heard. To his surprise, Cherry was not interested in listening to him. He repeatedly got the cold shoulder. He quickly began to look for another candidate.

Political kingpins all over Arkansas got the same rough treatment and, by 1954, were ready to jump to someone else. One was Maurice Smith Sr. of Cross County, who had offended Cherry by supporting McMath. A group from that part of the state went to ask Cherry's help with a problem. He opened the discussion by asking whether they were friends of Maurice Smith. They said they were. He said, "Well, I'm not going to do anything for any friends of Maurice Smith." One of them said, "Governor, we supported you.

We're friends of Maurice Smith, but we supported you in the campaign when you were elected." He refused to listen.

In Little Rock, the influential owners of printing companies that had done business with the state for years—and had shut out outsiders through questionable bidding practices and close ties with the right officials—were angry at Cherry because he had tried to reform the system for stationery and printing contracts. They were looking for another candidate.

Cherry undoubtedly had morality on his side against the printing company owners and perhaps in his dealings with other political heavyweights, as well. But he was unskilled in the art of not antagonizing such people. As one man put it years later, "Cherry didn't have a damn lick of political sense."

After the 1954 campaign got under way, Cherry was manipulated by some of the more gifted local pols. One was Paul Van Dalsem, the bluff and crafty legislative representative from tiny Perry County, up the Arkansas River from Little Rock. One night after a rally at Perryville, the governor was invited to Van Dalsem's house to meet the county judge, Carl Adams. Van Dalsem wanted Cherry to install Adams as head of the state welfare department. Cherry, thinking he did not need the likes of Van Dalsem and Adams in his corner, refused to promise the job. Unknown to Cherry, Van Dalsem had the other three Democratic candidates parked in other rooms of his house waiting for his pitch. None knew the others were there. Before the night was over, Adams had been promised the job. The promise came from Orval Faubus, who might not have known that he was part of an evening's entertainment but who had the ready instinct to recognize a supply of easy votes.

Not surprisingly, Cherry went into his reelection campaign in 1954 confident that virtue would reward him and that the voters would understand the logic of what he had been doing as governor. When his people discovered Orval Faubus's secret history, Cherry made the purely rational assumption that the story would sink the Faubus candidacy. The voters of conservative Arkansas surely would not elect a man with ties to a discredited Communist-controlled institution. The only question was how to handle the issue. The smart way was to let someone besides the incumbent run with it. Wells, one of the most virulent critics of McMath and anyone associated with him, was one logical choice. And he had a printing press.

It was Wells who had first brought the Commonwealth story to Cherry's attention. He came to the governor's mansion late one evening and laid out what he had found. The next day, the governor's young driver, David H. Pryor of Camden, drove to Mena with a state trooper and picked up a bound volume of the Commonwealth newspaper, the *Fortnightly*. Rumors started spreading that Cherry was about to accuse Faubus of being a Communist. But the governor seemed not to know what to do with his explosive information. He waited several days while his advisors argued strategy.

William J. Smith, the ubiquitous political handyman who had been a friend or advisor to every governor since Carl Bailey in 1940, told Cherry that smearing a war hero, a soldier who had fought in the Battle of the Bulge, would backfire. "You never heard gunfire," he said. "You spent the whole war in Washington, D.C." If the governor wanted to use the Commonwealth information, he said, they should persuade Boyd Tackett to go on statewide television and raise the issue. Tackett as prosecuting attorney had taken the college to court and knew the whole story. Cherry seemed to agree.

Smith brought Tackett from Texarkana to Little Rock that night. But the governor's assistant Leffel Gentry won the day with the argument that an issue as important as this had to be raised by the candidate himself. "You'll get him beat," Smith warned. Tackett was sent home angry, threatening to work against Cherry.

Meanwhile, Faubus, who also understood strategy, was not waiting. He knew that his first task was to force Cherry to make a mistake. That he did so by lying is made a little less reprehensible by the context of history. He himself was being made the victim by association of one of the great lies of American history—the assertion endlessly repeated by the grasping classes and their political servants that a small band of zealots, encouraged by a foreign power, constituted an urgent threat to the world's most stable democracy, not just to the government but to the entire collective, spiritual, and cultural idea of the American nation, the world's contrariest people with no historical tolerance for dictatorship, and that the Red conspiracy was about to turn us all into cowering, authoritarianized puppies. Anyone who disagreed with that squalid assertion or who, like Sam Faubus, expressed skepticism about the virtues of capitalism risked being hounded into disgrace.

What made Faubus's lying remarkable was its sheer imaginative vigor and virtuosity. It was not just that he skillfully laid his fabrications end to end to meet each day's new demands, but that he layered the daily fictions so delicately that he persuaded a willing and gullible public to at least look the other way even if it did not fully believe him. The lying and dissembling also confused, outwitted, and infuriated his opponent. Cherry announced triumphantly at one point that he had counted five differing and contradictory versions of the Faubus story. He sounded genuinely baffled.

Faubus set the trap on that Saturday morning at Tuckerman when he saw Wells's newspaper being handed out in the crowd. He started his speech with an aggressive answer to something that had nothing to do with Commonwealth. The governor, trying to capitalize on the highway audit of the McMath administration, had charged that the old political highway commissioners were trying to regain control by putting their friend Faubus into the governor's office. That was a credible charge. The challenger's two biggest financial contributors were Truman Baker and Jim Crain, highway commissioners who had profited by their association with state government. Faubus replied that "holier-than-thou" Cherry had ordered many state employees, including employees of the highway department, to take two weeks' vacation to campaign for him.

He seemed to be ignoring the men at the back of the crowd as he went through his favorite issues: welfare; 100 percent assessment; utility rate increases; the feed, seed, and fertilizer tax.

Then he paused. The reporters became alert. The opposition, he said, had started "a whispering campaign of smears." But it would prove futile "because I am as American as the corn bread and black-eyed peas on which I was reared. I am just as free of subversion as the spring that flows from a mountain to form the White River."

That was all. The reporters were waiting at the next stop at Newport. Several of them had heard the rumors about Commonwealth, the left-wing school at Mena that had been closed and branded by the authorities as subversive in 1940. They had agreed not to write about it unless it was injected into the campaign. Now the challenger himself had injected it. They wanted a statement.

"They are saying that I am either a former student or faculty member at Commonwealth College," he told them. "This is not true. I have never been a student or faculty member at the school and have never attended a class there."

Lie Number One: The bait.

One of the reporters warned him that Cherry would "beat you to death with it" if he denied it. Apparently talking off the record, he said he knew that, and did not intend to deny that he had had contact with Commonwealth. But this was all he wanted to say "at the present time."

Cherry was indignant. "He seems to want to make this an issue," he said. "We'll see what we can find." His people had been busy since Wells's late-night visit gathering information on Faubus at Commonwealth. Their investigators had combed the state, even calling on Orval's boyhood friends. One had approached Carl Vanlandingham, a respected teacher who as a boy had been a pupil of Orval's at the country school at Pinnacle. "He said, 'I understand you got some correspondence from Orval when he was down at Commonwealth.' I said, 'That's mine and his business and nobody is going to get it.'" But the investigators had found at least a few who were willing to share what they knew. And in Little Rock, Wells had been busy with the old files of the college paper and other documents brought from Mena. Large piles of his *Arkansas Recorder* containing the story were already stacked around the Cherry headquarters waiting to be distributed. A campaign worker had contacted various newspapers asking whether they would accept the *Recorder's* "Who Is This Man Faubus?" editorial as an advertisement.

Two days later, on Monday, August 2, Faubus issued a statement purporting to elaborate on his teaser of Saturday. Actually, it was designed to draw his opponent in deeper. The statement traced his teaching career and said he had received an offer of a scholarship to the Mena college. He said,

> Arriving on the campus during the organizational period, preceding the beginning of a term or semester, I was elected president of the Student Association. I was not acquainted with a single student or faculty member prior to my arrival at

the college and could not account for my selection. I shortly
discovered that members of the college staff were very much
interested in obtaining students from Arkansas.

Before enrolling and paying the cash tuition, I inquired
about accreditation with other colleges. I found that the work
at the College would not be accredited toward a degree at
the University of Arkansas or other reputable colleges.

By this time I had observed other things not to my liking,
nor in conformity to my philosophy of life, such as the testimony of the head of the College, before a Legislative Committee, that he did not believe in a God.

I left the College after being on the campus as an un-
enrolled student for a few days, and returned home, not
having enrolled, not having paid any tuition and not having
taken any courses.

He concluded by saying that neighbors and friends had known all
this for nearly twenty years.

The strategy worked. Cherry shoved Wells aside and took charge
of the issue personally. That night, he went on statewide television
and radio. The *Arkansas Gazette* reported that for three-quarters of
an hour he "bludgeoned" Faubus over Commonwealth. Far from
never having been a student or never having attended a class there,
Cherry said, Faubus had spent at least a month on the campus and
might have been there as long as three months. He noted that
Faubus just that day had told reporters that he had indeed had a
brief connection with the college, but had been there no more than
two or three days. The governor then displayed the college paper,
the *Fortnightly,* which reported that Faubus had not only been on
campus but had been elected president of the student body, had
delivered the May Day speech, and had been part of a delegation
to a left-wing labor and civil rights conference at Chattanooga.

He bore down on the May Day speech. Here was "this man
Faubus," he said, "making the principal address on May Day in
the afternoon of Commonwealth's great celebration of the Red
holiday."

Cherry's aggressive tone camouflaged misgivings. He was not at
all sure he was doing the right thing, even though he was convinced

that Faubus was a Communist. His uncertainty made him sick. As he left for the television studio Monday evening, he vomited on the front porch of the mansion.

His confidence returned when the reaction set in. During the first twenty-four hours after his speech, hundreds of people called the mansion and his campaign headquarters to vent their anger. The Communist scumbag ought to be hung or run out of the state, several said.

During the next four days, Cherry repeated his charges in every corner of the state. Faubus-at-Commonwealth was page-one news every one of those days. But after the first day, a change in public sentiment began to be seen. Certain veterans' groups and influential figures spoke up to vouch for Faubus's loyalty and to praise his war record. As for Faubus himself, his response was a combination of fact, half-truth, and outright falsehood. Some of it was cold calculation, some instinctual, instantaneous recoil, and some the blind stumbling of a man trapped in fear and danger. During those four days he or his campaign workers told seven outright lies, nimbly layered, as it developed, into an artful pattern of evasion and dissembling:

1. He never attended a class at the college.
2. He was on campus only two or three days. (Years later, he refused to take credit for this one. He said his campaign office had put it in a statement without his knowledge, that he had tried to stop it, but that one newspaper already had it and printed it.)
3. He was not acquainted with a single student when he arrived there.
4. He stayed not more than two weeks.
5. He did not deliver the May Day address.
6. He never went to the meeting at Chattanooga.
7. He was not there as early as February, meaning he did not stay for the full spring term of February through May.

Through it all, Faubus's main goal was to mislead his opponent and tempt him to make mistakes. It is doubtful that he fretted over the corollary consequence of misleading the public. He could make it up to the people later. His main enemy was not even Francis

*This sign on a storage building
at Commonwealth College fairly
represented the spirit of the institution
when Faubus went there in 1935.*

Cherry; it was time. The runoff campaign lasted two short weeks. He had to decide very quickly whether to keep quiet and hope the damaging issue never surfaced or to force it into the open. He knew that if the revelation broke during the final days, there would be too little time to deal with it. Communicating with the public can be maddeningly slow, like stirring quilts in a washpot. And it would be necessary not just to inform the public but to create the necessary emotional reaction—a backlash against dirty tactics.

Hidden behind all his calculation was something else. Faubus was afraid. He had worried for years that the Commonwealth experience would derail his career. He had seriously considered going public on the issue in the first speech of his campaign at Fayetteville. The original handwritten speech contained a page and a half saying he knew all about communism because he had encountered it at the left-wing institution at Mena. "I was one time there," he wrote. The wording of the paragraph suggested that he had stayed just long enough to see Russian names painted on two buildings and to hear the director say he did not believe in God. He cut that section before delivering the speech.

He had also discussed the Commonwealth problem with a few close friends and advisors before getting into the race. One night during the winter of 1953–54 he drove to Mountain View for a long talk with Truman Baker, an associate from his days on the highway commission, and Harold Sherman, the writer and lecturer whom he had befriended on a highway matter. Sherman had a feel for the unpredictable way of public opinion. Commonwealth, he said, need not be fatal to Faubus's candidacy. It would depend on how adroitly he handled the issue.

For all his planning, Faubus was afraid. His fear seemed justified on the morning after Cherry's television speech. Faubus arrived at his headquarters and found it practically deserted. Instead of bustling with dozens of workers and volunteers, the place was quiet. A handful of loyal friends manned the phones and tried to work, but the spirit had gone out of them.

Nevertheless, the first part of his plan had worked. He had quickly enticed Cherry to abandon the role of gentleman above the fray and assume the unseemly pose of mudslinger. Now his task was to make sure the voters viewed him with sympathy and not contempt. To accomplish that, he had to stick tenaciously to his story, no matter how fictitious it was. The truth was more interesting, but far too risky.

CHAPTER
9

When Orval left his pregnant wife in the winter of 1935, he traveled in pursuit of a dream that she did not share. He had begun to look beyond the classrooms of the country schools to the security and prestige of elected office. To get there, he needed a college education. The problem, as usual, was money. The state's university was only a few miles away in Fayetteville, but he thought it was out of reach of the likes of him. As it happened, he knew of another institution of higher learning.

One day a few years earlier, Sam Faubus had taken his family to hear a speech by the Socialist party candidate for governor, Clay Fulks. Sam and the candidate had become friends. Fulks was involved with Commonwealth College near Mena and had Sam put on the college's mailing list.

In 1934, during the darkest days of the depression, Sam remembered the left-wing college. He wrote and asked for help in organizing the hard-hit farmers of Madison County, hoping they might find some economic relief. Roosevelt's New Deal had not yet taken hold. Sam and his neighbors were almost destitute. Statewide, the average annual income per person hovered around three hundred dollars. It almost certainly was less than that in southern Madison County. Social Security would be inaugurated in another year, and eleven thousand elderly people in Arkansas would qualify. And the federal government was busy distributing $19 million in depression-fighting projects to the state. But little or none of this was reaching Greasy Creek.

The college sent two young men in response to Sam's letter. One was a member of the Communist party, perhaps one of only a dozen or so in Arkansas at that time. They spent a few days at Sam's house trying, without success, to start a farmers' union. The organizing might have been ineffective, but Sam and Orval spent some jovial and stimulating evenings with the visitors.

One night as the men sat on the porch talking politics, an elderly relative in a wheelchair sat listening inside. The visitors started reciting irreverent poems about religion, and the men all laughed. After breakfast the next morning, the old woman asked Sam to take her to another relative's. She was affronted by "those poems they quoted about Jesus Christ and all that." Sam was delighted.

Sometime after he graduated from high school, Orval was looking at the Socialist tracts and magazines in his father's house and came across material on Commonwealth. He was reminded that the college was a self-help institution with low tuition—ten dollars a semester—scholarship help, and a chance to work part-time to pay much of the student's expenses. Not only that, the curriculum appealed to his liberal mind. He remembered the Socialist candidate and the entertaining visitors. Orval resolved to try the place.

He finished his term of teaching at Pinnacle before leaving. Alta, unsure of her own future, went to stay with her parents at Lincoln until the baby arrived. Then, on a late February day in 1935, Orval packed a few clothes and hitchhiked south. The next three months would not only haunt but, in a small way, enrich the rest of his years.

The Ouachitas are the only mountains in the lower forty-eight states that run east to west. The ridges rise with exaggerated drama from broad valleys, leaving an impression of substantial altitude. One of the most appealing farms in western Arkansas lies in one of those valleys twelve miles west of Mena, four miles from the Oklahoma border. The productive part of the farm is pancake flat. Running along the southern edge of this bottom land is Mill Creek, and on the other side of the creek rises a low bluff. A tended landscape of pines and hardwoods rolls back from the bluff into the forest. To the north, across the flat bottom land, you can see Rich Mountain, one of the pleasure spots of the Ouachitas.

A small band of strangers came looking for land here in 1925 and were so taken with this farm that they bought it. The farmers who moved in were unlike any the conservative residents of Polk County had ever known. They were eight teachers and about thirty-five students of an itinerant college looking for a home. The college set about sprouting not only beans and potatoes but also ideas that at once fascinated and repelled the neighbors. Other students, some seemingly too old to be in school, began to arrive from all over the United States. By the time Commonwealth died at the hands of the state in 1940, it had produced one of the richest mixtures of controversy and idealism that Arkansas had ever known. Half a generation later, the memory of the college still had the potency to become the main issue in the election of a governor of Arkansas.

Commonwealth had its roots in the Socialist party dissent that erupted before, during, and after World War I. One of its antecedent institutions was the brainchild of Job Harriman, once a candidate for vice president on the Socialist ticket headed by Eugene V. Debs. Harriman founded the Llano Cooperative Colony in California in 1914. The group moved to northern Louisiana a few years later, and there, in 1923, invited the famous Socialists Kate and Frank O'Hare and others to establish a self-help college. After a squabble and a split, the college removed itself to the Ouachita Mountains, briefly to the Polk County village of Ink, then, after another squabble and split, to rented quarters in Mena, and finally, led by its director, William E. Zeuch, to the farm west of Mena.

Commonwealth's first 80 acres cost eight hundred dollars. The farm included a barn and a double-wing log house divided by a dogtrot. When additional money was provided by the Garland Fund—run by Roger Baldwin, the director of the American Civil Liberties Union—the college expanded its holdings to 320 acres. That meant the institution owned about enough land to support in comfort a single family of respectable pretensions. With labor and a small tuition from each of its students, the college stretched the farm's productivity so that, in the manner of the loaves and fishes, it fed and housed several dozen people a year for fifteen years.

The school turned out scores of idealistic men and women during its short life. Some organized for labor unions. Others went into social work and education. A few joined the professions. A few Commoners, as might be expected, fought for the Loyalists in the Spanish Civil War. They fought in even larger numbers for America during World War II. A small number of alumni became famous. Lee

Hays and Agnes "Sis" Cunningham went on from Commonwealth to join Pete Seeger in founding the Almanac Singers. Hays wrote the words to the song "If I Had a Hammer" and other folk ballads.

Others, less well known, became influential in their cities and states. Frances Reissman Cousens returned to her native Detroit, became a professor of sociology, and served as a consultant on race relations and urban affairs. Pete Hoedemaker became a leading member of the electricians' union in Little Falls, New Jersey. Lucien Koch, for a time director of Commonwealth, organized ship-builders in Boston and became a negotiator for airline pilots after World War II. His brother Raymond was educational director for the Midwest district of the United Radio and Electrical Workers Union. Kneeland Stranahan served as port agent for Harry Bridges' Longshoremen's Union in Portland, Oregon; his wife, Lois, daughter of one of the college's neighbors in Polk County, worked in the peace movement in Oregon. David Kaplan became chief researcher for the Machinists Union. A Minnesota farmer named Richard Bosch with not even an elementary-school education came to Commonwealth to broaden his outlook. He went on to get a master's degree from the University of Wisconsin, then taught agricultural economics. Alice Cook ended at Cornell University, where she did research on working women. Harold Coy wrote several books for youngsters, including a history of Mexico that so impressed the government of that country that he and his wife were invited to spend the rest of their lives there. Winifred Chappell became an official of the Methodist Federation for Social Service. Bill Cunningham became a writer and journalist and eventually worked for the Soviet Union's news agency Tass in New York.

Commoners were trained in the intricacies of organizing: how to get workers to join industrial unions with systems of stewards and committees, how to coordinate with churches and other organizations, how to influence politics. Most of the students and teachers were leftists of one stripe or another, and some number of those spent their lives in pursuit of the goals of the Communist party.

Even though many Commoners were Marxists, they attracted the support of American luminaries left and right, from the conservative iconoclast H. L. Mencken to the first Jewish member of the Supreme Court, the liberal Louis Brandeis. Albert Einstein sent a needy young friend to study there and provided his tuition. Erskine Caldwell and Ezra Pound sent exhibits for a "worker's museum." The writer Upton Sinclair was on the school's advisory council, as were Roger Baldwin, a founder and the first executive director of the American Civil Liberties Union, and Scott Nearing, the left-wing economist who later would become a guru of the back-to-the-land movement. Debs was a frequent correspondent; the college secretary, Charlotte Moskowitz Koch, remembered as a child being dandled on Deb's knee when he visited her parents.

But of the entire lot of brilliant, passionate students who went through Commonwealth's doors, all were eventually eclipsed by the notoriety of one Arkansas hillbilly: Orval Faubus of Madison County. Few of his compatriots at the Polk County farm would have voted him most likely to succeed, certainly not in the politics of the left that most of them adhered to.

Orval had caught a ride in a truck to Mena on that February day, then had walked the last twelve miles to the college. He had arrived after dark, tired and hungry. The others made him welcome, gave him food, and found him a roommate in the dormitory. He settled in for the spring semester. With his amiable ways and his easy hill-country humor, he quickly made a place for himself.

Two weeks after his arrival, he found himself in the middle of a statewide controversy. The college had caught the attention of the Arkansas General Assembly. Commonwealth's years of agitation for workers' rights, of haranguing the delta planters, of aligning itself with coal miners in Arkansas and elsewhere, all coupled with a growing mistrust in its own community, had finally produced enough anxiety in the conservative populace of the state to translate into political pressure. Members of the legislature were ready to act.

The first step was a sedition bill. If it had passed, and in the unlikely event that the courts had upheld it as constitutional, it probably would have shortened Commonwealth's life by five years. The bill would have made it a felony to advocate crime, violence, or terrorism as a means of political reform. It passed the House of Representatives, but was killed in the Senate after it drew fire from outside the state and from prominent liberals in and beyond Arkansas.

Shortly afterward, on February 13, just days before Orval hitch-hiked to Mena, the legislature passed a resolution calling for an investigation of alleged Communist activities at Commonwealth. A four-man committee of legislators, including Rep. Marcus Miller of Commonwealth's home county of Polk, spent all of the following Saturday and into the small hours of Sunday morning on the campus and in the neighboring community. They started by visiting classes and questioning teachers and students. Then they moved to the courthouse in Mena and took testimony from local citizens. Some of the latter claimed to have witnessed mixed swimming and "free love" at the college, which they saw as a lack of morality and Christian standards on the campus.

The investigation continued a few days later in Little Rock with more hostile witnesses. Then another bill was introduced. This one would have empowered the chancery courts to shut down any institution that advocated overthrowing the government or that engaged in anarchy or communism. A hearing was set for March 9 before the House Judiciary Committee. Among those traveling to Little Rock to defend the college was Orval Faubus.

The Commonwealth group, led by the director, Lucien Koch, and his wife, went to the capital in cars. It was Orval's first visit to the Arkansas Statehouse. He was probably the least sophisticated member of the Mena delegation. All the others had had experience in one kind of political activism or another. Orval's activism, if one did not count the free-wheeling conversation at his father's table, had been limited to a single public debate on the merits of socialism.

Young Lucien Koch set the tone. Showing more courage than wisdom, he did not shrink from telling the conservative legislators precisely and colorfully what he thought. Yes, the Communist government of the Soviet Union had some advantages over that of the United States. Yes, some Commonwealth teachers probably adhered to the Soviet government's teachings. No, he did not believe in a Supreme Being, and neither did most of his faculty colleagues. As for the legislature's revised proposal, it was still a threat to civil liberties and was clearly unconstitutional. In rewriting the proposed legislation, he said, "you are just swapping a carbuncle for a boil."

A teacher named Carl Parker accused the legislators of "looking for a Communist hidden under every twin bed." Another teacher, Mrs. Harold Coy, said the proposal had been born of hatred.

Then came the testimony of the only Arkansawyer in the college delegation. The reporter spelled his name Arval Faubaus and added with apparent skepticism that the fellow said he was from the Ozarks. The audience must have been let down by the mild testimony that followed.

Orval offered the opinion that the bill under question was un-American, but was otherwise uncritical. He did deny being a Communist or having been taught to overthrow the government. The bulk of his testimony seemed aimed at demonstrating the ordinariness of life at Commonwealth. It was "not unlike other schools" he had attended, he said. As for the background of the students, he himself had been affiliated with the Boy Scouts for eight years— suggesting perhaps that the typical Commoner was just the kid next door.

The reporter made no attempt to gauge Orval's effectiveness with the committee. Neither did he mention that the teacher Carl Parker, who had made the wisecrack about looking for Communists under twin beds, was from Finland, that he had settled in the American Midwest and Anglicized his name, and that he once had taken part in a traveling left-wing educational and propaganda effort known as the School on Wheels. The writer also had no way of knowing that the Americanized Finn had a sense of humor that would stay in his Commonwealth roommate's memory for half a century. His roommate was Orval Faubus.

There was one detail in Faubus's testimony that would have loomed large in the future if his political enemies had dug it up. He told the committee that he had been a student at Commonwealth about two weeks. That means he arrived at Mena in late February in time for the beginning of the spring term. He stayed through May, or a total of more than three months. None of the reporters covering the 1954 election and none of Cherry's workers—not even the energetic John Wells—happened upon that information even though it was in the same old *Gazette* files that they combed for days.

The Commoners made one other stop in Little Rock before driving back to Mena late in the day. They stopped to eat at Zeni's Cafe. This was a curious establishment built to look like a windmill. It sat, inexplicably, on the capitol grounds. Even more inexplicably, it was owned by a Greek immigrant who was probably the only openly avowed Communist in the state of Arkansas. A generation later, when the state went through still another Red scare and an ambitious but dull attorney general scoured the territory for Communist subversives past and present, he haplessly overlooked the proud Red who had once served hamburgers and Marxism in the very shadow of the Statehouse.

The legislature's heavy-handed treatment of Commonwealth provoked something of a national outcry. The famous lawyer Arthur Garfield Hays stood ready to defend it in court. About one thousand artists and writers sent a telegram from Paris saying, "Hands off Commonwealth." H. L. Mencken invited the college to move to his native Maryland where he would guarantee it free speech. "You will be at liberty to teach spiritualism, vegetarianism, communism, Calvinism, or cannibalism, or all of them together," he wrote to the school's faculty. "I engage to find 200 head of revolutionary young professors to help you and give a seminar in moral theology myself."

In spite of having been attracted by Commonwealth's leftist leanings, Orval did not align himself there with either of the two main left-wing groups, the Communists or the Socialists. True, he regarded himself in those days as "an extreme liberal." He liked what the Socialists had to say about Social Security and looking after the little man. He admired Norman Thomas, the Socialist party's perennial candidate for president. But something held him back from joining the organized left at the college. He made a point of running with the nonaligned, independent students.

His middle-of-the-road stance made him attractive as a potential leader. His fellows promptly elected him president of the student body, even though, as he later maintained, he apparently never formally enrolled as a student. He went to classes, anyway. Commonwealth was not rigid about such matters. It seems likely that the same compulsion that later drove him into politics in Madison County made him go after the presidency of the student body. He couldn't keep from competing when he had a chance.

But perhaps a more important reason for his being named president was his Arkansas connection. The college didn't have many Arkansawyers and, for public-relations reasons, needed more. Its mission to educate poor southerners was compromised somewhat by being known as a hotbed of Yankee radicals. The leaders had already reached out to some of the better-known liberals in the state. Vance Randolph, the folklorist, was a friend of the college and made even closer bonds with it after his nephew Lee Hays enrolled. Charlotte Moskowitz, the college secretary who later married the teacher Raymond Koch, became friends with a young Fayetteville woman named Helen Finger. Miss Finger was the daughter of the writer Charles Finger and later the wife of the distinguished legal educator Robert A. Leflar. Miss Moskowitz spent several weekends at the Finger home where she rubbed elbows with Arkansas up-and-comers like J. W. Fulbright. But Commonwealth had not attracted many ordinary young people from Arkansas as students. Orval's arrival was welcomed.

The make-up of the student body was of more than casual interest to the institution. As it happened, Orval had arrived on campus during a time when the college was beset not only by outside threats but also by a new eruption of internal squabbling. The Socialists and Communists on campus had both proseletyzed through the years, and both had gained converts. But now the Communists had decided to move more aggressively. Whenever a Communist student heard a teacher or another student make a point that did not conform to party theory, he or she challenged it on the spot. The policy was leading to considerable disruption, especially in courses on Socialist theory. Classes were becoming mired in controversy. Tension and bad temper became such problems that the director, Lucien Koch, had to call an assembly and lay down the law. The college was devoted to free expression, he said, and interference with that would not be tolerated.

To further suppress divisiveness, a United Front was formed. It was this group, representing the three political factions, that sponsored Orval for student body president.

He was also selected to present the main May Day address on the afternoon of May 1. The campus paper, the *Fortnightly,* reported that his topic was "The Story of May Day." The talk was part of a full day of festivities and speeches culminating with supper and an evening of drama and music. Neighbors were invited, and some of them applauded Orval's talk. The same issue of the *Fortnightly* carried a statement, written two years earlier, on the origin of May Day by eighty-eight-year-old Frederick Cuno, "probably the last surviving member of the intimate group which included Marx and Engels."

Part of the reason for Orval's ready acceptance was his personality. The young man who showed up at Commonwealth was far removed from the shy boy who had fled to the backyard to avoid strangers. The years of teaching, dealing with both pupils and parents, had brought him confidence. He had developed into a fairly good-looking man. Interestingly enough, the young women at the college did not find him particularly attractive in spite of his mild attempts at flirtation. But he made a place for himself and seemed to be enjoying the experience.

He clearly liked some aspects of campus life—the stimulating classes, the work in the fields and woods, the scintillating conversation, the play of ideas. He appreciated the challenging range of coursework: Marxism, labor journalism, psychology, imperialism, labor problems, public speaking, working-class history, current events, labor drama, English for the foreign-born, stenography, labor orientation. He read perhaps more systematically than he ever had before: books by Upton Sinclair and other leftist authors, newspapers such as the *New York Times,* magazines that only a library could afford. The campus boasted lawyers, musicians, dramatists, and writers. One man was writing a book about the Socialist uprising in Oklahoma. The college broadened the young man from the hills just as it did scores of others from around the country.

Commonwealth's middle years, before the radical left took over and dampened the play of ideas, were marked by an intellectual vibrancy that is rarely achieved in higher education. The college became a clearinghouse for left-wing magazines that carried the work of writers like Nelson Algren. The students read and discussed them avidly. Visiting speakers included the novelists James T. Farrell and Jack Conroy along with leftist luminaries like Ella Reeve (Mother) Bloor. Some students expelled from the University of

Orval and an unidentified fellow student at Commonwealth College during the spring of 1935.
AUTHOR'S COLLECTION.

California at Los Angeles for expressing radical opinions were invited to enroll at Commonwealth. Lenin was memorialized in a series of speeches a few weeks before Orval's arrival, and later that year a group of faculty and students traveled to Moscow to spend the summer session at Moscow University.

Even the play must have seemed exotic to a hard-working farmer and teacher. Men and women swam together in Mill Creek. One day Orval and seven or eight other students packed a picnic lunch and hiked to the top of Rich Mountain. At Greasy Creek, hiking was a form of transportation, not pleasure. The campus paper reported in a jocular tone that Orval and another fellow had caught some eels in Mill Creek and had had trouble persuading the other students to eat them.

Commonwealth, by the time Orval arrived, was deeply involved in most of the political rebellion that was sweeping the region. Coal miners in western Arkansas were rising against the mine owners for better pay and working conditions. Sharecroppers in the delta of eastern Arkansas were organizing for minimal standards of decency, and paying with their lives. All across the South, desperate men and women were fighting not only the economic depression but also generations-old systems of exploitation: planter domination of black and white sharecroppers; yankee colonialists siphoning raw materials and paying lower wages to southern workers than to northern workers employed by the same companies; railroads charging higher freight rates in the South than in the North; local bankers enforcing their political will through economic muscle; powerful interests throwing thousands of farmers off the land; whites denying the vote and other rights of citizenship to blacks. Some of those wrongs would be righted only by time and the turning wheel of history. But others, such as sharecroppers' being thrown off the land, had to be opposed at once if the victims were to avoid starvation.

In January 1935, while Orval was still teaching at Pinnacle, Lucien Koch received a telegram from the Southern Tenant Farmers Union saying one of their chief organizers had been jailed at Marked Tree, Arkansas. The group asked him to come and help. The union was the creation of two Socialists from Tyronza, Arkansas, H. L. Mitchell and Clay East. It was an interracial group that eventually spread across the Deep South. In Arkansas and elsewhere, it was opposed by planters and their political allies using everything from the judicial system to murder and terrorism. Some of the most brutal force in the South's violent history was used against the sharecroppers. Like the civil rights movement of the 1950s and 1960s, the tenant farmers union was seen as a threat to the southern way of life. Indeed, it was.

Koch and two students went immediately to the delta. They learned that the croppers around Marked Tree were on strike demanding a wage increase of twenty-five cents a day—from seventy-five cents to one dollar. The planters had already started evicting their striking tenants. Within hours of his arrival, Koch was arrested. He was dragged from a meeting in a black church by a drunken riding boss from one of the plantations. The boss was accompanied by four other pistol-brandishing men, including sheriffs' deputies. The men beat and kicked Koch and another man, then jailed them. A mob of planters and deputies invaded the jailhouse and threatened to lynch the prisoners. The Commoners finally were freed, thankful to be alive.

Meanwhile, the college plunged into another cause nearer to home. Thousands of western Arkansas people were out of work. Relief from the government was slow in coming, prompting hungry people to organize. That was Commonwealth's strong suit—organizing. Lucien Koch's brother Raymond joined that effort. He and nine others from Fort Smith and other western Arkansas communities were chosen to travel to Washington in January 1935 to seek help from the Roosevelt administration and Congress. They cadged food and lodging all the way there and back, staying in the capital long enough to badger their representatives and to attend a conference of unemployed people.

Arkansas's senator Hattie Caraway arranged housing for the visitors in Washington and helped them get two tires and gasoline money for the trip home. Mrs. Caraway, who had filled the remainder of the term of her deceased husband, was considered sympathetic to Sen. Huey P. Long's share-the-wealth movement. The Louisiana neighbor had ensured her election to a full term in 1932, as the depression spread, with a whirlwind seven-day tour that saw him deliver thirty-nine speeches in thirty-one Arkansas counties.

The year Faubus hitchhiked to Commonwealth was one of the worst in the nation's history. Drought descended on top of economic collapse, and the heartland shriveled into dust. Commonwealth's farm had been hard hit during the previous summer; the area went 109 days without rain, and most of the crops were ruined. A fourth of the national work force was unemployed in 1935. Millions were hungry. And before the end of that fateful year, Mrs. Caraway's mentor would be assassinated in Baton Rouge.

Raymond Koch joined a relief rally of five thousand people in Fort Smith. Scores were beaten by the authorities. Raymond was jailed overnight. Years later he wrote,

> I spent a night in a cell in which the steam had been deliberately turned up, and may owe my life to a crack I found in the outside wall near the floor. By lying prone, with my nose to the aperture, I managed to continue breathing.

The main political excitement for Orval occurred when the college sent a delegation, led by Raymond Koch, to Chattanooga for the All-Southern Conference for Civil and Trade Union Rights. Orval was one of four from Commonwealth. They arrived there about May 26 expecting to spend the next few days discussing how to repeal the poll-tax requirement and the federal sedition law—the one that had ensnared Sam during the First World War. Other topics included the disbanding of "all armed fascist bands" and an end to racial lynching and capitalist persecution. The conference was racially integrated, a bold move for the time.

Before the conference could begin, a vigilante group of Chattanooga policemen and members of the American Legion got wind of it and threatened violence. The delegates left before the vigilantes arrived and secretly reassembled at Highlander Folk School at Monteagle.

Orval missed the excitement. He had gone to visit acquaintances in a nearby community. He rejoined the group at Monteagle in time for part of the program, but it is doubtful that he got much out of it. While he sympathized with the aims of the conference, the trip to Tennessee seemed to be more of an outing for him than an experience in activism.

That reluctance to engage himself seriously in a purely ideological cause would show itself time and again during his career. It troubled some of his Commonwealth associates at the time. As they recalled it years later, Orval was personally ambitious but politically unsophisticated. As seen by those dedicated leftists—who happened to be well-read Marxists—he had only a superficial grounding in history and economics in spite of his exposure to Socialist thought at home.

Perhaps so; but his reluctance was grounded in something more than a poor understanding of history and economics. What he already possessed in abundance at age twenty-five was an instinctive realism that made him shy away from danger. The only surprising thing about his Commonwealth experience is that he surrendered to his father's urging and went there in the first place. It is clear that he had already set his sights on elected office, and he had to have known the dangers of a close association with the political left.

Orval was ambitious in a way that set him apart. While the other Commoners yearned to be part of a larger cause—organizing workers and farmers, abolishing child labor, establishing a more rational economic system, saving the world—Orval's ambition was personal. He yearned to be somebody, a "big shot" as one person put it. His acquaintances noticed that he was always sizing people up but withholding his own inner thoughts. He showed a certain care in what he professed to others, indicating, as they saw it, that he had already decided on his life's goal and understood that his ambitions might be thwarted by a careless utterance that could be resurrected by opponents.

And while he might have been unsophisticated in book learning, he possessed a certain rural wisdom that was lacking in his more educated colleagues. For example, they had dismissed his argument that they would make more headway in organizing rural people if they would stop openly condemning religion. Then one organizer returned from a mission trip to the black sharecroppers and reported, with some surprise, that "you cannot get anywhere with these people unless you join them in a church."

His fellows also noticed that he made sure to display the best side of his personality. And his personality was winning. At age twenty-five, he had blossomed into a natural storyteller, using tales of possum hunting and country life to make people laugh and to drive home a point. The classroom had honed his skills as a public speaker. He found a ready audience for that skill at the college. The students were encouraged to practice public speaking not only in the classroom but also spontaneously wherever an audience of three or four could be gathered—waiting in the food line, working in the field.

There was a revealing moment during the public-speaking class. The teacher asked each student to explain why he or she wanted to become a public speaker. Everyone else talked of serving one cause or another, of becoming part of a larger movement. When Orval's turn came, he said forthrightly that he aspired to become a public person. He wanted to represent the people, he said.

The others were a little shocked at what they took to be so bold an admission of personal ambition. Probably some of them wondered why a person who had grown up in a Socialist household had no more concern for the larger good. There is no doubt that his father's teachings had made him more aware than his childhood friends of social and economic injustice. There is also no doubt that he wanted to improve the world. But somewhere along the way, the cause of saving the world had become less pressing than his own advancement. It might be remembered that personal ambition was admired in most of American society at that time. Only in a community of idealists would it be seen as a flaw. For the rest of Orval's life, there would be those who accused him of betraying his father's ideals for his own advancement. If betrayal is the word—and more needs to be said about that—then it began to be visible during his tenure at Commonwealth.

In public, he protested repeatedly in later years—not just during the 1954 election campaign, but for years afterward—that he had stayed at Commonwealth only a short time, a few weeks at most. He said he first found that the school was not accredited. Then he discovered—this with a profession of shock as he spoke of it years later—that Commonwealth was trying to indoctrinate young people with Marxism. The last straw, he said, was hearing an assertion by a Communist refugee from Germany, speaking to an orientation class, that marriage was simply legalized prostitution. He took that as an insult to his mother and shook the dust of Polk County from his feet.

This was, at the least, selective memory. In a letter to Gov. Carl Bailey two years after he left the college, he urged the governor to take a "progressive and liberal viewpoint" by opposing a legislative proposal aimed at Commonwealth. He wrote, "I personally have first hand knowledge that the school is not guilty of the things of which it stands accused, namely that it teaches Communism and free love." Much later, he acknowledged that he had been aware of the Communist influence while he was a student there. He told two interviewers before he died that by 1935 he had already begun to think about running for office and had been worried about the college's growing identification with the Communist party. "My discontent was when the Communists were becoming too prominent, and I knew if I became connected with it too strongly, you know, that it would just eliminate me from any role in public life in Arkansas."

There is considerable evidence that Commonwealth did fall increasingly under Communist domination, especially during the five turbulent years after Faubus was there. Lucien Koch, for all his youthful excesses, had exercised some restraint on the doctrinaire Communists. But after the legislative investigation, he apparently saw little future at the college. He left a few weeks after Faubus during the summer of 1935. The directors who succeeded him included some who made little secret of their Communist party sympathies, and the college's advisory committee included a number of Communists. Historically, these were relatively safe years for left-wing activists; the nation was midway between the anti-communist rages of the late teens and the early 1950s. Nevertheless, rural Polk County reacted predictably as the creature in its bosom came to look more and more, in the eyes of the home folk, like a viper.

Locally, the fight against Commonwealth was led by the Rev. Luther D. Summers, pastor of the First Baptist Church of Mena. For three years, he denounced the faculty and students as "immoral, atheistic, and bestial." He accused them of practicing communism, free love, and nude bathing. Political pressure built steadily. Finally, in 1940, the authorities filed a number of charges aimed at demonstrating that Commonwealth was trying to overthrow the government. A justice of the peace hurriedly tried the case and fined the institution $2,500. The property was auctioned to satisfy the judgment. The library's valuable collection of books, perhaps the best resource on left-wing thought in Arkansas at the time, was bought by the Rev. Mr. Summers. He got 5,442 books for $360. He said he wanted them for "further use against Communism."

That was not the end. Commonwealth's memory was revived during the post–World War II Red scare that came to be named for the Republican senator from Wisconsin, Joseph R. McCarthy. Even before the war ended, the Special Committee on Un-American Activities of the House of Representatives in 1944 branded the college as a "Communist Enterprise." Then in 1949, Atty. Gen. Tom C. Clark, a Democrat appointed by Pres. Harry S. Truman, put his own stamp of Communist on the defunct but somehow still-threatening college. Five years after that, during the election summer of 1954, the ghost still had the power to frighten Arkansawyers.

CHAPTER

10

A mystery: Why would the voters take to their bosom Sen. John L. McClellan, who had the bearing of a mob boss and spent the brutal summer of 1954 dressed in a white suit and riding in a lavender Cadillac, while turning their backs on upright Francis Cherry, whose only obvious lapse in judgment was showing up at rallies in an air-conditioned Oldsmobile while his listeners cooled themselves with funeral-home fans? Somehow, the one was perceived as a man to look up to while the other was seen as a snob.

True, that peevish view of the governor was subtly encouraged by his hillbilly opponent, but Cherry seemed unaware of his problem. At one midafternoon rally, in the scorching July heat, he sat in his car with the air conditioning running, well away from the distracting crowd, and listened to a St. Louis Cardinals baseball game while he waited his turn to speak. Faubus, in shirt sleeves and sweating, spent the time working the crowd with a match stem in his mouth.

Faubus's appeal was easy to understand. His style was one of rural dignity, not aloofness but appropriate distance, overlaid with a hint of personal concern. He was not good at remembering names, contrary to popular belief. He compensated for it at political gatherings by huddling head to head, he attentive to the ground, like a pitcher listening to his manager, as first one voter and then another leaned close and spoke confidentially.

When the candidate finally looked up, the voter found himself confronting one of the extraordinary faces of modern politics. It was striking not for its symmetry but the lack of it. Everything in the face was regular and even quite handsome except the nose, which was crooked from every angle. In profile, it was a hesitantly drawn question mark. It bulged at the bridge, narrowed in its descent, and jutted forward and upward like a ski slope at the end. This Cyrano's appendage seized the attention of anyone close at hand, and from the nose it was a short distance to the place where Faubus was most dangerous: his eyes. At a glance, they seemed unremarkable. They were a dull light brown (or were they hazel?) and of ordinary size and setting. But they were unquestionably a weapon. At one moment, they might be clouded and distant as if he were lost in thought or had forgotten where he was. Then in an instant they would fix the other person in a gaze of such interest and intensity that anything he said was taken as true. And then he would smile slightly and the eye frames would wrinkle and the deal would be closed.

Thousands of voters had already seen Faubus and Cherry at close range when the Commonwealth storm broke. Behind the contrasting images the opponents had established, only a few close associates of the challenger knew that he possessed another quality that did not show in public. He was capable of great cunning.

Faubus waited precisely four days after the first primary to bait the trap for Cherry. It was on Saturday, July 31, that he revealed the "whispering campaign of smears." That meant the story would land in the big Sunday newspapers. Cherry on that same day was still hammering at Faubus's highway commission experience, warning that the old crowd was using Faubus to try to regain control of the lucrative highway construction business.

There was another running story in the newspapers that week, one that until that Sunday had no apparent connection to Arkansas. Sen. Joseph R. McCarthy of Wisconsin had finally overreached in his Communist hunt. The Senate was debating whether to censure him. A national backlash against his tactics had set in.

Cherry's obvious satisfaction at having Faubus raise the issue was not the only reaction after the Sunday papers came out the next day. Guy H. (Mutt) Jones, one of the defeated candidates, chose that day to announce his support of Faubus. He went on to denounce the smear tactics against his new ally. Faubus pointed to his World War II combat as proof of his loyalty. He told reporters he had gone to Mena to look over Commonwealth but left after "a few days, not more than two weeks." Twenty-four hours later, Jones fired another barrage at "Joe McCarthy Cherry."

Then on Monday evening came Cherry's forty-five-minute "bludgeoning" of his opponent, strongly suggesting that the Commonwealth connection made Faubus unfit to be governor. The trap was sprung.

That same evening, Faubus telephoned Kenneth Coffelt, a lawyer friend, and got a quick lesson in libel law. Early Tuesday he sent a bluntly worded telegram to the governor and two of his main advisors, John Wells and Boyd Tackett, who had returned, a little grumpily, to the Cherry campaign. Tackett was a former congressman and one-time prosecuting attorney for the Mena district who had investigated Commonwealth. Faubus's wire dared them to use the word that had thus far been unspoken in public:

> The issue is now based on the insinuation of your crowd that I am a subversive and have engaged in subversive activities. Now I charge you to make this statement that I am a subversive or that I ever participated in any subversive activities and if you do, knowing that you do not have any proof of any such charge, I will sue you immediately in the courts of my native state. Now you men get down to the point and get on the line and either stand or fall on this proposition.

The confident tone of the telegram masked a growing anxiety. Faubus was aware that he and his workers had told contradictory stories—first that he had never been a student there, then that he had stayed two or three days, then that maybe he had been there two weeks—and that these scattershot reports had opened him up to a charge of dishonesty. From Texarkana, where he was speaking after firing off the telegram, he telephoned Henry Woods, an old friend in whom he had confided his Commonwealth story while both worked in McMath's office at the Capitol. "What do you think?" he asked. "Orval," Woods said, "you've got to get one story and stick to it."

Faubus heeded that advice, first by firmly repeating that he had not made the May Day speech and had not gone to Chattanooga as part of the college's delegation to the labor and civil rights conference. Unknown to Woods, Faubus had taken the precaution, before issuing his teaser on Saturday, of dispatching a trusted Madison County friend to Tennessee to collect a box of damaging evidence, material that presumably would have tied him to the conference. The friend met a man at a prearranged spot, spoke only his name, was handed the box, and drove back to Arkansas with it. The friend said he never opened the box. After it was handed to Faubus, it disappeared. For the moment, the candidate ignored the troubling variations on the length of his stay at the college. He trusted that Cherry's people would not be able to prove, decisively, that he was short-changing the truth on that and other details. Taking the offensive, he hurled an accusation of his own. Cherry, he said, was using "McCarthy tactics."

The Cherry camp sidestepped the charges of McCarthyism. It continued to rely on what it regarded as a case built on facts. Tackett invited Faubus to sue him. "The real issue is whether Faubus is truthful," he said. He apparently was confident that Faubus would not sue because under court rules of sworn testimony the damning details of Faubus's stay at Commonwealth would be revealed. Tackett took a swipe at Faubus's new ally, Jones, saying that Jones had tried to peddle inside information on Faubus at Commonwealth to the Cherry campaign three or four days before the first primary vote.

Faubus and his staff feverishly set about constructing the one story that he could stick with. Jim Malone, a young campaign worker from Lonoke County, was tipped off—by Mutt Jones, he said later—that he could find evidence supporting Faubus in the old files of the *Arkansas Gazette*. Malone found the newspaper's report on the legislative hearing of February 1935. In it was a reference to one Nat Brown of Chicago as president of the

Commonwealth student body. The young sleuth then persuaded Secretary of State C. G. (Crip) Hall to give him copies of the official record of the legislative hearing to back up the newspaper report. The record listed what purported to be all the enrolled students as of February 1935, and the name Faubus was not on the list.

Faubus was elated. He had sent Alta to Huntsville to look for written evidence to back his claims, but the documents she was looking for had disappeared. "This is it!" he told Malone. Campaign workers and advertising experts stayed up late Monday night writing Faubus's definitive answer to Cherry's charges.

On Wednesday, a full-page advertisement appeared in the *Arkansas Gazette* laying out Faubus's case. "How do you define 'decency,' 'Frantic Francis'?" the headline said. The ad, in "fact" versus "fiction" format, presented all of Faubus's denials: that he had enrolled as a student, paid tuition, attended any classes, or made the May Day speech. On Cherry's assertion that he had showed up at the college in February, the ad said that Cherry had the records of the state legislature and that those records

> contained something very important that he didn't quote— sworn testimony that Orval Faubus was not a student at Commonwealth College. He knew that the record—which listed all the students of the college—contained no mention of Orval Faubus anywhere in it.

The ad omitted an important fact. Faubus had indeed been at the college in February. If Cherry's people had searched the old newspaper files more thoroughly, they would have found the *Gazette* story tucked away on an inside page of March 9, 1935—two and a half weeks after the first legislative hearing—in which Faubus was quoted, in testimony before a second legislative hearing, as saying that he had been a student there about two weeks. Before he died, he admitted that that information would have been "quite damaging" to his prospects if his opponent had found it.

The ad dealt cleverly with Faubus's having been elected president of the student body. Yes, it said, he was elected to the presidency, and he was also named as a delegate to the Chattanooga conference (but never went) and selected as May Day speaker (but never spoke), only because the college was trying to put up an

"Arkansas front" during the legislative investigation. "IT'S AN OLD COMMUNIST TRICK AND ORVAL FAUBUS WAS ITS INNO-CENT VICTIM," the ad said.

Four days into the Commonwealth controversy, a casual observer would have been hard put to judge which candidate was more appalled by the Communist conspiracy to seduce the depression-era youth of Arkansas with its Mena college. Faubus, in teasing out his own fictive history there, found himself denouncing the place almost as often as his opponent did. He had been itching to run against communism from the start. In the section about Common-wealth that he had cut from his announcement speech, he had noted that the authorities had finally closed the abominable place before World War II. He also had asserted in the deleted paragraph that more alert state leaders would have closed it sooner, thus pre-venting "this attempt at Communist indoctrination of our youth."

Alongside the bluster, defiance, and revisionism, a more subtle narrative was also being laid down by Faubus. Arkansas in those days had large numbers of people who were proud to call them-selves liberal or moderate Democrats. To them, Cherry's tactics amounted not just to mudslinging but to the lowest form of politi-cal combat: questioning an opponent's patriotism. The most promi-nent in this group was Harry S. Ashmore, executive editor of the oldest daily newspaper west of the Mississippi River, the *Arkansas Gazette*. Ashmore, a native of South Carolina, had come to Arkansas with the fresh viewpoint of postwar southerners influenced by W. J. Cash and his *The Mind of the South* and by a new breed of real-istic historians such as C. Vann Woodward. The editor brought with him a broadened national perspective that fit well with the young progressives surrounding McMath. In 1952, he had taken leave to work as a high advisor to Adlai Stevenson, the Democratic nominee for president.

Ashmore, although disappointed by McMath's defeat for a third term, had given some editorial support to his successor. He liked some of Cherry's reforms even though he considered the man a stuffed shirt and a political amateur.

When Cherry raised the Commonwealth issue—and the corol-lary suggestion that his opponent might be a Communist traitor—Ashmore was incensed. So were many other progressive Democrats, including people of influence in all parts of the state. Even conservatives who considered themselves strongly anti-Communist were troubled by what they saw as the unfairness of Cherry's tactics. Many of these same conservatives were already disgusted by McCarthy's national campaign, not because they disagreed about the threat of communism, but because they had begun to see McCarthy as a bully. Arkansas's own Fulbright was leading the Senate fight to censure him.

Word had got around before Faubus forced it into the open that Cherry was considering using Commonwealth. Three friends who had halfheartedly supported Cherry in the first primary—Edwin Dunaway, a former law professor and former state Supreme Court justice, one of the few white leaders in Little Rock who had personal friends in the black community; Frank Newell, another leader of the Little Rock progressives; and Tom Downie, who had been nominated for prosecuting attorney without a runoff—paid a visit to the governor early in the runoff period. As they waited in an outer office of the campaign headquarters, they overheard John Wells telling another Cherry supporter that their man should use the Commonwealth issue. The other man was Jimmy Karam, a Little Rock clothier with a past reputation as a tough and a strike breaker. The three men confronted Cherry in private. Dunaway told him, "If you use this Commonwealth business, accuse Orval of being a Communist, in my opinion you will be defeated, and in my further opinion you should be defeated."

Shortly afterward, a Cherry operative approached the *Gazette* with an advertisement attacking Faubus over Commonwealth. The paper's management sent him packing with a warning that the paper would condemn Cherry editorially if the tactic were used.

When Faubus telephoned Woods from Texarkana, it was clear to the latter that the candidate was on the verge of panic, his cool public performance notwithstanding. Woods made an instantaneous decision. Before the election season started, he had been one of the main friends advising Faubus not to run. He not only believed that his friend could not win; he was also troubled by the damage a Faubus candidacy might do to McMath's race against McClellan. The two candidates would rely on many of the same political operatives in the McMath organization, a group that Woods, an organizing genius, had carefully put together. But now his best friend had been defeated in the first primary, and Woods had to decide whether to swallow his resentment. He opted to help his other friend.

He told Faubus that he had just seen Harry Ashmore and that Ashmore was disgusted with what he saw as Cherry's Red-baiting. He would ask the editor, one of the most fluent writers in the state, to help write a speech for Faubus.

Woods and Dunaway went to Ashmore's house in Pulaski Heights. Dunaway, who had jumped to Faubus with enthusiasm after Cherry's attack, had put up his own money to buy radio time and was shaking the bushes for contributions. The three of them worked on the speech much of Tuesday night, using material supplied by the candidate and Malone. Ashmore was the wordsmith. Like Woods, he had known about the Commonwealth episode for some years, but was dismayed by Faubus's seemingly abrupt denial and his later dissembling over how long he had stayed there. Handling those contradictions required "pretty fancy footwork," as he recalled later. They settled on the assertion that Faubus in his early statements had been misinterpreted, that he had meant to say that he had been there only a short time, and that when he found out what was going on, he left. The speech, as it developed, was a gem of persuasion.

Unfortunately, it was too long. Dunaway had bought thirty minutes on a statewide radio network to originate from an open-air meeting at Pine Bluff. Ashmore's ringing cadences stretched to about an hour.

Faubus, who had arrived in Little Rock late in the afternoon, worked on it frantically, adding here, cutting there. It was still too long. His car arrived at the Pine Bluff baseball field eight minutes before air time. He had to finish the editing as he spoke, discarding whole paragraphs as he stood in front of the microphone. A well-dressed figure materialized out of the dark fringe of the field to hold the pages for him to keep them from blowing in the wind. It was Jimmy Karam, the man Dunaway had seen in Cherry's office days earlier. Faubus never knew whether Karam had come as a spy; whatever his motive, he became a convert.

The speech turned out to be the most important of Faubus's life.

It dwelt first on his reasons for going to Commonwealth and his need as a poor mountain boy for a better education. One of Ashmore's clauses stuck in his mind the rest of his life: "When I went out from the green valley of my youth . . ." The speech—fact, fiction, and all—became his story, and he stuck with it.

Midway through it, Faubus glanced up from his text and saw the spectators moving closer. They made no sound, but he saw women wiping away tears. He knew before he left the playing field that night that his campaign had turned the corner.

The next day, Ashmore wrote a blistering editorial. Appearing on page one of the Friday paper, it did not attack Cherry directly for his Commonwealth tactic but took his campaign to task for an advertisement in the *Arkansas Democrat*. The ad, signed by a Cherry supporter, accused the *Gazette* of taking Faubus's side in its reporting on Commonwealth. "This is a deliberate and calculated untruth," Ashmore wrote, adding that the *Gazette* deeply resented the attack on its integrity.

Faubus tossed out another denunciation of his alma mater. He asked the voters to choose which documentation to believe, his own, taken from official state records, or Cherry's, relying on the newspaper files of this "bad college."

He wound up his campaign at Batesville with a warning. "If by these slimy unfair tactics," he said, "a cloud is cast upon my good name, upon the peace of my family and the heritage of my son, and my rights as an American citizen are jeopardized, then the same can be done to you and yours."

The voters went to the polls the following Tuesday, August 10. They chose Faubus by 6,585 votes, most of that margin could have been provided by Cherry's insults to Jim Crain and other local chieftains. Faubus won a majority of about 4,000 in 31 precincts controlled by old friends on the highway commission and various other bosses who had been offended by Cherry. Crain's domain alone went with Faubus by a majority of almost 1,500. The candidate's home county of Madison gave him all but 50 of the 2,994 votes cast and put him over the top. The county turned out 104 percent of its registered voters, a display of civic zeal that was never fully explained.

There might have been questionable vote handling on the other side, as well. Late in the evening of the election, the ballot totals

Alta Faubus congratulates her husband on his first statewide electoral triumph in 1954.

PHOTO BY LARRY OBSITNIK, COURTESY OF THE *ARKANSAS DEMOCRAT-GAZETTE* AND SPECIAL COLLECTIONS DIVISION, UNIVERSITY OF ARKANSAS LIBRARIES, FAYETTEVILLE.

from Garland County suddenly stopped coming in. Faubus's people suspected tampering. By one account, Truman Baker winked at another worker, and the two quietly went to a telephone in another room and took care of the problem.

By a second account, the problem was solved by still another old politico whom Cherry had offended. Leo McLaughlin had been forced out of the Hot Springs mayor's office, after years of overseeing open-but-illegal gambling, by the young marine veteran Sid McMath. McLaughlin had been happy to support Cherry in his successful campaign against McMath in 1952. But, like others who had befriended Cherry, McLaughlin felt that he had been snubbed. He no longer influenced a lot of voters, but he still had contacts.

On election night, as the story is told, McLaughlin stationed himself below the second-floor room of the Garland County Courthouse where the votes were being counted. He had an accomplice inside who dropped slips of paper out the window containing the true vote returns. As the returns being reported to Little Rock began to diverge from the correct ones, McLaughlin phoned Faubus headquarters, identifying himself to a knowing campaign official as "the man with the gardenia," an allusion to his trademark boutonniere. (His lapel flower was actually a carnation.) Faubus's man then phoned the ballot counters in Hot Springs and let them know they had been caught.

At 2 A.M., the Garland County votes still had not been reported. Homer Adkins, the former governor, who was working in Faubus headquarters, telephoned Hot Springs and said, "You all might as well unlock this thing because we're holding out stuff in North Arkansas." He named several boxes still unreported there and added, "You can't outlast us, so you might as well give up." Then the candidate himself placed a call to the holdouts. "If you count me out over there," he said, "you better do a damn good job of it, because if I get to be governor . . ." The Garland County boys folded. Cherry still carried the county, but his margin of victory from the first primary was reduced by more than eight hundred votes.

Ashmore weighed in with a postprimary editorial strongly condemning Cherry's use of Commonwealth, calling it "a shabby political device" and "essentially spurious on its face." The editorial expressed a little regret, saying that Cherry's reform record had not deserved to be repudiated. It took a shot at Faubus for demagoguery but concluded with the hope that he would rise to meet the opportunity that he had unexpectedly been given. The *Gazette* also revealed that its letters commenting on Commonwealth had run 8 to 1 for Faubus even though the editors, in the interest of balance, had finally published 25 for him and 19 against.

There had been a final revealing moment late in the campaign. A Faubus ad published August 5 mistakenly claimed that the candidate had been under fire 392 days during World War II. That would have covered most of the time he was in Europe, including several months after the war ended. Ted Lamb, whose agency handled Faubus's advertising, visited the candidate that morning to apologize. He explained that a typesetter had added an extra digit in the figure. It should have read 32 days. Lamb promised to correct it before the ad ran again. Faubus was undisturbed. "Aw, just let it go," he said.

<table>
<tr><td>CHAPTER

11</td><td>Wilton R. "Witt" Stephens made his money by being agile. As a novice salesman fresh off the family farm in Grant County, he once sold belt buckles at an army base. He set up next to the paymaster's table and, as the young</td></tr>
</table>

privates picked up their money, made no effort to correct their impression that they were required to buy his buckles.

Some years later, he was dickering to buy a natural gas company and had to defend the purchase before the Securities and Exchange Commission. An austere and skeptical Harvard lawyer asked the shambling rube how he expected to raise enough equity to get the firm going. Witt pulled a $150,000 cashier's check from his hip pocket and said, "Judge, I brung it with me." He got the company.

He was equally agile in his politics. He was a McMath man until Francis Cherry defeated his hero. Loyal literally to the end, Witt stayed at McMath headquarters until late on election night and watched the bad news come in. At 8 o'clock the next morning, a Little Rock man walking to work saw a tall, slouching figure ahead of him with his arm around the shoulder of Francis Cherry's campaign manager. It was Witt.

W. R. (Witt) Stephens, financier and political kingmaker.

His loyalty to Cherry was cut short by the political accident of Orval Faubus's victory in the Democratic primary of August 10, 1954. Stephens's blunt warning not to run that year was fresh in Faubus's memory on the morning of August 11 when he and Truman Baker arrived in Stephens's office. The conversion was neat and fast. "I was for him before the day was over," Stephens recalled.

Faubus and Stephens were natural allies, the differential in their finances and economic philosophies notwithstanding. Stephens made money, lots of it, until the day he died. He believed that a person never had enough, and he was hesitant about giving it away, even to good causes. He reportedly helped numerous people in totally private ways, but he was careful never to advertise his generosity. He had the Medici's craving for power without the Florentine disposition for taste and community.

Faubus had no interest in moneymaking, was a poor manager of finances, and died virtually broke. But in important ways, he and Stephens were alike. Both came from farms and knew hard physical work as youngsters. They feared failure, although their definitions of it were different. They were proud. They distrusted city people and took satisfaction from besting them. Each rose to the top, but neither was accepted by the elite of the state. They represented the populist ideal in all its yearnings, rewards, and disappointments. It was natural that Stephens should become Faubus's chief financial supporter.

Many of the men whom the new governor surrounded himself with were as rough-hewn as Stephens. They included businessmen, planters, hungry lawyers, and political operatives. Not many would have appealed to Sam Faubus. They were long on ambition and short on idealism.

Truman N. Baker came to be seen, perhaps unfairly, as the typical Faubus crony. Even Faubus soured on him eventually. Baker owned a Chevrolet dealership in Searcy and used his political connections to sell large volumes of vehicles. He was heavily involved in the highway commission problems of the early 1950s. He was one of Faubus's closest colleagues on the McMath highway commission and one of the first financial supporters of Faubus's campaign for governor. He and James H. Crain, another colleague on the highway commission, pledged enough money to keep the Faubus race going even during dry periods. It was fitting that Baker, one of the most effective political manipulators in central Arkansas, leapt into action to stop vote tampering on the night of the runoff election.

Another early supporter who understood the vote-delivery system in Arkansas was Sheriff Marlin Hawkins of Conway County. Late in life, he wrote a memoir facetiously titled *How I Stole Elections* in which he tried to answer the widespread accusation that his political machine had voted dead people and other unsuspecting citizens. Whatever his method, Hawkins was known for two qualities: an ability to throw large numbers of votes to a favored candidate and loyalty to his political friends. He was a Faubus friend to the last.

The governor-elect found another friend in one of Hawkins's neighbors, state representative Paul Van Dalsem of tiny, rural Perry County. Van Dalsem, who owned a large and prosperous farm in the Arkansas River bottom, ran his county like a Balkans principality. In Little Rock, he bullied government employees and fellow legislators where he could and made deals where he could not. The deal for his friend Carl Adams to be Faubus's welfare director was typical. Adams was one of the new governor's first appointees.

Dozens of others, risk takers all, clambered aboard the Faubus bandwagon during the days and weeks after the runoff primary. What they were betting on was not just financial advantage, although that was a consideration for some. Many simply liked the prestige of being on the inside. It was exciting and gratifying to be known as a friend of the governor. Wallace Baker, a young nephew of Truman Baker and a political apprentice in the Faubus campaign, suspected that his leg was being pulled when he got a call after the election asking whether he would like to lease a box at the Oaklawn horse track in Hot Springs. He took it and when he visited it the first time was delighted to see that it was on the finish line a few feet from the governor's box—and just back from his uncle's.

It was revealing that Faubus sought out Stephens the day after the runoff primary. Ordinarily, the winner would bide his time and let the losing bigshot crawl forward, making peace offerings. But Faubus understood that for the first time within memory, the Democratic nomination did not mean automatic election to office.

First, some Cherry supporters tried to get their man to enter the November general election as an independent. Then the Republican mayor of Little Rock, personable, good-looking Pratt Remmel, entered the governor's race with realistic expectations of capitalizing on lingering resentment among Cherry's voters. Cherry declined to run again, but did nothing to keep his supporters faithful to the Democratic party. Someone organized a Democrats-for-Remmel group composed of alienated "Cherry pickers." Cherry got into an unseemly squabble with his insurance commissioner, Harvey Combs, because Combs, a Madison County man who had known Faubus since the latter was a boy, campaigned for his friend.

Faubus knew that he would need money for more advertising and get-out-the-vote drives, even though his campaign against Remmel was deliberately quiet to avoid giving an impression of concern. He made peace not only with Stephens but also with other prominent money men who had supported Cherry. One notable convert was W. E. "Bill" Darby, president of Old Line Insurance Company. Men like Stephens and Darby were happy to buy into a new administration at what must have seemed a low price. Darby's peace offering was the loan of a Cadillac for a Faubus family vacation trip. Stephens was more generous. He helped substantially to pay off Faubus's primary campaign debt.

Two weeks before the general election, Stephens made the next move to increase his fortune. He bought the Arkansas Louisiana Gas Company and began grooming it to challenge the Arkansas Power and Light Company for political dominance among the state's utilities. Whether Faubus knew Stephens's plans, or was made part of them during the fall of 1954, is uncertain. His main concern in any event was getting past November 2 and the election. He did so with ease. He defeated Remmel almost 2 to 1.

Winning did not remove the hostility of many Arkansawyers. They saw the state moving backward with Faubus's election. They believed him to be a pawn of crooks, an uncouth hillbilly, and probably a crypto-Communist. He was especially unpopular in Little Rock, a reasonably sophisticated little city that perceived itself on the morning after the election as Rome delivered into the hands of the Vandals. Pulaski County had given Cherry a margin of 12,800 votes in the runoff. Faubus cut that to fewer than 3,000 against Remmel, but he was under no illusion that he was popular in the capital. Several thousand well-to-do people had a chance to show him how they felt at a football game at War Memorial Stadium shortly after the general election. He was invited to crown the state Jaycees' Miss Hospitality at halftime. When he walked onto the field, the stands erupted in booing.

Faubus was disturbed by the hostility, but not so much as his opponents might have wished. He knew the value of a good enemy. He sometimes saw himself as a modern, somewhat subtler version of Jeff Davis, the famous turn-of-the-century governor who profited by using the capital as a foil. Davis delighted rural audiences with his colorful denunciation of Little Rock's "silk-stocking crowd"—an epithet used by Faubus when he and the capital had their most serious misunderstanding during his third term. Davis enjoyed running against insurance agents and other "high-collared roosters" who "wear collars so high they can't see the sun except at high noon." He told his country audiences, "If you farmers will stay with me, we'll lick the gang in Little Rock one more time." He told country voters to save their money when they came to Little Rock by staying at his house instead of a hotel. His wife might be busy making soap, he said, but just tell her to put on some hog jowl and turnip greens.

Faubus's wife, though a good country woman, would have been appalled if her husband had issued any such invitation, even in jest. She had not been keen on leaving the comforts of Huntsville. Little Rock was as forbidding as New York. A few of the capital's established women tried to make her feel at home, but she knew that most of that crowd looked on her and Orval wtih disdain. Her clothes might have been less than fashionable, and her conversation might not have sparkled with the latest cosmopolitan gossip. Nevertheless, she had the hill person's pride. She knew that the booing at the stadium was for her as well as for her husband.

Even so, he quietly cultivated them. Part of his motive no doubt was the purely political desire to neutralize an enemy. But there probably was another reason. He saw those establishmentarians as his betters, and he had always been impelled to get the approval of that kind. Back at Combs, he had cultivated the merchants and their families, the town's establishment. A hill man's unremitting torment is his pride, his compulsion to prove that he is as good as the next man. One of his first meetings as governor-elect was with a group of Little Rock businessmen and country clubbers, the capital's best. They fired questions at him all evening: Did he intend to punish business? Would his liberalism hurt them? Would they have access to him? How did he feel about communism? He left the meeting convinced that he had satisfied most of their concerns. He also sensed that he had held his own with the best that the city had to throw at him.

Their questions about communism were a reminder that Commonwealth would nag him for a long time. The issue during the campaign had made many wonder about his loyalty, in spite of his war record. Wells, in the *Arkansas Recorder,* accused Faubus of lying about his attendance at Commonwealth when he signed a loyalty oath to become an army officer. He pointed out repeatedly during the fall election campaign that the oath Faubus had taken in 1942 required an applicant for a commission to state whether he had ever attended any of a list of subversive organizations. Faubus ignored Wells, but the army did not. He drove to Denver to bury a favorite aunt during the Christmas holidays of 1954, and when he returned he found Gen. Arthur G. Trudeau of the United States Army waiting for him. The general had been investigating his experience at Commonwealth. Now he had come to Arkansas to interview the governor-elect.

The interview ended with General Trudeau decrying the hysteria of McCarthyism and the many reputations that had been ruined by that hysteria. He might well have had in mind Senator McCarthy's ill-fated attempt the previous summer to smear the army as a hotbed of Communists. The governor-elect was cleared, at least by the army.

Faubus took office January 11, 1955, four days after his forty-fifth birthday, and immediately hunkered down. He understood the frailty of his political muscle. His problems went beyond the skepticism of Little Rock's power structure. More urgently, there was the legislature. Most members of the General Assembly had, rationally enough, backed Governor Cherry. A first-term governor is supposed to be reelected easily. Mere coolness would have been surmountable, but there was more. Ten years after the war, Arkansas was in the grip of a severe antitax phobia, a feeling that was not just reflected but perhaps magnified in the legislature. That in itself was not remarkable—antitax sentiment in the state has always ranged from hostile to explosive—but the tightfistedness of the voters and their representatives happened to coincide with increasingly serious problems that state government was expected to handle, almost all of which required tax money.

Public schoolteachers, as usual, were among the most poorly paid in the nation. Large numbers of citizens still survived on subsistence farming, and the state's per-capita income was near the bottom in the national rankings. What little industry the state had was mainly low paying and situated far from the dying farm communities that needed it. State services were patchy to poor. More than two hundred patients at the state mental hospital were sleeping on the floor because the hospital had too few beds and no space for more in any event. Money for schools was so scarce that some districts had had to cut their terms to six and seven months. Drought and economic recession had reduced state revenues further than usual; the revenue commissioner estimated that they were declining by $2 million a year.

Adding to the general grumpiness, the gas company that Witt Stephens had bought had an undecided request for a rate increase pending before the public service commission when he bought it.

It would have been hard to find a time in Arkansas history, except for the Great Depression and the Civil War and Reconstruction era, less propitious for a tax increase. Nevertheless, some of the needier groups began to press for a rise in the sales tax, which had been at 2 percent for a generation. Faubus quietly polled key members of the legislature and determined that such an increase would get no more than a fourth of the votes in the House. He publicly endorsed the tax, mainly to satisfy the *Arkansas Gazette,* a major advocate of higher spending for education. But he made almost no effort to wring votes for it in the legislature, and it was defeated. His general attitude toward the legislative session of 1955 was hands off. One editorial cartoon showed him lolling in the back of a wagon drawn by horses named House and Senate, the whip

parked, reins tied loosely to the seat. He is saying, "Lead on, boys—
I may suggest a turn now 'n then . . ."

Faubus did exert himself to fulfill some specific campaign
promises. He persuaded the legislature to repeal two laws: the seed
and feed tax that had so exercised the poultry industry and the
requirement that welfare recipients had to seek help from relatives
before they could draw state aid. The former showed that he was
capable of arm-twisting. The bill was headed for defeat in the
Senate until he began calling members and bringing pressure.
By the next morning, he had secured enough votes to pass it by 25
to 9. Political insiders took note.

From the first, Faubus showed a canny ability to read not only
public opinion but also the needs and desires of legislators. His style
was back-scratching when possible and, when that occasionally was
not enough, hardball. During his first term, he knew he had too
little clout to get away with tough power plays. He concentrated on
building goodwill.

He began by picking a respected veteran legislator, Rep. James L.
"Bex" Shaver of Cross County, as his legislative advisor. He struck
a deal with the leading candidate for Speaker of the House, Charles
"Rip" Smith of West Memphis. Smith and the Crittenden County
machine that he was part of had thrown their considerable support
to Governor Cherry in the primary. When their man lost, Smith
had to come to the new governor to plead for help. He needed
Faubus's support to win the speakership. Faubus held out the hand
of peace—in exchange for a pledge that Smith would not block
Faubus's legislative proposals or join any combine against him. He
cultivated other powerful members of both houses such as Senators
Clifton "Deacon" Wade of Fayetteville, Roy Milum of Harrison,
W. E. "Buck" Fletcher of Lonoke, and J. Lee Bearden of Leachville
and Representatives Carroll C. Hollensworth, Marion H. Crank,
Glenn F. Walther, and Van Dalsem.

He exercised similar care in staffing his own office. His aim was
to surround himself with a variety of hometown friends and political pros. J. L. Bland, the Walnut Ridge newspaper publisher who
had joined the Faubus campaign as coordinator after the first
primary, became his executive secretary. Jim Bland had years of
political experience. He had helped manage a number of statewide

campaigns and for a time had been Gov. Carl E. Bailey's executive secretary. In spite of his qualifications, he quickly became an embarrassment. His style was brusque; stroking egos did not interest him. Perhaps more disabling was his reputation as a Bailey man. Arkansas politics during those years was divided not by party but by faction, and the two main factions were headed by two former governors, Carl E. Bailey and Homer M. Adkins. Faubus learned that he had offended the Adkins people by placing a Bailey man in the sensitive post of executive secretary. Three months into his administration, he persuaded Bland to become head of the Employment Security Division—one of the state's most prominent agencies—and replaced him with an Adkins man, Arnold Sikes. Sikes had been an early supporter of McMath and had served as McMath's purchasing agent for a time. He could not have guessed that he would be the governor's executive secretary for eight years and would set a state record for longevity in that job.

Working with the executive secretary as administrative assistants were Rolla Fitch, a Huntsville friend, and Claude Carpenter, an ambitious young Little Rock lawyer. Knowing that someone had to understand the hard mathematics of state finance, Faubus chose two veterans with impeccable reputations, Frank A. Storey as director of the state finance department and Julian Hogan as budget director.

The new governor made one appointment that brought favor from two important sources, organized labor and the *Arkansas Gazette*. Clarence T. Thornbrough, a well-liked printer for the *Gazette* and a prominent member of the Typographical Union, became commissioner of labor.

Faubus suffered a temporary setback when he reached into the ranks of Cherry's closest associates to get a legal advisor. William J. Smith was known as a lawyer who could get things done in state government. He had worked officially and otherwise as an advisor to every governor but one since Bailey. He had been Gov. Ben Laney's executive secretary. Smith had smoothly made himself indispensable to Cherry as his legislative liaison, making it possible to pass a package of bills that Cherry's inexperienced staff had not been able to push through.

More pertinently, he had worked hard to defeat Faubus. His deal with Mutt Jones to back Cherry in the runoff might have changed

William J. Smith (behind Faubus) *watches as the governor signs one of the many bills that Smith shepherded through the legislature.*

Arkansas history if Mrs. Cherry had not botched it. Faubus sent peace feelers to Smith early in the 1955 legislative session. His legislative advisor, Bex Shaver, approached Smith and said the new governor wanted him to help with his legislative program. Smith turned him down, saying that wouldn't work because Faubus knew that Smith was opposed to him. Shaver picked up the phone and told Faubus that Smith didn't want to have anything to do with him. Smith later related that he had remonstrated with Shaver. "I said, 'Bex, wait a minute, I didn't say that. You didn't have to cut my throat.'" Faubus waited until Smith came around. That did not happen until 1957, just in time for a momentous session of the General Assembly. Smith would eventually outlast even Sikes as a Faubus lieutenant.

Unlike his predecessor, Faubus had an almost unnatural ability to forget a grudge, or at least to paper over it. One of his first instructions to his cabinet and staff was not to hurt the administration's friends but to take every opportunity to turn an enemy into a supporter or to neutralize him. He gave them a profitable example five months into his first term. One of Francis Cherry's loyal and generous backers had been John Cooper of West Memphis, a lawyer, businessman, and prominent member of the Crittenden County machine. During the next generation, Cooper would change the face of much of Arkansas with his up-scale retirement villages. His first, Cherokee Village in Sharp County, was under way during the 1954 election year. On June 11, 1955, Faubus braved a perilous thunderstorm and flew to Sharp County to help dedicate the project. Cooper became a loyal and generous Faubus man that day.

Faubus's knack for combining liberal and conservative, idealist and hack, was evident from the first. Some of the more high-minded people, those who had trouble seeing the sun except at high noon, deplored his appointments. What they failed to appreciate was the political strength that he was crafting.

He used that strength sparingly during his first term, but he managed to make progress. He supervised the completion of the University Medical Center at Little Rock. He signed legislation raising unemployment compensation and extending the period of eligibility, and he vetoed a bill to deny benefits during strikes—all of which cemented his ties to labor. He lobbied for and got a law requiring a utility to wait 120 days to start collecting higher rates after applying for them. He cooperated with the legislature in establishing a publicity and parks department to promote tourism. In 1956 he presided over the opening of two new state parks, Queen Wilhelmina, near Mena, and Mount Magazine. He signed a bill authorizing construction of a new justice building on the capitol grounds.

Two programs enacted during his first term affected the state for years to come. One was property reassessment, a device for equalizing property taxes statewide, which forced many laggard school districts to tax themselves more heavily instead of sponging inordinately off state revenues. Reassessment became an issue so contentious that it threatened to unseat Faubus at the next election. He rode it out, however, and the program eventually produced improved schools all over Arkansas.

The second was a systematic effort to industrialize a state that, from the beginning, had relied on the perennial uncertainties of agriculture for its economic base. Other southern states were well ahead of Arkansas in this as in other areas. Faubus and important business leaders decided on a crash program to catch up. As a signal that the state meant business, he persuaded Winthrop Rockefeller to head the campaign. Rockefeller, as a symbol of American capitalism, was perfect for the job. He had become a resident of Arkansas a few years earlier as part of an effort to shed an unwanted wife and rebuild a wastrel life. Now he was given a chance to redeem himself by performing valuable public service. He jumped into the task with enthusiasm, and his adopted state soon forgave his playboy transgressions and luxurious lifestyle.

They made an interesting pair, the heir of a robber baron's fortune and the son of a hardscrabble Socialist. Faubus brought to the combine a growing network of political connections that could smooth the way for out-of-state industries. One of his first actions was to pressure the highway department to cooperate with Forrest City in persuading the Yale Lock Company to build a plant there. The department had been reluctant to tell the company where it intended to build roads in the area, and the company had refused to select a site until it knew. Faubus solved the problem using the method he understood best—political pressure.

Rockefeller for his part understood his own celebrity value. He used his show farm and home on Petit Jean Mountain to entertain industrial prospects and Arkansas business leaders. He never hesitated to spend his own money. As chairman of the Arkansas Industrial Development Commission (AIDC), he was entitled to reimbursement for expenses. But what was a state expense account to a man who used his own jet airplane to go to New York for a haircut?

The partnership paid off quickly. Before the end of 1955, plans were announced for a tire plant at Magnolia and a paper mill at Pine Bluff. New industries cropped up all over the state in 1956— Fort Smith, North Little Rock, Lepanto, Fayetteville, Searcy, Arkadelphia, Waldron, Mount Ida, Clarksville.

Faubus and Rockefeller appeared together frequently. Rockefeller's being a staunch Republican was, at this stage, nothing more than a laughing matter between them. When the governor was asked whether he intended to attend a Republican fund-raising dinner put on by his AIDC chairman, he replied, "I made them this kind of a proposition. I told them I would go to their dinner and contribute to the Republican Party in proportion to my wealth, if Winthrop Rockefeller would come to my Democratic dinner and contribute in proportion to his wealth. I haven't heard from them." They remained friendly partners until the middle of Faubus's second term.

Within weeks of taking office, Faubus had demonstrated more skill in the art of governing than Cherry had in two years. If the purpose of state government is to provide services and safeguards, and if the governor's role is not simply to supervise the governing bodies but also to balance competing interests, then Orval Faubus clearly had a talent for the job. Furthermore, he came to it better qualified by experience than any governor since Carl Bailey in the late 1930s. He had been trained in politics since young manhood, first in his father's house, then in county office. He had worked in state government both as a policy maker and as an executive in two of the most demanding agencies, the governor's office and the highway department. He had learned governing from the inside. From that vantage point, he had dealt with the most powerful forces in Arkansas. But, like a meterologist tracking a hurricane, he knew that learning and skill were sometimes not enough. A successful governor must rely on his instincts.

One day years later, after the governorship had come to feel as comfortable as an old coat, he sent for a new man who was struggling through his first term in the legislature. Rep. Lloyd George, fresh from Yell County and green as corn, had no idea why he was being summoned. He was nervous. The governor administered the expected pleasantries, then suddenly spread a map of Yell County across his desk and said, "Mark the roads you'd like paved." Young George knew the highway commission was independent in theory, but he understood that Faubus had appointed almost all its members and could deliver roads. He marked several in his county starting with the road to Mount Magazine, a popular park. Faubus asked, "If you got those roads paved, would you vote for a one-cent gasoline tax?" George said he would. Faubus folded the map and bade him goodbye.

A month after the session ended, George had a call from the governor's office saying he should go to Little Rock for a press conference. Faubus got up to face the cameras, put his arm around George, and announced that the road to Mount Magazine was going to be paved. Then he soberly told the press that George had given him no choice. He said the persistent young man had made him do it, that he had harried and ragged him and stayed after him until the governor had finally caved in. George listened in astonishment and kept his mouth shut. When the voters of Yell County found out that their rookie had that kind of clout, they insisted on sending him back to the House at the next election. He was still there thirty years later.

CHAPTER	The Arkansas Power and Light Company ran things to suit itself for many
12	years. If it wanted to dam a river, it dammed it. If it wanted families to pay higher rates to subsidize industrial customers, they paid them. Regulation

by the state was perfunctory to nonexistent. Senators, congressmen, governors, and state legislators were routinely put in the company's debt, and they routinely did the company's bidding.

Hundreds of thousands of country people had no electricity to light their houses, wash their clothes, or cool their food because the power company refused to run expensive lines to sparsely settled rural communities. It was a rare public servant who saw anything wrong with that. One such, a congressman named Clyde Ellis, had the gall to criticize the power company and speak up for public power. When he ran for the Senate in 1942, thugs in the company's pay tore down Ellis's billboards all over Arkansas. John L. McClellan won that election and became a favorite of AP and L for the rest of his career.

Sid McMath, another public power advocate, let it be known in 1952 that he intended to run against McClellan in 1954. The power company's friends arranged a damaging audit of Governor McMath's highway department. The bill to establish an audit commission was introduced by AP and L's best friend in the state senate. The chairman of the audit commission was a member of the board of AP and L. Two company officials were on the grand jury that subsequently investigated. There was a flurry of legal action that came to very little—except to destroy the political career of McMath.

Sam Faubus, no friend of private power companies, was one of the legions of country people who circulated petitions to get power lines installed by the federally supported Rural Electrification Administration (REA). Orval saw the old women weep with relief to get electric irons and washing machines. He supported public power in his weekly newspaper after World War II. When he ran against their man Cherry, the high-collared roosters at AP and L fought him. To rub it in, they raised the company's rates during the 1954 election campaign and dared the voters to do anything about it. Faubus took note of that in every campaign speech, making sure that his opponent shared the blame. Perhaps his most satisfying triumph was whipping AP and L along with Cherry and then, in due time, forcing the power company to fall in line and become a solid Faubus supporter.

Even that triumph was handled in his own quiet way without gloating. Sometimes, he seemed to fight the giant with reluctance. For example, AP and L had always taken what it wanted in the division of territory between it and the cooperatives of the REA. The cooperatives ran the expensive lines through the countryside to the

Sam Faubus after his son became governor.

outskirts of the towns because the private company refused to do it. Then when the towns expanded into public power territory, AP and L took the rural customers without compensation. The cooperatives tried without success to persuade the legislature to remedy that, first in 1953 and again in 1955. They finally passed the bill in 1957 with not a vote to spare.

Faubus in his memoirs later took credit for providing the necessary votes. Harry Oswald, executive secretary of the Arkansas cooperatives during the 1950s, remembered it a little differently. He said one senator, the deciding vote, was holding out against them. Then Oswald found that the senator had a secret agreement with Faubus to go to work on the state payroll. Faubus apparently was reluctant to use his obvious leverage to get the man's vote because he did not want to anger the influential men at AP and L when he needed their support for other programs, such as raising taxes for education. He tried to persuade Oswald and his allies to wait another two years to get justice on territorial allocation. Only after Oswald told Faubus that he knew of the senator's job deal did the governor lean on his new employee and pass the bill. The practical men at AP and L understood that when a man was pushed against the wall, he had to act.

On another front, Faubus was less equivocal. The state public service commission, which was dominated by Faubus appointees within weeks after his inauguration, understood what was expected. Witt Stephens persuaded the commission to give his newly acquired Arkansas Louisiana Gas Company (ARKLA) two hefty rate increases in eighteen months during Faubus's first term. One of those was a sharp rise in what he charged AP and L for gas used in generating electric power. AP and L objected. Predictably, the Faubus-friendly commission paid no attention. The power company's managers, apparently unable to believe their new situation, went to the public service commission twice during that same eighteen-month period and asked for rate increases. Each time, they were turned down. They went back a third time. The commission finally granted a fraction of the requested increase. It was just enough to pay for the increase in the power company's gas bill.

While AP and L was being hung out to dry, Stephens and his interests, including his gas utility company, prospered. He found friends in every state agency that mattered. He expanded his alliances in banks, courthouses, city halls, and school-district headquarters across the state. His company was one of a handful in the state trading in bonds. Bonds for municipalities, school districts, and other public bodies were almost always handled through Stephens, Inc., or one of its Little Rock allies such as T. J. Raney & Sons, Inc. Dallas P. "Pete" Raney was part of Witt's political combine, along with John Cooper, the retirement community builder; Harry Parkin and Jack Lynn, printing company leaders; Bill Darby, the insurance company owner; Leon Catlett, a Little Rock lawyer; and other powerful businessmen around the state. The Stephens combine became the money engine that drove the Faubus machine for twelve years. Before every election, Witt rounded up the big shots and their many underlings and funneled their contributions to the Faubus campaign.

What these men got in return was sympathetic treatment from state government and its friends at the local level. That treatment ranged from tax breaks to relaxed rules that meant higher profits.

The most persuasive proof of a new order came during a single week at the beginning of Faubus's second two-year term. Between Monday and Friday of the last week of February 1957, Witt Stephens and Orval Faubus planted the flag that announced a new power structure for the state of Arkansas. The same four days set Stephens on the road to being a very rich man.

Wallace Baker was sitting in his office one day that winter when he got a telephone call from his Uncle Truman. "Boy," the uncle said, "borrow all the money you can borrow. Get every penny you can." When Wallace asked why, Uncle Truman told him that he should buy every share of ARKLA Gas stock he could get his hands on. The word was being passed in the tight inner circle. With the governor running interference, big money was about to be made on the Arkansas Louisiana Gas Company. Wallace did not take the advice, to his lifelong regret.

Witt Stephens had taken over ARKLA in the fall of 1954 in what amounted to a fire sale. The giant Cities Service Company had been ordered by the government to sell its majority holdings in the gas company. Few wanted it because ARKLA was a notoriously poor moneymaker. Only a visionary like Witt could see the possibilities.

But to turn the company around would take two things: lots of borrowed money and ruthless political action.

The purchase price for a controlling interest in ARKLA was $24.5 million. Stephens put up $1.2 million of his own money, borrowed $2.5 million from the Mississippi River Fuel Company of St. Louis, and borrowed the remaining $20 million from the First National City Bank of New York. To escape federal requirements concerning holding companies, he pledged to sell a large share of his stock by December 15, 1956. That meant that he had to perform whatever magic he had in mind in two years, a short time in the life of a large business enterprise. Witt, as usual, had a plan.

First, he cut expenses drastically. He fired and retired dozens of unproductive employees. He sold dozens of company-owned cars. Wall Street noticed and started to bid up the price of ARKLA's stock.

Then he went to work on the political front. His new friend in the governor's office had gained a 2-to-1 majority on the public service commission during the first month of his administration in 1955. The third member, a Cherry appointee, quickly became a Faubus man—which is to say, a Stephens man. The commission allowed Stephens to raise the price of gas twice that first year, mainly to large industrial customers like the big aluminum companies and Arkansas Power and Light Company. That further quickened Wall Street's interest and prompted another rise in the stock price.

Meanwhile, it was revealed that Wallace Baker's Uncle Truman was the owner of three thousand shares of ARKLA stock and that a number of other Faubus administration insiders had taken similar advantage of the stock's low price. They included Walter L. Hinton Jr., whom Faubus had appointed to head the public service commission's assessment coordination division, a new agency to oversee an overhaul of property taxes. They also included two members of the governor's staff, Arnold Sikes, his executive secretary, and Claude Carpenter Jr., an aide. Also in on the action were Orville Cheney, state revenue commissioner, and Rolla Fitch, Faubus's Madison County friend who had become director of the Alcoholic Beverage Control department.

How many others owned ARKLA stock, how they got it and

when, how much they paid—these questions were not fated to be answered. The only serious attempt to get them answered came during the 1957 legislative session when Rep. Hardy Croxton of Benton County pushed for an investigation. He was thwarted at every turn by powerful legislative leaders, all of whom turned out to be warm friends of Witt Stephens. Croxton's resolution was bottled up in committee after fearful pressure was put on some of the more reluctant members. One south Arkansas legislator came to Croxton in tears and apologized. "He said, 'Hardy, I just had to change, but you're right. Goddamn, you're right.' And he just cried like a baby."

Flattery was as useful as pressure. Members of the public service commission were seen from time to time in the prestigious ARKLA boxes at Oaklawn.

Stephens did not depend entirely on deals made in smoke-filled rooms. He was a public-relations genius. While he gouged the big industrial customers—openly blackmailing them at one point, telling them publicly that if they did not sign expensive new contracts guaranteeing him higher rates they might see their gas shut off—he played dramatically at the same time to the small domestic users of his gas. These latter he called the biscuit cookers. They became the populist symbol of his campaign. Over and over, he demanded to know whether the industrial giants should be pampered at the expense of the biscuit cookers. This was dema- goguery worthy of the great Earl K. Long, who, during this same era, governed Louisiana and who, whenever some foe threatened to cut the state budget, would indignantly demand to know whether the rascal intended to abolish the school for spastic children. Witt's dig at his rivals at AP and L was hardly subtle. They had been pampering the big guys at the expense of the little ones, and now they were being called to account.

Faubus was not an automatic ally of Stephens in every contest. Not many people were aware of it, but he was under strong pres- sure from the big aluminum companies to side with them against ARKLA. The pressure came from his friend Leon Catlett, a Little Rock establishment lawyer to whom he was indebted. Catlett had been called in to help protect Faubus's interests when it appeared that some of his votes were in jeopardy in the Democratic primary in 1954. Now Catlett was representing Reynolds Aluminum Company in Arkansas. He met with the governor several times in the quiet of the mansion. But Faubus's allegiance to Stephens was greater, and finally he made it clear to Catlett that he was not willing to "blackjack" the gas company. At that point, the big users sat down to serious negotiations with Stephens. The latter gave a little ground, but not nearly so much as his adversaries. The aluminum interests threatened to fire Catlett afterward, and Faubus intervened to save his job as Catlett had saved his two years earlier.

Much of the negotiating was being handled in public, to the chagrin of the power company people and their industrial friends. But an important part of Witt's strategy was being conducted out of sight. His multi-million-dollar debt was real and pressing. A lesser man would have been satisfied to get it paid without losing money. Not Witt. He began repaying the loan a few million dollars at a time, selling stock to do so. Then, with a deadline for shedding the bulk of his stock, he sold—at a price almost double what he had paid for it, thanks to the generous rate increases granted by Faubus's public service commission. He thus managed to repay the loan and have several million dollars left over. With continued cooperation from the PSC, he pushed ARKLA's earnings to more than 10 percent, or 4 percent above the customary figure allowed for utilities, ensuring high profits for many years to come.

At the heart of the gas company's high earnings was a device known as the fair field price. That was a revolutionary theory that a gas company should be allowed to receive as much for the gas that its own production department produced as for the more expensive gas it had to buy from other production companies. The U.S. Supreme Court ruled in the fall of 1956 that a large gas company in another state could not use that pricing device. Furthermore, neither Texas nor Louisiana, with two of the most complaisant governments in regards to oil and gas interests, allowed it. Stephens, unintimidated, installed the device at ARKLA. The Faubus PSC approved it. When some big customers appealed to the courts in protest, the state supreme court stepped in and prohibited fair field pricing.

ARKLA stock declined on the news. Witt's big plan was threatened, but he was ready. Obviously anticipating a reversal in the state supreme court, he had a bill already drafted to override the court decision. The court ruled on the last Monday in February. Witt's bill was introduced in the legislature on Tuesday, endorsed by the necessary committee on Wednesday, passed by the House on Thursday, and seconded by the Senate on Friday. Faubus signed it the next week. The effect on ARKLA stock was predictably restorative. The price started rebounding when the House voted for Stephens 83 to 7 and climbed further when only one member of the Senate opposed him. It had fully recovered by the time the governor signed the bill. The stock continued to climb for years, so that the substantial holdings still in Stephens family hands became worth much more. Thus was born one of America's great fortunes.

Stephens demonstrated his gratitude to the legislature in various ways. A young member who voted right, Knox Nelson of Pine Bluff, got the ARKLA account for his gasoline station. Later, Nelson borrowed money from Stephens to buy a farm. The company's insurance policies were passed out among legislators in the insurance business. There were reports that Stephens sent cash gifts to a large number of legislators. Sen. Clarence E. Bell of Parkin eventually went on ARKLA's payroll as an industrial representative. By the end of the next decade, seventeen of the thirty-five state senators were said to be on Stephens's payroll as public-relations consultants, lawyers, et cetera.

And what did Stephens do for Faubus? Much of that remains a mystery, but the quid pro quo apparently amounted to relatively small but consistent favors for most of Faubus's life. Stephens once told an interviewer that simply being in office cost a governor money and that a poor man could not afford it. "Faubus got his support from people like me and a lot of other people who would chip in and pay the expense," he said. Witt was still chipping in until he died, long after Faubus left office. He helped get jobs for friends of Faubus. He lent money to him several times when the former governor was down on his luck.

The eventful week in February 1957 had a profound effect on Arkansas politics. Stephens and Faubus had broken the hold on the state of the Arkansas Power and Light Company. The new establishment would have its own questionable impact, but for the moment it seemed enough to celebrate the death of the old one. The winners were entitled to gloat. What they had to say in private at the time is not known, but Faubus finally offered his opinion after a generation of reflection. With just a trace of irony, he said that the men who ran AP and L during his time as governor had become good corporate citizens.

CHAPTER

13

The oldest rule of politics looks simple enough: Reward your friends and punish your enemies. Faubus found it easy, for example, to oppose a permit for dog racing at West Memphis. The big man behind it was W. B. "Bill" Ingram, a former Crittenden County judge who had delivered the county overwhelmingly to Cherry in the 1954 Democratic primary.

The game becomes confusing, though, when the winning candidate cannot figure out who his friends are and who his enemies. Faubus confronted that dilemma on another sporting proposition— horse racing. Sometime during 1955 he began to hear rumors that an eastern combine had designs on the horse-track monopoly at Hot Springs. That sounded like another easy decision. All things being equal, a good politician sticks with the home crowd against outsiders. True, John Cella, the owner of the venerable Oaklawn track, had not supported him in the election. Furthermore, he had for years retained Little Rock's premier political law firm, Mehaffy, Smith, and Williams, to look out for his interests at the capital. Those lawyers were not allies of Faubus—not yet. Still, it was expected that the state racing commission, all Faubus appointees, would keep out the interlopers.

Then the situation became sticky. Some members of the racing commission were said to like the new outfit, which operated Suffolk Downs at Boston and other enterprises. A quiet investigation revealed that six of the eleven members had agreed to take the franchise away from Cella's Oaklawn. Faubus also learned that several leaders of organized labor, friends of his, had been promised cooperation and numerous jobs for their members and were pushing the new company. Cella had always operated a nonunion track. Then Faubus found out that the law firm of his old friend and mentor Sid McMath had been hired to represent the eastern interests. Here was a chance to reward friends and punish enemies. The opposing law firm was a hotbed of Cherry supporters who had shown little regard for Faubus. Indeed, one of its partners, Smith, had worked hard for the other side in the recent election and had turned down a chance to go to work for the new governor.

Imagine then the amazement in the political grandstand when Faubus came down on the side of his enemies. On the day the racing commission was to award the new contract, he dramatically fired the whole body and, a few days later, reappointed the five Oaklawn loyalists. The only reason he ever gave was a never-substantiated claim that the easterners had tried to bribe him and that they had underworld connections. Some observers saw an additional calculation, however. The McMath firm was on the political outside after its leader's loss in the 1954 Senate race. Mehaffy, Smith, and Williams was on the inside and rising fast. Faubus was looking to the future. Within a decent period, Smith formally shifted his allegiance and became Faubus's legislative liaison. And his law firm became the third side in a power triangle that included Stephens, Inc., and the governor's office.

Faubus often worked eighteen hours a day as governor. He answered every letter. Occasionally, he would reply to a one-page note from Illinois or Montana with four pages of philosophy and agony. And there was more to the job than sitting behind a desk. He traveled the state constantly. No group was too insignificant to receive a speech from the governor, no ribbon-cutting too out-of-the-way, no opening of a new industry or shopping mall too far from Little Rock. In his introverted way, he liked the limelight.

Several times, his health gave in to overwork and stress, and he sought relief away from the capital. One of his favorite places was the Buffalo River, where he canoed and camped with friends. More often, he slipped away for a quiet weekend at someone's hunting camp for languid days and nights of talking, sipping whiskey, and playing poker. There his friends saw a side of Faubus that most people never knew. For example, he could talk for hours on esoteric subjects. One night at Truman Baker's fishing camp, someone mentioned the Bible. Young Wallace Baker said to himself, "Orval Eugene Faubus, this will be one thing you won't be able to talk

Adlai Stevenson, the Democratic presidential nominee in 1952 and 1956, shakes hands with J. E. Dunlap, an Arkansas newspaperman, in 1955 at Jerome, Arkansas. Looking on are Faubus and Sen. J. W. Fulbright, sometime duck-hunting companions of Stevenson.

about." He was wrong. "He started in Genesis and ended up in Revelation five hours later."

It was customary in those days for the state prison to send convicts—usually murderers, because they were dependable and less likely to cause trouble—to work as servants at the hunting camps of the well connected. One day at a duck camp where Faubus and his friends were hunting and relaxing, a prisoner approached Witt Stephens and said, "Mr. Witt, let me borrow your shotgun and some shells." Witt pointed to his gun in the corner, and the murderer took it. He came back in about forty-five minutes with a wheelbarrow full of ducks. Someone said to him, "What you going to do if the game warden was to catch you?" He replied, "What can you do to a man serving life?" Everybody laughed, including the governor.

The homely pleasures of the camp suited Faubus's modest taste in company and pastimes. In this, he followed a long southern tradition. The nation's founding fathers went to some pains to make sure that an intellectual and political elite percolated to the top of the national government. They were less successful in ensuring that state and local governments were led by the best and brightest. Especially in the South, the people have delighted in thrusting parochial leaders to the top. Ordinariness has in fact been a requirement of office for southern politicians since the memory of Jefferson and Madison faded. The southern electorate has chosen the occasional genius who was not ordinary, flambeaux like Huey and Earl Long and the dark visionary James K. Vardaman, and the occasional Ivy Leaguer like Bill Clinton or Al Gore, and a few rustic con artists like Lyndon B. Johnson and Sam Rayburn. But all of them have had to masquerade as ordinary and hide their brilliance under earth tones to appeal to the populist taste. Only rarely has the South thrown up a J. William Fulbright, who never apologized for his erudition and world view, or a Richard B. Russell, the Georgian who refused to disguise either his gentility or his intellect. But the southern voter, left to his own devices, has almost always favored the limited leader of narrow vision, the man he perceives to be most like himself.

Judged only by the people he surrounded himself with, Orval Faubus fit the mold of narrow and parochial. Most of his employees and advisors were competent, but only a few could be called distinguished. Some were little more than political hacks. A few were outright crooks. Virtually none outshone the man who appointed them. Faubus was no different in this regard from most of his predecessors. Some of Arkansas's first officials in the 1830s were white-collar criminals who found government more lucrative than land-grabbing and common thievery. One of the tasks of a governor has always been to find enough knowledgeable, hardworking men and women to run the government with some efficiency while paying his honest political debts to mere job seekers. Faubus achieved this balance with some skill, but without noticeable distinction.

And yet, the ordinariness that he cultivated in public and reenforced with the people he chose to help him was in fact a deception. The man himself was anything but ordinary. His vision was pedestrian, but the fierceness of his desire and the breadth of his understanding placed him beyond ordinariness. He wanted to be thought a clever hillbilly, a man of whom it might be said, "He don't have much book-learning, but he's handy with tools." At one level he was exactly that. His education was rudimentary. He had a scattershot knowledge of history, but no reasoned grasp of it. His reading was undirected and unfocused.

What set him apart was an impulse toward specific goals. In the tumult of his upbringing, he had acquired a sense of direction. That sense had come to him because he had had to struggle for every toehold and advantage and because he had had the intelligence and intuition to discern it. There are no hillbilly aristocrats. In the Ozarks, there is no natural nobility thrown up from lush circumstances. A Franklin Roosevelt or a Nelson Rockefeller can slouch through his boyhood in the sure knowledge that someday all this will be his. In a Faubus habitat, leadership goes to the tough and sure-footed, and such a person emerges into the world knowing what he wants. Faubus's vision might have been narrow, but it was not vague.

When he became governor, he knew with some precision what he wanted to accomplish. He wanted to make life better for the people he had sprung from, the have-nots. Specifically, he had in mind the old people of the countryside living in near-penury, the hardscrabble farmers, the small shopkeepers and tradesmen, and those who knew hard work and low pay. When he became persuaded that better schools and better jobs would help all of these, he became an enthusiastic advocate of public education and industrialization. Out of those concerns and entwined with the political necessities of the day, he fashioned a program. At the center of it was improved education. How to pay for that was the first great challenge of his tenure.

If it had not been for the events of that autumn, 1957 would have been remembered as the year of unalloyed triumph for Orval Faubus. He managed a feat that had been thought impossible: a landmark increase in state revenues, mainly to finance the public schools. No governor had done that since J. M. Futrell had grudgingly acquiesced in imposing a 2 percent sales tax in 1935 to help pull the state government and public education out of the Great Depression.

Faubus approached the matter with his usual deliberate preparation. He had risked little of his meager political capital for a tax increase in his first term, and he was still wary. But he had won reelection decisively in 1956. That put him in the odd posture of having more clout in his second term than in his first. He made sure he used it wisely.

Unlike some other governors of the late twentieth century—most notably Gov. Bill Clinton—Faubus never waited until the last hour to share his plans with the legislature. He consulted with the General Assembly's leaders early and at length. Then he deftly planted news leaks so that the public was in on his plans, as well. A full month before the 1957 legislative session began, he announced the rough outlines of his tax plan. He would ask for rises in sales, income, and severance taxes. He plugged the plan several times between Christmas and the opening of the session in mid-January, arguing with mounting persuasiveness that the increases were necessary to finance the improved educational system needed to support industrialization and jobs. The state's notoriously underpaid teachers got special attention. While many influential state agencies would share in the higher revenues, most of the increase would go to teachers.

The statewide teachers' organization, the Arkansas Education Association, went to work full-time lobbying legislators. The Governor's Advisory Committee on Education, which included such prominent people as Hugh B. Patterson Jr., publisher of the *Gazette,* went into high gear with publicity. The needs were spelled out repeatedly. Dozens of districts could not afford to keep their schools open more than seven or eight months a year. Arkansas rolled the dice annually to determine whether it or Mississippi would claim last place in the nation in teachers' salaries and per-pupil expenditures.

Faubus's second inaugural speech on January 15 was devoted almost entirely to the tax program. He knew by the end of the day that he was gaining. Reaction of the legislators was predictably cautious, but much of the hostility of two years earlier was gone.

The bills were on the members' desks within twenty-four hours. There was a brief sign of trouble four days later when a batch of counter proposals was introduced.

Faubus was not idle. The southern counties that still produced considerable oil had enough representation in the General Assembly to pass or defeat a bill in a tight vote. The increased severance tax that Faubus had proposed, while never onerous on any of the mining and drilling interests, was a convenient area for compromise. He cut an early deal with the oil people to exempt stripper wells from the tax; that relieved an important source of pressure.

The judges and prosecuting attorneys were lobbying hard for a pay raise out of the new tax revenues. Two weeks into the session, Faubus went on television to plead for his plan. He once again spelled out the needs for education and other state services. Then he mentioned the judges and prosecutors. He said he would veto their raises unless the legislature passed the whole tax program and provided for the teachers, welfare recipients, and others equally needy. The threat ensured that the judges and prosecutors did not get behind a lesser program that would benefit their cause alone.

There was serious opposition. While the *Gazette* editorialized for the program, its smaller afternoon rival, the *Arkansas Democrat,* opposed it. Several other papers around the state were skeptical or outright opposed. One of the most powerful members of the legislature, Sen. Ellis M. Fagan of Little Rock, led the opposition in the Senate. Faubus had seen Fagan's power before when the senator and his allies at Arkansas Power and Light Company had destroyed Sid McMath's career.

This time, Faubus was ready. He had carefully cultivated his own centers of power in the legislature. His floor leader in Fagan's chamber was a quietly powerful man from east Arkansas, Lee Bearden of Leachville. The governor converted Rep. Paul Van Dalsem of Perry County, the House bull, who had repeatedly killed tax legislation in the past. Virtually all of Fagan's fellow veterans in the General Assembly went over to Faubus's side, thanks largely to Bearden's crafty work. Both houses passed the plan by overwhelming margins.

Significantly, the bills got more than the two-thirds needed to attach the emergency clause, meaning the tax increases would go into effect soon after the session ended. Faubus knew that the opponents planned to gather petitions to refer the legislation to a popular vote. Without the emergency clause, the new laws would not have gone into effect until after the next election in November 1958. The matter was placed on the ballot, but by the fall of 1958 the voters were able to appreciate what their increased taxes were providing. Faubus's tax package coasted to victory.

Part of the new money enabled the public colleges and the university to replace and renovate large numbers of old buildings. At the spring commencement of 1957, Orval Faubus finally got a degree from the Fayetteville institution that he could not afford to attend when he was young. The university made him an honorary doctor of laws. The *Democrat*'s editorial cartoonist Jon Kennedy portrayed him striding across the campus in cap and gown with a citizen in the background asking, "Don't they have a 'Doctor of Politics' degree?"

The state's children gained more than he did. For the first time, all of Arkansas's schools during the 1957–58 year were open for nine months. And for the first time in many years, their teachers were paid enough to keep most of them from leaving the state.

Another beneficiary was the state hospital for the mentally ill. That institution had struggled for years because of a lack of money. Dr. A. C. Kolb, the superintendent during the 1930s and 1940s, had stretched the hospital's resources by starting a dairy and raising produce for the patients. He scrounged materials to build cottages for his doctors. He once came into a railroad carload of Ku Klux Klan costumes that had been forfeited for nonpayment of freight charges. Female patients who could sew converted them into bed sheets. The General Assembly took the view that the hospital, operated so resourcefully, didn't need much state money. It was the same with the state penitentiary, which for years turned a profit from its extensive cotton lands. The hospital had about five thousand patients, and Dr. Kolb took care of them at a per-patient cost to the state of fifty-six cents a day. When he asked Gov. Ben Laney for an increase to sixty-three cents, he was rebuffed until a young reformer in the legislature named Paul Van Dalsem forced the governor to relent.

Early in his tenure, Faubus learned of patients sleeping on the floor because there were too few beds. Legislators inspecting the place found conditions so deplorable that they vomited. There was an occasional horror story in the press. An elderly woman with cancer was turned away, and the ambulance driver parked her outside the capitol and invited the press corps to take a look.

The superintendency had passed to a bright but politically awkward doctor named Ewing Crawfis during Cherry's administration. His political problems accumulated steadily. A small, rowdy unit of the Congress of Industrial Organizations began organizing the workers. Important members of the legislature—those who controlled the state budget—began to be alienated. Crawfis made the mistake of firing a friend of Van Dalsem, a powerhouse who by the mid-1950s had outgrown his youthful idealism. Then he resisted pressure from the governor's executive secretary, Jim Bland, to fire certain staff people and replace them with Bland's friends.

Threatened with losing political control of an important state agency, Faubus went on the offensive. He lambasted the hospital's deplorable conditions in the press. He publicly feuded with Crawfis. During a public debate with Crawfis one night, Faubus held up a jar of milk from the hospital dairy and asserted that he could see bits of manure floating in it. Crawfis soon decided to return to his home state of Ohio.

Faubus and the legislature suddenly became warmly attentive. With the new tax revenue of 1957, the hospital was given new buildings, more medicines, more staff with better training, and improved programs. One of the buildings was named for Faubus.

But the hospital staff were reminded periodically that they worked at the sufferance of political egoists. Dr. Payton Kolb, the acting clinical director—and the son of the long-time superintendent—had the bad judgment to complain in a series of personal letters that one of his programs had been halted "due to political interference." He found himself hailed before a legislative investigative committee. Van Dalsem, the chairman, accused him of frightening away qualified staff applicants. Kolb got the message: Keep your mouth shut or get out. He also understood that the message was coming not just from the bluff boss of Perry County but from Van Dalsem's circumspect friend Orval Faubus. Dr. Kolb was luckier than some. Little Rock had a shortage of psychiatrists in private practice. He slipped easily into new work away from the demeaning pressure of petty politics.

CHAPTER 14

Americans from afar harbor a vague notion that Arkansas is distinguished, if at all, by political corruption. It is true that since statehood in 1836, not a decade—perhaps not a single gubernatorial tenure—has passed without some besmirching of political honor. The sins have ranged from petty favoritism to egregious giveaways to railroads and land-grabbers.

However, the uncomfortable national truth is that Arkansas has never been more corrupt than the rest of the country. Indeed, the state's corruption looks bush-league against the examples of New York, Illinois, Rhode Island, and Louisiana. The graft and extortion budgets of a dozen American cities rival the legitimate annual budget of the state of Arkansas.

What really sets Arkansas apart, if a distinction is honestly sought, is a history of deciding public policy by force. Perhaps more than that of any other state, Arkansas's politics until quite recently has been marked by a raucous and unnerving physicality. The reason may lie in the state's beginnings. With the Indian Territory on its outer border until the twentieth century, blocking the historical urge to drift west, the state had to accommodate the restlessness and violence of its citizens within itself. Some of the meaner sort slid off the bottom corner into Texas, where they were welcomed, but most of the raw-tempered settlers stayed in the Bear State. They had no one to vent their hostilities on except their neighbors. Much

Gov. Earl K. Long of Louisiana, who once declared that he would forfeit the highest office in the land before he would "sell out the colored people of this state," bends the ear of a fellow southern moderate at the Democratic National Convention of 1956.

of the bad humor was expended on politics. Well into the twentieth century, election day was often a kind of quarrelsome holiday with eruptions of drunkenness, fistfights, and gunplay.

On one election day when Faubus was a young teacher, hundreds of Madison County Democrats and Republicans massed across the street from each other prepared to shoot it out over what the Democrats saw as a Republican attempt to steal the election. Men came to Huntsville armed with pistols, hunting rifles, blackjacks, and clubs. The sheriff set up two machine guns in a second-floor window of the courthouse. When the election commission chairman emerged to declare the Democrats victorious, he carried the election certificate in one hand and a pistol covered with a handkerchief in the other. No one challenged him, and the day passed miraculously without bloodshed.

Violence and quarreling were not confined to election days. Any disagreement, whether on policy or points of personal honor, might lead to bloodshed. Countless numbers of nineteenth-century public figures died in duels. Many others died in ordinary shooting scrapes. One memorable shootout occurred in the editor's office of the *Arkansas Gazette* when a leading public figure shot to death an intruding rival. No one has ever tallied the casualties of knifings, fistfights, and eye-gougings among political opponents. The Speaker of the House killed another member with a Bowie knife during the first session of the legislature in 1837. Four prominent public figures, including a former Confederate general, were assassinated during Reconstruction. Armed gangs, vigilantes, and freelance terrorists roamed the hills and delta for years after the Civil War, often operating under the authority of state government. Any neighborhood feud might erupt into a countywide political contest, with blood spilled on all sides. In 1874, Arkansas had its own shooting war over a disputed gubernatorial election between Joseph Brooks and Elisha Baxter. It lasted more than a month and produced dozens of casualties, including about twenty deaths. Baxter won.

Most of the nineteenth-century political violence had little to do with the race issue or was at least race-neutral as in the case of the Brooks-Baxter War, in which the hastily recruited soldiers on both sides were mainly Negroes from the plantation country. Later, when racial violence spread across the South, Arkansas held its own in the bloody competition. There is some evidence, in fact, that Arkansas holds the title to the all-time worst escapade of race-related murder. A disturbance in the Phillips County community of Elaine in 1919, a massacre sometimes misleadingly labeled a "race riot," resulted in the slaughter of at least dozens and perhaps hundreds of black people after black sharecroppers tried to form a union to put an end to a generations-old system of peonage. Responding to an interracial shooting and rumors of a black insurrection, white planters sent their families to a neighboring town, then roamed the countryside in gangs shooting black men, women, and children. The National Association for the Advancement of Colored People estimated that as many as 250 blacks had been murdered.

There was another outbreak of racist nightriding during the 1930s when a pair of home-grown Socialists organized an integrated union of tenant farmers. Violence followed as the Southern Tenant Farmers Union spread from the Arkansas delta to other parts of the South. All this was in addition to the periodic lynchings, Ku Klux Klan beatings, and cross burnings, not to mention the everyday racial antagonisms that blew into open fighting when trouble-hunting youths and louts encountered like-minded members of the other race.

By the fall of 1957, when Orval Faubus tapped into the historical reservoir of Arkansas violence, the state had been relatively quiet for a generation. That is, its political competition was being settled by ballots, not bullets. But the old habit, although dormant, was not dead. He had seen evidence of that in his campaign for a second term when the race issue threatened to bring out the beast once again.

Young Jim Malone had expected that his campaign speeches might be received with coolness or even hostility. But when a mob at Bearden threatened to cut the throats of him and his workers, he was shocked. Nevertheless, they drove on to Hampton for a night rally and tried to put the episode behind them. At Hampton an old man greeted him with this message: "They're going to shoot you off the stump." Malone told him to take his message back: "Tell them to get ready because I'm going to make the speech." Minutes into the speech, a convertible with a rifle hanging out its window circled the courthouse square. Malone interrupted his remarks to make sure his listeners saw the car. Seconds later the car approached again and the audience, on Malone's instruction, turned to stare at it. It left and no shots were fired. That was his most unnerving moment during the angry summer of 1956, but he had to face threats of various kinds in other towns. At Paragould, an enraged man attacked him and was pulled off by plainclothes policemen.

This violence was not directed personally at Jim Malone, a member of a respected political family in Lonoke County. It was meant to send a message to the candidate he was campaigning for, Orval Faubus. It was not as if the governor had created a scandal or plundered the state treasury or run off with another man's wife. His sin was that he had sent gestures of friendship to the black community of Arkansas. He had helped open the Democratic party apparatus to black participation and had appointed black leaders to the party's state committee. He had started equalizing the salaries of black and white state employees. He had overseen the quiet desegregation of the public schools in five districts. He had helped Arkansas to become the first state in the South to open all its white colleges to black students. He had appointed a few blacks to state boards. He had even given an Arkansas Traveler certificate, the state's official honor, to Mrs. Daisy Bates, president of the Arkansas branch of the National Association for the Advancement of Colored People.

Among professional southerners and die-hard white suprema-cists, these were acts of betrayal or perhaps even treason. A lot of people still suspected that Cherry's hatchet men had got it right, that Faubus was a crypto-Communist. Large numbers of white southerners were becoming persuaded that racial integration was part of an international Communist plot to disrupt the United States and place a dictatorship at the head of its government. To many of his enemies, Faubus was at the very least a traitor to the southern way of life. He and his friends were disconcerted to learn that Arkansas still had plenty of men who were willing to settle their political differences with force.

The southern way of life that Faubus was betraying meant that black people knew their place and stayed there, not just in schools but at every point where the two races might brush together in public. Drinking fountains, toilets, and waiting rooms were labeled "White" and "Colored." Jobs carried unwritten labels. Office workers and skilled craftsmen were "White." Janitors, field hands, and maids were "Colored." Across the Deep South, a black person who tried to vote risked his livelihood and sometimes his life. The hill country governor saw the system as unjust and silly, and he would hit it a lick here and a lick there. But he did not see himself as a champion of change.

His caution and moderation notwithstanding, the 1956 gubernatorial election was in many ways more dramatic than the one that had put Faubus into office two years earlier. During the interim, the Supreme Court's *Brown v. Board of Education* decision of 1954, declaring school segregation unconstitutional, had begun to sink in across the South. Most white southerners reacted calmly at first, especially in the upper South states like Arkansas and Tennessee. But determined segregationists in the Black Belt of the Deep South vowed at once to oppose the ruling with everything they had. For some, that included violence. Political leaders talked of obstructing it through legal means—courts, legislatures, political pressures—but among those with lesser reputations and even less sense of responsibility, there was dark talk of taking up arms and picking up where Appomattox had left off. Southern nationalism was being reborn.

Most white supremacists, even those with no intention of using violence, based their beliefs on personal observation overlaid with a thin sheet of legalism. They thought Negroes to be biologically inferior, and to support that theory they pointed to high rates of crime, ignorance, and family dysfunction among them. State laws sanctioning segregation were justified on the grounds that they accorded with local custom. Folkways could not be altered by law, they said. Anyway, public education was the business of the states, and the federal courts had no constitutional voice in matters of states' rights. Beyond the legal argument, there was a widespread belief that integration was the work of the international Communist conspiracy.

A vast majority of southern whites held one or more of those views with varying degrees of intensity. Only a few, a politically ineffective minority, believed that school desegregation should proceed as soon as possible. Those few saw the federal courts as the highest authority in all matters of law, including racial segregation. A somewhat larger group, known as moderates, tended to dislike the prospect of integration, but reluctantly bowed to the authority of the federal courts. The moderates thought integration should be implemented gradually at a pace that would do the least harm to local custom. Polls indicated a slow, grudging acceptance of the distasteful change among the latter, especially outside the Black Belt.

It appeared during the first months after the *Brown* decision that the gradualists would be a significant force. Upper South officials took the public position that their states would comply, albeit without enthusiasm. Even a few Deep South governors like James P. Coleman of Mississippi, Earl K. Long of Louisiana, and James E. Folsom of Alabama cautioned their segregationist citizens against overreacting.

But, in an echo from the 1850s, the gradualists lost ground as the Deep South mounted its resistance. Dissent against the prevailing sentiment was suppressed. White Citizens Councils sprang up from Jackson to Richmond, all working energetically to build fear, anger, and resistance. While the councils in the small towns included many established white leaders, those in the cities and larger towns tended to attract second-rate lawyers, hustling clergymen, and hot-eyed parvenus who suddenly presumed to speak for all white people. It was as if Ab Snopes had come in from burning a barn and announced that he had been called to preach. These people were quick to exploit the natural anxiety of ordinary white parents, otherwise decent people who had been reared to be wary of the dark-faced stranger, church-going white people who would not think of poking fun at a cripple but who, from infancy, had been taught to make jokes at the expense of black people.

The aim of the councils was to build obstruction to the Supreme Court decision. Their legal scholars threw up one scheme after another: pupil placement laws to allow white children to be moved out of integrated schools, laws to close integrated schools, abolition of compulsory education laws, and several other legislative measures. The quaint doctrine of interposition, holding that a state could interpose its authority between the Supreme Court and local school districts, caught the fancy of editors, lawyers, and public officials. Nationally respected public figures like former secretary of state James F. Byrnes of South Carolina and Sen. Richard B. Russell of Georgia joined the call for massive resistance to the Supreme Court edict.

By 1956, when Faubus had to face reelection, the resistance had gathered such force that virtually every southern member of Congress, even those with no stomach for it, signed an extraordinary document called the Southern Manifesto. The paper challenged the legitimacy of the Supreme Court's school decision and urged southerners to resist it. The legal scholar Alexander M. Bickel called it "a calculated declaration of political war against the Court's decision."

Throughout the months of rising resistance, Arkansas remained cautious. The state had a strain of liberality that often baffled outsiders, especially in light of its history of political violence. It boasted a significant intellectual elite nurtured by the state's institutions of higher learning, especially the University of Arkansas and privately endowed Hendrix College. Then there was the statewide influence of one of the nation's great newspapers. The elderly *Arkansas Gazette* never let its readers forget its credentials, its authority, or its stern advocacy of public decency. J. N. Heiskell, the owner, believed that his newspaper's mission was to lead Arkansas out of darkness. The paper reached every corner of the state and had about 100,000 subscribers. Its moderate, reasoned editorials and its comprehensive news coverage were responsible for much of the tone of civility that prevailed in Arkansas during the 1940s and 1950s.

It was Heiskell who brought to the paper Harry Ashmore, a new voice, to become the *Gazette*'s executive editor just as the race issue became a national preoccupation after World War II. A Carolinian, Ashmore had come to maturity on the same newspaper that had nurtured W. J. Cash. He had spent a year at Harvard University on a Nieman Fellowship, then, like Orval Faubus, had gone to war as an army officer. In Little Rock, he and Faubus seemed to have much in common. Both identified with the progressive politics of Sid McMath and Harry Truman. They seemed to share a belief in equal

J. N. Heiskell, editor and chief owner of the Gazette, in the 1950s and (inset) in 1913, the year he was appointed to fill the unexpired term of Sen. Jeff Davis. Heiskell was editor of the paper from 1902 until 1972 when he died at the age of 100.

rights for Negroes. They distrusted concentrations of wealth. They were casual friends and ran in the same political circles, up to a point. But there were differences that would finally rend the friendship and turn them into fierce enemies.

The *Gazette* was not the only editorial voice of sanity. The *Northwest Arkansas Times* at Fayetteville, run by Sen. J. W. Fulbright's mother, Roberta, joined the *Gazette* and several other respected southern newspapers in urging respect for the *Brown* decision.

A number of Arkansas school districts quietly complied with the ruling. Fayetteville, home of the University of Arkansas, became the first town in the South to go along with it. Four days after the decision was handed down, the Fayetteville School Board, led by Senator Fulbright's brother-in-law, Hal C. Douglas, voted to begin integration in the fall. The university itself in 1948 had been the first institution of higher learning in the South to admit Negroes.

Arkansas found it easy to be a little high-minded on race. Its population never contained as many African Americans as most other southern states, and only in the low country dominated by that old slaver, the Mississippi River, were there consistently large concentrations. By 1950, after years of black flight to the North, Arkansas had only six counties with black majorities. But high-mindedness was not the same as justice. The state was spending $102.25 a year on white students and only $67.75 on black students in 1954. Separate-but-equal was a mockery in Arkansas as it was across the South.

Faubus's progressive record on race was not surprising. Sam had preached racial equality. Orval and his brothers and sisters had rooted for the black prizefighter Joe Louis during the 1930s, which was seen as unusual even in the politically cranky confines of Madison County. He had seen only a few African Americans before reaching manhood. Black workers came to Combs occasionally to load railroad ties. A black baseball team from another county sometimes came to play a local white team. There was the little band of black folk at Wharton Creek, whose affection Orval had courted and won in his early election campaigns. Later, on the state scene, no one was surprised when he appointed blacks and helped integrate the state Democratic party. During the early years of his tenure as governor, he quietly cultivated the goodwill of integrationists. He once told a small gathering at Winthrop Rockefeller's farm that he saw the Supreme Court's school decision as the law of the land and morally right. He said, "If I had been on the court, I would have voted that way myself."

But there were other signs that he was far from committed to racial equality, that indeed he could take either side with equal facility. During and after the war in Europe, he had exhibited some race antagonism. He found that he resented black servicemen's dating white girls. In his opening speech for governor in 1954, he had made an ominous statement on the *Brown* decision, warning against pressure and mandatory methods to establish "a complete and sudden mixing of the races in the public schools." He called desegregation the number-one issue in the campaign. The *Gazette* scolded him for that, and he didn't mention it further in public.

The *Gazette* might have been even harder on him had it known his private thinking at the time. Well ahead of other public figures, he had spotted the explosive potential in the *Brown* decision on school segregation. He thought the issue wasn't yet ripe, but eventually would elect a governor of Arkansas. He matter-of-factly told a small gathering of campaign associates at the Marion Hotel one day in 1954 that if he could find a way to capitalize on the race issue, "they'll never get me out of office."

He found a way. But first he had to get past the 1956 election, and in that he was again blessed with the right opponent. He had the good luck to be opposed by one of Arkansas's most gifted hell-raisers, a man so volatile in his eloquence that he frightened large numbers of otherwise receptive voters into the security of the political center—Orval Faubus's natural habitat.

CHAPTER 15

Jim Johnson's prospects in 1956 were better than many people understood. Faubus had hurt himself severely by supporting a politically risky reform of the county property-tax system in 1955. Reassessing property to equalize the tax burden sounded good on paper, but in practice it meant that everyone who had to pay more became, in his own eyes, a victim of an unjust law. County assessors were the first to feel the backlash; many were defeated at the next election. Johnson marveled at the courage Faubus had shown in pushing the program through the legislature. "It took the balls of a four-ball rabbit to put that over," he once told an interviewer. Nevertheless, he was ready to capitalize on an unexpected opportunity as the governor prepared to ask for a second term. The issue the challenger seized on was one that caused even stronger emotions than taxes.

James D. Johnson, dark-haired, handsome, ambitious, grew up in the rowdy lumber town of Crossett, just north of the Louisiana line. He served in the Marine Corps during World War II, then returned to Crossett to practice law after getting his degree from Cumberland Law School in Tennessee. He vaulted to a seat in the state Senate at the age of twenty-five. He stumbled when he tried to move to the state political stage as attorney general. But as the segregationist reaction began, he saw his chance.

He had made valuable contacts in the states' rights movement in 1948 working for Strom Thurmond, the Dixiecrat presidential candidate. All through 1955 and the winter of 1956, he traveled the Arkansas low country speaking at Citizens Council rallies. Capital reporters who had known him only as a somewhat reform-minded young senator began to notice that he had a genuine talent on the stump. He was fast on his feet. He established instant affinity with an audience. His public style was Old Testament: thunder, lightning, and dark warnings. Privately, he had an astonishing gift for ribald imagery. He was altogether the most effective wielder of the language that Arkansas had seen in many years.

His message was stark. The Supreme Court's school decision was unconstitutional and should be opposed by a massive show of resistance. Beginning in the summer of 1955, six months after Faubus took office, Johnson added the governor to his message. Faubus, he said, was a traitor to the southern way of life. He assailed his target not only on the stump but also in the lurid pages of *Arkansas Faith*, a publication of the White Citizens Council of Arkansas, of which Johnson was state director. He had teamed up with a shadowy figure named Curt Copeland, who had been forced to leave Hot Springs for publishing a recklessly libelous periodical called the *Hot Springs Rubdown*. Copeland's many enemies eventually learned that he had

Jim Johnson, who frightened Faubus with his appeal to segregationist voters in 1956.

been arrested in a counterfeiting scheme in Texas, among other brushes with the law. He found work as editor of Johnson's paper just as massive resistance began to bubble across the South.

In a typical attack on Faubus, the paper complained that the governor had appointed a black man as a highly paid investigator for the Alcoholic Beverage Control agency and that the deal had been consummated over breakfast at the governor's mansion. In another issue, it denounced Faubus and his friend Winthrop Rockefeller as politicians "who would trade YOUR daughter for a mess of nigger votes." A cartoon showed Faubus patting the rear of a seductive black woman labeled "NAACP." The January 1956 issue reported that Faubus was "supposed to be" a member of the NAACP and had colluded with Daisy Bates, state president of the organization, to enroll Negro students in every white school in Arkansas that spring.

But that was all largely speculative. What Johnson needed was a visible outrage that he could blame on Faubus. He got it in the summer of 1955 in the town of Hoxie on the edge of the rich cotton land of northeast Arkansas. Hoxie's consolidated school had one thousand white and twenty-five black students. The school board for years had sent the black youngsters to nearby Jonesboro, paying tuition and transportation. Always shy of money, the board saw a chance to save a few dollars when the Supreme Court outlawed segregated schools. In July 1955, at the beginning of the split term customary in many cotton areas—allowing students to take leave and work in the cotton harvest during the fall—it kept the black students home and sent them to the white school.

It appeared that Hoxie would accept the change as readily as the other Arkansas towns that had already integrated. Then *Life* magazine featured the town's desegregated classes in its August issue. When the magazine reached Hoxie, trouble began. White supremacist organizations, including Johnson's and a number from other southern states, flooded the town with racist handbills. Local segregationists began to speak out. They were quickly joined by outsiders such as Johnson, Copeland, and Little Rock's leading segregationist lawyer, Amis Guthridge.

The rhetoric grew meaner. Guthridge in one speech said he would not be responsible if someone should throw a rock through a school board member's windshield and put out his eye. Johnson discussed a racial lynching in Mississippi. Other speakers more or less openly advocated lynching, saying firearms and grass ropes might have to be used to keep "the nigger out of the white bedroom." People thought to be integrationists began to get anonymous phone calls late at night.

Tensions rose in the school. Parents became anxious, and about half of them pulled their children out of classes. By mid-August, petitions were circulating demanding the ouster of the school board. The board responded by closing the schools early for the fall break.

Johnson and Copeland went back to Hoxie for a large rally on September 18. They were cheered with enthusiasm when they urged white people to stand up against forced integration, mongrelization of the races, a treasonous Supreme Court, and the Communist plan to destroy the southern way of life. Then they lambasted Faubus, the weak-kneed fence straddler, for failing to join the struggle against that conspiracy.

The governor's response was to keep a low profile. He refused to condemn the segregationist agitators, but he also refused to help the besieged school board. Hoxie's trouble, he said, was a local matter and he would not intervene. The U.S. Department of Justice did intervene, mostly through an elaborate subterfuge by Arthur B. Caldwell, an Arkansawyer who headed its civil rights section. He had been ordered by his superiors to keep out of the quarrel. But he quietly encouraged a bold young Jonesboro lawyer named Bill Penix to push the Hoxie case into federal court. Then the Justice Department, finding itself on its legs, entered the case as *amicus curiae*. The department and Penix persuaded a federal judge to enjoin Johnson and his cohorts from further interference at Hoxie.

The injunction eventually led to the peaceful desegregation of Hoxie's schools, but its immediate impact was to give Johnson ammunition in his fight against a "tyrannical" federal court system— and against Orval Faubus. By early 1956, he had found a way to tie Faubus not only to Hoxie but also to the perceived worldwide integration conspiracy. Speaking on statewide television, he said the white people of Hoxie had been betrayed first by their school board, then by their governor. Faubus, he said, was spineless. Not only that, he was a left-winger.

"Don't you know that the communist plan for more than fifty years has been to destroy southern civilization, one of the last patriotic and Christian strongholds, by mongrelization, and our negroes are being exploited by them to affect [*sic*] their purposes."

Arkansas Faith underscored the attack with a cartoon. It showed Faubus as a butcher holding a dog labeled "Arkansas." Using a cleaver labeled "Gradualism," he lops off the dog's tail a little at a time, each piece representing another town falling to integration. Faubus is saying, "This will please the niggers and confuse the white folks!"

Johnson's statewide reputation was enhanced by the Hoxie episode, which made news daily for months. But there was a danger that he might find himself cornered at the outer extreme. He found ways to be seen as often as possible with men of unassailable respectability. When he addressed a huge segregationist rally at the town of England in February 1956, another speaker was former governor Ben T. Laney, a favorite of businessmen. Johnson's growing political instinct also led him to cultivate the friendship of well-known officeholders from other states, notably Georgia's senator Richard B. Russell and governor Marvin Griffin and Mississippi's senator James O. Eastland. He became especially close to Eastland, who favored his young friend with a biting public attack on Faubus's cautious integration stand in late spring, just before the primary season.

If Johnson used his famous acquaintances, they in turn used him. Leaders like Eastland and Griffin made no secret of their desire that Arkansas should stand up to the federal courts and preserve Confederate unity. One of the other speakers at the England rally was Roy V. Harris of Georgia, a friend of Governor Griffin, president of the Citizens Councils of America, and one of the South's chief segregationist strategists. Harris fervently wanted the upper South to stand united with the Deep South. Urged on by Eastland and other southern leaders, Johnson became Arkansas's point man for massive resistance.

He and his fellow segregationists seized on still another respectable association to further their cause. James J. Kilpatrick, the editor of the *Richmond News-Leader,* one of the South's most influential newspapers, became the intellectual guru of massive resistance.

His efforts in reviving the old doctrine of interposition gave the resistance not only respectability but also the patina of constitutionalism that it needed. Using interposition, a state could do whatever it deemed necessary to maintain segregated schools. Kilpatrick relied on the initial constitutional authority of 1787 when only certain enumerated powers were delegated to the national government and all others were reserved to the states. The constitution he saw had lain undisturbed and unchanged for two hundred years, in the manner of Rip Van Winkle, and, in his mind, should remain unviolated by such whims as the passage of time, changed circumstance, or shifting court interpretations.

Taken to its logical extremes, interposition could supposedly nullify a Supreme Court decision. That, of course, could lead to massive disobedience of court orders and a blunt confrontation with the federal government not unlike the one of 1861.

Most of the southern states adopted interposition measures of varying severity. They ranged from mere resolutions of defiance in the upper South to outright requirements for massive disobedience in the states of the Deep South. The theory behind the latter was that if enough states "nullified" the *Brown* decision, the federal courts would have to decide whether to imprison thousands— perhaps hundreds of thousands—of angry southerners to enforce their orders.

Johnson wrote a proposed constitutional amendment for Arkansas and led a petition drive to get it on the ballot in the general election of November 1956. He deliberately drafted it to require that Arkansas move in with the Deep South and strike the most severe possible stand: nullification.

Reflecting on it years later, Johnson said, "That amendment was damned near a declaration of war against the United States. It'd kill corn knee-high. It was strong. Actually, too strong for me."

The proposed amendment became the foundation for Johnson's unannounced candidacy for governor. He charged at one point that Faubus had ordered state employees not to sign his petition. Faubus had to deny it, but both the charge and the denial swelled Johnson's publicity.

On April 30 in Little Rock's largest auditorium, Johnson made his candidacy official in a triumph of theatricality. The occasion was a rally of two thousand people. The crowd had become increasingly enthusiastic as it heard repeated cries against the communistic, atheistic, integrationist threat. Then Herbert Brewer, the farmer who had led the opposition to desegregating Hoxie's schools, strode to the stage and declared that their friend Jim Johnson ought to run for governor. That ignited a twenty-minute demonstration during which people walked the aisles to toss money into the orchestra pit to pay the filing fee. The hero finally went to the microphone and consented. "I'll run for governor if you'll support me," he said, and the crowd, not unexpectedly, signaled its approval.

Faubus was not at the rally, but he was not forgotten. Ben Laney, who had tried for a comeback by unsuccessfully opposing Faubus's friend McMath in 1950, was master of ceremonies. In a twenty-five-minute speech, he proposed a way to deal with politicians who ignored the views of him and his friends. "Cut a few political throats," he advised.

Faubus did not have to be reminded that his was the throat in jeopardy. Some of his advisors saw Johnson as no threat, but he knew better. He had fretted over the younger man's growing popularity since the fall of 1955. In January, Mrs. Bates applied pressure from the left by trying, without success, to enroll black students in four Little Rock schools. The effect in the white community was exacerbation of the growing fear. A Faubus poll the same month showed 85 percent of white Arkansawyers opposed integration; there was no reason to doubt its accuracy. In the spring, he instructed his pollster, Eugene F. Newsom, to measure his popularity against Johnson's in selected south Arkansas counties. The poll confirmed his suspicion. Johnson was dead even with him there.

Orval Faubus's flawed appreciation of history came into play as he considered how to meet the threat. To rationalize the course he began to set, he marshaled an argument against the *Brown* decision that went as follows: The nation had operated under the *Plessy v. Ferguson* decision, which legitimized segregation, for ninety-two years. That judgment had been repeatedly confirmed through the years by some of the nation's best jurists. Now the *Brown* decision was being condemned by other great legal minds and defended by only a few respected lawyers.

It was not clear whether he realized that his reading was the opposite of the actual reaction among the nation's constitutional scholars. Nevertheless, armed with his historical argument, he was ready to move to the right. He could ignore the left, the NAACP, and the noisy but small band of white liberals. Still, his own inherent sense of moderation—coupled with a fine political instinct—bound him with a kind of centrifugal force to the center, or as near it as he could get.

He knew that if Johnson defeated him, it would be with votes from eastern and southern Arkansas. He had to move faster to consolidate his strength there. It was no longer enough to pay attention to that region's desires on highways and economic priorities. He had to undercut Johnson on the race issue, not by out-shouting but by outwitting him.

The more substantial leaders of the Arkansas low country had not jumped on the resistance bandwagon that was careering across the rest of the Deep South. They opposed integration, but, unlike their peers in most of the rest of the Black Belt, they had little respect for the *arrivistes* running the Citizens Councils. In Lincoln County, the sheriff and other white leaders refused to let the council hold an organizing meeting. These traditional leaders wanted no tampering with the customary power structures in the delta. When he made his move to the right, Faubus went over the heads of the council hotheads and reached out to the established leadership.

In February, well before the primary season and just after the NAACP had sued the Little Rock School Board in federal court to compel integration, Faubus appointed a committee of some of the low country's most respected citizens. Their assignment was to study Virginia's plan for opposing the court decision. The committee included Marvin Bird, an Earle banker who headed the state board of education; state representative Bex Shaver of Wynne, a former lieutenant governor; R. B. McCulloch of Forrest City, a graduate of Harvard Law School with years of experience; Bert Dickey, a Crittenden County planter; and Charles Adams of Hughes, Faubus's old friend from the 1954 campaign.

The Faubus plan that grew out of the committee's work was, in the context of the times, a model of restraint. It was similar to the plans of other moderates across the upper South. It called for an initiated act to establish a pupil-assignment scheme to allow whites to opt out of integrated classes and a resolution of interposition that was little more than a throttled cry of defiance. It hardly mattered that nothing in the plan was likely to be deemed constitutional by any federal court. Both measures would be on the November ballot alongside Johnson's radical amendment proposal.

Faubus's rapprochement with the powers of eastern Arkansas produced another result. When the governor called on the legislators of the low country for help with his tax increase the following winter, they remembered his efforts to try to stall integration. Their votes provided the margin of victory for the state's biggest educational improvement in a generation.

Another candidate of some substance, Jim Snoddy of Alma, who had served briefly as Cherry's executive secretary in 1953, was also on the primary ballot. Faubus did not worry about him except for his capacity to draw votes and possibly force a runoff. Snoddy's message on race was similar to Johnson's, but he lacked the latter's electrifying appeal. Faubus devoted most of his energy to the south Arkansas firebrand and to walking the fine line that, he hoped, would hold the political center in his camp.

He discovered just how hazardous it could be walking that line. On July 9 he attended a rally at Pine Bluff, the largest town in Arkansas's Black Belt. He was jeered when he said integration was not an issue in the campaign. By the time he spoke at Marianna, deeper into the Black Belt, two days later, he had added to his speech the line, "No school district will be forced to mix the races as long as I am governor of Arkansas." That seemed to satisfy the crowd.

In mid-July, he turned up the heat on Johnson. He began by aiming at one of the Johnson campaign's most vulnerable spots, his association with Copeland. He devoted time in speeches and television appearances to Copeland's biography, waving a copy of his FBI record, his mug shot from the El Paso Police Department, and the court documents from his criminal libel trial in Arkansas. He called Copeland a bully and a liar. He suggested that the man would be a close gubernatorial advisor if Johnson should be elected.

As for Johnson himself, Faubus labeled him "a purveyor of hate" who was profiting from stirring racial tensions. Speaking on Little Rock television July 16, he described the magazine published by

Copeland and Johnson as "one of the vilest, most dissolute, neo-pornographic publications it has ever been my disgust to see." Then he added:

> This opposition candidate for governor readily and will-ingly supplements the filth contained in this publication with hate-filled mouthings of intolerance, suggestions of violence, totalitarian proposal of changes in our methods of govern-ment, and an advocacy of mob rule.

The best answer to the Supreme Court challenge, he said, was his own interposition plan. "I don't have to jump up and down and stomp on my hat to tell you that."

Johnson's response was to send workers out with a leaflet por-traying Faubus flanked by four black people—a picture that Faubus quickly branded as fake.

Finally, the violence that had thus far been directed only against Malone and anonymous campaign workers, and that had gone unreported, threatened the governor himself. He began to feel the rising tension as he campaigned in the hamlets and county seats of eastern and southern Arkansas in mid-July. One day at Monticello, in the pine woods of southeastern Arkansas, his friend the police chief had to intercede to shut down a Johnson loudspeaker that had been set up to drown out Faubus's speech. A Johnson crowd was waiting later that evening when he reached the nearby town of Warren. Faubus realized he was traveling with only three workers who might be able to protect him. He had deduced that Johnson's strategy was to send toughs to disrupt his talks and thereby distract the media and the audiences from Faubus's campaign message. He figured that, if unchallenged, the opponents would try to drive him off the stump and create a publicity coup.

He arrived at Warren well ahead of his 8:30 appearance. Sensing trouble, he telephoned Jimmy Karam in Little Rock and asked him to hurry down. Karam was a former football coach and one-time goon who had terrorized labor organizers in other parts of the South. He now owned a clothing store and had worked for some time to achieve respectability. But when he heard of the possibility of a brawl, he could not stay away. Carrying a large club around the courthouse square, Karam led the little band of Faubus workers in keeping order through the governor's speech. They forcibly shut down a loudspeaker and so frightened its operator that he fled to the police station for protection. Another protester was manhandled so roughly that he vomited.

There was no further trouble until some days later when Faubus spoke at Pocahontas in northeastern Arkansas. There the hecklers set in again. One advanced toward the speaker's platform and was knocked down by a Faubus protector. He raced to his car and reached for a pistol but was struck again, this time by a monkey wrench wielded by a Faubus worker who had been a University of Arkansas football player.

That was the end of the violence, but Faubus had the satisfaction a few days later of confronting Curt Copeland in person. Johnson in later years contended that none of his 1950s followers were capable of real violence. The Faubus people saw it differently. When Copeland turned up at a Faubus rally at Mountain Home, the governor suspected another plan to disturb the peace. He took the initiative by pointing to Copeland in the crowd and showing some of his more sensational magazine pictures. Then he said, "Always in the Ozark Mountains we have heard of two kinds of liars. One is a natural-born liar, the other is self-made by practice. I'm telling you, he's both. And there he sits, right there." Copeland took the microphone later and tried to respond, but the crowd made it clear that it belonged to Faubus.

So did the election. He carried sixty-seven of the state's seventy-five counties and defeated Johnson by more than 2 to 1. But the segregationist challenger drew more votes than any other Faubus opponent would get until Winthrop Rockefeller opposed him in 1964. More ominously, the anti-integration measures backed by Faubus and Johnson were approved overwhelmingly in the general election in November. The Faubus pupil-assignment plan was approved almost 2 to 1, while his interposition resolution got 61 percent. Johnson's declaration of war got 56 percent, thanks in part to thousands of black votes controlled by white planters. Even the fraud seemed portentous.

Jim Johnson cast a large shadow by the end of 1956, and it fell most luridly across the frame of Orval Faubus. A long generation later, the two old men were riding in the same car on the way home from a funeral and fell to talking about the campaign of 1956 and its aftereffects in 1957. Faubus was moved, perhaps by the emotion of the day, to acknowledge his debt. "You made me take positions that served me well politically," he said.

<table>
<tr><td>CHAPTER
16</td><td>The violence during the 1956 primary campaign was not just an attempt to run Faubus off the stump. What really fueled it was an anger that had been spreading in Arkansas and across the white South since the Brown decision two years</td></tr>
</table>

earlier. The more anxious segregationists felt increasingly desperate as they saw schools desegregated without trouble in border states like Oklahoma and in small towns in Arkansas and Kentucky. They watched in alarm and amazement in 1955 and 1956 as the Rev. Dr. Martin Luther King Jr. led a silent, maddeningly nonviolent black army in Montgomery. That army, casting its own fearful shadow, humiliated the frustrated hordes of white people who threw everything they had into the fight to keep black people at the back of the bus. To rub it in for Arkansas's resisters, in April 1956, their own capital abolished segregated seating on its city buses. Just a month after Johnson's defeat in August, they and their fellows in the Deep South suffered the further indignity of seeing the huge public school system of Louisville, Kentucky, abandon its racial barriers with quiet acceptance. All in all, they felt increasingly cut off from polite society. Jim Johnson would eventually come to see it as a visitation of plague, as if he and his kind had contracted a corruption of blood.

Nevertheless, there were signs of encouragement for them. Negroes trying to integrate the schools at Mansfield, Texas, in the fall of 1956 were physically threatened by a band of thugs, the violent minority who seemed to inhabit every community of segregationists. Gov. Allan Shivers sent Texas Rangers not to help the Negro children but to enforce the segregationist threats. The Rangers took the Negroes back to the black school. And while Louisville integrated peacefully, several other Kentucky towns saw violent opposition. In Tennessee, Gov. Frank Clement sent the National Guard with tanks to put down segregationist trouble-makers at Clinton and Oliver Springs. Several people were injured, but segregationist morale was boosted. White boycotts crippled numerous districts in Tennessee and Kentucky during the fall of 1956. Segregationists of the Deep South were heartened.

It began to appear that Martin Luther King was the only American, white or black, who understood the implications of what was going on: that someday the provocations of the resisters would produce a reaction from an authority higher than a police chief, a mayor, or a governor, and that when that molasses-paced monster called the federal government was finally urged into motion, it would not be to support white people with clubs and guns but to suppress them, and that from that instant their movement would be doomed. Already, middle-of-the-road southern whites were slipping the bonds of conformity and rejecting the more extreme bombast. In a few years they would desert wholesale and not just reject but fiercely oppose the cross burnings of Jackson, the bombs of Birmingham, the mobs of Bogalusa, and the lynchings still ravaging the Ku Klux Klan belt.

Before that happened, though, there was one last flowering of hope for the lost cause. It occurred in tolerant, progressive Little Rock.

Virgil T. Blossom had a plan, and it suited him fine that it was called the Blossom Plan. He had moved from Fayetteville to become superintendent of Little Rock's schools in 1953 and had started energetically preparing Little Rock for the change as soon as the court handed down its desegregation decision the next year. By the time the schools opened in September 1957, he had held about 225 meetings with influential organizations and civic clubs to explain his scheme. There seemed to be no way it could fail. His promotion of gradual integration won him the honor of "Man of the Year" for 1955 in an *Arkansas Democrat* poll. Only a few people realized that Blossom's ambitions lay beyond the realm of education. He wanted to be governor of Arkansas. Further success as a handler of the South's most difficult problem would surely widen his reputation throughout the region, perhaps the nation.

Superintendent Virgil Blossom, the harried leader of the desegregation of Little Rock's public schools.

PHOTO BY LARRY OBSITNIK, COURTESY OF THE *ARKANSAS DEMOCRAT-GAZETTE* AND SPECIAL COLLECTIONS DIVISION, UNIVERSITY OF ARKANSAS LIBRARIES, FAYETTEVILLE.

The Blossom Plan was as simple as it was cynical. Desegregation would start at the top with one high school, then proceed to the junior highs in two or three years. Desegregation of all grades would come by 1963. The catch was in the arithmetic. Only a token number of highly qualified Negro students would be allowed at each stage. Seventeen were accepted for Central High School—in the working-class part of town—for the first term. Another handful would be added the year after. Any significant integration would be put off for years, maybe generations. A member of the school board was quoted as saying, "The plan was developed to provide as little integration as possible for as long as possible legally." As some said in bitter jest, the Blossom Plan was a plan of continued segregation, not integration.

Nevertheless, it fit the mood of the white leadership, not only in Little Rock but in much of the upper South. Those leaders typically disliked the Supreme Court ruling and believed that the only practical way to implement it was slowly, grudgingly, appeasing the opponents of integration while seeming to comply with the court orders. Virtually no one in a position of political power advocated integration as a moral duty or portrayed segregation as wrong in the same way that apartheid in South Africa would come to be portrayed as wrong. The news reports of white thugs beating black demonstrators in Montgomery stirred no sympathy among a majority of southern whites but rather indignation against the victims for disturbing the peace. A few white ministers joined their black colleagues in Little Rock to argue for ending an immoral system. But they were outnumbered and, in most cases, got only tepid support from their congregations.

Integration in Little Rock was to be a one-man show. Blossom spoke to more than two hundred groups, but he pointedly did not ask their advice. A leader in the desegregation of the schools of Washington, D.C., appeared in Little Rock and offered suggestions. Blossom ignored them. Teachers and students expressed interest in preparing for the big change; Blossom rebuffed them repeatedly. He was invited to speak at Ninth Graders Night during the spring to tell the new Central High students what to expect when the first Negroes were admitted. He greeted the parents and students, welcomed the youngsters to Central, and sat down without mentioning integration. Several civic leaders discussed bringing in a law enforcement expert to help prepare for any disturbances. Blossom told them he needed no outside help. The Parent-Teacher Associations volunteered to help. He told them to stick to PTA programs and stay out of integration. The Negro ministers' organization suggested a biracial committee to study the matter. Blossom rejected it. The white ministers' organization wanted to endorse his desegregation plan publicly. He asked it not to. What then could they do to help? "Keep quiet," he said. "Do nothing."

On the surface, his campaign seemed to be working. The plan was endorsed by numerous civic groups. The business establishment saw wisdom in its cunning. The country-club set applauded it. Pulaski Heights, the silk-stocking district, was all for it. The newspapers promoted it. Afterward, the city's establishment leaders expressed surprise at some unexpected turns. But before it was put to the test, Blossom convinced them that he had the situation in hand, and they were more than willing to abdicate their responsibility and let him handle it.

Black leaders, who were virtually ignored by Blossom, were skeptical and a little sullen, but they got nowhere. A lawsuit by the NAACP demanding speedy integration was dismissed by two levels of federal courts. Even the federal judiciary gave the Little Rock voluntary plan the stamp of approval.

The integrationist cause was not helped by a simmering division in the black community. Many black parents saw L. C. and Daisy Bates as radicals bringing trouble. The newspaper published by L. C. Bates, the *State Press*, spearheaded the integration campaign alongside the Arkansas chapter of the National Association for the Advancement of Colored People, headed by his wife, Daisy. But a second newspaper serving Negroes, the *Southern Mediator Journal,* published by C. H. Jones, was more cautious. While polls showed a large majority of blacks favoring school integration, many were anxious about pursuing it aggressively. This diversity of opinion was not well understood in the white community. Only a handful of white people, none of them in the business establishment, had any social or professional contact with black leaders.

The flaw in the superintendent's campaign turned out to be its audience. Nobody in Little Rock's top ranks noticed the little band of zealots in the Capital Citizens Council, who lived cheek to jowl with the city's lower middle-class white people. Their public statements were dismissed as the rantings of cranks. Nobody heard the muttering from the fundamentalist congregations in the working-class wards or the muttered threats from the gas stations and body repair shops along gritty Asher Avenue. But there was one who noticed.

Governor Faubus had sent a signal in January, for those who were listening, that he was open to advice from beyond the silk-stocking precincts. His January address to the legislature had included warnings to both sides: violence, disorder, and hate were not the answer, but neither was "forcible integration of our public schools." He noted that the voters just two months earlier had overwhelmingly approved certain measures to evade desegregation. Before the legislature adjourned in the spring, it would pass four more segregation laws with Faubus's acquiescence, including one establishing a state sovereignty commission with troubling investigative powers. Winthrop Rockefeller warned that it could establish an "Arkansas Gestapo."

The Citizens Council had its own plan and was ready to offer advice. In May, the council president, Robert Ewing Brown, published an open letter to Faubus reminding him how Governor Shivers and his Texas Rangers had dealt with a court order to integrate the schools at Mansfield and urging Faubus to do the same. The governor's reply seemed to contradict the message he had sent in his address to the legislature. No, he would not intervene at Little Rock. That's a local problem, he said. Then, kicking the segregationists in the shin, he followed that a week later with a call for more Negroes on the state Democratic Party Central Committee. That strengthened the long-held opinion of many that their governor was an outright integrationist. As suspicions rose, so did tempers.

While the moderate mass remained largely silent, letting Blossom play the role of the lone paladin, the immoderate core in the Citizens Council began to organize rallies. The organization had only about five hundred members, and at first its rallies were not well attended. That changed as the summer wore on and the less prosperous citizens began to see the Blossom Plan in a new light.

One aspect was particularly offensive to the white working class. Most of them lived in the older parts of the city near the black population. Their children would go to Central, the city's only high school for whites, the first target of integration. It made little difference that Central would remain the state's premier high school, that for years to come, as in years past, it would send large numbers of its graduates to Ivy League colleges.

As it happened, the governor's son, Farrell, had been a student there briefly. Farrell had grown into his teens with little attention from his father. He was shy and had become overweight and ungainly during the years at Huntsville. When he entered Central High, he made an easy target for physical and emotional abuse. The young toughs on the football team, for which he tried out, tackled and blocked him with cruel relish. Some of the more intellectually inclined taunted him for being the son of a "Communist." After several months, he persuaded his parents to let him return to Huntsville High.

Farrell's experience at Central would shortly take on a dark significance in the minds of some. But for now, the white people in Central's neighborhood were upset over something else. The more fashionable suburbs lay to the west, and for those youngsters the school board had started building a new high school. Hall High would attract few Negroes. The Blossom Plan had ignited class conflict on top of racial antagonisms.

The larger world added another layer of anxiety. In June and July, Fort Smith, Ozark, and North Little Rock announced that they would integrate their schools in the fall. Congress debated a sweeping civil rights bill throughout the summer, and southern delegates, including Arkansas's, portrayed it as one more threat to states' rights, public order, and the southern way of life.

The Citizens Council stepped up its pace. It bought a full-page advertisement in the *Arkansas Recorder* urging people to pressure the governor to stop race mixing. Many responded by sending him letters. Amis Guthridge, the council's lawyer, and the Rev. Wesley Pruden, pastor of Broadmoor Baptist Church and a council leader, very publicly asked the school board its policy on integrated dances and other social functions. There won't be any such affairs, the board said. A segregationist preacher from Dallas addressed a council rally and warned that if integration took place, "there are people left yet in the South who love God and their nation enough to shed blood if necessary to stop this work of Satan." Guthridge added his own prediction: Little Rock schools would never be integrated, and if they were, there would be "hell on the border."

Aside from all this, the governor was having a bad summer. His exertions during the legislative session of the winter and spring had left him exhausted and sick. He had undergone a minor operation in June, then had treated himself to a reunion of Arkansawyers at Fullerton, California. He and Mrs. Faubus had planned to take a leisurely train trip from there to Mexico. Instead of relaxing with old friends, he had fallen ill again. He canceled the Mexico excursion, went back into the hospital at Little Rock, and emerged into the spotlight just in time to answer new demands that he do something about integration.

He sounded a little snappish. He claimed that he had not even read the Citizens Council's flamboyant advertisements. As for the recently passed state laws opposing integration, enacted with his lukewarm support, he said, "Everyone knows that no state law supersedes a federal law. If anyone expects me to try to use them to supersede federal laws they are wrong." Earlier in the year, in a private conversation, he had made his views clear on the authority of the Supreme Court. He had told a couple of old liberal friends that the *Brown* decision was the law of the land and that, if he had been a justice of the court, he would have voted in favor of it.

The segregationists expanded their organizing and increased the pressure. Weeks before school was to start, they formed a Mothers League of Central High School to resist integration. Another group filed a lawsuit to force Faubus to stop procrastinating and appoint the members of the new state sovereignty commission. He scoffed, seeing the hand of Jim Johnson behind the suit. But within two days he had made the appointments. They included the same prominent east Arkansas leaders who had studied Virginia's massive resistance. These men lacked the heated enthusiasm of the Citizens Councilers, and the commission made little history except to relieve pressure on the governor.

Nevertheless, the resisters were encouraged. What they slowly came to realize was that they had stumbled on to Faubus's vulnerability, a secret then known only to his inner circle. The governor's weak spot was that he seldom reached out for advice from knowledgeable people outside his administration. There were such people, men like Witt Stephens, but they, not the governor, initiated the contact. For his part, Faubus was excessively accessible to anyone with a problem or a request. It was as if Jeff Davis's friends from the backwater had taken up his invitation and descended on his successor two generations removed, moving in to eat his hog jowls and peas and instruct him in how to govern the state. George Douthit, the chief capitol reporter for the *Arkansas Democrat,* who came to be close to Faubus, noted the consequences of that. "Faubus will fall for any story, however fantastic, if it is told with sufficient conviction," he wrote.

Faubus could easily have had informed advice from his new friends in the east Arkansas establishment. Richard McCulloch, for example, the legal genius behind much of Arkansas's scheme to maintain segregation by stealth and torpor, understood that minimal, token integration was necessary. That would make it easier for the courts to uphold pupil assignment laws and the other legal dodges currently in favor. Little Rock's plan fit his thinking neatly.

Neither did Faubus ask the advice of his old liberal friends like McMath, Woods, and Ashmore. And they shrank from offering it at first, perhaps unwilling to believe that a man with Faubus's history would align himself with his natural enemies. They failed to understand that Faubus was instinctively impelled to make peace with his most insistent and dangerous opponents, people like Johnson and his high-pitched segregationists.

Thus it was that the people who got the governor's ear, to their good fortune, were the leaders of the Capital Citizens Council and their far-ranging network. Two Little Rock men emerged as the most visible. The Rev. Wesley Pruden had seemed destined for the obscurity of a second-tier Baptist church, a man whose ambition out-paced his abilities. His friend Amis Guthridge had enjoyed even less professional success. His law practice was so unrewarding that he had had to supplement it by refinishing furniture in his wife's antique shop. But when integration threatened, they found their niche. Each had the gift of oratory and invective.

They knew the council members were with them, and they had

seen the polls showing that 85 percent of the state's white people disliked school integration. But they could not be sure they were reaching anyone in authority. Then one day in July, Guthridge got a phone call from Jimmy Karam. He might well have been surprised because Karam was known as an integrationist. He was active in the Urban League. Many of his men's store customers were black. He had boasted of having played football against black teams when he was young.

What Guthridge had no way of knowing was the extent of Karam's flexibility. He had carefully cultivated the friendship of Faubus, seeing in him not just the state's chief executive but also a fellow outsider. While Faubus had grown up in the hills, Karam had come of age at the opposite end of the state in Lake Village. As a child of Lebanese extraction, he had felt the scorn of his schoolmates. He had fought his way to manhood and earned a reputation as a strike breaker and a tough. He had spent his years in Little Rock struggling for respectability. Now that he had a foot in the door with the governor, he wanted to make sure that his man was elected to a third term, and maybe a fourth.

Karam got right to the point. "Amis, would you all support Orval Faubus for a third term if he would stop the integration of Central High School?" The startled Guthridge said yes. Karam said, "All right, he wants to meet with you."

The meeting took place in an upper floor of Karam's store and lasted upward of two hours. It included Guthridge, Pruden, Karam, Brown, a council member named Will Smith, and the governor. Guthridge said later, "He indicated to us very strongly that he was going to stop it, the integration of Central High School." He could not recall Faubus's exact words but said, "We had a thorough understanding." Brown recalled that Faubus was agitated about the prospect of the national Republican party's dictating what happened in Democratic Arkansas. "I don't know exactly what I will do," Faubus told them, "but I will do something. I'm not going to let the Republicans dictate to me."

There were other secret meetings. Some took place late at night at the governor's mansion. Sometimes the council leaders were summoned by Karam. They came away from every meeting a little more reassured.

Jimmy Karam, Faubus's friend who appeared to be a leader of the white resistance in the streets outside Central High.

PHOTO BY LARRY OBSITNIK, COURTESY OF THE *ARKANSAS DEMOCRAT-GAZETTE* AND SPECIAL COLLECTIONS DIVISION, UNIVERSITY OF ARKANSAS LIBRARIES, FAYETTEVILLE.

Then there was one further effort, breathtaking in its audacity. The leaders of the resistance organized a secret campaign to send panic through the capital. The targets were the governor's office and the school-district headquarters.

Jim Johnson had returned to Crossett after his defeat, but he had not fallen into lassitude. He knew that Faubus had been frightened by his electoral challenge and that in time he would look for a way to court Johnson's voters—his most dangerous opponents. Almost sixty thousand of those had signed petitions demanding a statewide vote on Johnson's interposition amendment. The candidate and his people had preserved those names and addresses. As the dreaded event loomed in Little Rock, Johnson and his friends used the list to organize telephone committees around the state. People were urged to round up a crowd for the opening of classes at Central High. Then Johnson and a few trusted associates from Crossett and elsewhere began systematically calling Faubus to warn that Little Rock would erupt in violence if Negroes were allowed in Central. They claimed to have inside information. Caravans of armed men, they said, were going to descend on the capital. Blood would flow.

"We were dedicated to hustling him," Johnson said long afterward. "Our people were phoning him from all over the state. Orval hid out, but our people in Little Rock got through to him."

While they were at it, the callers tied up the phone lines to Blossom's office, giving him the same message. "We had Blossom climbing the wall," Johnson said.

Blossom had already shown signs that he was unable to handle the gathering fury. He had confided his anxieties to Faubus and others. Weeks before the beginning of school, he had considered sending his children to board with relatives in Jonesboro during the coming school term. He did send them away to visit relatives for several days at the end of August after an anonymous telephone caller told his older daughter, "You girls will not be alive this time tomorrow." Now with the daily telephone threats as the opening of school drew near, he became increasingly agitated and fearful.

Where Blossom saw danger, Faubus saw opportunity. He made a phone call of his own as the panic calls increased. Johnson described it: Faubus hinting, speaking in calculated indirection because both men suspected that the line was tapped by the feds. Faubus, knowing that a protest could be useful, communicating his desire that Johnson should help get out a crowd at Central. Not wanting to be too explicit. Then ending with these words, more or less, as resurrected from memory thirty-two years later: "Jim, expect—I'm going to do something that ought to please you very much, and it may be that you'll want some of your friends to be here, be present, when school opens on Monday, or Tuesday, morning."

Johnson of course had already been at work on that task. Now he was joined by certain of Faubus's own people. Claude Carpenter Jr., an aide, helped the telephone committee along with his sister, who was active in the Mothers League of Central High School. But for Johnson it was bizarre to be asked by his main enemy to sacrifice his own career, to help destroy his own chances of becoming governor at the next election.

"And when he did this," Johnson said, "when he did this in 1957, that pulled every tooth I had in my head."

Jim Johnson could only stand and watch in a kind of pained satisfaction as his followers found a new hero to advance his cause while permanently altering his life.

CHAPTER 17

John E. Miller was one of dozens of federal judges in the South who inherited the distasteful task of enforcing the Supreme Court's desegregation ruling. Like most of his fellows, he had earned his job by long years of service in state Democratic party politics. A crafty politician, he had won election to the U.S. Senate against long odds and afterward had settled into the security of the bench. When the Little Rock case landed in his lap, he did what he had to do without enthusiasm. He approved the Little Rock plan of minimal integration in 1956. His superiors at the U.S. Court of Appeals for the Eighth Circuit seconded his approval and ordered that he oversee its implementation.

Miller had more than one opportunity to crush the segregationist resistance at Little Rock. On June 27, 1957, just over two months before the opening of school, he was paid a quiet visit at Fort Smith by two men who had grown concerned about the shrill protests of the Capital Citizens Council. Archie F. House, who in two days would be sixty-five years old, was there representing the Little Rock School Board. House was one of the most highly regarded lawyers in the Little Rock establishment. He was the senior member of the Rose Firm, the state's oldest law firm. He was literate, smart, and tough. With him in Miller's chambers was Arthur B. Caldwell, head of the young civil rights section of the Department of Justice. Caldwell was from the Ozarks. His father was an old friend of House's, and the young lawyer had important connections in the state. It was he who had surreptitiously involved the Justice Department in the Hoxie case.

House and Caldwell gently inquired what might be done to damp down the Citizens Council's increasingly incendiary attacks on everyone it perceived as part of the "Communist" plot to destroy the white race, including the justices of the Supreme Court, the Little Rock School Board, and Miller himself. The judge suggested that if they believed the council was conspiring to prevent his order from being carried out, someone, perhaps the school board or the NAACP, should ask him for an injunction. He indicated that he not only would issue such an injunction but also would probably declare Arkansas's basket of resistance laws to be unconstitutional, thus removing two obstacles at one stroke.

House said his clients would be "extremely reluctant" to ask for such action. Maybe "certain colored attorneys" would bring such a suit. Later, he declared that he would not allow his clients to collude in such a sham. A gentleman of nineteenth-century sensibilities, a lawyer since the administration of Woodrow Wilson, House took the view that the judge should have been outraged by the segregationists' "slanderous and contemptuous" attacks on him and his office and should have put a stop to them on his own. He made a second trip to Fort Smith, this time with Blossom, to urge the judge to act. Once again, Miller brushed aside the attacks, saying he had been called worse things by other people. House went away thinking that Miller had missed a chance to stop the agitation. He and his clients felt even more isolated and unprotected.

Caldwell returned to Washington after the June meeting and pondered whether the Federal Bureau of Investigation should investigate the segregationists. He thought the bureau might build a case against Guthridge and the others under the same federal civil rights law that had been brought into play at Hoxie. But for the present, he told his superiors, it might be wiser to wait until they had more evidence against the Citizens Council. Judge Miller was not the only one who missed a chance to damp the rising flames.

Several members of the school board were as nervous as Blossom as the phone calls and rumors of violence escalated. In public, they assured anxious parents that they had no reason to expect trouble. In private, they were less certain.

Besides the prospect of disorder, there was the seeming conflict between state laws and federal court decisions. That was an apparently easy problem in legal terms. The Constitution's supremacy clause says that federal law prevails when it conflicts with state law and that state officials are bound to uphold the federal Constitution. But the conflict in Arkansas, up close, was fraught with political consequence. Wayne Upton, a board member who was also a lawyer, suspected that someone, possibly from the Citizens Council, would try to block integration at the last minute by persuading a state court to enjoin the board from going ahead with its court-approved plan. The plaintiffs probably would rely on the anti-integration measures passed by the state during the past year.

On August 13, Upton found himself in Fort Smith arguing a case before Judge Miller. Privately, after court, he expressed his concerns. The judge gave the first indication that he might be weakening in his determination to carry out his own order. He suggested that someone of standing, not a radical segregationist, might file a suit in a state court to test the state's anti-integrationist measures. He told Upton that if a state court enjoined the school board from going ahead, he would consider suspending the board's plan until the matter was litigated. It was obvious that both men saw this as a tactic of expedient delay, not a serious challenge to the final authority of the federal courts.

Upton and Blossom joined Faubus for breakfast a day or two later. Faubus agreed that such a lawsuit was a good idea and volunteered the opinion that the state statutes on integration, almost all of which carried his signature, were illegal. More significantly, the news delivered by the two men was a signal to the alert Faubus that he could move boldly without fear from Judge Miller. This gave him an opening for making friends among Johnson's followers. For the benefit of the latter, he would be careful not to utter publicly any heresy about the doubtful legality of the laws.

Blossom, Upton, and Harold J. Engstrom, another board member, went to Fort Smith to see Judge Miller August 18 and showed him a copy of a lawsuit in state court that had been filed days earlier by William F. Rector, a Little Rock real estate man. The suit had been quietly inspired by Bill Smith, the governor's legal advisor. It asked for a declaratory judgment on the constitutionality of the state laws and the Johnson amendment. Miller said he saw no way he could act on the basis of such a judgment, that only a state-court injunction interfering with the board plan would give him a reason to issue a restraining order.

Such an injunction could be arranged.

This was the great game at its most dangerous. Surrounded by watchful opponents. Traps and hazards everywhere. There were the high-collared men of the Little Rock establishment still looking down their noses at the hillbilly governor, needling, demanding, cajoling, trying to trick him into saving their necks without risking their own. There was the intimidating apparatus of the federal government waiting to pounce on any mistake. There was Jim Johnson, alert, ready to attack from the other side. Even the state attorney general, white-haired, amiable, reckless Bruce Bennett, was talking openly about running against Faubus in 1958. Like Johnson, Bennett was solidly segregationist.

Here was the chance Orval Faubus had worked for all these years, the moment when he would walk into the courthouse at the end of the fight with all eyes fixed on him in admiration and awe. Only a few more days and a few more moves and it would all be ready.

On August 21, he telephoned the Justice Department in Washington. He spoke to the deputy attorney general, William P. Rogers, and asked what the government planned to do if violence should erupt in Little Rock. Rogers said he would send someone to talk to him.

Before the emissary arrived, Faubus found his situation shifting fast. One of the South's most effective prophets of massive resistance hurtled into the picture. On August 22, Gov. Marvin Griffin of

Georgia, a failure as a chief executive but a first-rate rabble-rouser, came to Little Rock to address a rally of the Citizens Council. His speech drew a predictable response at the rally, but its effect was felt far beyond the ballroom of the Marion Hotel. Griffin's appearance quite suddenly convinced large numbers of white people that the entire integration problem could be solved quickly and simply.

His message, greeted by "Amens" and rebel yells from the councilers, was that constitutional government was dead if the South surrendered its schools to the federal government. He vowed that the public schools of his state would never be integrated, and he said that Arkansas and the rest of the South should likewise resist the "ruthless decisions of the Supreme Court." The way to do that, he said, was just to assert state authority and refuse to obey the federal courts.

His traveling companion, Roy V. Harris, a Georgia kingmaker and a chief architect of massive resistance, put it more explicitly: "If this happened in Georgia, we'd call out the National Guard."

Faubus pointedly stayed away from the council rally. Following custom, however, he put up the Griffin party at the mansion and ate breakfast with them the next morning. He reported that they talked about bird hunting. That was probably the extent of the conversation because neither governor had any regard for the other's racial politics. Griffin had made it clear that his main motive in coming to Arkansas was to push Faubus into a corner.

Overnight, opinion makers and political leaders saw a change in attitude all over Arkansas. People who had paid only modest attention to the controversy began asking why Arkansas had to integrate its schools while Georgia had not. Faubus later credited Griffin's appearance with creating an abrupt and massive increase in pressure from the segregationist camp. If he had had any lingering inclination to oppose the tide of protest, Griffin's visit removed it. "The situation was not that clear to me," he confessed later, "but I could read public sentiment and events."

Rogers sent the Arkansawyer Arthur Caldwell to explain the Justice Department's position to Faubus. On August 28, Caldwell, eluding reporters (Little Rock's cadre of reporters was above average, but it missed practically all of the behind-the-scenes maneuvering leading up to the opening of schools), spent an hour and fifteen minutes with the governor. He began by noting that the recently passed civil rights law had been crippled and left powerless to deal with school desegregation. He then outlined various ways the Justice Department might intervene under old statutes, as it had in Hoxie and in Clinton, Tennessee, to suppress violence.

"It became apparent," he reported to his superior afterward, "that the Governor was not so much interested in the application of the law as he was in explaining to the Department what he planned to do." Faubus told Caldwell of his growing anxieties about violence; of Governor Griffin's visit and his stirring of emotions; of the upcoming lawsuit in Chancellor Murray O. Reed's court. He said he was on the spot because of the state's anti-integration laws, which he was obliged to enforce even though they were of questionable constitutionality until ruled otherwise. He hoped Judge Miller would delay integration for a semester or at least until the Arkansas laws could be tested. Caldwell found out that Faubus had gone to the school board during the previous week and urged it to seek a delay. Archie House had squelched the idea.

When Caldwell asked the governor for evidence of impending violence that he could turn over to the FBI, Faubus replied that his information was too vague to be of any value to law enforcement agencies. Caldwell said his own inquiries had given him no reason to fear violence, and he told the governor that his agency could not approve the course of obstruction he had embarked on.

Faubus and the school authorities continued their dance. It appears in retrospect that his consistent desire until the last moment was to avoid an abrupt showdown over integration. Until House put a stop to it, Faubus apparently thought the school authorities agreed with his strategy of delay. But Blossom and the board, protected from public anger to some extent by being under a federal court order, became anxious to get it over with. The governor's expressed hope for a delay was not given much credence by his critics at the time, but there is reason to believe that he was sincere. He could not be sure what the political fallout might be from a dramatic confrontation—using armed officers, say, to block integration. Whether by court action or armed men, either delay would be temporary, as he knew. Political advantage, if any, might be roughly the same in either case, but delay through the courts would bring less wrath down on his head.

Publicly, the state-court lawsuit that began to germinate in Judge Miller's office in mid-August appeared to be a creature of immaculate conception. A Mrs. Clyde A. Thomason, a member of the Mothers League and a citizen enjoying no previous notice beyond family and friends, suddenly appeared in Chancellor Reed's court demanding that he enforce the state laws and stop the integration of Central High. Only later was it revealed that a number of players on all sides, including some of Faubus's closest political and legal advisors, had had a hand in the suit. The plaintiff's lawyer of record in the beginning was Arthur G. Frankel, who confided that he was acting at Bill Smith's request—a statement denied by Smith. Smith acknowledged that his partner, Pat Mehaffy, had taken a quiet role. So did Leon Catlett, another Faubus confidant. The governor himself was involved, as were Blossom and Upton, according to Faubus's memoirs and recollections shared with interviewers years later. He told of seeing the two school men at the mansion and of being asked whether he would file a lawsuit to stop integration. When he said he would not, they asked whether he would arrange to have it filed if they provided the complaint. He said he would. Two or three days later, he received it from Blossom, surreptitiously, during a large gathering at the mansion, and passed it to his own people the next day with instructions to find someone to file it.

That was Faubus's version. Blossom told the FBI he had simply acted as a conduit from Miller and Faubus to Smith to let the lawyer know that those men wanted such a lawsuit filed.

Testifying in Reed's court, Faubus and Blossom gave convincing portrayals of innocent detachment combined with sincere concern. Blossom: No, he had no reason to anticipate violence when school opened. Faubus: Pistols and knives were being sold in huge numbers; caravans of armed men were preparing to advance on the capital; there may well be bloodshed. Neither man acknowledged paternity of the lawsuit or let on that he knew anything about it. Chancellor Reed obliged with an injunction stopping Central's desegregation.

Then came an unexpected development that exploded the scheme. Miller suddenly changed his mind. Instead of seizing control of the case, plodding through hearings, and finally overruling Reed's injunction and declaring the state laws unconstitutional—a process that he might have stretched out for months—he called his superiors in the federal judiciary and asked to be removed from the case. It seems likely that he saw a chance to get out of a highly controversial lawsuit in which his personal sentiments were at odds with his official duty. Beyond that, he might have been swayed by a new private message from Little Rock. The school board, its spine stiffened by its no-nonsense lawyer, Archie House, sent word that it wanted no further delay, that it preferred to "go ahead and get it over with."

Federal district judge Ronald N. Davies of Fargo, North Dakota, took Miller's place. He flew to Little Rock and immediately ordered an end to the charade. No deals, no drawn-out hearings, no more delays. Desegregate Central High the first day of school, he said.

Later, after the FBI was thrust onto the scene to demand answers, the principals across the divide of the ill-fated lawsuit called each other liars. Smith and Faubus insisted that Blossom had pestered them for weeks, sometimes several times a day, with his fears of violence. Smith told of Blossom's pleading with him to file a lawsuit to stop the Blossom Plan. He said the superintendent once grabbed his lapels and cried that the blood of children would be on his, Blossom's, hands if Smith did not help him stop integration. Another time, Smith said, he brandished a pitcher and ordered Blossom out of his house after Blossom, furious and threatening, advanced on him as if to attack. Faubus and Smith described Blossom as wild-eyed and "scared to death." Faubus said Blossom told him over and over that he knew of caravans of troublemakers poised to descend on Little Rock, that a secret society of seventy men intended to take the law into their own hands, that white and Negro boys were arming themselves with pistols and knives, that his own life and those of his family members had been threatened.

Blossom said most of that was untrue, that he had simply expressed normal concern for the safety of his charges. He confirmed that he had told Faubus of a report from Amis Guthridge about seventy armed, angry men who considered the Citizens Council too law-abiding. But his aim, he said, was to persuade Faubus to assume the role of leadership that his office required. He said he had tried repeatedly and with no success to persuade Faubus to state publicly that he wanted no disorder or violence when school opened. Faubus refused, Blossom said, because he was afraid that such a statement would be misconstrued as supporting integration.

Federal judge Ronald N. Davies, Faubus's on-the-scene bête noire *during the desegregation crisis.*

Sometime during the week before Labor Day, Faubus called in the commander of the Arkansas National Guard, Maj. Gen. Sherman T. Clinger, and Herman Lindsey, director of the state police. He instructed them to screen their personnel files and find out which of their men had had experience in riot control.

On Friday, August 30, four days before the beginning of classes, he met secretly with his department heads and his top aides. He asked what he should do. Some said do nothing; others, a majority, advised a preemptive strike using the guard or the state police if he had evidence that violence might occur. Faubus, repeating what he had heard from Blossom and from Johnson's telephone banshees, said he had information that students were arming themselves with guns and knives.

He called them together again Saturday morning. They went over the same discussion. A couple of close aides sensed that he was leaning away from taking action, and they huddled with him privately after the others had left. They advised him that he would forfeit a third term if he did nothing. Clarence Thornbrough, the commissioner of labor, said, "We think that in order to get elected to a third term, you have got to take a stand on this thing. We think that you have got to call out the troops." Thornbrough had heard that certain white boys intended to kill the Negro students and throw their bodies from one of the school towers. "And if that happens, you're going to get the blame."

Faubus decided to get his own evidence. After lunch on Saturday, he summoned Sgt. Melvin DeLong of the state police and instructed him to survey the sales of guns and knives in the area's stores. DeLong had only an hour and a half before the stores closed. He went to eight pawn shops. One was closed. Two managers reported small increases in the sale of knives, one didn't know, and four had sold no more guns and knives than usual. DeLong's report to the governor was that while gun sales had been normal, he had found an above-normal sale of knives. He apparently based that ominous conclusion on a rumor he had heard about knife sales at another store that he had not visited. True or not and scant as it was, DeLong's information gave the governor a little more cover if he should be called to account in federal court.

Very late, Faubus's liberal friends and advisors realized they were about to lose him to the segregationists. They heard a rumor that he intended to call out the National Guard. Harry Ashmore talked it over with Hugh B. Patterson Jr., the publisher of the *Gazette* and son-in-law of the owner. Faubus owed Ashmore for turning the tide against Cherry in 1954. "Faubus said that I had a blank check," he said. "Should I try to cash it?" Patterson said that would be embarrassing and probably wouldn't work, anyway.

Sid McMath tried to talk to Faubus. Abide with the federal court orders, he advised; defying the courts would be a dead-end street. Faubus listened but gave his friend no encouragement. McMath telephoned Harry Truman at his home in Independence, Missouri, hoping that Faubus's old hero from the war and the 35th Division would talk sense into him. Truman said he wouldn't dignify the governor's scheme by calling him.

Adolphine Fletcher Terry, the grande dame of the Little Rock establishment, had befriended the Faubuses in 1955. She had given a reception for Mrs. Faubus at her old mansion on Seventh Street. Now she came to the mansion at the other end of the historic district. She pleaded with Mrs. Faubus to intercede with her husband. Blocking integration would flood Little Rock with bad publicity, she said. Alta mentioned the visit to Orval and got no response.

Winthrop Rockefeller, at the urging of Blossom and R. A. Lile, a member of the school board, spent part of Sunday afternoon, September 1, trying to persuade Faubus to keep away from the school situation. His argument was that the state's industrialization would suffer from a violent confrontation or a highly publicized conflict between the state and the federal government. Faubus replied that if he did anything to encourage integration, especially if he used state law enforcement to protect the Negro students entering Central, the state would be taken over by Jim Johnson, Bruce Bennett, and Amis Guthridge. Rockefeller reported to the school men afterward, "I don't think I got very far."

Rockefeller might have stirred Faubus to another bout of intro-spection, however. Late that night Blossom was awakened by a phone call from the governor asking him to get dressed and come to the mansion. The two men talked for three hours, and Blossom thought once or twice that Faubus wanted to help the school board. But his last words were, "I'll call you when I decide. But I don't think I'm going to let you do it." Blossom took that to mean the die was cast.

Of all the meetings held to deal with the coming fury, one of the quietest took place on the Sunday before Labor Day in J. N. Heiskell's cluttered office on the second floor of the *Arkansas Gazette* at Third and Louisiana Streets. The paper's owner was eighty-five years old, a stately, gentle man with a taste for whimsy and civic virtue. His strongest drink was sherry. He loved libraries and trees.

He also loved his newspaper. When his young publisher once tried to save money by skimping on supplies for the newsroom, his employer told him not to worry about profits, that his job was to earn just enough money for Heiskell to publish the kind of newspaper he wanted—that is to say, a first-rate one. In newspaper circles, it was appreciated that the old man never used the title of president or chairman or chief executive officer. His title was editor.

Patterson and Ashmore went to his office that day to tell him that it was decision time. Ashmore put it forthrightly. "The position you have to take is to support the school board, but I can't make that decision. It's your newspaper and costing you the money."

Ashmore knew what to expect from the city's business leadership. He remembered a conversation he had had in the early 1950s with C. Hamilton Moses, then head of the Arkansas Power and Light Company and perhaps the most powerful man in Arkansas. Ashmore had just finished a landmark study on segregated schools and knew what was coming. When he told Moses that soon the Supreme Court would probably order the schools desegregated, Moses said, "Oh, my God, they can't do that. If they do that, there'll be race riots, there'll be trouble. We'll never be able to sell another bond issue in New York." Ashmore asked whether he was willing to rally the business community and start preparing people for the change. Moses replied, "Oh, God, no, I can't get mixed up in a thing like this."

It was clear that the *Gazette* would be practically alone among the city's leaders in supporting the board. The rival *Arkansas Democrat* would waffle and fade, as would the chamber of commerce and the big businessmen. The segregationists would clamor for Heiskell's head, neither suspecting nor caring that in his heart this nineteenth-century southerner was bereft at the passing of his world. Just as they would never understand his hard core.

Heiskell heard out Ashmore and Patterson and turned away and looked for a long minute down Louisiana Street. Then he said, "I won't let people like that take over my town."

Daisy Bates and her young charges were hunkered down, waiting. She adopted an oddly detached attitude toward Faubus, resentful but not personally hostile. She understood that his class antagonisms were not directed toward her people. Mrs. Bates saw her friend Edwin E. Dunaway, the white lawyer, one day during the tense time, and they talked about Faubus. She said, "He's against you and the people in the Heights, and I'm going to have to pay for it."

CHAPTER 18

Two things occurred in Virgil Blossom's office on Labor Day less than twenty-four hours from the beginning of classes. First, eight of the seventeen Negro students who had been accepted at Central came in and withdrew their applications. The tension was too great for them. Second, Blossom's secretary took a telephone call from an anonymous man speaking barely above a whisper.

Investigators got a description of the scene later from Lt. Carl Jackson of the Little Rock Police Department, who was hastily summoned. "Mr. Blossom appeared to be excited, and upon first contact with Mr. Blossom, Lt. Jackson could not get much information from him. Mr. Blossom seemed to calm down and handed Lt. Jackson a list of names of persons and towns in Arkansas. Mr. Blossom informed Lt. Jackson that one of the ladies in the office had received an anonymous telephone call, which call advised her that 150 to 200 people were coming to Little Rock to cause trouble."

The caller told the secretary that several well-known segregationist leaders, including Jim Johnson, were already there. He said the troublemakers were "out to get Blossom."

Daisy Bates, the NAACP leader who guided the nine black students through their painful first year at Central High.

PHOTO BY LARRY OBSITNIK, COURTESY OF THE *ARKANSAS DEMOCRAT-GAZETTE* AND SPECIAL COLLECTIONS DIVISION, UNIVERSITY OF ARKANSAS LIBRARIES, FAYETTEVILLE.

The superintendent called the governor. The ensuing conversation was a dance of evasion. Blossom said he asked Faubus whom he should call in case he needed state help to put down trouble at Central High. Faubus asked him, "Do you want protection?" When Blossom replied, "Do you think I need protection?" Faubus said, "Yes, I do." Faubus then asked Blossom to put his request in writing. Faubus's version was that Blossom, after weeks of growing anxiety, initiated the plea for protection. They agreed on one point: Blossom refused to put anything in writing. He said it was unnecessary. Faubus's view was that Blossom understood that putting it in writing would explode his public statements and his court testimony that he had had no reason to expect violence at the school opening.

Both Faubus and Blossom had in their possession evidence of impending violence—evidence that was either real or handcrafted by Jim Johnson's invisible army. The one man, while tumbling into a private panic, publicly denied knowing anything about it. The other grabbed the tale of alarm and ran with it.

At 10:15 Labor Day evening, the governor's face appeared on television screens all over Arkansas. He was a picture of worry. He did not tip his hand at once, but alert listeners caught the drift in his opening sentence. "In view of the decisions I have made," he said, "I think it is well to review for the people of the state and the nation some of the background in the tense situation which has now developed relative to the forcible integration of the public schools of Little Rock."

In a speech that would become a symbol of rabble-rousing, he devoted almost the entire first half to reciting the state's progressive record in race relations and his own part in that: Schools, buses, and political parties integrated. Negroes elected to local offices. Negroes hired in state government and appointed to state boards.

Then a warning note: Little Rock's desegregation plan had been constructed before the voters had had a chance to express themselves. He outlined the various anti-integration measures approved by popular vote and legislative action, all by overwhelming majorities. He wanted time to test those in state court, but a federal judge had said no. The judge's ruling, he said, had caused a deluge of anger.

Now there were threats of violence and disorder. The unsubtle suggestion was that the coming turbulence would be the fault of Ronald N. Davies, the North Dakota judge, and the dictatorial federal apparatus that had sent him to meddle in Arkansas's affairs.

He laid out just enough evidence of the imminent explosion to let the audience know that he had grave cause for his concern. A police check had revealed a sale of unusually large numbers of weapons in the Little Rock area. Negro youths had bought large numbers of knives at one store. Revolvers had been taken from white and black students. Now, he said, a massive telephone campaign was under way to assemble a crowd at 6 A.M. Tuesday at Central High. Faubus told the viewers:

> I have reports of caravans that will converge upon Little Rock from many points of the state, and the members of the caravans are to assemble peaceably upon the school grounds in the morning. Some of these groups have already reached the city—are here now—and some of the information of these caravans has come to me from the school authorities themselves.

Because of "the harm that may occur on the morrow," he concluded, he had sent the National Guard to Central High and had alerted the state police to mobilize as an arm of the state militia. The troops would not act as segregationists or integrationists. But order and peace could not be maintained if forcible integration went ahead. "The schools in Pulaski County, for the time being, must be operated on the same basis as they have been operated in the past."

The telephone campaign did produce a sizable crowd of white protesters the next morning. Faubus declined to take credit for the assembly, although a number of those who received calls said the organizers claimed they were acting at the governor's behest. In any event, the crowd had nothing to protest. The school board quickly got word to the nine remaining Negro students to stay home. Before the day was out, Judge Davies ordered the board to delay no further. He also ordered the FBI to find out why his orders had been thwarted.

Harry Ashmore's page-one editorial Wednesday morning was titled "The Crisis Mr. Faubus Made." Deriding him for protecting life and property against a mob that had never materialized, the editorial went on:

> Now it remains for Mr. Faubus to decide whether he intends to pose what could be the most serious constitutional question to face the national government since the Civil War. The effect of his action so far is to interpose his state office between the local School District and the United States Court. The government, as Judge Davies implied last night, now has no choice but to proceed against such interference or abandon its right to enforce its rulings and decisions. Thus the issue is no longer segregation vs. integration. The question has now become the supremacy of the government of the United States in all matters of law. And clearly the federal government cannot let this issue remain unsolved, no matter what the cost to this community.

The country and much of the world waited that morning. The crowd of white antagonists gathered again. A few minutes before the opening bell, the Negro students arrived, some on foot and some by car. The National Guardsmen turned away most of them and they left. A tenth student, Jane Lee Hill, came with the others, although she had not pre-enrolled. She returned to Horace Mann High School for black students after the rebuff at Central.

One girl had failed to get the message that all were to go to the school together. At the front of the school, fifteen-year-old Elizabeth Eckford arrived alone. She walked toward the nearest entrance. The solid line of guardsmen blocked her path. She tried two other entrances with the same result. Then the crowd of white people, numbering some five hundred, spotted her. They screamed and hounded her as she walked the long block to a bus stop. A friendly white woman sat with her until the bus came. She tried to comfort the girl, but the youngster could not talk.

The president of the United States was equally tongue-tied. His comments at a White House press conference that week were nearly incomprehensible. He seemed to say that while the Supreme Court's school decision was "probably" correct, he could understand the strong emotions on the other side. Eisenhower almost certainly was more of a segregationist than Faubus was. He had

Elizabeth Eckford was taunted and cursed when she appeared to enter Central the first morning. After Faubus's National Guardsmen turned her away from the school, she waited for a bus to take her home.

taken a few steps to end segregation in the government—most notably, he had ended segregation in Washington's public institutions, from jails to restaurants, and he had advanced the desegregation of the military that Truman had begun—but he had never thrown the weight of his office behind the Warren court's school ruling. His tepid response to the federal court's actions disappointed and angered many people outside the South.

As for any help that Davies and the school board might expect from Ike's Justice Department, that would have to come virtually without his cooperation. As it happened, Atty. Gen. Herbert Brownell Jr. was not cowed. He was after all the man who had flown to Europe to persuade the famous general to come home and accept the Republican nomination. He had helped Ike select Earl Warren as chief justice. He had persuaded his boss to appoint more than twenty enlightened federal judges in the South, who in the coming years would open the political process to black southerners for the first time since Reconstruction.

Even so, Brownell hesitated to get into the Little Rock fray without sound cause. Some of his eager young lawyers thought the school board was dragging its feet and was not sincerely trying to desegregate the schools. They wanted to jump into the lawsuit on the side of the NAACP. That was seriously considered. But the prevailing view, and Brownell's, was that the department had to wait for the Little Rock School Board to ask for help, as the board at Hoxie had done, before sending marshals or some other form of aid. For their part, the board members hesitated to ask for help because they thought that would send an unwarranted message that they feared violence, a message that in itself might make violence more likely.

While the confrontation simmered in court and the Negro students cooled their heels, fifty FBI agents scoured the city. They quickly demolished Sergeant DeLong's hour-and-a-half study of weapons sales. Even his superior, state police director Herman Lindsey, dismissed DeLong's survey as having shown nothing significant. When the investigation was finished less than a week later, the agents had produced thirty-one exhibits and 501 pages of confidential interviews. The summary was damning. "Not a single individual had any knowledge of any act of violence or actual threats of violence prior to the time the Governor called out the Guard on September 2, 1957," it said.

The agents found just two stores that reported small increases in gun sales. One owner told them, "Since July 1, 1957, I have received calls for about four or five pistols . . . by unidentified Negro men." The bureau concluded that that was the whole basis for the governor's concern about gun sales. The agents checked more than one hundred businesses that might sell guns and knives and found no significant increase in sales of either. One of the most titillating rumors had a barbershop burglarized and its entire stock of razors stolen. The FBI found the barber. He confirmed the burglary. He said the only thing stolen was a straight razor with a red handle.

Toward the end of his life, Faubus acknowledged that DeLong's report had produced no alarming evidence of a weapons build-up before school started. But he insisted that there had been an explosion of gun and knife sales a few weeks later after real trouble developed.

As for caravans descending on Little Rock, the FBI learned that one small group from northeastern Arkansas had intended to form a motorcade to the capital but had called it off after the Citizens Council found out Faubus's intention of using state lawmen to keep Negro students out of Central.

In his old age, Jim Johnson put it bluntly. "There wasn't any caravan. But we made Orval believe it. We said, 'They're lining up. They're coming in droves.' . . . The only weapon we had was to leave the impression that the sky was going to fall."

Faubus sent a telegram to the president complaining that the FBI's investigation was aggravating an explosive situation. If they touch off violence, he said, the blood would be on the federal government's hands, not his. Ike replied that he intended to uphold the Constitution and he felt sure Faubus would cooperate with the federal court.

On September 6, the governor again wired the president saying federal authorities reportedly had tapped his telephone and were preparing to take him into custody by force. Eisenhower replied that the complaint had "no basis of fact."

Little Rock had become a worldwide story. The New York Times led page one with it almost every day during September, and on one day covered the front page with seven articles about the Arkansas situation. It was big news all across Europe and Asia. The Communist press distorted it shamelessly for its propaganda value in illustrating America's racial disharmony. Radio Moscow one day reported that Elizabeth Eckford had been "brutally murdered." The *Times* of London credited Faubus with inspiring a segregationist bombing several hundred miles away in Tennessee.

Although many American reporters were personally sympathetic to the nine Negro students, most managed a reasonable showing of objectivity in their coverage. The most notable exceptions were the Luce magazines, *Time* and *Life*. Both portrayed Faubus as a witless redneck with no education or refinement. That angered the governor's Arkansas enemies as well as his friends and gave him the chance to play the underdog and the friend of the common man, the role he excelled in. He compared himself to Lincoln and Franklin D. Roosevelt, both of whom had had to deal with unending hostility from newspapers.

Faubus was seen as an unprincipled bigot in much of the North. For a time, his stand threatened to slow down the industrial development of Arkansas that he had worked hard to improve. For example, he and Rockefeller, chairman of the industrial commission, received letters in September from an executive of Seamprufe, Inc., which had announced an upcoming expansion in Arkansas, expressing his disappointment in Faubus's defying the law of the land.

Beyond Arkansas, Faubus became an instant hero to the same southerners who a year earlier had derided him as a closet integrationist. Roy V. Harris, the fiery Georgia editor who had accompanied Governor Griffin to Little Rock, playfully pretended to be puzzled. "I sat there . . . just scratching my head and wondering if he called 'em out *for* us or *agin'* us," he said. When the Faubuses attended a football game in Atlanta a few weeks later, the spectators went wild with applause after he was introduced.

Others offered more than cheers. Many sent telegrams saying they would bring weapons and fight behind Faubus. An out-of-state man representing himself as part of the Confederate Air Force volunteered to bring a squad of planes with bombs. One telegram said simply, "Have gun will travel." A truck driver saying he spoke for a group of eight drivers telephoned from St. Louis to say they all were prepared to run guns from Illinois and Indiana. Thousands of telegrams and letters, most offering merely moral support, poured into the governor's office.

Not all the encouragement came from the South. Numerous correspondents from the North joined the chorus. A man from the Bronx did not want Negroes in his schools, either. "They are born Savage's, its in their blood, a nigger will always be a nigger," he wrote. A more literate man from Brooklyn commiserated over the threat to state sovereignty and offered sympathy for Faubus and the people of Arkansas. A man wrote from Cicero, Illinois, to say, "We the people of Cicero, with the help of many friends, drove the Negro from our midst," and urged Arkansawyers to take heart. People from California and Illinois volunteered to bring guns and help defend Arkansas and its sovereignty. Altogether, Faubus received some 250,000 letters and telegrams, and most supported his actions.

As tension rose, Arkansas's own freelance defenders of the southern way of life offered their services. A hill-country supporter of Faubus drove to Little Rock with a loaded rifle and a case of shells prepared to shoot anyone who threatened his hero. In Little Rock, a veteran of World War II who believed that the federal government had taken away his liberties made it known that he intended to kill the first Negroes to enter Central High. "I'm just going to take my pistol and go up there and see how many of them I can get before they get me," he said. Faubus heard of him and sent Herman Lindsey, the state police director, to tell him to back off. The man agreed. Lindsey, as insurance, collected his weapon.

Not all white Arkansawyers backed Faubus. A substantial number in Little Rock were angered and dismayed. Up the Arkansas River at Ozark, a small-town editor scolded the yahoos who had been bullying the three Negro children assigned to the previously all-white school there. Elizabeth Burrow, co-owner of the *Ozark Spectator*, was dying of cancer. In one of her last columns, she said of the racism among her readers, "Here's a malignancy worse than my cancer and I wouldn't swap with you."

Now it was the turn of black leaders to apply epithets to Faubus. An editorial September 6 in the Bates's newspaper, the *Arkansas State Press*, expressed shock at the governor's calling out the guard and said Negroes must protect the use of the ballot "before Awful

Faubus uses the power of his office to thwart that." Hurry out and get a poll-tax receipt, the paper urged.

While waiting to use the ballot, they pressed their case in court. Thurgood Marshall, chief counsel for the NAACP, who had argued the Supreme Court case that resulted in the 1954 desegregation ruling, came to Little Rock to lend his prestige and knowledge to the cause.

Marshall and the Bateses were fighting on two fronts. While pressing the white legal establishment, they were at the same time trying to persuade a skeptical population in their own community that it ought to get tough on integration. While most blacks favored integration, not all were willing to push forcefully for it. The Bateses and a few young activists were at times perilously ahead of the mass of the black population. The rival black newspaper favored deseg-regation but took a more conciliatory line than the *State Press*. It eventually attracted much more advertising from white businesses.

When Faubus blocked the nine students, some black leaders argued for suspending the integration effort until passions cooled. But the Bates activists prevailed. They contended that pulling back would cost them valuable momentum in the black community. Ozell Sutton, who later became an important organizer across the South, pressed the activists' case. He used the analogy of the Israelites who got cold feet just as they reached the door of the Promised Land.

Daisy Bates, strong-minded and determined, had greater reason than most for pressing ahead. From hard experience, she trusted few whites. Her mother had been raped and murdered by three white men when Daisy was a baby. The girl was brought up by foster parents in the ragged southern Arkansas town of Huttig. There she was subjected to all the cruelties of white supremacist scorn. She married L. C. Bates, a native of Mississippi who had learned journalism in Ohio, and they moved to Little Rock and started the *State Press* just before World War II. They became active in the NAACP and a few interracial activities, allowing themselves to begin to hope for improved cooperation between the races. Then they got a lesson in a more subtle form of racism. When Daisy wrote a series of articles on police brutality of Negro soldiers from nearby Camp Robinson, the white business establishment tried to crush the paper by withdrawing the advertising of large stores.

By the time of the Blossom Plan, the Bateses were in no mood to invest much trust in the city's white leaders.

The school board asked Davies on Wednesday, September 4, to suspend his integration order temporarily. He refused. The following Monday, he received the FBI report and asked the Justice Department to enter the case as a friend of the court. That was the signal Brownell and his civil rights lawyers had been waiting for. At the judge's request, they quickly petitioned the court for an injunction to get Faubus and his National Guard out of the way so that desegregation could go ahead. A hearing was set for September 20.

The Citizens Councilers, who had been restlessly waiting for the call, now swung into action. Five carloads left West Memphis at 2:30 A.M. Monday, September 9, and arrived in front of Central High at 7:30. There were motorcades from Blytheville, McGehee, and other places. A spokesman said they wanted Little Rock to know how the people of east Arkansas felt about integration. One man told a radio interviewer, "I don't believe it would take us in Eastern Arkansas over two days to raise a regiment to come over here and surround this schoolhouse to keep them Negroes out of it." He had brought his .32 caliber Smith and Wesson revolver with him. All of them had shotguns at home.

The council militia was not needed that day. The National Guard was still there to keep the Negroes out.

Meanwhile, Rep. Brooks Hays, Little Rock's congressman and one of Arkansas's most liberal politicians, entered the controversy. It would end his career in a year, but at the time it seemed that a respected public figure with friends in the right places might defuse the constitutional crisis. He called his friend Sherman Adams, Eisenhower's assistant, and arranged for a meeting between Ike and his one-time infantry officer. It took place September 14 at Newport, Rhode Island, where Ike had gone to play golf.

The meeting was a fiasco. Faubus, the sometime integrationist, almost persuaded Ike, the would-be segregationist, that he should order the whole process stalled. Give us a little more time. Ten days, a few weeks. The old general saw nothing wrong with that. His lawyer, Brownell, spoke up firmly and told him that he couldn't give Little Rock anything. Even a president is not above a court order, he said.

*Brooks Hays, one of the state's best story-
tellers, campaigning for reelection in 1958.*

Eisenhower, for his part, apparently thought he had persuaded Faubus to go home and let the black students into Central with the National Guard's protection. If he indeed thought that, he seriously misread Faubus's situation. Any Arkansas governor who used his troops against a segregationist mob would be seen not as suppressing violence but as supporting integration.

The participants cobbled together a public statement that had Faubus saying that the *Brown* decision was the law of the land and had to be obeyed. But when he got home, he refused to change the guard's orders. Eisenhower was furious. Faubus had tricked him, he thought. Faubus later said he had made no such agreement and went so far as to suggest that someone, perhaps Brownell, had doctored Eisenhower's after-the-fact memo saying there had been. As for his saying that the *Brown* decision was the law of the land, that line had been forced upon him by the president's men, he said. Then he added an off-handed remark that would be thrown in his face the rest of his life: "Just because I said it doesn't make it so."

Hays had miscalculated. He believed in the goodness of people. Any misunderstanding could be relieved by good faith negotiation. But Faubus had passed the point of negotiating. Once he ordered General Clinger's guardsmen to surround Central High, he was committed, and talk would not solve the problem. This was no mere misunderstanding, no failure to communicate.

And yet, Hays had a point. As a lawyer, he understood Brownell's insistence that court orders had to be followed and that it was a governor's duty "to suppress violence and to remove any obstruction to the orderly enforcement of the law." He also saw the wisdom of an old-fashioned back-room compromise, the kind he had learned at his father's knee in Yell County—a little fudging of compliance, a few days of cooling off, a face-saving that would let Faubus go home with something to talk about before he slipped back into the shadows and moved out of the path of history's irresistible tread.

Herbert Brownell had a different political upbringing, one that perhaps made him less receptive to compromise. He was a proud member of the Republican party's liberal wing. Like Earl Warren, Thomas E. Dewey, Henry Cabot Lodge, the Rockefellers, and even Richard M. Nixon, he saw not just moral correctness but also political advantage in civil rights for Negroes. The Republicans might lure some of the black votes back to the party of Lincoln in 1960. And smiting the stubborn South was still good politics for a national party. In any event, he had already prepared the Justice Department for just this sort of trouble. He had foreseen that massive resistance of southern officials would inevitably lead to "a clash of historic importance" between them and the president. His young lawyers had thoroughly researched the legal background and the president's power to intervene to put down disorder and protect the Constitution.

Faubus came to see Brownell as his chief antagonist in the Little Rock crisis. There would be bad blood between them for more than thirty years afterward. It originated in the few minutes they spent together at the Newport meeting. He thought that Brownell, who had advised the president that it was the duty of state authorities to suppress violence and enforce the law, was making him the goat and sloughing off any federal responsibility.

Faubus gradually developed a conspiracy theory to explain Little Rock. Speaking in 1990 at a school desegregation conference at Abilene, Kansas, he asked rhetorically why Little Rock was chosen for a showdown, who chose it, when and where, who was told beforehand, why the governor of Arkansas was not told. He plainly wanted to suggest that Herbert Brownell, the Yankee schemer—Brownell, a fellow panelist at Abilene, sitting in the audience not more than thirty feet in front of him—was behind the plot. Had not Brownell just confessed, there at Abilene, that he had anticipated "a clash of historic proportions?"

Brownell's explanation contained its own hint of double-dealing, if not conspiracy. He had advised Eisenhower against the Newport meeting because Faubus had "soiled" himself. He didn't trust Faubus; he thought it especially ill-advised for the president to meet him alone with no witnesses. He recalled at Abilene that when Eisenhower and Faubus had finished their private session of about twenty minutes, and after continuing their discussion in the company of Hays and Adams, he had been called in.

> And the President told us that Faubus had agreed to let the black children into the high school. Just as flat as that. And

Faubus was standing there. I can't recall that he said anything. And I was absolutely amazed because Faubus was capitulating. I knew from my sources that politically he couldn't afford to let the black children into the high school. It would defeat him for re-election. I just didn't trust Faubus any more than I trust him today. I think he is a small-town politician. So I congratulated them and went off by myself to a Yale Law School reunion. And then from there I went on down to Washington. And then the President called me the next day and said, "You were right." And he said that "Faubus has gone back on his word."

Brownell was not the only one of Eisenhower's advisors who thought that meeting Faubus was a bad idea. Vice President Nixon, who was considered a progressive on civil rights and who even then was a master tactician, saw the conference as a mistake and apparently told the president that. He confided to Sid McMath that J. Edgar Hoover, who remembered Faubus's flirtation with left-wing politics, felt the same way and also advised against the meeting. The thinking was that such a conference would inflate Faubus's importance and help to make him a hero to the massive resisters right across the South. But Sherman Adams, who favored the meeting, carried the day.

Brooks Hays had his own problem with Faubus. He could never determine whether Faubus had any core of integrity or set of beliefs that a compromise could be built on. After one of his visits with the governor, he confided to an aide, "I can probe him and probe him to find what the core is here, and I'm not finding any core."

Hays did satisfy himself that Faubus was not acting out of any committed opposition to integration. While the two of them were arranging the Newport meeting, they had long discussions about the whole problem. At one point, Faubus suggested trying to persuade the Eisenhower people to delay integration at Little Rock for a semester and, when it resumed in January, starting the process at the first grade instead of at the high-school level. That put Faubus in the company of a number of integration scholars who argued that first graders would accept students of another race more readily than older students would.

Six days after the Newport meeting, Judge Davies enjoined Faubus from using the guard to interfere with integration. The governor's lawyers walked out of the courtroom before the hearing started, creating a mild sensation. Davies sided with Brownell, saying that Faubus should have used the guard to uphold the federal court order, not to thwart it.

The federal government made a startling, inexplicable miscalculation at the hearing. Its lawyers failed to use the FBI's damning investigative report on Faubus's scant evidence of impending violence. That left the public free to believe whatever version of events it chose without challenge from the nation's premier investigative agency. It also left Faubus free to continue insisting that he had surely prevented violence by scotching integration. If the FBI investigators had found nothing to disprove his claim, he said, why didn't the government lawyers call as witnesses those two-hundred-odd people whom the FBI had interviewed? Within sight of his death more than thirty-five years later, he was still saying that his action had proved the old adage, "An ounce of prevention is worth a pound of cure."

On the day of the court hearing, he was somewhat harsher. He portrayed the government's selective use of witnesses as a transparent attempt to get the result it wanted: a court order making him the villain. "Now begins the crucifixion," he said.

Three hours after the judge's ruling, the governor ordered the guard removed from the school. He left the next day for the Southern Governors Conference at Sea Island, Georgia.

There might have been another reason for the government's reticence at the court hearing. In at least one case—which the FBI might or might not have known about, and Jim Johnson's disclaimer notwithstanding—Faubus had a credible reason to expect violence.

He maintained all his life that his evidence of impending violence was real. He insisted that several carloads of segregationists had converged on Little Rock from various parts of the state, some of them lodging at the Marion Hotel. Years afterward, he confided that he had received a telephone call from a prominent east Arkansas person a day or two before the opening of school in

September 1957. The person warned him that he had just intercepted two carloads of angry men from Phillips County who were headed for Little Rock. He had told them to wait and see what the governor did with the National Guard. He had persuaded them to leave their guns with him before driving on. Faubus refused to name his source.

The man who called him was Joe Foster, the town marshal of England. Foster was a respected political figure in Lonoke County. He was also a leader of the segregationist movement. His grandson, Bill Foster Jr., a college student, was at his grandfather's house the night the armed men stopped to talk. The scene was engraved on the young man's memory: There was a sizable group, more than one carload. They were businessmen and farmers from Phillips County, somewhere around Helena or West Helena. One load came in a blue and white Chevrolet. They had "lots of guns"—shotguns, deer rifles, and pistols. Their intention was to go to Central High and keep the Negro students from entering.

Bill's grandfather, a commanding figure, told the men not to take guns to Central High, that he happened to know that Governor Faubus was going to call out the National Guard. That satisfied them. They unloaded their weapons, stacked them on Joe Foster's back porch, and went on without them.

Wherever Faubus traveled in southern and eastern Arkansas during the early fall of 1957, he saw a hardening of attitudes and at least a mental preparation for violence. A clergyman seated next to him at a dinner in Warren warned of violent men from there who would travel to Little Rock to oppose integration with force. A moderate sheriff in southeast Arkansas supported Faubus but, to protect his own interests, made himself visible at a meeting of the hard men. Every day, Faubus found more evidence to back his claims.

The Negro students at Central High were not the only targets of armed and dangerous men. The state police received a message one day during mid-September. It was coded in numbers and took a while to decipher. When the detectives finally decoded it, the words said: "Ten men have sworn to kill the gov if he allows integration." Before the crisis was over, Faubus would get threats from both sides.

The black students returned to Central on Monday, September 23, and the violence that Faubus had predicted was waiting for them.

About one thousand white people had gathered early. Their first victims were four black newsmen walking toward the school. Someone yelled, "Kill them, kill them!" Two of the reporters were beaten and kicked.

The students entered at a side door while the mob was distracted in front. A white woman cried, "Oh, my God, they're going in. The niggers are in!"

A ringleader shouted, "They tricked us, the yellow bastards. Come on, let's go in the school and drag them out."

The crowd surged against the police line. About one hundred officers from the city and state police had been sent to replace the National Guardsmen. The state troopers mainly served as reserves. The city officers stunned a few belligerents with billy clubs and the crowd yelled, "Nigger lovers!" Law enforcement had been made more difficult by an abject refusal of support from the fire department. The mayor had ordered the fire chief to use high-pressure hoses on the mob, and he had refused.

A radio newsman at the scene broadcast live panic, including a number of inaccurate and inflammatory details. The broadcast added to the anxiety of parents all over town. It might also have encouraged more angry men to drive to Central and join the mob.

At 11:30, assistant police chief Gene Smith decided that the black students had to be removed—quickly. His men were not able to hold back the assault. Several people were already headed into the building, and others had moved to surround it. Smith and a group of bodyguards led the students through a dark basement passage to waiting cars. While the youngsters sat with their heads down, the white drivers roared at full speed through the crowd that was trying to stop them with bricks, stones, and bare hands. The nine made it safely home, having survived just over three hours of integration.

Back in front of the school, a man asked reporters, "Do you think that's violence? What do you think of Faubus now?"

A question asked repeatedly during the months and years afterward was whether the disturbance had been inspired or even manipulated by Faubus to justify his actions. There was one report, never confirmed, that he had instructed his department heads to call all over the state and round up protesters to descend on Little Rock. The question of Faubus's direct involvement was never answered definitively. It was once said of another southerner who had the gift of politics that he moved at oblique angles, that his hand seemed to be in everything but without leaving fingerprints. If Faubus's fingerprints were on the violence at Central, they were visible only through the web of the mob's leadership and its vaporous ties to the governor's office.

There was little doubt that the crowd had been assembled systematically and that its leaders were intent on producing the violence that Faubus had predicted. All the leaders of the Citizens Council and the Mothers League were there that day and came back every day for some time afterward. When the protesters had been called to the school on opening day, September 3, one of the telephone leaders for the Mothers League was Claude Carpenter's sister, Anita Sedberry. Carpenter was one of Faubus's aides.

Many members of the crowd on September 23 were organized segregationists from east Arkansas and beyond the borders of the state. The police had checked 477 cars around Central during the first week of school and found that 129 bore out-of-state licenses. Many of those apparently returned to serve in the mob later. *Gazette* reporters counted licenses in the neighborhood during the week of violence and found cars from nine other states. Most were from Texas.

The crowd was egged on by invective from strategically placed leaders. "I hope they bring out eight dead niggers," one leader shouted. The Rev. Wesley Pruden of the Citizens Council was more circumspect. He limited himself mainly to quiet words of assurance to the members of the mob, although once, when the crowd rushed the barricade, he raised his voice. "That's what we have got to fight—niggers, communists, and cops!" he said. Speaking to a reporter, he noted that the police chief's daughter was a student at unintegrated Hall High School, while his men were here forcing integration on others.

Several other clergymen were on hand. One came to the attention of the police because his strong language seemed unusual for a minister. He was not arrested, but the FBI interviewed him and recorded his denial that he had agitated the crowd.

Some of the women were as outspoken as the men. Mrs. Clyde Thomason, a leader of the Mothers League and the plaintiff in the August court case in which Faubus had testified, managed a cadre of girls who went in and out of the building spreading alarm. She tried to break through the police line. Failing that, she urged the men to do so. "Where's your manhood?" she yelled. "Why don't you do something to get these people?" Finally she surrendered to hysteria and cried, "My daughter's in there with those niggers. Oh, my God! Oh, God!"

Thirty white people were arrested, twenty-six from Pulaski County and the rest from other Arkansas towns. Many of them protested that they had only come out of curiosity. A planter from Altheimer who had become overwrought told the police that he would not have been there at all if it had not rained the day before and made it too wet to work. One Clarence Whitehead of North Little Rock, who weighed 205 pounds and who was pictured in a newspaper photo riding the back of a Negro, explained when the police tracked him down that he had come to Central merely to see whether the black students would show up. He had no sooner arrived, he said, than he was knocked to the ground by a Negro man running from a crowd of white men. He joined the chase, rode the Negro to the ground, and beat him up. He stood around for an hour or so and presently heard a Puerto Rican photographer using abusive language to some girls. He knocked the man down. Then the Negro driver of a green pickup truck called him a son of a bitch. He punched the Negro in the face, bounced the vehicle up and down, and threw the man's shovel through his back window. A trooper tried to subdue him with a billy club. Whitehead took it away from him. He told the officer not to hit him any more. When he was finally arrested, he told the police, "I did not go to the school with any intention of starting any trouble or raising any excitement."

Faubus's friend Jimmy Karam was also there during the disturbance. His intentions seemed to be as innocent as Clarence Whitehead's. Karam said he was there merely as an interested parent of two Central High students. He acknowledged that he was close to Faubus, that indeed his wife was a guest of the Faubuses at Sea Island while the trouble was going on back home. But in his conversations with reporters on the scene, he repeatedly deplored the violence.

There was reason for skepticism about Karam's story. First, he had had a mysterious conversation with Superintendent Blossom in the bar at the Marion Hotel at midnight the night before. "I like you personally," Karam said, "but don't make a martyr out of yourself. Don't go out there tomorrow." When Blossom asked why, Karam would say only that meetings were being held all over the city.

Then there was his behavior at the school. When a black photographer was kicked repeatedly, Karam used language not expected from a member of the Urban League. He shouted, "The nigger started it!" The crowd ran after another black man, and Karam shouted, "Are you going to let him get away? There he goes. Get him." He tipped off newsmen to keep an eye on Patrolman Tommy Dunaway. The policeman, in an apparently prearranged show of disgust, threw his badge to the ground and told the crowd, "I'm through." The photographers snapped pictures while leaders of the mob took up a collection for him.

Furthermore, Karam was identified by several newsmen as a leader of the mob—not violent but acting in a supervisory role. He held whispered consultations with first one and then another person who would then move into the crowd where a new eruption would occur. A government document said that "some unknown individual was apparently communicating orders to Karam at the scene." The other person was never found.

The anger of the mob was not easily assuaged. It burnt throughout the night, and all over the city young men, white and black, vented their passions on one another. There was an interracial gang fight at 15th and Main Streets; it was broken up by state police. Teenagers broke windows and car windshields with bricks, stones, and bottles.

More ominously, at about 10:30 P.M. the police intercepted a caravan of about one hundred cars filled with angry whites driving into the Negro community where the Bateses lived. Breaking it up required fifteen carloads of policemen. An officer assigned to guard

When Alex Wilson, a Memphis reporter, showed up to cover the mob scene at Central High September 23, 1957, white men in the crowd yelled, "Run, nigger, run!" He said, "I fought for my country, and I'm not going to run." They attacked him.

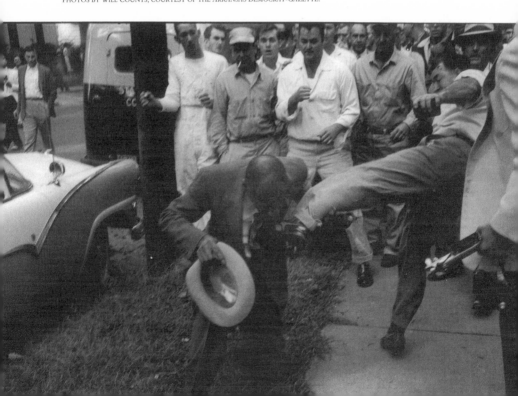

the Bates house roared away to help. When he returned, he told them the police had found dynamite, guns, and clubs in the cars. After midnight, Mrs. Bates answered the telephone and heard a man say, "We didn't get you last night, but we will. And you better not try to put those coons in our school."

The nine black students knew, by now, that life at Central High would be unbearable without more protection. They declared that they would not go back until the president of the United States guaranteed their safety.

He did so the next day. At 10:22 A.M. September 24, Eisenhower issued an executive order for the removal of "an obstruction of justice within the state of Arkansas." He first took the National Guard away from Faubus and placed it under federal command. Then he ordered one thousand soldiers from the 101st Airborne Division of the U.S. Army to leave Fort Campbell, Kentucky, at once and go to Little Rock. The first paratroopers got there just after nightfall. The white soldiers camped in the high-school football stadium. Black troops were housed at an armory in western Little Rock. Some remained on duty until the end of November, and federalized guardsmen stayed through the school year.

The citizens of the town were stunned, saddened, infuriated, relieved, or all of those, depending on their point of view. Faubus likened Little Rock to Budapest, where Russian troops had invaded to stop a revolt against the Communist regime, and even to Paris's occupation by Hitler's army. Once, in a fit of pettiness, Faubus sent a letter to the general in charge of the troops addressed to "Major General Edwin A. Walker, Commander of the Little Rock Occupational Forces." Faubus's state police had had a comic encounter with General Walker five days before he led his troops to Little Rock. The general and an aide had quietly visited Little Rock to determine what they would need to do if the president decided to send troops. Dressed in civilian clothes, they were circling Central High on the evening of September 19 when Trooper Floyd Weaver stopped them. Walker became belligerent when Weaver asked him to identify himself. Only after the trooper threatened to run him in did he reveal his name, rank, and serial number. He curtly explained his business and was released. That episode set the tone in federal-state relations in Arkansas for the next several months.

Probably everyone sensed at some level that they were suddenly and for all time a part of history. As for the principals, virtually none of them escaped censure from some quarter. Hundreds or even thousands of people in and out of Arkansas would eventually involve themselves in the crisis and spend time, money, and passion on it.

But on the day the army arrived, it became clear that the chief antagonists over the long haul would be two centers of power less than a mile apart in the capital of Arkansas—the governor and the *Arkansas Gazette*. Ashmore's editorial written as the army jeeps and trucks moved in on Tuesday evening laid down the theme the paper would follow during the coming months. History was being rolled back to the Reconstruction era, he said.

> And so the reckless course the governor embarked upon three weeks ago has raised old ghosts and tested the very fiber of the constitution. And, the greatest irony of all, he has by his acts and words dealt a major and perhaps a lethal blow to the cause of segregation which he purported to uphold . . . Mr. Faubus and the angry, violent and thoughtless band of agitators who rallied to his call may well have undone the patient work of responsible local officials.

Then, the following day:

> The day Orval Faubus put armed and uniformed men around Central High School under his personal order to nullify the order of a United States District Court he invited a show of federal force. When he refused to accept the conciliatory gestures of a mild and patient president he made such a show certain. Now we have it.

The *Gazette* led a small minority of Arkansas newspapers in opposing Faubus's actions. Even the Fulbrights' paper at Fayetteville, where the town had led the South in desegregating its schools, decried the president's sending troops as an attack on states' rights.

The acrimony between Faubus and Ashmore and their seconds would grow worse during the coming days and years, and only when they had reached old age would they be able to speak of each other with even a hint of their early friendship.

Faubus's reply to Ashmore's Reconstruction blast was to charge that the editor himself had been part of a local conspiracy responsible for bringing the army in. In this case, he was partly right. When Eisenhower decided to use military force, deputy attorney general William P. Rogers telephoned Ashmore, who had been an infantry officer in World War II, and asked his advice on how many troops would be needed. About a battalion, Ashmore said.

Ashmore and several others, including McMath and Woods, had been meeting feverishly for days to address the growing stalemate and to discuss options for protecting the black students. Several local leaders, including Blossom, Hays, and Mayor Woodrow Mann, had tried in vain to persuade Brownell and others in the Eisenhower administration to send federal marshals to protect the students. In the end, Eisenhower decided that a decisive show of armed force would be best. A presidential assistant asked the mayor to send a telegram requesting troops, and Mann did so.

Little Rock's lame-duck mayor, who had lost a confidence vote when the city decided to change to a city manager government, was the chief official critic of Faubus's action. He called it a political hoax. For his efforts, he found a cross burning in his yard in the early morning of Friday, September 6. He was not intimidated. He repeated his assertion that Faubus's evidence of violence was all fabricated and added that, in the absence of the real thing, violence was being manufactured "to keep the citizens keyed up."

Afterward, Eisenhower's decision to use troops was criticized in some quarters as overreaction. His critics had second thoughts in 1963 when Pres. John F. Kennedy used marshals to try to control violence at the University of Mississippi. Two men were killed there, and 166 of the marshals were injured. Kennedy then had to send in the army troops he had placed on standby alert.

Eisenhower might have avoided sending soldiers if he had heeded the advice of his attorney general earlier. Over much of 1956 and 1957, Brownell had tried to persuade Congress to let the Justice Department initiate civil suits and get injunctions to stop interference with court-ordered school desegregation. The department had participated in such an action at Hoxie but only in the guise of friend of the court after the school board had requested its help, a requirement of the old law. Brownell believed that the government needed the power to intervene on its own to head off criminal obstruction of court orders. Even the most determined resisters would usually obey an injunction, backed up by a threat of jail, rather than force a fight with armed marshals or soldiers. Unfortunately, Eisenhower opposed the idea and refused to support it until Brownell tricked him into a grudging endorsement. Southern senators and representatives defeated it handily when the proposed change in civil rights law came before Congress.

"If we had been given this authority in the 1957 civil rights bill," Brownell said later, "we would have been able to take such action that would have made it unnecessary to send in Federal troops to keep order."

One who was not surprised by the president's show of force was Faubus. He was taken aback by Ike's sending soldiers; he thought marshals were more likely. But he had known all along that the federal courts would push ahead and that, ultimately, he would have to give way. He could not afford to say that publicly. He also knew that fighting the feds with guns, as some hotheads were eager to do, was insane. He reflected afterward, "You couldn't fight the federal government on this without starting the Civil War all over again." Nevertheless, the lines were drawn once again—black against white, integrationist against segregationist, North against South.

| CHAPTER 20 | Eight of the nine black students finished the school year. Minnijean Brown was expelled for repeatedly fighting back. The several dozen determined segregationists in the student body took it as their mission to vilify, curse, harass, and |

torment the Negroes every day. Some days they assaulted them: pushed them down stairs, struck them with fists and hands, kicked them, stepped on their heels, set off firecrackers in their lockers, dumped food in their laps, spat on them. The victims went home many days with bruises, cuts, and bloody clothes. White students were not immune to the consequences of the hatred. Those who tried to befriend the black students were ostracized and threatened. Classes were regularly disrupted by bomb threats.

The soldiers and guardsmen were in and around the school at all times, but they were not always able to protect the youngsters. Some of the guardsmen, after the federal troops left in November, made little effort to do so. On a single day, for example, three incidents occurred. Two black boys were overtaken by six white boys. They shoved them repeatedly, knocked their books from their hands and kicked the books across the floor. Two black girls were struck by pencils. A black boy was kicked. All this took place within twenty feet of National Guardsmen, and the troops did nothing to stop it. Years later, Faubus got a letter that indicated the sentiments of many of the guardsmen. The man had been at Central and, he said, "The Arkansas National Guard people would have gone to war, to a man, behind you, had you rebelled against Isenhower's [sic] order to you."

The boldly declared aim of the white radicals was stark: to run the black students out of Central, to return the smaller districts like Fayetteville and Hoxie to segregated status, and to defeat integration for all time. For most of the school year, they had reason to believe they were winning. They would have been even more optimistic if they had known the pain and doubt that the Central High Nine and their families were feeling. Week after week, they had to remind themselves that their goal was worth the suffering.

Outside the school, the legal and political battles wore on. The NAACP and a group of Negro ministers challenged Arkansas's anti-integration measures in federal and state courts. Judge Davies refused to order the troops out. A segregationist lawyer vowed to see Davies impeached. Faubus threatened to sue to have the troops sent home. A group of moderate southern governors worked out an agreement between Eisenhower and Faubus in October. Faubus would guarantee that the federal court orders would be peacefully enforced and not obstructed if the president removed his troops. When Faubus added to his statement that the court orders would not be obstructed "by me," the president stopped trying to deal with him. He was convinced that Faubus aimed to stir up so much trouble across the South that there would not be enough federal troops to control the situation. And every day brought new doubts that he could trust any Deep South political leader on the integration question; all of them apparently put their careers ahead of their intellectual honesty and what they patently knew to be right.

L. C. and Daisy Bates and Little Rock detectives examine a partly burned cross on the Bates's lawn during the tension of autumn 1957.

COURTESY SPECIAL COLLECTIONS DIVISION, UNIVERSITY OF ARKANSAS LIBRARIES, FAYETTEVILLE.

The school board asked the court for a two-and-a-half-year delay, citing the chaos of the first year. An Arkansas federal judge agreed, but the U.S. Court of Appeals for the Eighth Circuit and the Supreme Court ordered integration to continue in September 1958. One of the briefs asking the Supreme Court for delay came from Sen. J. W. Fulbright. The Supreme Court's ruling, styled *Cooper v. Aaron*, removed any doubt that state officials had to obey the U.S. Constitution on school questions. The decision became a judicial cornerstone of the long campaign to stamp out state-sanctioned segregation in public schools.

Brownell resigned in October 1957, and his Arkansas enemies were certain that Eisenhower had fired him for giving bad advice on Little Rock, even though he had indicated for some time his intention to leave the job. His successor, William P. Rogers, declined to prosecute the troublemakers at Little Rock. U.S. District Attorney Osro Cobb had tried to have some of the mob leaders arrested, but Rogers's Justice Department overruled him. He and his aides apparently feared that a trial with its open testimony would compromise the FBI informants who had infiltrated the segregationist organizations.

On May 25, Little Rock had a distinguished and controversial visitor. The Rev. Dr. Martin Luther King Jr., then in the youth of his fame, came to sit in the stands of Quigley Stadium at the Central High commencement. He was there to pay tribute to Central's first black graduate, Ernest Green. The youngster ignored threats on his life—rumor had it that anyone who assassinated him would be paid ten thousand dollars—and, with King sitting next to Green's mother, walked the aisle to get his diploma. Green was of pioneer stock; his family had lived in Little Rock since before the Civil War. It was in Little Rock that they had been set free from slavery.

Faubus kept his resistance in the news by deriding Mayor Mann, the Justice Department, the FBI, and the *Gazette*. His supporters started a boycott of the newspaper that eventually cost it $5 to $6 million in lost advertising and subscription revenues and nearly 20 percent of its circulation. Subscriptions were canceled at the rate of one thousand a day for thirty days after Ashmore's first editorial blast. Enraged segregationists blocked a *Gazette* delivery truck at Clarendon and refused to let the driver unload papers there.

*L. C. and Daisy Bates invited the nine black
students enrolled at Central High for
Thanksgiving dinner November 25, 1957.*

PHOTO BY WILL COUNTS, COURTESY OF THE *ARKANSAS
DEMOCRAT-GAZETTE.*

The *Gazette* was not the only Little Rock business to suffer. The capital's steady growth in industrialization ground to a halt after the Central High crisis. In 1957, the city had attracted eight new plants worth more than $3 million and employing more than one thousand people. In 1958, no new plants came. The slowdown continued into the 1960s.

Little Rock business and church leaders tentatively tried to solve the crisis, but little progress was made. Faubus stirred up emotions in early October by charging that federal troops had invaded the privacy of the girls' dressing rooms at Central. School administrators painstakingly proved that it had not happened, but Faubus's followers ignored them. Words like "Gestapo" and "tyrant" were used on all sides.

Faubus never got around to revealing his sources for the caravans, guns, knives, and marauders who had threatened Central High. He did, however, find other causes of turmoil beyond the *Gazette* and its friends. Grace Lorch, for example, the white woman who had befriended Elizabeth Eckford in front of Central, and her husband, Lee, who taught at Philander Smith College, were Communists, Faubus said. They refused to reply.

Opinion was more divided among Little Rock white people than was understood beyond the state, where the name of the Arkansas capital would soon become an easy cussword for sneering at southern racism. In addition to the liberals and moderates who followed the lead of the *Gazette,* a sizable number of church members, especially of the Roman Catholic and mainline Protestant congregations, rallied behind the Blossom Plan. Six thousand people attended Columbus Day prayer services supporting the moderate to liberal position. A third of the Catholics of Little Rock and North Little Rock were in that number. The city's leading rabbi was among the organizers.

A few white ministers risked their positions by preaching that segregation was immoral. The Rev. Colbert S. Cartwright lost 10 percent of his members at the Pulaski Heights Christian Church. Those remaining constituted one of the most liberal congregations in the state. The Rev. Dunbar Ogden, pastor of Central Presbyterian Church, also spoke up for integration. He first lost his pastorate when well-to-do members stopped contributing money to the church. Then, in 1960, Ogden's son killed himself because of a depression that his friends traced to the Little Rock crisis and to a campaign of harassment against him by segregationists and by friends who considered him a traitor.

Even the Faubus household was quietly divided. Alta Faubus thought her husband had made a mistake in blocking integration. Afterward, she wished she had summoned the courage to tell him. She remembered the visit before school started from Adolphine Terry, the doyen of Little Rock liberals, pleading with her to intercede with the governor not to side with the segregationists. She spoke to him, but too many of the Faubuses' friends were giving him opposing advice.

Other members of Faubus's family also disagreed with him. Sam held his tongue so as not to embarrass Orval, but late in his life he confessed to one of his daughters that he had been disappointed. Another who disagreed, and who told him so bluntly, was his sister Bonnie Salcido. She had lived for several years in California and was married to a Mexican American. Her children were harassed by their schoolmates when they learned that the Arkansas governor was their uncle.

The tension was taking its toll on both Orval and Alta. He fainted one day at a reception, and to relieve his stress and fatigue he spent several days on the Buffalo River. He had so much trouble sleeping, tossing and squirming, that Mrs. Faubus didn't want to stay in bed with him. There were threats on his life, which frightened her perhaps more than they did him. The state police gave her a pistol to carry in her purse. At one time, she feared she was close to a nervous breakdown. She told Orval she wanted to leave. He told her she could not. If she did, he would send the state police and have her brought back.

Just as the election season of 1958 began, the *Gazette* won two Pulitzer Prizes. One went to the paper for its coverage of the Little Rock story and the other to Harry Ashmore for his editorials. The largest crowd in the history of the Marion Hotel turned out for a dinner honoring the paper's leaders. Ralph McGill, editor of the *Atlanta Constitution,* was the speaker. The display of affection for the paper was a signal that the class division in Little Rock was opening wider, with blacks and prosperous, often liberal whites on one side and Faubus's disaffected blue-collar whites on the other. During the coming years, the paper would become an object of hatred of the sort usually reserved for people, not institutions. *Gazette* editors and reporters were casually denounced as Communists.

To the surprise of some, Faubus's appeal to the Snopes sensibility brought out the rube in some of Little Rock's cosmopolites. When William F. Rector, a wealthy real-estate developer, accused Faubus of costing Little Rock a $10 million business investment from New Jersey, Faubus said that that was false and that Rector was an integrationist and a Republican. Rector, who traced his ancestry to a Civil War governor, was furious. He said Faubus was a skunk.

By the winter of 1958, Faubus had begun using the term integrationist as a pejorative. Months earlier, he was still pointing with a kind of defensive pride to the state's record in integrating public institutions. Now he was sliding into the separatist rhetoric that would mark his public discourse for several years. Eventually, as his attitudes hardened, he would add other right-wing tones to his thinking.

Jim Johnson, making the best of his changed situation, offered his services once or twice a month during this troubled year. He periodically advised the governor, in public, on ways of resisting integration. He urged a special session of the legislature. He announced that he would not run for office in 1958 but instead would submit an amendment to the state constitution providing for the closure of integrated schools. The state supreme court frustrated that effort by ordering it off the ballot. Before that ruling was made, he changed his mind about running for office and filed for the state supreme court seat held by Minor W. Milwee, an unassuming justice who commanded the respect of lawyers across the state.

Johnson said later that Faubus had encouraged him to enter the race. Faubus in fact was lukewarm about supporting his fierce foe of just two years earlier, but he told his people to help Johnson in various places around the state. Then his advisor Bill Smith, acting with Faubus's knowledge, tried unsuccessfully to persuade Johnson to withdraw two weeks before the primary. Johnson had suffered a series of setbacks that threatened to sink his candidacy. He was distracted by the terminal illness of his mother. Having one of his candidates lose would have hurt Faubus's growing image of invincibility.

Harry S. Ashmore, executive editor of the Gazette, won a Pulitzer Prize for his editorials on Faubus and the school crisis. The paper won another for its news coverage of the event.

Amis Guthridge also sought to capitalize on his growing reputation by running against Brooks Hays in the Democratic primary. Hays showed little concern. Less than a month later, he was elected to his second term as president of the Southern Baptist Convention, one of the nation's largest religious bodies.

Two men with only regional reputations, Lee Ward of Paragould and Chris Finkbeiner of Little Rock, offered themselves as sacrifices and opposed Faubus in his bid for a third term. The race was bitter but one-sided. Finkbeiner, a businessman and political neophyte, stood for segregation and efficiency in government. Ward also supported segregation—by this time, with massive resistance in full cry, it was nearly impossible for a candidate to admit to integrationist tendencies anywhere in the South—but he attacked Faubus vehemently. He called him a "fence-straddling, pussy-footing demagogue" who was in league with Witt Stephens. He accused him of trying to take over all state boards and commissions, in particular the sensitive highway commission.

Arkansas had not had a three-term governor since Jeff Davis. Three terms would allow Faubus to appoint three of the five members of the highway commission. He was able to finesse the issue through luck. A member died in May, before the election, and Faubus appointed the Pine Bluff lawyer Lawrence Blackwell, co-author of the Mack-Blackwell Amendment that had supposedly removed the highway commission from political influence.

The *Gazette* weighed in with frequent editorials against Faubusism. He in turn devoted most of his attention not to Ward and Finkbeiner but to Ashmore, the *Gazette,* and Sid McMath, the supposed sponsor of the opposition candidates. Johnson decided that the same villains were opposing him, and he adopted a similar stance.

The governor took special satisfaction in pointing out that the *Gazette* (like most southern papers of the time) had no Negro employees in the news and editorial departments. He also exploited Ashmore's non-Arkansas roots. "The basic choice in this campaign," he said, "is not between me and the other two candidates but between me and Harry Ashmore and the other outsiders who are assisting him."

Faubus's campaign was not all negative. He knew that he was not seriously threatened, so he spent most of each speech pointing to the achievements of his administration. Teachers' salaries and educational facilities were improving. The state hospital was on the mend. During May, ground was broken for two important new facilities, the Children's Colony at Conway to care for mentally retarded youngsters and, at Pine Bluff, the state's first vocational training school.

The big money of east Arkansas was no longer in doubt. The delta planters and businessmen lined up to support Faubus. Dan Felton of Lee County, a planter, civic leader, and second-generation political boss, expressed the sentiment of virtually everyone in that part of the state except for the black underclass. Along with his contribution, he sent a letter expressing gratitude "for what you have done." He did not need to be more specific.

Only Johnson's race was close. He narrowly defeated Milwee. Hays swamped Guthridge. Faubus won 69 percent of the vote and carried all seventy-five counties. In the delta, they showed their gratitude by giving him more than 80 percent of the vote.

Oddly enough, Faubus won large numbers of black votes. Negroes were still blatantly "voted" by their employers in many of the eastern counties. In and around the capital, the situation was more complex. Certain black leaders could deliver votes through the use of persuasion, charisma, and financial incentives. One of the most effective was Bishop O. L. Sherman of North Little Rock, a regional leader of the African Methodist Episcopal Church. His pitch to his followers in 1958 was similar to Faubus's: The Yankees are coming down here trying to tell us what to do, how to run our schools. We know how to take care of our people. You stay with those of us who have been here trying to help, and we're going to work this thing out. And let's keep it quiet; we don't want any trouble.

Sherman was paid by the candidate, and he earned his stipend. He delivered the votes. His organization was hierarchical with himself at the top, two or three trusted lieutenants next, then supervisors who worked the telephones. Under them were knockers, rousters, and drivers.

William F. (Casey) Laman, mayor of North Little Rock at the time and a political friend of Sherman's, described how it worked. "The knockers go out on Friday, Saturday, Sunday and Monday before the election," Laman said. "They knock on the door and hand out the literature and tell them why they're working for this candidate. Then they have the rousters. On election day, the drivers would drive the car. The rouster would go to the door and roust them out of the house; they won't come. And they'd roust them out of the house and get them in the car. In one of my campaigns, they said, 'Mayor, you're going to need at least two creepers.' I said, 'Now, what's this creeper?' He said, 'Well, you know, the opposition is having some meetings. Someone has got to creep in there to see what's going on.'"

The segregationists were winning, or so it seemed. They had successfully intimidated the moderates at the center of public opinion. They had made their own rigid position the standard of discourse. Anyone who opposed that position risked opprobrium and perhaps danger. Businessmen dared not speak against the Citizens Council for fear of boycott and ruin. Now the segregationists had further concrete evidence of their gains. Federal District Judge Harry J. Lemley had granted the school board a lengthy delay in resuming Central's integration, leading thousands to believe that the federal enforcers were on the run. The case had not yet reached the higher courts for its inevitable reversal. And the victorious campaigns of Faubus and Johnson had pumped up the cause enormously.

While the followers were exultant, the leader had to be more circumspect. He knew that he had pushed about as far as he could go in defying the federal courts. Even as Faubus was winning nomination to a third term, the new federal attorney general, Rogers, was laying plans to thwart any repetition of the 1957 episode when integration resumed at Central High in September. On August 18, Rogers sent a memorandum to the president saying, "If Governor Faubus calls out the National Guard and prevents the attendance of the Negro students, the course is clear. The Department of Justice would immediately file a petition with the District Court asking that Governor Faubus and the commanding officers of the National Guard be cited for contempt of court." He pointed out that Faubus and his commander were already under a federal court injunction to stay out of Central's business. Faubus knew that it was unlikely that a governor would be sent to jail, but—as Rogers noted in his memo to the president—he could be assessed a heavy fine for every day he remained in contempt.

Faubus decided on a strategy that would be less risky but still give a strong appearance of continued defiance. He enlisted most of the state government in his effort. Less than a month after the primary, he called the legislature into special session. He willingly shared the spotlight with Atty. Gen. Bruce Bennett, even though he knew that Bennett was edging in from the right to position himself to run for governor in 1960.

Bennett's special target was the NAACP. The passions unleashed at Little Rock had spread across the state. The NAACP, which had been regarded tolerantly when it was noticed at all in the white community, now had become demonized everywhere. At Bennett's urging, the legislature passed measures to force politically suspect organizations to reveal their memberships and financing. He drafted a model ordinance allowing cities to pursue their own local chapters of the iniquitous NAACP and any other troublemaking nonconformist groups. Little Rock's City Council, which had already parted company with the mayor and announced its support of Faubus's action at Central High, passed such an ordinance in October. The idea spread to a dozen other Arkansas towns, then to other southern states. The NAACP had to spend thousands of dollars in court getting the obviously unconstitutional laws declared so. In December, Bennett and a committee of the state legislative council held three days of highly public hearings to expose what they saw as Communist party meddling in Arkansas's integration problem. They judiciously overlooked the left-wing connections of the Faubus family.

Faubus's contribution to the special session was more dramatic, if equally unstable as constitutional law. He persuaded the legislators to pass a law allowing him to close public schools to avoid integration. The closed schools would be leased to private school corporations. Two weeks later, he closed Little Rock's four public high schools and called a city election to ratify the action. The ballot choice on September 27 was closed schools or total integration. Predictably, the vote was one-sided against integration. Wealthy supporters of Faubus opened T. J. Raney High School, a private school for white students. The school board agreed to lease the closed schools to the corporation, but the federal court stopped that within hours, leaving the private school to find its own building and funding while the rest of Faubus's legislative package made its tortuous way toward death in the federal court system.

There is some evidence that the school board, which was running out of nerve and stamina, conspired with Faubus on the school-closing legislation. It held a lengthy meeting with him and several leaders of the legislature just before the special session. Most school officials took no part in the school-closing election.

Closing the schools hurt Faubus with thousands of Little Rock parents, but elsewhere in the South his action was applauded. Sen. Strom Thurmond of South Carolina wrote to praise the "courageous fight you are making in order to preserve the principles of Constitutional Government through the maintenance of State control in the field of education." He issued a public statement at the same time urging southerners to "oppose integration orders regardless of Federal force," which struck some as a call for another attack on Fort Sumter.

Little Rock's 3,698 high-school students scratched for schooling wherever they could find it or simply dropped out that year. More than 750 whites enrolled in the T. J. Raney High School. An attempt to divert public money to the private school was promptly squelched by the federal court. Other students, black and white, moved to other towns and states and lived with relatives or friends while they attended strange schools.

On November 12, 1958, the frustrated Little Rock School Board, having just been ordered by a federal appeals court to get on with integration even though it had no high schools to integrate, bought up Virgil Blossom's contract. Then five of the six members —all except Dr. Dale Alford—resigned. A new board was elected December 6 with its membership evenly divided between those favoring compliance with the court's integration orders and those favoring continued resistance. The stage was set for the final confrontation in the Little Rock school crisis.

Brooks Hays was relieved at drawing no stronger an opponent than Amis Guthridge in the Democratic primary. What he failed to see was the depth of resentment that could be stirred up against him in the right hands. Dr. Alford, an opthalmologist, had been alone on the school board in opposing implementation of the Blossom Plan. The acclaim that resulted gave him a taste for higher office. Eight days before the November general election, he announced his candidacy for Hays's seat. It was far too late to get his name on the ballot, so he resorted to an unusual device. He asked voters to write in his name. To make it easier, he had thousands of stickers printed bearing his name. His workers handed them out at the polling places, sometimes with the help of poll workers.

Faubus repeatedly denied taking any part in Alford's campaign. He insisted that he had tried to talk the eye doctor out of making the race. He secretly did not like Alford, whom he considered a political chameleon and a fake. To underscore his distance from the contest, he was pointedly absent from the state during that week.

While he took no overt part in the election, the considerable weight of his political organization was thrown behind the write-in candidate. A chief gubernatorial aide, Claude Carpenter Jr., resigned to manage Alford's campaign. Several other close associates worked hard for the challenger. Mack Sturgis, Faubus's purchasing agent, was a visible presence for Alford in up-river counties where he had courthouse contacts. Rep. Paul Van Dalsem of Perry County, a leading Faubus man in the legislature, worked hard and openly to unseat Hays.

Some worked with stealth. Sam Rorex, a Pulaski County chancery judge who had been appointed by Faubus, was a long-time political rival of Hays. A Yell County landowner, he had opposed Hays for Congress in the early 1930s and, in a disputed three-way race, had helped David D. Terry of Little Rock, Adolphine's husband, defeat Hays in the runoff. In the fall of 1958, he went home to Yell County with a two-fold mission, to smite his old enemy and to help his friend Faubus. Without fanfare, he went from one political leader to another with the message: "The governor doesn't want Brooks Hays." Other Faubus associates quietly carried the same message throughout the Fifth District.

Faubus was in a delicate situation. He dared not forbid his troops from working for Alford because word would get out and hurt him with the high-riding segregationists. The Citizens Council leaders were working feverishly for the challenger. Jim Johnson borrowed fifteen hundred dollars in his own name to do "missionary work" (and had trouble getting reimbursed by the campaign committee). On the other hand, Faubus disliked offending Democratic party loyalists who resented Alford's insurrection. What he managed was a semi-public wink that let him have it both ways.

One of Hays's die-hard supporters was Sheriff Marlin Hawkins, the boss of Conway County. Hawkins was a friend of Hays and his father before him. He was a yellow-dog Democrat, and he saw Alford's write-in ruse as a threat to the party's effectiveness. The title of his sunset-years book, *How I Stole Elections,* was meant ironically, but that was not fully understood by many of the old-timers who had witnessed his uncanny skill at delivering votes. The common belief, fair or not, was that the sheriff could deliver a total to within one hundred votes of the number required for any candidate whose name appeared on the Conway County ballot. Faubus had benefited from that skill and might need Hawkins's help in the future.

One night after Alford had made his ambition known privately, Faubus and Carpenter drove to Morrilton. Carpenter was ordered to stay in the car. Inside, Hawkins and his friends made their pitch for party loyalty. They understood that Hays had become an irritant for Faubus, what with his liberal mouth stirring up compassion for blacks and making segregationists feel guilty. But wait another two years and Hays probably won't run again, they said.

After four hours, Faubus told Hawkins that he would pull Alford out of the race. He knew that Hawkins would repeat that promise in all the right places to people who expected a Democratic governor to support the Democratic nominee for Congress. The next morning, he instructed Carpenter to talk to Alford and "get him out." Carpenter rebelled. He thought Alford could win, and he was eager to run his campaign. If Faubus wanted him out, he said, he should tell Alford himself. Faubus quickly wrote a letter on a note pad telling Alford he couldn't win and that if he ran he would do so without Faubus's support.

Carpenter delivered the letter but urged Alford to run, anyway. Carpenter told him, "The newspapers will say that Faubus has put you in the race, which will get all those fired-up people out there. And the more he says he didn't put you in the race, they're going to be that much more inclined to vote for you because they're going to think, 'Hey, you know, he's just got to say that.'" Carpenter was convinced that his boss "deep down" wanted Alford to run but knew he had to pretend otherwise to assuage the feelings of Hawkins and save Conway County's votes for himself at the next election.

Hays was among those who eventually heard about Faubus's pledge to Hawkins. He took it to mean that Hawkins had successfully appealed to Faubus's sense of loyalty, only to see a weaker side of Faubus prevail. "If his political conscience had really been stirred," Hays later wrote, ruefully, "he could have publicly renounced the Carpenter-Alford plans." Hays obviously played The Game by different rules.

Carpenter, the campaign manager, played boldly on racial emotions. He put his Citizens Council friends to work licking stamps and making telephone calls. He found a newspaper photograph of Hays sitting between two black Baptist ministers in another state. He reprinted the picture in a full-page newspaper advertisement. The caption said, "We know you, Brooks." In the temper of the times, that was enough to convict the congressman of being an integrationist.

When the votes and the stickers were counted, Alford was declared the winner by 30,739 to 29,483. Both John F. Kennedy and Richard M. Nixon sent messages of condolence to Hays. Some four thousand other people from across the nation wrote and wired to express their dismay and outrage. Ripples from the Hays–Alford contest could be seen years later. In 1963, former governor James P. Coleman of Mississippi was defeated in his attempt to regain the governor's office. The most damning issue against him was that he was a racial "moderate" and not a full-bore segregationist. To back up the charge, his enemies pointed out that, as governor in 1958, he had publicly supported Brooks Hays in his electoral contest.

The House Special Elections Committee investigated Alford's election, but the leaders of the House, including Speaker Sam Rayburn and Arkansas's Wilbur Mills, chairman of the Ways and Means Committee, gave Hays no support. Indeed, Hays became a pariah among his old associates in the state's congressional delegation. Rep. Oren Harris of El Dorado was driven to deny that he had defended Hays.

Dr. Dale Alford (center) *celebrates his write-in victory over Rep. Brooks Hays in 1958.*

PHOTO BY LARRY OBSITNIK, COURTESY OF THE *ARKANSAS DEMOCRAT-GAZETTE* AND SPECIAL COLLECTIONS DIVISION, UNIVERSITY OF ARKANSAS LIBRARIES, FAYETTEVILLE.

Hays declined to contest the election in spite of considerable evidence of voting irregularities. Hawkins was in the uncomfortable position of advising his friend against it because some of his own boys might have "got excited and did a little something wrong" that a contest would uncover. Hawkins told, with some indignation, of numerous polling frauds in neighboring counties. For example, there was a precinct in Faulkner County that took four hundred votes away from Hays and gave them to Alford. Hawkins knew that stealing votes was easy. "If you had the judges and the clerks, you could wipe out a whole box."

Many years later, Hawkins reflected on the race with some sadness. "The only time in my life I wished I had stole the election," he said.

Hays typically accepted the defeat with a joke. He said he felt like the man who was kicked in the head by a donkey, then pleaded with his doctor to keep him alive long enough to catch pneumonia because he did not want his tombstone to say, "He was kicked to death by a jackass." Equally to the point was the humor of Herblock, the *Washington Post* cartoonist. He drew Faubus standing behind Hays, plunging a dagger into his back and saying, "I said I wouldn't stand in your way."

CHAPTER

21

There was no longer any doubt who the boss of Arkansas was. Orval Faubus had whipped the establishment roosters. He had shown that he could punish any politician who crossed him or who simply posed an inconvenience. He controlled the legislature so thoroughly that only an occasional maverick dared oppose him, as demonstrated by the overwhelming majorities for his school-closing legislation. He had the Citizens Council irregulars at heel, and even when they eventually turned sour, he had so much power and popularity that he could shuck them off with impunity. His fame was worldwide. Only the morally fastidious saw it as a poor reflection on Arkansas. He would soon be touted for president by the right-wing fringe, an honor that his ego appreciated even while his judgment scorned it as hopeless.

His power was never complete, though. All through his long years in office there would be pockets of influence that he could not own. They never threatened his hold on the state government and its network of money and privilege. They did, however, keep him alert and fretful. A number of small newspaper editors followed the lead of the *Gazette* and criticized almost every move he made. John Wells, never forgetting his original suspicions and antagonisms, filled his paper every week with mini-scandals from the state records, the kind that dog many public officials in a democratic society.

The most troublesome pocket of dissenting influence was Little Rock and its environs. The opposition there was slow to recover its wits. J. N. Heiskell's vow that he would not let Faubus and "people like that" take over his town looked sterile for more than a year after Central High's inauspicious integegration. The segregationists of Little Rock seemed to be winning, and they were heartened to see that their brothers across the South were strengthened in their resistance. The final lesson, that opposing federal power was futile, had not soaked in. Indeed, new thousands had taken inspiration, especially in the Deep South states, from Faubus's confrontation in Little Rock. The violence in Arkansas paled beside the bombings and lynchings in Alabama and Mississippi during the late 1950s and early 1960s. School desegregation appeared to be stalled for a time. During Eisenhower's last three years in office—after Little Rock—only forty-nine school districts were desegregated, most with token numbers.

But Little Rock's story was not finished. Before it was over, Faubus would suffer his most serious setback, and integration would continue its slow, uncertain progress.

Most of the men who fancied themselves as leaders in the capital city were thoroughly intimidated by the Faubus juggernaut. They made intermittent and ineffectual attempts to get past the crisis, at first trying through legerdemain and public relations avoidance to soften its economic impact and only later, reluctantly, confronting it as a political and moral problem. Twenty-five former presidents of the chamber of commerce talked themselves into a stupor after the 101st Airborne arrived before finally issuing an unenthusiastic call for peaceful compliance with court orders. The school board tried repeatedly to get an audience with Eisenhower; its failure prompted one member, R. A. Lile, to write a testy letter of frustration to the president. An insurance executive, Herbert L. Thomas Sr., proposed suspending Little Rock's integration for a year and forming a state interracial commission to help school boards meet the problem. His plan got considerable publicity, but nothing came of it.

One of the more imaginative efforts came from an Arkansas native who had left. Harlan S. Hobbs, who in the 1930s had attended Little Rock High School, had settled in Ohio with a successful career in public relations and corporate business. He used a White House connection to urge an unusual idea on the president. He suggested sending a delegation of Little Rock student leaders to see Ike. As a one-time editor of the high-school paper himself, he reasoned that the youngsters, carrying no political baggage, could be received as emissaries more readily than could adult leaders. He hoped the trip, which would be well-publicized, would help to calm the national turmoil over Little Rock. Hobbs' quietly-pursued scheme became just one more failed effort.

The men of the town fell silent. And into the silence walked a handful of women who were willing to risk their standing, their tranquility, and even their family livelihoods.

Velma Powell, secretary of the Arkansas Council on Human Relations, an affiliate of the Southern Regional Council in Atlanta, had attended business college with the considerable help of Mrs. David D. Terry and had lived for a year in the Terry mansion. Her husband was the vice principal at Central High.

Shortly after the city's high schools were closed, Powell wrote to Mrs. Terry urging her friend to take the lead in solving the school crisis. As it happened, Mrs. Terry had been pondering the matter. She was very much aware of her place in the city. She was a sister of John Gould Fletcher, the Pulitzer Prize–winning poet. Their family were proud descendants of Hanoverians who saw civic virtue as an obligation of their class. She recalled that years earlier an organization of southern white women had effectively put a stop to wholesale lynching in the South. Such an organization might put a stop to the madness in Little Rock. She and Powell called in their friend Vivion Brewer, the wife of a federal civil servant, and they set to work. The Women's Emergency Committee to Open Our Schools, made up of white women largely of the middle class, held its first meeting September 16, 1958, in the living room of the old Albert Pike mansion, Mrs. Terry's home.

The Emergency Committee lost the first election on closing the schools, but it set to work at once to reverse the decision. During the winter and spring, the women compiled voluminous lists of voters with addresses and telephone numbers. By late spring, they had built an effective political organization.

Alarmed by the continuing loss of business and industry, the Little Rock Chamber of Commerce finally took a stand in March 1959. It voted 819 to 245 in favor of reopening the schools "on a controlled minimum plan of integration acceptable to the federal courts." Even then, the businessmen protected their flank. The chamber's statement urged continued support for the private segregated high school. That caution was not considered remarkable. Few Little Rock opponents of Faubus and the Citizens Council admitted to being integrationists. Most in fact favored segregation but saw the council's resistance as hurting the city.

The turning point came May 5. The three radical segregationists on the school board, supported by Faubus, tried to fire forty-four teachers and school employees who were suspected of integrationist sympathies. This was in line with a broad attack on teachers across the state. When the teachers' main organization, the Arkansas Education Association, went on record as favoring the preservation of public education, the state legislature showed its displeasure by delaying the budget of the state Department of Education. The state Democratic party, now a personal tool of the governor, pressured teachers to get in line. It asked every principal to solicit five-dollar donations from teachers and send it a list of the contributors. It was not necessary to point out that those not on the list would be identified as enemies.

The three moderates on the board walked out and refused to participate in the meeting. The radicals went ahead with what became known as the teacher purge.

Civic and educational organizations reacted angrily. Three days after the purge, 179 business and civic leaders—most of them men who had finally been shamed into action—met at a bank and organized the committee to Stop This Outrageous Purge, or STOP. Its aim was to recall the segregationist members of the board. A counter group sprang up calling itself the Committee to Retain Our Segregated Schools, or CROSS. STOP won the battle of the acronyms in spite of Faubus's heavy support of the other side. His contribution to the rhetoric of the battle was to condemn his opponents as members of "the Cadillac brigade." The segregationists were replaced on the board by three moderates.

The political know-how of the furious women of the Women's Emergency Committee made the difference. They provided most of the STOP campaign's workers. Faubus never forgave them. Two years later during a reelection campaign, he held both the committee and Mrs. Terry up to scorn. He called her "the strongest integrationist you ever saw" and declared that she believed not only in integrated schools but also in interracial marriage. She replied that he had forsaken his progressive roots and would be remembered in history in the company of such demagogues as Eugene Talmadge of Georgia and Theodore Bilbo of Mississippi.

The committee did not stop at electioneering, and Faubus's people did not stop at name-calling. The committee began to look into the general performance of the Faubus administration. It found some questionable practices, especially in awarding contracts and buying merchandise. Mack Sturgis, the purchasing agent and a longtime friend of Faubus, fought back. He telephoned a Little Rock engineer whose partner was married to one of the women activists who had been investigating the purchasing office. Sturgis told the man to tell his partner to "get his wife out of nosing around in our offices." He added, "She's going to cause you problems."

On June 18, a federal court declared the school-closing law unconstitutional. The new school board announced that it would reopen the high schools in September. The members were far less confident than they sounded in public. Privately, several worried that the reopening would bring new violence. They also fretted that the all-white Raney High School would drain away many students. Late in the summer, a majority decided to approach Faubus with a confidential offer of a compromise, a merger with Raney High. They drafted a letter to the governor and dispatched one of their number, J. H. Cottrell, to deliver it. Cottrell was also a member of the legislature and was friendly enough with Faubus to start quiet negotiations. He drove to the capitol one day in early August. Before going to the governor's office on the second floor, he encountered a friend in the downstairs lobby who gave him a piece of news that changed everything. What the board members did not know was that Raney High was almost broke. Faubus had been helping raise money for it and had collected thousands of dollars from around the country. But the money had run out. Cottrell's friend told him that, minutes before, the directors of Raney had announced that it was closing. Cottrell never mentioned the letter. "I just turned around and drove home," he said.

Days later, the board announced its integration plan for the fall. Three Negroes would go to Central. In a nod to class antagonisms, three were assigned to Hall High. Then, to confound Faubus and the Citizens Council, it announced that it was opening the schools early—just days hence.

Segregationists from across the state hurriedly gathered in the capital for what was seen as a last-ditch stand for Arkansas's way of life. They assembled at mid-morning August 12, school-opening day, on the capitol grounds and listened to martial music and a brief address by Faubus. He guardedly advised them against any rambunctious protest, saying he saw no reason for them to be "beaten over the head today by the forces in the field, or to be jailed." The city police, now headed by the fearless Gene Smith, found a box of tear gas in the trunk of a car and speculated that it was to be thrown into the crowd to make it look as if the police had done it. The tear gas was eventually traced to the state police via connections in the Citizens Council. The embarrassed state owners went to city police headquarters and claimed it.

A determined crowd of about 250 people set off to Central High to thwart its integration once again. Smith's men blocked their path and arrested the leaders. When the incipient mob refused to disperse, Smith called in fire hoses and cooled off the remaining hotheads.

That effectively ended the threat of mob violence. The angrier radicals went underground. Several buildings were bombed, with minimal damage. The most flamboyant effort occurred on Labor Day when bombs damaged the fire chief's station wagon and the offices of the school board and the new mayor's private business. The culprits were rounded up within days. One effort to bomb a school was frustrated when an FBI infiltrator emptied the powder from the plotters' dynamite sticks and substituted sawdust. Agents watched as the men planted their castrate devices at the target, then arrested them. The most prominent bomber was E. A. Lauderdale, owner of a building materials company and a member of the board of the Capital Citizens Council. He served less than six months of his three-year sentence. Faubus reduced his term, made him eligible for immediate parole, and returned his five-hundred-dollar fine. Two other bombers served even less time. Only one bomber freely admitted his guilt and went straight to prison. Faubus never commuted his sentence, and he served almost two years.

Many years went by before Little Rock's schools could boast more than token integration. The process accelerated after Faubus left office, although he had long since stopped opposing it. By the 1969–70 school year, Central was 25 percent black, and two years later all grades were finally desegregated to some extent. The city's schools eventually were overtaken by problems of white flight, violence, and threatened standards. But those came to be seen as problems owned by no one region.

The hero who stood down the mob on its way to Central High survived only a few months. Under relentless pressure from angry segregationists, Gene Smith slowly came unhinged. He began to drink heavily. More than once, including a night when he had driven into a ditch, acquaintances in the state police removed him from his car and quietly drove him home. He blamed leaders on all sides for his problems but was especially angry at Faubus. He got out of bed one day, picked up his pistol, and told his wife, "I'm going out to the mansion and kill Orval Faubus." She stopped him. Added to the pressures of politics and work were a number of personal problems. A son was arrested for burglary in another town. His marriage was troubled. Finally, about midnight on March 18, 1960, after a long quarrel, he got the pistol that he had wanted to use on Orval Faubus and killed his wife. He walked the floor into the early hours of the new day, then turned the gun on himself.

Arkansas's civil rights movement ebbed and flowed. Faubus watched with a mixture of amusement and irritation. The Bateses'

Gene Smith (center) and Little Rock policemen halt a segregationist march on Central High in 1958.

PHOTO BY LARRY OBSITNIK, COURTESY OF *ARKANSAS DEMOCRAT-GAZETTE* AND SPECIAL COLLECTIONS DIVISION, UNIVERSITY OF ARKANSAS LIBRARIES, FAYETTEVILLE.

newspaper, the *Arkansas State Press*, had to suspend publication in the fall of 1959 after most of its remaining white advertisers withdrew. Later that season, Mrs. Bates accompanied a foreign dignitary to Faubus's office. The two adversaries were photographed smiling and shaking hands, and for months afterward the governor had to fend off snide comments from segregationists. Early in 1960, the home of one of the Central High black students, Carlotta Walls, was bombed. There were no injuries. Faubus could barely contain his satisfaction when the culprits turned out to be two Negro men. They were sentenced to prison. Faubus and others speculated that the event had been staged to draw contributions for the Walls family. Shortly afterward, the black sit-in movement spread west to Arkansas. Again, Faubus was gratified to point out that his despised enemies in Little Rock's business establishment were hypocrites, that they wanted to foist school integration onto the town but were unwilling to serve Negroes at their lunch counters and restaurants.

Faubus's turn to the right obscured a number of progressive advances. While he was accommodating the segregationist clamor, he was at the same time moving the state ahead in important ways. Public school and college teachers were enjoying the highest pay they had known, thanks to the tax increases he had engineered. The state hospital continued to improve. He oversaw the opening of the state's first vocational technical school just five weeks after his segregationist followers had fallen to Gene Smith's batons outside Central High. And two weeks after that, the Children's Colony for housing and training retarded youngsters opened at Conway. It would brighten the lives of thousands of children and their families for years to come.

Perhaps the most important step the state took during the aftermath of the Central High crisis was a change in its industrialization program. Arkansas had been losing population for years, and the decline would continue through the 1950s as high-school and college graduates poured into more prosperous regions to earn their living. Per-capita income was going up, but not as fast as in the rest of the country. The Arkansas Industrial Development Commission had been operating since Faubus's first term and had attracted a number of new businesses. Some paid good wages, and others were blatant sweat shops that in a few years would move south where wages were even lower and union restrictions even less demanding. The Central High problem slowed growth dramatically in the Little Rock area.

In a special legislative session in January 1960, Faubus sponsored a proposal that would show gratifying results. The idea was Bill Smith's. It would allow local communities to issue revenue bonds to build plants for new and expanded industries. The companies would lease the buildings from the communities. The arrangement would cost local governments property tax revenue, but by boosting the economy it would increase revenues from sales taxes and property taxes on new homes and stores.

Before long, industrial experts from around the country began traveling to Arkansas to see how it worked. Generally, it worked well. The device brought in a predictable number of low-wage companies, but it also helped to lure a substantial number of high-quality businesses. Within weeks after the new law was passed, the voters of Batesville and Jonesboro approved revenue bonds to build plants for new industries. Serendipitously, the largest plant lured to the state that winter came without the sweetener of revenue bonds. The Norge division of Borg-Warner announced plans to build a $10 million plant employing up to two thousand people at Fort Smith. That set in motion a flow of attractive new manufacturing operations into the state, many lured by Act 9 revenue bonds. Several built plants in the northwestern quadrant around the university town of Fayetteville, setting off an Ozarks boom that would continue for the rest of the century. During his lifetime, Faubus would see more than $2 billion worth of industry financed through Act 9 revenue bonds.

But his progressive actions were overshadowed by his exploitation of the race issue. No longer did anyone accuse him of being a closet integrationist or of flirting with the left wing. Much of his political behavior during the next several years was a blend of coded white supremacy and McCarthyism.

Before the Little Rock crisis, he had vetoed a bill passed by the increasingly reactionary legislature that would have required state employees and teachers to sign a loyalty oath and swear they belonged to no subversive organizations. Those who refused would be fired. Faubus said it was not possible to obtain loyalty that way. But in 1958 the legislature passed a new version of the law as part of its broadside attack on integration. It required state employees and teachers to list all the organizations they belonged to or supported financially. The lawmakers wanted to ferret out any members of the NAACP—or, worse, even more radical groups— who might be drawing taxpayers' money. Faubus still suspected that such a law was unconstitutional. So did his legal advisor, Bill Smith. But this time, looking over his shoulder at Bruce Bennett, a certain challenger at the next election, he signed the bill. It became Act 10 of 1958.

The law received only cursory attention at the time, but when teachers at the public schools and state colleges were asked to swear their allegiance to the state and nation and list their organizations, many rebelled. Lawsuits were filed. One was argued by Faubus's friend-turned-enemy Edwin Dunaway. In 1960, on a vote of 5 to 4, the Supreme Court confirmed Faubus's original estimate and declared the law unconstitutional. Act 10 caused rancor that lasted for years. The University of Arkansas was censured by the American Association of University Professors because the board of trustees would not rehire four teachers who had lost their jobs for refusing to comply with the act. Faubus played both sides, first meeting with university faculty for an amicable discussion, then deriding the same people in his news conferences. He drew the applause of the know-nothings when he quipped that it would be a pleasure to cut the university's budget—a threat to other professors who might have been thinking of further nonconformity.

There was no longer any doubt that he would punish his political enemies. Members of his family had seen his ruthless, hard-hearted streak since his youth. Now it became more pronounced. Shortly after Dunaway challenged him over Central High, Faubus fired Dunaway's sister as secretary of the public service commission, a job she had held since the McMath administration. Josephine Knowles, the registrar at the state hospital, lost her job after she was identified as an integration sympathizer. Her sympathies were established when it was learned that she was a prominent member of Bert Cartwright's congregation at the Pulaski Heights Christian

Church. The governor's staff entered into the spirit of the hunt. When an executive at the state-supported University Hospital went to work for the STOP campaign, a staffer wrote a note to the governor saying, "Let's get him." The message throughout the administration was blunt: get on the governor's side or get out. Several were fired when they refused to bow.

For its part, the federal government proved that it also could play dirty. Shortly after Faubus closed Little Rock's high schools, the Internal Revenue Service subjected him to a rigorous audit of his taxes. The agency then billed him for income tax on the rental value of the governor's mansion and on all the state money to maintain the mansion and pay the salaries of its employees. That was an outrageous demand that no other governor had to contend with. Sen. John L. McClellan intervened, and the IRS backed off and apologized. Nevertheless, the episode deepened the antagonism between the state and the federal government.

In Arkansas, the hatred for integration and for its local and national advocates became almost frenzied. Anyone suspected of integrationist or left-wing tendencies became a target. Amis Guthridge typified the style. At the height of the Act 10 controversy, he sent a statement to the student newspaper at the university suggesting that both the Arkansas Education Association and the university were controlled by left-wingers. He said the latter might well be a headquarters for Communist brain-washing.

Much of the state government joined the chase behind Faubus. Politicians outdid each other in establishing their white supremacist credentials. The legislature passed an absurd bill requiring blood collected in hospitals to be labeled by race. The governor signed it with the explanation, "A lot of people were afraid of contamination from Negro blood." The same legislature combined forces with Attorney General Bennett to investigate the suspicion—the certain knowledge, in the minds of many—that the Communist party was behind the integration campaign. For days, Bennett conducted televised hearings and smeared people like Ashmore and his cohorts.

The effort proved persuasive. As a young reporter, I was stunned one day to hear an otherwise sensible citizen of North Little Rock refer matter-of-factly to my editor as a Communist. Ashmore did not have to put up with much more such abuse. Attractive employment was offered in California, and he took it. He turned the *Gazette's* editorial page over to James O. Powell of Florida, who slowly ripened into a liberal even more unpalatable to the conservatives than his predecessor.

Most of the state's congressmen bowed to the prevailing sentiment. Rep. Wilbur D. Mills, probably the most powerful member of the House of Representatives after Speaker Sam Rayburn, went out of his way to praise Faubus's stand against the integration menace. So did Rep. Oren Harris. Rep. E. C. (Took) Gathings was embarrassed to learn that one of his aides, Parker Westbrook, a member of a prominent southwestern Arkansas family, was friendly with one of Faubus's opponents and was also sympathetic to integration. When Gathings upbraided him, Westbrook resigned in anger and went to work for Senator Fulbright. Fulbright was alone among the delegation in speaking out against Faubus, and it took him two years to get the courage to do it. Answering a question on national television, he said he thought Faubus had handled the Central High situation wrongly. Faubus replied that he had not questioned Fulbright's judgment when he signed the Southern Manifesto. That began years of bad blood between the two men.

CHAPTER 22

The governor named for Eugene Debs was now a darling of the Right. He had been enormously pleased at the height of his notoriety over Central High to be named in a Gallup Poll as one of the ten men most admired by Americans. Now in the season of a new presidential election came another flattering development. Conservatives across the Sun Belt began urging him to run for president. Faubus-for-President clubs sprang up. Campaign buttons were handed out.

He encouraged the attention for a while, prompted not by any belief that he could become president but by the chance to exploit the national publicity. He said the Democrats needed a man of courage—meaning himself—and that none of those being mentioned, such as Lyndon B. Johnson and John F. Kennedy, qualified in that regard. Various conservative groups such as the Constitution

Faubus greets well-wishers with Gov. George C. Wallace during the Alabamian's visit to Arkansas in 1964.

party and the National States' Rights party got behind him. He first accepted then declined an invitation to speak to a right-wing group in Los Angeles after a promise of television time was withdrawn by the station and after learning that Gerald L. K. Smith, the noted anti-Semite and right-wing troublemaker, was involved in the event. The States' Rights party nominated him only to have him snub the offer. One who was not surprised was his father, who told newsmen that Orval had too much sense to run for president at that time.

The attention paid him by out-of-state conservatives coincided with a shift in his ideological posture. His language and public utterances and even his private observations became more tinged with racial intonations. In late 1959, fighting back after his humiliation over the reopening of Little Rock's high schools, he declared that gradual integration was like cancer, that it would spread to all social contact once started. Negroes, he said, were governed by excesses and had not learned self-denial and self-restraint.

His estimate of black Americans had not improved five years later. "It is my opinion that the Negroes have not been especially discriminated against," he wrote to a Wisconsin man in 1964. "Usually people get in this world about what they have earned and what they deserve. Whenever the Negro improves his life morally, and especially in the moral field does he need improvement, educationally, physically, and otherwise, then much of the so-called prejudice will fade away and disappear."

When young blacks brought their sit-in campaign to Arkansas to pressure restaurants and other businesses to abolish segregation, Faubus chimed in with other southern leaders and blamed the resulting unrest on outside agitators, the modern version of the carpetbagger. Writing to Congressman Alford in 1960, he noted that only seven of seventy-six people recently hired by the Veterans' Hospital at North Little Rock were white. He added that "because of the preference shown for Negroes at this institution, some of them do very little work and are quite negligent in their duties." Whites acting like that would be fired, he said. A few weeks later, one of his trusted associates suggested that the Arkansas secretary of state think carefully before flying a flag on the capitol honoring the Negro scientist Dr. George Washington Carver.

He endorsed a radical school-closing measure, a 1960 proposed amendment to the state constitution that would have allowed the panic-stricken white patrons of a school district to abolish their schools and funnel tuition directly to students to avoid desegregation. Even though the measure had only limited support beyond the Citizens Councils, Faubus argued for it, saying he might need it in his running fight with the federal courts. The voters turned it down almost 3 to 1.

This defeat, like his earlier ones in Little Rock, barely dimmed his star among his throng of admirers. People continued to look to him for protection against the black peril and to join him in his right-wing campaign. The imperial wizard of the United Klans of America wrote to assure him that the Klan stood behind him in the fight for state sovereignty. As late as 1963, an official of a big Little Rock factory got word to the governor that agitators were trying to integrate black and white female workers on the assembly line. Just letting him know, in case of trouble. A white woman from Malvern telephoned the governor's office urging him to fire her niece from her state job because she had gone to Washington with a bus load of Negroes to take part in a freedom march. Some of Faubus's followers went so far in their bigotry as to embarrass him. When he appointed a retired Air Force colonel, Carl Hinkle, to head the Arkansas Industrial Development Commission, Hinkle promptly produced an outcry by uttering a blatantly anti-Semitic remark. Speaking to the southeast Arkansas Chamber of Commerce, he apologized for bringing a certain industrialist to look at the area. He referred to the industrialist as "this kike."

As his racial thinking shifted to the right, Faubus began to take a greater interest in the University of Arkansas. The Fayetteville campus had a disproportionate number of liberals, and he found them nettlesome. He was particularly upset when the Rev. Wyatt Tee Walker, an aide to Martin Luther King, was invited to speak to the Law School. He urged various people to protest with letters to the university administration. His close political associate Dallas P. Raney, chairman of the university's board of trustees, sent a bluntly worded letter to Pres. David Mullins saying he had made a mistake by allowing a radical like Walker to appear on campus. Faubus, replying to one concerned citizen, condemned "these left-wingers and Negroes" like Walker, then got in a dig at Winthrop Rockefeller, who had begun thinking about opposing his old friend for the governorship. He warned that if Rockefeller should be elected, the citizen could expect to see a Negro running the state police "and probably a number of patrolmen in your area." Shortly afterward, Raney and his fellow trustees voted not to integrate the university's dormitories. This was some years before the athletic program was integrated, with notable success. Faubus was yet to be converted. In 1963, he wrote to a Texas correspondent that he had "never known of any good to come from integrated athletics."

More ominously, the governor sent a veiled threat to any university faculty who went too far in promoting integration. When a Fayetteville man wrote to Faubus complaining that certain professors had threatened to boycott his restaurant if he refused to integrate it, he wrote back asking for the teachers' names. "We will then have a much better opportunity to correct the situation," he said. The governor's office kept a list of university teachers and staff members known to be anti-Faubus.

His rancor toward the university continued for years. In his last year as governor, he interceded with the institution's board of trustees to suggest that an unfriendly law professor be fired. The man had made a speech to the Young Democrats criticizing the Faubus administration. He found work in another state one jump ahead of the axe.

Part of this was traditional power politics. Faubus, like other politicians, wanted to reward his friends and punish his enemies. He was not above reminding state employees who had been patronizing the wrong motel at Lake Village that they were expected to do business with one owned by a friend of his. When a Little Rock legislator began to cause trouble for the state Employment Security Division, the agency's director tried to persuade a banker with a large deposit of state money to put his vice president into the race against the legislator. As leverage, the director pointedly reminded the banker that the governor could put that state money in another bank. The ploy didn't work.

But what was happening to Faubus on the race question was politics of a different order. Here was an issue that threatened to violate the rules of the great game. There is evidence that some of the shift in Faubus's public utterance during those years was more than gamesmanship or cynical opportunism. For a few years, his beliefs on race seemed to match his public image.

Sometimes it was difficult to know whether an utterance was something he believed or simply a provocation to annoy his enemies. After a series of ownership changes, the paper that had been John Wells's prickly *Arkansas Recorder* became Faubus's. He renamed it the *Arkansas Statesman* and turned it into a vehicle for segregationist and states' rights thinking. The paper reprinted a sympathetic appraisal of Carlton Putnam's book *Race and Reason* claiming scientific evidence that the brains of Negroes were physically undeveloped in the areas governing higher intelligence, thus limiting their ability to reason and exercise judgment. In later years, Faubus said he did not believe that and that all such racist material was put into the paper not by him but by his paid editor. But during that same period, although he had carefully avoided labeling himself as a segregationist, he seriously considered the possibility that a segregated society might be preferable. In any event, he wanted nothing to shake the loyalty of his segregationist admirers.

Occasionally, he pulled back from the racial abyss. He scolded a zealous Little Rock follower, saying, "I think you go too far when you object to Negroes participating in sports." It was clear that he referred to segregated sports. Just weeks after comparing the federal court in New Orleans to Nazis for enforcing desegregation, he shunned a chance to join Louisiana's white supremacist leader Willie Rainach in bolting the Democratic party. And a few months later he ridiculed a publication of the States' Right party that declared the trial of the Nazi Adolf Eichmann to be a "propaganda hoax."

Nevertheless, the state he led during this period was more bitterly divided than at any time since Reconstruction. Even the raucous Jeff Davis, a master of divisiveness, had always diluted his harsh rhetoric with a wink and a nudge. Faubus never winked. His campaign rallies were intensely partisan, and his followers let their anger show in their reactions to his words. I remember a rally at the farming town of Hazen sometime in the early 1960s. It was the governor's last appearance of the day. The crowd heard him in a clearing on the edge of town, well away from any store or house. He began speaking as the sun went down. Half an hour into his standard speech, he brought up his favorite enemy, the *Arkansas Gazette*. This was part of every campaign speech. I was long since accustomed to hearing my paper and its editors denounced. But on this night, Faubus's anger rubbed off on the east Arkansas crowd. Just before he went on to another subject, he said, "The *Gazette* has a man here in the crowd tonight." A dozen men glared at me in what felt like pure hatred. After the crowd thinned out, Faubus half-apologized, saying he hoped I didn't take his remarks personally. A few years later, I would feel the same hostility in the crowds of George C. Wallace as he fanned the emotions of his people with his them–against–us rhetoric.

Faubus found ways to amplify his racial populism beyond Arkansas. He never got the credit he deserved for his instruction in how to exploit the hundred-year-old willingness of southerners to hate the central government. In addition to his early efforts against Brownell and the federal judiciary, he anticipated the later adventures of Wallace by picking fights with the Kennedy administration, supposedly populated by liberals, at every opportunity. The Freedom Riders who tried to integrate buses and bus stations across the South in 1961 gave him a chance to assail one of the South's favorite villains, the president's brother Atty. Gen. Robert F. Kennedy, in a tart and well-publicized exchange of telegrams. The Justice Department tried to protect the riders with marshals; Faubus labeled them outside agitators.

He found another national forum for his views when President Kennedy visited Arkansas in 1963, six weeks before his death, to dedicate Greers Ferry Dam. In his welcoming speech, the governor delivered a scarcely disguised attack on Kennedy for his civil rights advocacy. Jim Johnson called afterward to congratulate him and to tell him that he was in better shape than ever with the segregationists, that he had knocked the wind out of certain extremist leaders who had started to turn against him and had "left them looking for a place to spit."

Faubus was as stunned as most other Americans when the president was assassinated. He clearly did not share the sentiment of some of his admirers who applauded the killing. One of them wrote to Faubus on the twenty-fifth anniversary of Kennedy's death to recall how pleased he and his friends had been to hear of the

*Pres. John F. Kennedy flanked by Faubus and
Sen. John L. McClellan at Fort Smith in 1961.*

shooting. But when Faubus elected not to go to Washington for the funeral, citing security and transportation problems, a number of ordinary Arkansawyers thought he was catering to the fanatical right wing again.

One who grieved was Sam Faubus. He had become an outspoken fan of Kennedy. One of the thrills of his life was shaking the president's hand and chatting with him at Greers Ferry. Sometimes under his own name and sometimes under the alias of Jimmie Higgins, Sam wrote several letters to the editor excoriating Kennedy's detractors among white supremacists and reactionaries. Replying to the claim that the Communists were behind integration and Negro voting rights, he wrote, "If that is true that is the best thing I have heard about the Communists." Orval finally wrote a letter to Sam urging him to stop writing to the newspapers, saying he was playing into the hands of Orval's enemies. He delayed mailing it, and when Sam fell terminally ill he forgot it.

Perhaps under the goad of the race conflict, Faubus began to reveal other conservative ideas that had lain dormant in him. Not surprisingly, he had always been partial to rural areas and rural values. Now he went further and lamented the growing urbanization of America, suggesting that country people were generally of a higher moral quality than city people. He declared himself solidly behind the biblical account of man's origins and against Darwinian evolution. He believed in capital punishment and—over the heartfelt objections of his friend Witt Stephens—presided over the execution of several murderers. He carried his states' rights conviction to the extreme of endorsing a scheme to erect a new supercourt of the fifty state supreme court justices with the power to overturn certain Supreme Court decisions. He defended Arkansas's so-called right-to-work law, even though it was anathema to his friends in organized labor. He opposed federal gun-control legislation and attempts in Congress to soften the restrictive federal laws on immigration. The 1960s counterculture enraged him. He saw the country under attack by "immoral hippies, dirty, shiftless beatnicks [sic], lawless demonstrators, and misguided college know-it-alls . . . directed by communists." He lamented the efforts of these people to discredit J. Edgar Hoover, the director of the FBI, and to corrupt the army. During that era, it was a rare Arkansawyer over the age of thirty, black or white, who did not share his view of hippies and college know-it-alls.

The lions of the Right recognized Faubus's value to the cause. He found himself in demand as a speaker and spokesman. H. L. Hunt, the Texas oil billionaire and financier of right-wing causes, became friendly. His Life-Line Foundation, Inc., which broadcast programs on more than three hundred radio and television stations, offered Faubus air time for commentaries. He declined, but maintained contact with Hunt and his political enterprises.

Anti-communism blossomed in the South during the late 1950s and early 1960s. It was as if the seeds sown by McCarthy in the early 1950s were blown south and lay dormant until they were watered by the showers of racial turmoil. For there was no doubt in the minds of the segregationists that they were fighting not just the Negroes but also the larger menace of international communism. All across Dixie, political leaders hastened to brand their enemies in the civil rights movement as Communists or fellow travelers. The Rev. Dr. Martin Luther King Jr. was widely libeled as a Communist or a tool of the party. The Mississippi Sovereignty Commission, financed by state funds, planted an article in Mississippi's largest black newspaper suggesting that King was linked to the Communist party. Faubus was happy to align himself with the Red hunters.

His right-wing contacts proved useful in a context somewhat more parochial than international conspiracy. It is a custom of politicians to keep track of the vulnerabilities of others in the trade on the theory that one might someday want to sue for the fellow's job. Faubus began compiling a file on Sen. J. W. Fulbright in the late 1950s. The senator would run for reelection in 1962, and Faubus figured he could defeat him if he tried. His Fulbright file was notable for its emphasis on communism.

Fulbright's enemies decided after his attacks on McCarthy that he was soft on communism. By the early 1960s, he had become one of the main targets of the far right. H. L. Hunt and his many associates used every forum at their command to tie Fulbright to the Communist conspiracy and its presumed goal of world government. Fulbright in 1961 exposed the U.S. military's involvement with the far-right movement, and that brought more wrath down on him.

Harding College, a Church of Christ school at Searcy, joined the military in sponsoring a seminar on anti-communism. The speakers found targets far beyond the Kremlin; virtually every American institution or person of liberal standing was tied to the Communist party in some manner. Fulbright, one of the main villains, fired back, calling Harding part of the extreme-right movement. Faubus was pleased to join the debate on the side of Fulbright's critics. He wrote to the college president, "I had always been under the impression that you people were regular, patriotic Americans, teaching the time-honored principles of industry, thrift, and virtue to your fine students."

Weeks later, Faubus wrote to the president again to say that a lot of people wanted Fulbright out of the Senate for smearing patriotic Americans. "A lot of work will be required in bringing about the Senator's defeat," he added portentously. To another correspondent, the governor accused Fulbright of Communist appeasement and said his misguided action "lends the greatest encouragement to the enemies of America." In the end, he decided against running for the Senate in 1962. But he kept his Fulbright file up to date. Communism continued to dominate it through the 1960s, especially after Fulbright became the leading Senate critic of the Vietnam War.

While Orval snuggled closer to the anti-Communists, his father conducted guerrilla warfare on the other side. Sam sent a letter to the editor of the *Gazette* denouncing Orval's friends at Harding College as "nothing but a gang of reactionaries doing everything they can against labor and everything else that is progressive."

Orval continued to blame the Communists for almost every initiative of the civil rights movement. He saw the hands of the Reds behind the various civil rights bills debated in Congress. When the Voting Rights Bill of 1965 was considered during the worst of the outrages committed against blacks trying to vote in Alabama, Faubus perceived the threat to the country to be the internal dissension created by "the very diligent and astute efforts of the Communists at propagandizing the people." He voiced no sympathy for the disfranchised millions of African Americans in the neighboring Deep South.

Nearer home, he happily signed a bill making membership in the Communist party a felony punishable by six years in prison.

His Department of Education hastily complied with a legislative directive to root out subversive and un-American philosophies from the state's public school textbooks. None was found, but the commissioner suggested that key legislators might want to sit alongside local school personnel and take a closer look. "We want it clearly understood," he said, "that the Department is making no claims with reference to the purity of all textbook materials."

The governor and his employees furthered the notion that any liberal organization that meddled in integration must be Communist or at least pink. At the top of the list, year after year, was the *Arkansas Gazette*. Heiskell's paper could raise Faubus's bile even at the end of his long tenure. He wrote to one man in 1966, "The *Gazette* seldom endorses any cause or action unless it is atheistic, immoral, or pro-Communist." His *Arkansas Statesman* regularly targeted another liberal institution, the Southern Regional Council. That Atlanta-based organization was a treasure-trove of information on the race issue. It made no secret of its liberal bias. The *Statesman*, repeating information from the right-wing circuit, accused the council of being infiltrated by Reds. An alert Hot Springs man notified the governor that he had spotted the director of that "Red front" as one of the speakers at a meeting of the Arkansas Council on Human Relations. The citizen seemed not to know that the Arkansas Council was an affiliate of the Southern Regional Council, a bond that certainly would have frightened him further. The governor thanked the man for his help, pondering, no doubt, the torment the poor fellow would suffer if he knew the truth about Faubus's own left-wing upbringing.

Orval Faubus was conducting a kind of war—not a shooting war but one that went beyond the normal verbal hostilities of American politics. Toward the end of his life, he passed off his angry rhetoric of the 1950s and 1960s as the natural assertions one would expect in a propaganda campaign. He was besieged, he said, and he fought back with harsh language. But it is clear from his actions and statements at the time that he was motivated by something deeper than cynicism. For a period of some years, he became a true believer. He had chosen sides. He fought with every weapon he could find.

It was as if Arkansas in the mid-twentieth century had become his personal battleground in still another engagement of the Civil War. He was choosing at last to join forces with his great-grandmother Minerva, the last Confederate in his boyhood home, the Union-hating woman who should have taken her bitterness alone to the grave. The running skirmish under Faubus's direction was a little like the Battle of New Orleans, which took place two weeks after the end of the War of 1812, except this time ignited, preposterously enough, a century after the war that it properly belonged to.

CHAPTER 23

The conspiracy was everywhere. There were the Little Rock husband and wife who were overheard "talking integration." Not surprisingly, they had a friend who was having mixed-race parties at his house.

Then there was the variety store with black and white customers who were said to favor integration. Two state employees had been shopping there; they needed to be identified.

An informant saw two white women driving cars carrying black children. The same informant a few weeks later spotted an even more alarming spectacle: a car with a white woman at the wheel and a black man in the seat beside her.

These and dozens of other episodes of similar gravity were quietly and seriously investigated by the Arkansas State Police during the years after the Central High crisis. Such Inspector Clouseau preoccupations might seem far removed from arresting speeders and drunk drivers. But from 1957 until the end of Faubus's tenure in 1967, his state police doubled as juvenile tricksters on a kind of year-round Halloween spree. It would have been ludicrous except for the threat they posed. The agency had its well-financed Criminal Investigation Division, separate from the familiar highway troopers. The CID busied itself as an instrument of harassment, intimidation, and spying. It made it its business to keep track of Faubus's political enemies. Those ranged from civil rights activists to the country-club establishment of Little Rock.

In pursuit of its mission, the CID infiltrated organizations, tapped telephones, secretly tape-recorded meetings, compiled lists of group members and suspected sympathizers, traced car ownership through license numbers, fingered state employees suspected of integrationist or anti-Faubus sympathies, and collected damaging personal information on political opponents and seemingly ordinary citizens. The gumshoes were especially alert for signs of adultery and homosexuality. But their long-term mission was to root out Communists, left-wingers, and others suspected of furthering the international conspiracy against the southern way of life.

Not much came of it all. A small number of people were fired or pressured to leave their jobs, and the threat of official blackmail was sobering. But compared to some other southern states, Arkansas escaped with minimal damage, unless you count the cost to the state's decent opinion of itself.

The same anxieties were being acted out across the South during that time. Mississippi used a sovereignty commission, which worked in effect as an arm of the Citizens Council in harassing integrationists. The commission collected damaging information and hounded people from their jobs. In Florida, the same work was done by a committee of the legislature. The committee and its staff investigated hundreds of Floridians looking for sexual as well as political aberrations. They used intimidating tactics to persuade people to confess, and they established a system of informants to spy on fellow citizens. Similar operations were conducted in other southern states.

In Arkansas, the state police detectives took their work seriously and passed all the choicest findings to the governor. They took special delight in uncovering sexual peccadilloes. They opened files on a number of well-known Little Rock businessmen who frequented a black nightclub and reportedly had sex there with black women. Their names were forwarded to Faubus by Herman Lindsey, the director of the state police. In another part of town, two investigators happened to see a black woman and a white man "embracing fondly" on a street corner. They followed the couple, traced a car license number, and found that the car belonged to a local television personality. They learned later that the man in the embrace was not the on-air showman but a faceless producer. Nevertheless, it made a titillating report. Lindsey's letter to Faubus said the incident "could be important." And a state police informant who spotted an attractive young white woman riding with a

Negro in a car commented, "Appeared to be more than a driver-passenger relationship." The police traced the car to an auto salesman who lived in Pulaski Heights.

Anyone who spoke favorably of integration risked being overheard and reported to the CID. A confidential informant reported that a woman employee of the Little Rock health department was a member of the NAACP and had received known integrationists in her office. Another informant reported that the principal of Forest Heights Junior High School was "an outright integrationist." A black porter at the Capital Hotel was said to be active in the NAACP. He was also said to be a pimp who sometimes slept with a white prostitute from North Little Rock.

Nat Griswold, a Methodist minister who headed the Arkansas Council on Human Relations, was an easy and obvious target because of the council's connection to the liberal Southern Regional Council. An investigator staked out a council meeting in October 1958 and traced auto licenses to a number of prominent Little Rock people, all known to sympathize with the integration movement. One man was identified as a professor at the University of Arkansas College of Medicine. "Subject was convicted of draft dodging during the Korean War," the report said.

Anyone drawing a state paycheck got special attention. An employee of the state health department was seen at an integrated meeting in September 1958. Someone in a state-owned car was seen entering a store known to be patronized by Daisy Bates.

The Bateses and their organization, along with the Urban League, were studied intently. NAACP chapters all over Arkansas were watched constantly. License numbers were recorded and traced by informants who shadowed the organization's meetings. An investigator spotted a newspaper advertisement soliciting members for the Little Rock Urban League and announcing a meeting. He parked outside trying to identify any white people who went in, but had to park too far from the door to be sure of the color of the faces. He satisfied himself by recording the license numbers of forty-four cars and tracing their owners.

The detectives kept a close watch on the personal lives of Daisy and L. C. Bates. Visitors to their home were regularly identified and their names placed in the files. The armed men who regularly guarded their house were harassed. Late on the night of August 12, 1959, an undercover state police detective arrested three of the guards who had followed his unmarked car out of the Bates neighborhood. One was a well-known black physician. The detective confiscated a checkbook from the guards' car and meticulously typed a list of all the checks recently written from it. Several were to "NAACP Home Office."

The finances of the Bateses' newspaper were subjected to scrutiny. A black man who had once owned a part interest in the *State Press* told the state police he was owed money by the Bateses. He named another Bates creditor, a Mississippian, and offered to persuade the second man to invite L. C. Bates for a poker game, then have the local authorities raid the party. Apparently, the scheme was not pursued.

A state police captain wrote to the police department of Youngstown, Ohio, asking for information on L. C. Bates. The reply named an Ohio woman as Bates's first wife and added that he had asked for a divorce in 1942, but she did not know whether he had obtained it. Another agent spent a day in the Shelby County Clerk's office in Memphis looking for a record of the marriage of L. C. and Daisy. They found none.

A confidential informant provided a thorough accounting of the Bates family finances including the amount they had paid for a city lot, how much life insurance L. C. had, his salary, and the annual revenue of their newspaper.

The police suspected anyone connected with the arts of being part of the leftist conspiracy. They learned that a white couple was giving dance lessons at a Negro community center. Another report began, "Indications point that anything pertaining to Fine Arts, such as acting, dancing, directors of such come from the controversial crowd." It went on to name several suspects, including a director of the community theater, an opera singer who was paid to sing at a Jewish synagogue, and Mrs. Winthrop Rockefeller, who promoted the arts at all levels.

The Women's Emergency Committee became a favorite target of the CID. The committee's meetings were infiltrated by women who reported the names of those attending and what was said. The investigators were shocked to learn that the wife of a highway department employee was one of the heretics. In case an informant missed someone, she copied the license numbers on all cars parked in front of each meeting place. Prominent members of the committee were followed by uniformed state police troopers when they drove through black neighborhoods.

Churches were watched. Any black church that had white people at its meetings was listed in the file. A member of the segregationist Mothers League, one of the agency's volunteer spies, submitted a list of seventeen people (identified by auto licenses) at a meeting of Unitarians. Her report said, "Reason for checking this meeting is subversion. It is my firm belief that these people have no religious background, and there is little actually known what their real purpose is in assembling." The suspects included a conductor for the Missouri Pacific Railroad and the dean of the College of Medicine.

A spy attended an integrated Christian Fellowship conference at Petit Jean Mountain and reported half a dozen "revolting" statements that had been tossed out, including, "Christianity hasn't added anything to the world that was not here before the birth of Christ."

The Pulaski Heights Christian Church was known as a hotbed of integration, and the CID lavished attention on it. At one Sunday evening service, the licenses of cars parked out front were checked to establish ownership. After the pastor offended some of his congregation with a sermon against segregation, a dissenting member surreptitiously obtained a copy of the sermon and passed it to the CID. Forrest Rozzell, executive secretary of the Arkansas Education Association and a frequent political ally of Faubus on school matters, was a leading member of the church. The state police informant reported that Rozzell was damned on two counts: he was a close associate of the pastor, Bert Cartwright, and he was connected somehow to the NAACP. "A further check of Mr. Rozzell's activities and his associates will be made in the future," the investigator wrote.

Faubus and his investigators took an ever more sprightly interest in the civil rights movement that was spreading across the South. Arkansas was little more than an afterthought to the national organizations promoting black equality, but the movement seemed to prove their suspicions. Here was conspiracy manipulated from afar. Never mind that almost all of the participants were home-grown. Several students at the predominantly black University of Arkansas at Pine Bluff, then Arkansas AM and N, were expelled for taking part in civil rights demonstrations in 1963. When a number of black leaders styling themselves the Pine Bluff Citizens Committee wrote to Faubus asking him to help reinstate the students, he briskly turned them down, then instructed one of the CID men to check out the activities of the members.

The CID was especially interested in William W. Hansen, a white northerner who had come south to lead Arkansas's Student Non-Violent Coordinating Committee. The agency got a full report when he married a black woman in the fall of 1963. Its investigators sounded miffed when the Pine Bluff police chief passed on word of the impending wedding to the FBI but snubbed the state police. Hansen worked to register blacks to vote. Agents followed him as he transported Negroes to the polls on election day. The state police revoked his auto registration after they arrested him for speeding, then arranged with a small-town police chief to have him arrested again for owning a car that was not registered. Hansen complained to the FBI that his civil rights had been violated. Federal agents tangled with the state investigators over that.

The FBI and the CID at times seemed on the verge of open warfare. The CID uncovered evidence that the FBI was tapping its telephones in 1962. An alarmed Lindsey sent along the evidence to Faubus, saying "it raises a question as to just how far have they gone or how far they will go in applying such methods."

The state agency apparently limited its own wiretapping to blacks and whites suspected of integrationist activities. In 1961, it tape-recorded a lengthy telephone conversation between two black political leaders as they discussed lobbying members of the legislature. They spoke with predictable candor about the reliability of certain central Arkansas legislators.

The CID continued its interest in the university. The state police enlisted the black house mother of a residence for black students to report on integrationist activities on campus. She submitted the names of students and teachers whom she observed crossing the color line in their friendships. She fingered a large number of white and black university people who were perceived as agitating for integration. She named leaders of civil rights organizations who visited Fayetteville.

When Faubus was picketed by a group of university students during a speech at nearby Springdale, the CID traced their cars and identified them. They included the president of the student body, the editor of the student newspaper, a homecoming queen described as "very pretty, but very silly," and about a dozen members of fraternities and sororities. One was David Watkins of Hope, an acquaintance of young Bill Clinton and, in time, a member of his White House staff.

The Ku Klux Klan occasionally found its way into the state police files. A mother complained that a Klan meeting just south of Little Rock, featuring a large burning cross, had frightened her children. A detective investigated and found nothing out of the ordinary. The group was in its usual meeting place where it had gathered for the last five years. He noted that the caller was new in the area. The CID stepped in when the Klan began to suspect one of its members of being an informant for the FBI. It learned by means not explained that his personal effects contained the names and addresses of several military people and of an intelligence officer in the U.S. Treasury Department. That seemed to confirm the Klan's fears. What became of the informant was not reported.

If the investigators took a tolerant view of the Klan, it cut no slack for left-wingers. Numerous people thought to be advocates of world government or Communist sympathizers were investigated. One suspect's children were named, and a son was "alleged to be effeminate." The same man was described as an excellent neighbor except that he had been having Negroes in his home regularly and had recently "come out in the open with some of his leftist inclinations." Another Little Rock person was seen passing out literature to teenagers. "It is believed that this is Communist literature," the report said. Then it added ominously that the subject "has numerous contacts in Hot Springs, both Negro and White." A white teacher at the predominantly black Philander Smith College was described as a member of the Communist party who had been charged with contempt of Congress for refusing to cooperate with a congressional committee. His state police file was lengthy. A *New York Times* reporter who allegedly admitted to having been a Communist during his student days at Columbia University was investigated after he came to Little Rock to cover the Central High story. The report noted that he was being furnished a desk and typewriter at the *Gazette* by a fellow Columbia alumnus, Harry Ashmore. Then it added, "Edwin Dunaway [a liberal lawyer and former state supreme court justice] of Little Rock is another alumnus of Columbia."

Lt. Howard Chandler was the most zealous of the CID Communist-hunters. He finally ran Arkansas's Red conspiracy to ground early in 1961 when he uncovered the entire membership of the Little Rock chapter of the Council on Foreign Relations. In a long report to Faubus, Chandler described the council as "the invisible government of the United States." Its aim, he said, was to convert America into a Socialist nation, then make it part of a one-world Socialist system. The council subverted ordinary Americans through a program called Great Decisions, in which leftist literature was spread across the nation through elitist discussion groups. Chandler's list of Little Rock people involved in Great Decisions was a Who's Who of the capital's business and professional establishment. On the list were industrialists, lawyers, real estate and department store executives, insurance agents, and investment bankers. "The above list is bound to be the source of irritation in Little Rock," Chandler wrote, "since these constitute the hard core nucleus of the 'extreme left wing.'"

While secret investigations were conducted by the CID, highway patrol troopers were occasionally used in activities related to integration. In 1965, troopers forcefully broke up a demonstration at the capitol. An integrated group led by the Student Non-Violent Coordinating Committee picketed to try to open the capitol cafeteria to black customers. Hansen, SNCC's white leader, was slightly hurt when a trooper hurled him against a wall. A white reporter for the *Pine Bluff Commercial* was attacked by another trooper. The CID took it from there. The reporter was investigated. The detectives learned that the reporter's marriage was in trouble and that he was "close" to Hansen, meaning that he was an integrationist and a bad husband. The bounder went on to a distinguished career in Philadelphia and Little Rock.

Faubus, in later years, denied ever ordering the state police to investigate his enemies. He said the CID agents themselves initiated the investigations, probably to please him and their other superiors.

"I never at any time instructed or even suggested or inferred or in any way indicated that I wanted any surveillance of my political opponents," he said. But the work of the CID coincided with Faubus's growing anger at his integrationist opponents, and there is no evidence that he did anything to discourage the harassment and secret surveillance. Indeed, he quietly encouraged some of it, especially when the information gleaned could be politically useful.

Faubus wrote to state senator Dan Sprick to pass on information about some troublesome constituents. The information almost certainly came from the state police. Sprick was curious about a group of women representing various ethnic backgrounds who were speaking to Parent-Teacher Association meetings. They had got Sprick's attention by advocating equality and integrated facilities. Faubus gave a little background on each panel member and added, "This is a propaganda group for the integrationists."

A north Arkansas family that had long been active in politics crossed Faubus early in his career. After he took control of the state police, he instructed the director to "keep an eye on those boys" when they visited Little Rock. Family members were tipped off by a friend in the state police who advised them that if they intended to have a drink at the Tanglewood Club—a Little Rock night spot—they should know they were being watched.

Faubus received word that a state employee in Yell County had supported one of his opponents, Dale Alford, in the 1962 gubernatorial primary. He asked the CID to find out. Lieutenant Chandler went to Dardanelle, made extensive inquiries, and reported directly to the governor. The employee's brother had briefly deserted to the Alford camp, but the state employee himself had been loyal to Faubus throughout. The governor's supporters there thought it would be a mistake to fire him.

Another police investigator volunteered his thoughts on a political squabble in Greene County. He wrote a memo to his boss, Lindsey, who passed it on to Faubus. The investigator advised Faubus "not in any manner" to have anything to do with a certain legislative candidate because the connection would hurt him with the prevailing powers in the county. He ended the memo by asking Lindsey to let him know if new information on Greene County surfaced because he would like to "weigh it and put in my two cents worth."

Lindsey apparently encouraged this sort of political activism in his subordinates. As a state government operative since the 1940s, he had his own contacts across the state, and he used them to keep Faubus informed. He wrote numerous memos to his boss giving his estimate of various local political intrigues.

The state police were used in Faubus's election campaigns. Supporters of Joe Hardin in the 1960 Democratic primary were tailed from one campaign meeting to another. Licenses were traced to identify those attending. State police surveillance revealed that a friend of a prominent Little Rock banker was supporting Hardin. It was suggested that the governor might remove state funds from the banker's institution. Lindsey passed on several rumors of disloyalty and anti-Faubus sentiment among employees and prominent businessmen.

Political use of the state police did not start with Faubus. During the 1954 election campaign, Cherry had sent state detectives to Alabama and Tennessee to try to uncover any left-wing connections that Faubus might have had there during his Commonwealth days. They went to Highlander Folk School looking for information that could be used against him.

Faubus owed much of his political success to his network of contacts throughout Arkansas. The reporters who covered him professed to believe that he had a kind of mystical power to divine what "the people" were thinking. It is clear that his divination was grounded in something less than the supernatural. The bloodhounds of the state police were merely one small part of a vast political apparatus that carried information to the governor's office and then, when necessary, carried favors, threats, or penalties back down the line.

The overriding purpose of the system was Faubus's reelection every two years. In that, he broke all records by being elected to six terms, double the old record set by Jeff Davis. He defeated twenty-eight men in general and primary elections before leaving office in 1967. He extinguished the political careers of twenty-six of them.

<table>
<tr><td>

CHAPTER

24

</td><td>

It came to appear that Orval Faubus was invincible. His enemies, meaning no compliment, compared him to Huey P. Long. Some considered him a dictator and grimly joked that he had become governor-for-life. But if this was dicta-

</td></tr>
</table>

torship, it lacked a certain firmness. Orval Faubus had captured Arkansas not so much by a ruthless, unceasing abuse of power as through shrewd gamesmanship and good luck. Like any gambler, his great fear was that his luck would run out.

To protect his longevity and extend his luck, he built an effective machine of local vote rousters tied to the weight of state government. The spooks and Peeping Toms of the state police were a troubling but insignificant part of that machine. Their gumshoe exploits provided little information that was politically useful, and their authors had only negligible influence on elections. The real work that translated into continuous victory at the ballot box was the day-to-day juggling of interests by the man at the top. In that task, he was aided by dozens of associates at the capitol and hundreds more in the network of agencies, commissions, advisory boards, and informal political connections from Bentonville in the Ozarks to Eudora in the Mississippi River flats.

It was little appreciated at the time, but the machine was not perfect. Faubus's stunning margin of victory in 1958 had led friends and enemies alike to assume that he had found the key to everlasting success. But he would never again approach the 1958 triumph, and he would become increasingly vulnerable as his administration aged.

In fact, there was just one more easy election. In 1960, he had four opponents: Joseph C. Hardin, a wealthy Grady planter who had been close to Faubus and Witt Stephens and who, along with his wife, had been appointed to important state boards by Faubus; the Rev. H. E. Williams, founder and president of Southern Baptist College at Walnut Ridge—Preacher Williams, Faubus called him; Hal Millsap Jr., a supermarket owner from Siloam Springs who campaigned in a gaudy bus, traveling as it turned out with an expired license; and Bruce Bennett, the showman who as attorney general had danced in Faubus's tracks for years.

Governor and Mrs. Faubus at a football game in Memphis.

PHOTO BY LLOYD DINKINS, *MEMPHIS COMMERCIAL APPEAL;*
FROM THE PERSONAL COLLECTION OF ALTA FAUBUS.

They attacked him vigorously. They suggested that he was becoming a dictator, noting that he had already, in three terms, appointed a majority of the members of 124 boards and commissions. Those included the most important regulatory bodies in the state, among them those that set rates for electricity, gas, transportation, and water.

The opponents would have attacked even more enthusiastically if they had known some of the tactics Faubus was using in the campaign. On his instruction, for example, Jim Bland, the working manager of the campaign, investigated rumors of disaffection among several business people. Faubus fingered one outspoken opponent, a Little Rock businessman who was a partner of a prominent banker. The banker had state funds among his deposits. He might be reminded of that to encourage him to shut his partner's mouth. Bland reported that the banker had solved the problem by contributing to Faubus's campaign. An employee of the Game and Fish Commission was reported to be supporting Hardin. Bland turned that over to Truman Baker, a member of the commission, and suggested that he fire the man after the election "if this bird is guilty."

On the race question, all the opponents professed to be segregationists. Nevertheless, they pilloried Faubus with a confusing avalanche of denunciation. Hardin joined the *Gazette* in lamenting the shame Faubus had brought on the state in 1957. Coming at him from the other side, Williams and Bennett echoed the disaffected Citizens Council and accused him of promoting integration. Bennett went so far as to accuse him of being secretly in league with Daisy Bates. Faubus replied that his real opposition was a hard core of integrationists led locally by the leftist *Gazette* and tied nationally to the liberal conspiracy and the federal government.

The attacks had two effects. First, Faubus was able to persuade the voters that no man could be as bad as his enemies painted him when they used words like tyrant, dictator, Benedict Arnold of the South, Caesar Faubus, and Nero of Arkansas. Second, being attacked from both sides on race left him looking like something of a centrist—traditionally, his most comfortable position.

In the end, the voters seemed impressed by the governor's claim of a "Proven Program of Progress." New industry was coming to the state, though not yet to Little Rock in any quantity. Half a dozen big plants opened during the campaign season in other parts of the state. The Children's Colony was completed in time for the first occupants to move in about ninety days before the first primary. Then there were the regular increases in welfare benefits, the well-publicized improvements in the state's highways (overseen by the "nonpolitical" highway commission dominated by Faubus appointees), and new buildings at the decrepit state hospital for the mentally ill. The progress that Faubus pointed to was real, although his enemies refused to acknowledge that.

He was nominated for a fourth term with almost 59 percent of the vote. Hardin edged out Bennett for a distant second place, a finish that discouraged both from further political advancement. In the November general election, Faubus demolished his Republican opponent, Henry M. Britt of Hot Springs, by more than 2 to 1.

An episode during the 1960 election season demonstrated the shifting reliability of political machines, which seldom belong exclusively to one officeholder. In Arkansas, what was known as the Faubus machine was the same alliance that provided money, energy, and expertise to a number of other politicians. Many of Faubus's powerful friends were also supporters of Sen. John L. McClellan, Rep. Wilbur D. Mills, and other members of Congress. The most notable overlap of support was between Faubus and Sen. J. W. Fulbright. The junior senator was in some ways the most vulnerable of the state's prominent public figures. He was aloof and uncomfortable with ordinary voters who did not share his intellect. But he paid attention to the big economic interests of his state, and they repaid the favor.

Faubus had only limited contact with either senator, but he was more at ease with McClellan. He remembered that McClellan, who could have made a difference for Cherry, had refused to interfere in the 1954 gubernatorial primary. Faubus declined when organized labor urged him to oppose McClellan in 1960. He was less protective of the other senator. Fulbright knew that he would almost certainly be defeated if Faubus chose to run against him in 1962. The polls made that clear.

The Fulbright camp made a decision in 1960 that threatened to wreck the machine that the senator and Faubus depended on. Hoping that someone would defeat Faubus and remove the threat to Fulbright's reelection two years hence, the senator's staff and close associates encouraged various candidates to get into the race against Faubus. They raised out-of-state money for them. They used national Democratic party connections to try to persuade Sid McMath to join the contest, but he refused. Some of Fulbright's Washington aides went to Arkansas and worked in the opposition's campaigns. One was Fred Livingston Jr., who left Fulbright's staff to work for Hardin. His father was one of Faubus's main supporters in Independence County. Faubus explained this filial impertinence by saying, "He got off up at the University, and he went his own way. That happens a lot of times in families."

The ploy backfired. Faubus, of course, learned of it. Even though his share of the 1960 vote was 10 percent less than in 1958, he still made a terrifying spectacle to any Arkansas politician holding an office that the panther of the Ozarks might covet. During the next two years, Faubus took every opportunity to make Fulbright think that he intended to take his job away from him. For example, when it was learned in 1961 that Fulbright had criticized military leaders for conducting right-wing political seminars, reminding them that the Constitution required them to stay out of politics, Faubus happily joined in attacking him for "muzzling the military."

Faubus was only mildly tempted by the Senate. Neither he nor Alta relished the idea of living in Washington. But he thought he would find enough conservative friends there—men like Strom Thurmond of South Carolina—to be happy and effective if he should displace Fulbright. And he was certain he could beat the junior senator, who had notoriously poor political skills. He was astonished one day in a meeting with Fulbright to learn that the one-time Rhodes scholar could not name half the county political leaders in the state. At another meeting, Fulbright proposed asking a leader of the Arkansas River development program to work for the Democratic slate in the upcoming election. Someone said, "Bill, he's a Republican." Fulbright replied, "The hell you say." It was well known in political circles that Fulbright was so little interested in the intricacies of politics that he refused to raise money for his campaigns. His aides had to handle that.

Fulbright was finally saved in 1962 by the big-money machine that he shared with Faubus, but not before he stirred up the panther's wrath once more. Because of a severe population loss during the 1950s, Arkansas's delegation in the House of Representatives was cut from six to four. The powerful Mills, who had not faced serious opposition for years, found himself sharing a district with the suddenly popular Alford. No one knew what Alford might do. He might contest the House seat with Mills. He might aim higher and run against Fulbright.

Mills and Fulbright cooked up a scheme to solve both their problems. Alford would be induced to run for governor. Faubus would handily defeat him and remove the threat permanently from Arkansas politics. There was a slight risk that an annoyed Faubus would jump to the Senate race, instead, and thrash Fulbright. But the senator was aware that Faubus and his wife had no real desire to move east. He also knew that Stephens and the other rich supporters whom he shared with Faubus were leaning on the governor to stay out of Fulbright's race. Thus armed, he and Mills enlisted Stephens and his wealthy pals in their scheme.

Alford was home for Christmas in 1961. It was a Sunday afternoon. He got a phone call from an important businessman, one of the Stephens cabal. The man said, "I have just left a meeting where the governor was. The governor is not going to run, and I am advising you tomorrow morning to call a press conference and announce for governor."

Alford fell for it. Faubus several weeks earlier had hinted that he would support Alford for statewide office—maybe even the governor's office—if he would leave Congress and not run against Mills. When he got the mysterious phone call, Alford mistakenly assumed that Faubus was in on the deal. Actually, the weary Faubus was thinking seriously of retiring, but had not made up his mind. Alford's abrupt announcement that he was running for governor nettled him. Nevertheless, he took his time making a decision. He waited a full three months—plenty of time for Fulbright to worry that he might have made a mistake. Then on March 31, 1962, the governor went on television and announced that he would not run for a fifth term.

He was relaxed for the first time in years as he felt the rigors of politics releasing their grip. He slept better, ate with better appetite. He quit smoking. Alta was content.

Then he grew restless. People from around the state, old supporters, leaned on him to reconsider. One night in their living room, Alta, without preface, blurted, "Well, I know what you're up against. If you want to run again, it will be all right with me."

That was a turning point. But he waited another month. With him apparently leaving the scene, at least thirty men were toying with making the race. And those were just the Democrats. On the other side, Winthrop Rockefeller was being encouraged to enter the contest. On May 3, just before the filing deadline, Faubus reentered the race and put an end to those dreams. Even after flushing most of the field away, Faubus still faced six Democrats and two little-known Republicans. That was the largest field of gubernatorial candidates since 1948.

The main opposition would come from Alford and two others. Sid McMath, Faubus's old mentor, was considered the strongest challenger. He had the backing not only of the Little Rock liberals but also of large numbers of old friends from his days in the governor's office. The third strong opponent was Marvin Melton, a Jonesboro businessman and planter and a former state senator and president of the state chamber of commerce. He had considered running in 1960. By one account, Melton had encouraged McMath to run in 1962 and had suggested that if one of them made it into a runoff with Faubus, the other would throw his support to him.

Less than a month into the campaign, Melton abruptly withdrew. He said Faubus's people had dried up his campaign financing. If true, that would have attested to the power of the Faubus machine. The real story was more intricate. Faubus and his friends learned that Melton had helped start an insurance company and had sold stock for fifteen dollars a share after paying one dollar for it. That was common practice at the time, and legal, but not the sort of thing that a candidate for office wished to explain publicly. Witt Stephens and others tipped off a newspaper reporter. When the reporter routinely asked Melton about it, the candidate realized that he had been quietly and neatly neutered.

Meanwhile, Alford began to understand that he had taken on a more complicated task than he had expected. Jim Johnson had warned him not to give in to the blandishments of the Stephens crowd. "They'll not give you all that money," he had told Alford.

"They're promising you support that they'll never deliver, and once you get in that governor's race, you will be left on your own." That turned out to be the case. Stephens eventually revealed the contempt in which Alford was held. Referring to the eye doctor's meteoric rise and fall in politics, he said, "Somebody said Dale Alford is liken to a wasp. He is bigger when he is first hatched than he'll ever be again."

The big money, like water seeking its natural path, went back to Faubus. If the latter had hard feelings over being used by his rich friends, he rationalized them away. "They figured I was so strong that I could beat the tar out of Alford," he said. "I don't think they figured on McMath getting in. Now, sometimes these people can out-maneuver themselves."

The money came back, but the Citizens Council did not. It made its alienation public. Faubus, the council said, had turned out to be "a toothless tiger." The council went for Alford.

The opposition candidates emphasized the growing concentration of power in the hands of Faubus and his friends. They said he had sold out to the gambling, utility, and liquor interests. Harry Hastings, who dominated the wholesale liquor business in central Arkansas, had become a friend of Faubus and inhabited a place of importance in the shadows of power. Illegal casino gambling was once again flourishing at Hot Springs. There were constant rumors of payoffs in high places. But the real power in Arkansas, McMath said, had become Witt Stephens. He admitted that Stephens had supported him when he was governor. "But he did not take over my administration, and he did not control my Public Service Commission." He said the state government had forty million dollars deposited in twenty-seven banks that were dominated by Stephens and that those bankers had been coerced into supporting Faubus.

Faubus denied it, even though all the while he was doing business as usual with Stephens. Two weeks after reentering the race in May, he wrote to Stephens urging him to build a pipeline to help a group of people get natural gas. Stephens did it. During the campaign, Faubus learned that a Stephens employee at Fort Smith was working to defeat him. Stephens investigated to find out who it was.

As in previous elections, Faubus concentrated on his record of improved services and growing industrialization. He won without a runoff. However, his margin was the thinnest since 1954. He had defeated Francis Cherry by less than 1 percent. He edged out the field of McMath and all by 1.6 percent. No one opponent did very well. McMath ran a poor second, followed by Alford, Vernon H. Whitten, Kenneth Coffelt, and David A. Cox. But cumulatively, the challengers piled up almost 200,000 votes. Faubus escaped a runoff by less than 6,500 votes. The cities went against him decisively; only his strength in the delta and the hill counties saved him.

He went on to an easy 73 percent victory over an unknown Republican in November, but the Democratic primary had shaken him. Since his peak of nearly 69 percent in 1958, he had dropped more than 17 percent of his support in four years. At that rate, he could not survive another serious election.

The 1962 general election was memorable for another reason. The voters approved a constitutional amendment to permit voting machines. It would be some time before any were bought, but the old corrupt system of the poll tax was on its way out. With voting machines, Arkansas voters would enjoy a genuinely secret ballot for the first time. Chicanery and miscounting had been common throughout the state's history. In the same election that saw voting machines approved, an election judge at Pine Bluff watched helplessly as the other workers at her polling place split up the ballots and retired to separate rooms to count them in private.

There was growing sentiment for an all-round clean-up of the electoral process. By the 1960s, even the old practice of influencing male voters with strong drink was disappearing. Faubus himself had used that device back in Madison County. He and a partner were making the rounds the night before the election of 1946, in which he was a candidate for county judge, delivering whiskey to be handed out the next day. They ran out before they reached St. Paul. "If you didn't have some there," he explained, "they would sull up and stay at home and you'd just lose a lot of votes." He and his friend forded the White River in an old Jeep just before daylight and rousted a moonshiner out of bed. His uncombed hair stood up, and he paused every few minutes to scratch his head and remember where he had hidden his bottles. Some were under bushes and

Rodney Dungan's photograph at the Guion Ferry dedication in 1962 became the most famous image of Faubus. Dungan leaned across another photographer seated beside him in a car and shot the picture through a closed window. When the picture appeared in the Arkansas Gazette, *a friend of one of the governor's opponents in the 1962 election telephoned the editor and demanded, "Who are you for in this campaign?"*

leaves. Others were in stumps. He ran back and forth gathering up bottles until he had enough to lubricate the election machinery of St. Paul. "We carried the township pretty good," Faubus said.

When the voting-machine amendment was proposed, Faubus was ambivalent. He said they might be a good idea in the cities, but rural areas didn't need them—an odd observation considering that most of the state's vote fraud occurred in rural precincts. But when his advisor Bill Smith agreed to be the chief spokesman for the voting-machine campaign, teaming up with Faubus's old adversaries in the League of Women Voters, that was taken as a sign that the governor secretly wanted them. No organized opposition developed. The amendment passed by about twenty-six hundred votes.

Some of the county political machines that might have been expected to fight the devices supported them with a surprising enthusiasm. Smith and Ben Allen, a young associate in his law firm who had helped organize the drive, were having lunch in downtown Little Rock the day after the election. The boss of one of the delta counties walked up to their table and congratulated them. He said, "Ben, I saw you and Bill Smith's name on that voting machine amendment, and I tell you what we did for you. We gave you an extra thousand votes and passed that son of a bitch."

Financed by Rockefeller, the Republican party took an interest in cleaning up elections. Young Tom Eisele, a Hot Springs lawyer, challenged several county political machines in court seeking to end the theft of votes and the forging of absentee ballots. During a trial at Morrilton, he had some harsh things to say about Sheriff Marlin Hawkins, the Conway County boss. Hawkins remonstrated with him as they made their way through the crowd afterward. Someone yelled, "Marlin, hit him!" Eisele escaped attack, there and elsewhere, but he operated under a threatening atmosphere for years.

In 1964, Faubus campaigned as the underdog for the first time in ten years of elections. He had only minor opposition in the Democratic primary, but in the general election the Republicans found a heavyweight, their most serious challenger since Reconstruction. Winthrop Rockefeller, the New York playboy who had settled on his ranch atop Petit Jean Mountain, had been patiently building a party structure in the state. Many believed that the Rockefeller fortune could put him in the governor's office. Faubus believed it; his steady loss of voters in recent elections reminded him of his vulnerability. He was tired and wanted to retire to the Ozarks. But he abhorred the thought of a rich Republican sitting in his chair firing his faithful servants and installing hundreds of his political enemies in positions of influence. He was encouraged in this thinking by the legion of bankers, planters, bond dealers, utility executives, and road contractors who had done well under the Faubus administration, not to mention the hundreds of members of state boards and commissions, every one of whom had been appointed by him.

The governor's first chore was to shape up his troops once again. Any state employees suspected of alienation were whipped into line by the threat of firing. Stern memos went to all department heads urging them to take this election seriously. An aide instructed an operative at the state hospital to check out a rumor that an employee there was "a known Republican." Faubus heard of a couple of highway department employees at Hoxie who were working against him. Disregarding the constitutional prohibition against meddling in that department's affairs, he wrote to one of his appointees on the highway commission and asked him to "straighten out" the pair. A tower man for the state forestry commission was suspected of being a Republican. After being talked to, the man pledged his entire family to the Faubus cause.

State employees contributed to the campaign fund each according to his means. In the state police, for example, majors gave fifty dollars each, captains and lieutenants twenty-five dollars, and sergeants fifteen dollars.

Jobs were provided for election-season supplicants. A central Arkansas legislator found work in the administration for a friend, a cousin, and both his brothers. Another political minor-leaguer wanted a campaign job for his daughter and was so angered at being turned down that he threatened to turn his back on Faubus. The governor wrote to his campaign handler, Jim Bland, and suggested making a place for the young woman. A long-time supporter was risking a split in the Faubus forces in another county over a local feud. He had to be reminded of his higher obligation; Faubus had provided jobs for the man's wife, son, and daughter-in-law. A businessman complained that the administration did not include a single Greek American. He hinted that he could deliver that ethnic vote if he were appointed to a state board—any board. He was assured of the administration's concern.

Some advisors urged Faubus to be tougher on turncoats and slackers. Young Jim McDougal, an ambitious Democrat who was destined for notoriety in his middle age, during the Clinton presidency, wrote him an angry note chastising him for giving patronage jobs to incompetents and known enemies. Instead of throwing patronage to loyal workers like himself, he said, Faubus had listened to a couple of men "who wouldn't throw water on you if you were on fire."

Before confronting Rockefeller, Faubus had to face the prospect of a primary fight that might cripple him for the main match. Dale Alford had announced during the winter that he would run if Faubus didn't, an obvious ploy to nudge the champ aside. It didn't work. Then Guy Jones, one of his opponents in 1954, threatened to take on Faubus again if Faubus didn't help him get back into the state senate. With a combination of counter-threats and placating gestures, he was kept in the senate race, which he eventually won. The gravest danger, though, was from Jim Johnson, who wanted to leave the state supreme court and move into the governor's office. Bill Smith called him to his office and read the riot act. "I guarantee you'll never be governor if you run now," he said. "If you wait for your time, you'll win." Then he showed Johnson a poll indicating that he could not win. Johnson said he didn't believe it. Smith slapped his desk and uncharacteristically raised his voice. "If you run this time," he said, "you might as well forget about being governor." For whatever reason, Johnson pulled back, ran for another term on the court, and left the gubernatorial primary fight to a couple of minor figures who had no chance.

In the general election campaign, outside help was offered. The secretary to a Republican county chairman in central Arkansas volunteered to spy on her boss and send copies of his party correspondence to the Faubus campaign. Witt Stephens directed his lieutenants in the Arkansas Louisiana Gas Company to see that all their workers had paid the poll tax so that they could vote—for Faubus, it went without saying. James A. Noe, a former governor of Louisiana, sent the campaign one thousand dollars and offered air time on his radio station at Monroe.

Rockefeller put together a workable campaign machine of his own using the skeletal organization of anti-Faubus liberals as well as the Republican party's own apparatus. He made a start at mobilizing the black vote. The candidate took to the road in a bus. He still flew to New York in his own jet now and then, but he tried to keep it out of sight. He rejected his aides' advice to stop wearing cowboy boots and hat on the simple grounds that he had learned to like them.

For the first time in years, Faubus was able to use class as a weapon. It was like coming home to his father's house. He touched every nerve in the Arkansawyer's defensive psyche: the resentment of wealth, of aristocracy, of high society, of anything from the East. He alluded to Rockefeller's well-known drinking problem, not directly but by mentioning the huge collection of liquor at Petit Jean. He quietly exploited Rockefeller's messy divorce from Barbara (Bobo) Sears Rockefeller. He made fun of him for flying to New York for haircuts.

The talk of jets, liquor, and wild parties was merely an opening to the real issue. Faubus knew the deep, almost hereditary anger in Arkansas at the rich and ruthless men who had used the levers of Wall Street and corporate power to rob the poor. Here, for the first time since he was a boy learning socialist theology, was a chance to get even with the bastards. It meant laying aside his friendship with Rockefeller and their years of cooperating in bringing industry. He genuinely liked the man. But friendship was forgotten when he took to the stump to deride this New York carpetbagger, this spoiled child of privilege trying to buy his way into office with the ill-gotten gain of his old robber baron granddaddy.

The high point of every speech Faubus made that summer on every courthouse lawn in the swelter of every dusty, ragged, dried-up settlement was a particular lesson from his boyhood on the evils of runaway wealth. He set up the story carefully each time. First, the black suit coat was peeled off to reveal, quite intentionally, the white shirt with French cuffs and expensive links; poor people appreciated fine dressing in their leaders. Then he stood a moment, waiting.

Finally he moved his hands to hitch up his trousers, and then let them rest, poised, on his hips. His head went forward a little, suggesting weary defiance.

Then the story, the accent straight from the hills, all polish gone from the language: When he was a boy, his Saturday afternoon job on the way home from Combs was to walk behind the wagon carrying the gallon of kerosene—"coal oil"—with a potato in the spout. His father could not risk spilling any by carrying the can in the wagon. And why was the stuff so precious? Because old John D. Rockefeller, the grandfather of this playboy pup who was trying to buy the Arkansas governor's office, had cornered the market and jacked up the price so high that poor people could barely afford it.

He told how Rockefeller's Standard Oil froze out independent oil companies; how it forced the railroads to charge ten cents a barrel for hauling Standard's oil and eighty-five cents for hauling the competition's, with seventy-five cents rebated to Standard; how, after paying a five-hundred-thousand-dollar fine for antitrust violations, old Rockefeller simply raised the price of coal oil another cent a gallon.

"All of us poor people paid that fine," he said. "Yes, I tell you, if we owe the Rockefellers anything, we've been paying it for a long time."

Out under the shade trees and up around the courthouse steps, the old men in overalls and the old women in gingham dresses nodded grimly, and their eyes were on fire.

Rockefeller never understood. His aides urged him to answer. His attitude was, "Why respond? Anybody knows there's nothing to that, and they're not going to be concerned with what happened a generation or two ago." He went on traveling in his bus, drawing deceptively large crowds with free barbecue and watermelons and entertainment by Johnny Cash. Not that he was disliked. His poor speaking skill and mangling of the language actually attracted a certain sympathy. And his message of reform and of the value of a two-party system to provide checks and balances struck a chord with many, especially in the cities and larger towns.

Faubus's polls had him worried. For six weeks during the summer and early fall, he and Rockefeller were dead even. There was a large undecided vote, bad news for any incumbent. To add to his woes, he came down sick with a stubborn respiratory infection.

Seeking votes in 1964 near Rison, Arkansas.
His wealthy Republican opponent, Winthrop
Rockefeller, had a well-financed campaign
to lure black voters, an effort that paid off
when he ran again in 1966.

Alta had to deliver his convention speech accepting the Democratic nomination. She filled in for him repeatedly during the fall, and she was indirectly responsible when his gambler's luck returned. She called in a former employee of the governor's office, Robert Troutt, to help with public relations. Troutt's first coup when the governor got out of the sick bed was to flag an old black man on a log wagon in southeast Arkansas and have Faubus photographed driving his mules for a few yards. That neatly underscored the poor-man theme and undoubtedly played well with black voters.

Then Troutt heard from out-of-state contacts that Rockefeller owned a casino in Puerto Rico. Faubus ran with it, even though the casino turned out to be owned by Rockefeller's brother Laurance. Nevertheless, the publicity blunted the challenger's criticism of Faubus for allowing gambling in Hot Springs.

The next break came when Rockefeller interrupted his campaign to go to a huge livestock show at Kansas City. He had a legitimate interest; he had pioneered in the breeding of Santa Gertrudis cattle at his ranch. But it looked like a trivial use of his time during a serious campaign. Then it was reported that he had slept through the show and never left his hotel. The public suspicion was that he was drunk, although he had sworn off drink.

Faubus had another stroke of luck when Rockefeller said in a speech that Arkansas's progress under Faubus had been illusory. The governor began quoting from the dictionary, relentlessly weaving a sarcastic definition of illusory into every speech. "Mr. Rockefeller, look down from your mountaintop, and perhaps you can see that new trade school at Morrilton where none existed before. Go down to Conway and go out to the Children's Colony. Kick the walls with your cowboy boots and see if they aren't real brick and mortar and not an illusion. You people in Little Rock, don't you drive out on that new freeway bridge. That's just an illusion, and you'll plunge right into the Arkansas River."

There were dirty tricks. Faubus unfairly attacked Rockefeller for having a country cemetery bulldozed on one of his farms. The episode had happened years earlier when a dozer operator had accidentally disturbed some tombstones in an overgrown cemetery. He had restored them and, for good measure, had erected a fence around the graveyard. Faubus refused to back off even after he heard

*Winthrop Rockefeller, who established
the modern Republican party in Arkansas.
He challenged Faubus for the governorship
unsuccessfully in 1964, then went on to
win the office two years later.*

the whole story. On the other side, Rockefeller's people were accused of wiretapping the telephones of Faubus and other prominent Democrats. Bland was told that Rockefeller people had taped a political conversation between Faubus, Senator McClellan, and former governor Homer Adkins.

The national Democratic party caused a problem for Faubus. Pres. Lyndon B. Johnson and his running mate Hubert H. Humphrey were considered too liberal. Sen. Barry Goldwater, the Republican nominee, was more to Arkansas's taste. Faubus tersely endorsed the national ticket, then kept quiet.

Rockefeller had his own party problems. Goldwater had just defeated his brother Nelson for the Republican presidential nomination, and Winthrop had to swallow hard to support the conservative Arizonan. His rebuilding of the Arkansas party had alienated many old-line Republicans who had used it as a private club and an avenue to federal appointments. Some of the traditional leaders were so angry that they endorsed Faubus. Osro Cobb, the U.S. district attorney who had had to oppose Faubus over Central High, publicly suggested that Arkansawyers vote a split ticket of Goldwater and Faubus. The following year, Faubus would reward him with an appointment to the state supreme court.

It was thought that the liberal Rockefeller would get a heavy black vote, even though Faubus had recently been careful not to jump up and down and stomp on his hat, as he had once put it, to please the segregationist constituency. Indeed, Faubus had quietly continued to cultivate his sources among old-time black leaders and had even got on speaking terms again with the Bateses. L. C. Bates had met with him a few times to discuss community needs and issues. Bates emerged from one session at the governor's office in a jocular mood, saying they had had a good talk. Faubus had promised to hire a Negro state trooper. Bates told Faubus he would provide some applicants, then added that he never intended to vote for him again, no matter what.

Faubus could not resist using Rockefeller's liberalism against him. He said the nickname Win meant "Wants Integration Now." Recent racial protests had taken the form of demonstrators lying in the street to block traffic. Faubus said if any tried that in Arkansas, they would be run over. He added, "If no one else will do it, I'll get a truck and do it myself." Rockefeller called that immoral.

The election results were surprising. The man who just seven years earlier had become a symbol of segregationist resistance got 80 percent of the black vote. Some of those votes were supplied in the time-honored east Arkansas way, but many were the result of diligent political workmanship. Black leaders like Bishop Sherman turned out the vote for Faubus all across the state. Thousands more had connections to state employment through schools, colleges, correctional institutions, hospitals, nursing homes, and dozens of state agencies. Faubus's campaign workers made sure they were reminded that they had a friend in the governor's office.

Faubus was able to lure back many Democrats who had worked against him after Central High. The Arkansas AFL–CIO endorsed him. So did the Arkansas Education Association, whose executive director, Forrest Rozzell, had bitterly opposed Faubus's school actions after the Central crisis.

Faubus survived the Rockefeller challenge with room to spare. He got 57 percent of the total vote. Rockefeller was encouraged enough by his showing to run again in two years, and in that race, against less formidable opposition, he would win.

Madison County managed to embarrass its favorite son. First, he won it by only 59 percent, a reminder that the mountain counties had always had a lot of Republicans. Then when Rockefeller's agents went to inspect the absentee ballots, which had been handled in a questionable manner, they were threatened and run out of town. They returned several times. One was attacked in the county clerk's office. They sued to see and copy the records, but before they could get at them, someone broke into the courthouse vault and stole them. The Republicans held the governor responsible. They reminded him that his brother Doyle was a member of the Madison County Election Commission and that his son, Farrell, was the deputy prosecuting attorney there. Faubus stood aloof. His spokesman dismissed the fuss with no comment, saying, "That's Republican business."

Faubus lost several urban centers, including Little Rock. But he triumphed over the best-financed campaign ever mounted against him and carried sixty-five of the seventy-five counties. In some ways, the 1964 election was his most impressive victory. It was also his last.

CHAPTER
25

Faubus was fifty-five years old when he took office for his last term. He seemed to be at the height of his powers. George Fisher's cartoon in the *North Little Rock Times* summed up the conventional wisdom: In the legislative hall where he delivered his sixth inaugural address, every face—even on the mouse crawling out of its hole in the baseboard—was that of Orval's familiar visage.

In reality, Faubus's power at this time was already on the wane. That was not evident to the outsider, but he knew. His administration was growing old. There was not enough young blood in top posts. Some of the old heads had given in to temptation and had tainted themselves and their agencies through ethical lapses. Some had left the administration and had used their connections with the state to enrich themselves.

In the middle years, when the Faubus administration truly was vigorous, he could crack the whip and get what he wanted as long as he worked within the confines of government and political intrigue. For example, he defeated the powerful Arkansas Education Association in 1961 over how to finance the state's teacher retirement fund. At one point he persuaded twelve House members to change their votes overnight. One who refused told how he did it. When Faubus demanded his vote, the man said he would be in trouble with the school superintendents in his district if he voted against them. Faubus said he would be in trouble with him if he didn't. True to his word, the governor arranged for someone to run against the recalcitrant man—unsuccessfully as it turned out—in the next election. Using such tactics, Faubus got twelve of the fourteen programs he wanted in the 1961 legislature.

Even then, however, he sometimes overreached. The voters beat him 2 to 1 later that year when he called a special election to try to pass a sixty-million-dollar bond issue for construction at the state colleges, the state hospital, and the Children's Colony. There was a strong suspicion that the program would further enrich Witt Stephens and his brother Jack, who already had made millions in the bond business.

Faubus delivering his sixth inaugural address to the legislature in 1965. The scene inspired one of George Fisher's best-known cartoons, in which every face in the room—even that of a mouse—is Faubus's, a comment on his domination of the state after ten years in office.

Fisher in the North Little Rock Times *January 10, 1965.*

It was another bond proposal, this time for $150 million, that brought him up short as he began his last term. He wanted to upgrade the state's roads on credit. As usual, the legislature went along with him. Six weeks later, with Rockefeller and the Republican party joining the opposition, the voters turned it down by 2 to 1.

Toward the end of the sixth term, he called in his department heads and assessed their performance bluntly. One had been seen too often in shady company. Another had let a problem come to Faubus's attention from another source, then the governor himself had had to investigate and straighten it out, doing the director's job for him. "Have I got to tell you about your department, or shouldn't you tell me?" he demanded of another. "Can none of you report? Have you forgotten how to write a memo?"

Many of the main members of his administration had been with him since the beginning in 1955. Just before Christmas of 1965, two of them had serious heart attacks. Mack Sturgis, who had become highway director after years as purchasing agent, was struck December 14. He recovered slowly. Rolla Fitch, who had moved from head of the Alcoholic Beverage Control agency to director of the Livestock and Poultry Commission, was rushed to the hospital December 20. Faubus went to see him and was himself taken ill. He stayed two days for examination and rest.

Little that could be called big-time scandal surfaced in his administration until the last term. However, it soon became evident that the scandals that were made public in 1965, 1966, and 1967 had been festering for years.

One of the worst was in the insurance department, run by his old friend from Madison County, Harvey G. Combs. Neither the commissioner nor his employees were thought to be personally corrupt, but their lax regulation allowed unscrupulous operators to steal millions of dollars from unsuspecting premium payers and stock buyers. The sharks and con artists moved into Arkansas after Texas cracked down on their illegal activities during the 1950s. Under Commissioner Combs, who believed that encouraging new capital-creating companies was part of his job, 673 insurance companies were established or moved in from other states during the Faubus tenure. Some were outright scams designed not to insure people but to entice them to buy stock and enrich the company founders. After the owners looted the companies, the stockholders were left with worthless paper.

Political influence was used to get charters for new companies and to countermand regulators who tried to ride herd. A call from a state legislator would do the trick. There is no evidence that Faubus profited from any of that, but people close to his administration did so. For example, certain lawyers were known to be the conduits to having the insurance department approve a new charter. An Arizona man came to Arkansas to go into the insurance business. He and his partner applied to the insurance department for a charter. They were ignored. One of the men paid four hundred dollars to an employee in another state agency to tell him the secret. He was given the name of a lawyer who had once worked for Faubus. For five thousand dollars, the lawyer signed the application, and it went through without a hitch.

The Arizonan's company illustrated how stock buyers were bilked. The prospectus said in large print that if the buyer was dissatisfied, he could get his money back and keep all the common stock he had bought, turning back only his preferred stock. There seemed to be no way to lose. But the fine print on the back spelled out a condition: Money would be refunded only during a period of a few days each year and only if the company had at least five hundred thousand dollars in unassigned surplus at the time, which effectively shut off any refunds.

The Arizonan's career was interrupted by a term in federal prison for land fraud back home. When he got out, he learned that his partner had stolen the company from him. He sought out an *Arkansas Gazette* columnist and said, "You all ought to do something about these crooks."

Companies were also allowed to make illegal investments in real estate and in the stock of affiliated companies—devices that made it easy to siphon away reserves that were supposed to pay claims to insurance holders. Officials of both respectable and questionable companies showed their appreciation to Combs and his people by giving lavish Christmas gifts. At one public gathering, Combs was given a box containing the keys to a new Oldsmobile, a gift from a group of companies. Far from questioning the propriety of the gift, he saw it as recognition of his efforts to promote Arkansas businesses.

As for Faubus, his main interest in the insurance agency was in keeping premium rates low. Over and over, he admonished Combs to keep an eye on companies that were trying to raise their rates. He even appeared before the commission himself after he left office to fight a rate increase for auto insurers. While in office, he occasionally urged Combs to look into some stock offering or, more often, some outlaw sales agent who was operating dishonestly. At his direction, the legislature approved creation of a securities division of the insurance department to curb the more blatant stock manipulation. But he took no consistent interest in the exploding growth of shady new companies.

Setting up an insurance company required permission from both the insurance department and, after it was spun off into a separate agency, the securities commission. The latter was headed by another old friend of Faubus, Clint Jones. When Rockefeller succeeded Faubus as governor, he appointed a tough former prosecutor and ex-marine named John Norman Harkey to head the insurance department. Then he brought an Arkansas man named Don Smith home from Emory University to run the securities commission. These two brusquely cleaned house and turned their agencies into the regulatory bodies they were supposed to be. Smith estimated that Arkansas investors had lost $100 million in watered stock and worthless securities since the mid-1950s. Besides cracking down on the easy chartering of insurance companies, Smith closed twenty-three broker dealers who typically had preyed on elderly widows. Faubus contended until the end that his administration had prevented any serious outbreak of insurance fraud.

Rockefeller's clean-up was too late for two thousand Arkansawyers who were defrauded by one imaginative scam. Attorney General Bennett and several friends, including the powerful Paul Van Dalsem, the state representative from Perry County, cobbled together a company called Arkansas Loan and Thrift. It was an industrial loan corporation based on a 1937 state charter that had lain idle for years. It operated something like a bank or a savings and loan association, but issued "bond investment certificates." It lent money supposedly for industrial development but in fact for the convenience of the company's officers. Predictably, it went broke. The victims lost most of the $4.2 million they had invested.

If it had been called a bank or a savings and loan, the company clearly would have been regulated by the state. The heads of the securities and the banking commissions, both Faubus appointees and allies, professed not to know whether they had that power. They went for advice to the attorney general. Not surprisingly, since the enterprise had been hatched in his office, he said the company was not covered by the state laws on securities, banking, or savings and loans.

Ernest A. Bartlett Jr., chairman of the corporation, testified in federal court that the legal opinion had actually been written not by the attorney general—who was worried about propriety—but by Faubus's legal advisor Bill Smith. Smith said Bartlett was a liar. Van Dalsem also dropped Smith's name. He told his fellow board members that the governor's advisor had researched the company's charter at his request and found it to be sound. Smith by now was indignant. He accosted Van Dalsem, "gave him a cussing," and threatened to sue if he repeated the assertion.

When federal district judge John E. Miller—the reluctant enforcer of school desegregation years earlier—forced the outfit into bankruptcy, the list of those who had profited included Bennett, one of his aides, and several members of the legislature. It also included Faubus's former office assistant Claude Carpenter, who testified that he had been paid twenty-three thousand dollars for legal services that seemed to include nothing more onerous than an occasional trip to a resort and long hours listening to his employer talk about the University of Arkansas's football team. Carpenter received the first ten thousand dollars of his retainer in late January 1967. Joe Purcell, who had defeated Bennett for attorney general a few months earlier, filed suit that same week to shut down the company. The suit went to the chancery court of Carpenter's law and business partner Kay Matthews—another former Faubus aide whom the governor had once appointed to head the state commerce commission. Matthews repeatedly delayed trial until, more than a year later, he discovered that he and Carpenter owned the building that rented an office to the Loan and Thrift Company. Acknowledging a possible conflict of interest, he passed the case to another judge. But the Rockefeller administration, tiring of the waiting game, pushed the case into federal court. Several company officials, including Bennett, were indicted for fraud. Carpenter was named as an un-indicted "co-schemer" and "co-conspirator." Three men served prison sentences. Bennett escaped trial after he became ill with cancer, which eventually cost him his life. Faubus maintained that he knew nothing about the scheme.

As the Faubus administration lost its muscle tone, more and more people surrendered to greed. Faubus approved a blatant siphoning of tax money into the pockets of friends during his last term. A friendly legislator sponsored a bill in 1965 to pay a state pension to seven members of boards and commissions who had never qualified for such. When a Faubus critic brought it to light during the gubernatorial campaign of 1966, the scheme was labeled "Pensions for Pals."

Nothing better illustrated Faubus's declining power than the highway department, where he had fulfilled the prophecy of the Cassandra John Wells by appointing all five members of the commission and by meddling at will in its affairs. Faubus routinely intervened for years to get jobs for political friends and to select routes to be paved and improved, all the while denying that he had any power over the nonpolitical commission. Then on April 9, 1966, just over two weeks after he announced that he would not run for a seventh term—a statement taken seriously, for once—the highway commission discovered that it was indeed independent of him.

Sometime earlier, Faubus's old friend Mack Sturgis had tired of the job of purchasing agent. Faubus had persuaded the acquiescent highway commission to install Sturgis as director of the highway department. After the heart attack slowed him down, Sturgis resigned to return to his former, more relaxed job. Before he went, he and his administrative aide, Y. W. Whelchel, secretly—without the commission's knowledge—raised the salaries of about 2,100 of the department's 3,500 employees. The raises would cost between $2 million and $3 million and were found to be illegal in some cases. The two men worked after hours on Sturgis's last few nights to arrange the deal, inspiring the label "midnight pay raises."

Faubus knew about the plan and told Sturgis to go ahead. He later said that he knew little of the details and that the whole thing was an honest mistake. When the raises became public knowledge through anonymous tips, the highway commission asserted itself. It fired Whelchel and other top officials, rescinded the raises, and let Faubus know that the romance with him was over. The affair was so politically damaging that it ended any hopes his cronies might have had of persuading him to run for reelection.

Another scandal surfaced late in his tenure and became, perhaps unfairly, a national sensation. Arkansas had operated its penitentiaries on a for-profit basis for generations, sometimes with pride, sometimes with shame. After the Civil War, Arkansas along with much of the South adopted a system of leasing convicts to private contractors. The contractors used the cheap labor ruthlessly on plantations and other enterprises. It amounted to slavery in another form and led to widespread corruption and brutality. Gov. George W. Donaghey ended convict leasing in Arkansas in 1913 and established a prison farm system, which was still in effect when Faubus inherited the office.

The prisons at Cummins and Tucker in southeast Arkansas became so profitable, thanks to their thousands of acres of rich land, that they were earning more than one million dollars a year for the state treasury by the 1960s. The land produced all the food for the prisoners and staff. Convicts worked the crops guarded not by paid officers but by other convicts—trusties—armed with guns. Escapes were few. Lee Henslee, superintendent during most of Faubus's tenure, once explained to an inquisitive guest, "It's not hard to get a con to kill a con."

The trusty system saved money and was stoutly defended by Faubus and most members of the legislature. As described by Faubus, who visited Cummins often, the farm was not so much a prison as an institution providing fresh air, exercise, and wholesome food for the inmates. Ideally, it might have been just that. Providing healthy, useful work for prisoners is a recurring idea in penal philosophy. Unfortunately, the prison farms had been overrun by the same greed, corruption, and brutality that Governor Donaghey had tried to stop half a century earlier.

Faubus had been alerted early in his administration. Prisoners and their relatives complained repeatedly of mistreatment. He chose to believe Henslee, who, credibly enough, portrayed the murderers and thieves in his charge as liars. However, Faubus slowly came to realize that prison conditions were becoming intolerable. When Henslee retired because of ill health, Faubus instructed his new superintendent, Dan Stephens, to stop whipping prisoners. Stephens made numerous improvements on his own. He built a new prison hospital and educational and recreation facilities. But he eventually put the strap back to work after a new eruption of disciplinary problems, and it was not until Winthrop Rockefeller became governor that it was permanently retired. By then, the state had spent a little of the farm's earnings on isolation cells and could lock away the angry men who once would have been flogged until their backs ran red. One hapless prisoner with eye problems had been beaten for not picking his quota of okra. He couldn't see the pods.

Faubus was finally moved to act after receiving a series of new complaints in 1965 and after threats of federal court action. A Fort Smith minister who worked with prisoners passed on first-hand knowledge of conditions at the farms. Faubus took two steps: First, he arranged for a study of Arkansas's prison system by a nationally recognized authority on penology. Second, late in the summer, he ordered the investigative division of the state police to make a secret study of prison conditions.

What the investigators found shocked even hard-bitten citizens who had no sympathy for convicts. Inmates were routinely beaten with hoes, clubs, belts, whips, and rifles. A warden used a primitive form of torture to punish and to elicit information. Known as the "Tucker telephone," it was an electrical device attached to the genitals. Kitchens were filthy and the food was disgusting. Many convicts were given only a piece of bread and one large serving of rice per meal. They got meat once a month and eggs once a year. Hundreds were seriously underweight. Authority had so broken down that corruption ran from the top to the lowliest convict. Bribes were commonplace. Employees extorted money from prisoners. Drugs and liquor could be had on demand; inmates drove prison vehicles to nearby liquor stores. Staff and inmates stole property with impunity. Inmates sent to work at the state hospital stole several air conditioners, which were used and sold back at the prison.

Faubus fired three wardens and a fourth resigned. Several compromised trusties were moved out of positions of authority at Tucker. But by then, Faubus had only a few months left to serve as governor. His actions proved to be inadequate, and the old conditions cropped up again before he left office. Effective reform had to wait for a new administration.

Throughout the Faubus tenure, there were reports of bribes to buy the release of prisoners. Faubus wrote repeatedly to supplicants explaining, sometimes brusquely, that he would countenance no such behavior. He fired one member of his staff after continuous rumors that the aide had "sold" paroles and commutations.

There was unrelenting pressure from influential citizens to obtain the early release of prisoners. A Texarkana lawyer wrote to Faubus's executive secretary to say, "I would be deeply grateful if I can secure some sort of executive clemency for this good colored man." A letter to Faubus from a member of his cabinet began, "Noel Easter is in the penitentiary and wants out." Faubus himself seemed to be acquainted with an uncommonly large number of families with black sheep. He reluctantly commuted an eight-year sentence of the son of old friends from home, making him eligible for immediate parole. In another case, he was so touched by the plea of an old farmer that he got his son released early so that he could help with the spring planting.

All this—securities fraud, prison brutality, benefits for political favorites—paled beside the one wide-open scandal that everyone in the state knew about: illegal gambling at Hot Springs.

The town sits in the foothills of the Ouachita Mountains seventy-five miles east of the ruins of Commonwealth College. With its reputedly therapeutic waters, it has been a destination for the sick and the weary since the days of DeSoto. It has also been an affront to the rest of the Old Testament South since its incorporation in 1874. It styles itself the Spa; its neighbors call it Hot Town and Sin City. Until the late 1960s, it was known for open bars, accommodating whorehouses, and gambling casinos. That all those were illegal was studiously ignored by local and state authorities, although there had been periods of rectitude when this governor or that prosecuting attorney had briefly enforced the statutes.

Rival factions of gambling operators shot it out in the streets in 1878 and three men died. An anti-gambling newspaperman was shot to death in 1882. In 1899, another gambling war left five dead and a large number wounded. That led to a reform that took the form of regularizing the illegal gambling under the control of leading businessmen. The reform disintegrated in an eruption of arson.

In 1927, the city and its industry were finally stabilized under the leadership of Leo P. McLaughlin, a brilliant trial lawyer who had learned the town's elastic politics as city attorney. He was tall, handsome, and imposing, and his voice filled any auditorium with authority. He campaigned for mayor on a platform of taxing the gamblers, bars, and prostitutes to build new streets and sewers and a new fire department. The tax would be a system of fines. Without requiring arrests, the violators would appear in police court each week and pay the tribute. He was forthright about his intentions. In his speeches, as he described what he would do with the illegal tax money, he noted that the mayor's salary was a meager fifteen hundred dollars a year and that skeptics might wonder how he expected to live on so little. He said, "When we have taken care of these things [the city improvements] then I'll take care of Leo."

He kept his promise. The city was rebuilt and services improved. Then he took care of Leo. He liked expensive clothes and the high life. He had a rakish way of reminding the citizens that he was in charge. Every day at the same hour, dressed in a suit and red tie, a red carnation in his lapel, the brim of his straw hat turned up, he drove his sulky from his big old house on Malvern Avenue down the main thoroughfare, Central Avenue, past the bathhouses and the swank Arlington Hotel where big-name gangsters from the North, come to take the waters, were often in residence. The sulky was drawn by a costly pair of horses. Even their names were an affront to the Baptist ethic that lapped at the shores of the town. He called them Scotch and Soda.

The McLaughlin machine stayed in office twenty years, partly by stealing votes with casual brazenness. Because cooperation from the state capital was necessary, the gambling interests tried to buy friendship there. It is said that the standard campaign contribution to a "friendly" governor in those days was fifty thousand dollars. The returning World War II veterans led by McMath finally overthrew the machine and temporarily ended the gambling and its attendant corruption. Two of McLaughlin's cronies went to prison. He escaped the charges against him by having his trial moved to a friendly jurisdiction in neighboring Montgomery County.

Gambling went into an unbecoming limbo, half secret, never

Orval and Alta Faubus and their first grand-child, Fara Faubus, in the governor's mansion. PERSONAL COLLECTION OF ALTA FAUBUS.

sure when the next state police raid would shut it down and frighten away the gaming tourists. Then Faubus became governor. He quickly sent a signal: gambling was a local affair for Hot Springs, and he did not intend to interfere unless the people there wanted him to do so. Since most leading businessmen of the town wanted gambling, that meant there would be no police raids from Little Rock. Casinos quickly sprang to life again.

Faubus's good friend, traveling companion, and hunting buddy Harry Hastings Sr. quietly insinuated himself into the action. He had served jail time during Prohibition, but had survived to become Arkansas's biggest wholesaler of liquor. At Hot Springs, he became the silent partner of his boyhood friend Dane Harris, who would become the dominant public figure of the gambling industry.

Harris was perfect for his role. There was a Gatsby quality to his past that Hot Springs appreciated. Stories were circulated of bootlegging in his youth. The legend of old trouble with the law was not unbecoming to his debonair bearing. He had gone to the University of Arkansas. He was a veteran of the Army Air Corps. He was one of the best amateur golfers at Hot Springs's toney courses. He was a friend of Sid McMath and had flown a plane for him during McMath's campaign for governor. In spite of that friendship, he was not allowed to operate a gambling business openly until Faubus took office. By the time Faubus met him, his respectability was complete. He had been elected president of the chamber of commerce.

During the Faubus years, the take from gambling reportedly reached as high as $100 million a year. Once again, city authorities imposed a system of fines—$500 per crap table, a lesser amount for blackjack tables and slot machines—in lieu of taxes. The tourists came back and the city thrived. Only the determinedly high-minded took offense.

How much of the gambling money went to Faubus is hard to determine. He acknowledged receiving campaign contributions from the gamblers, but scoffed at the speculation from Hot Springs sources that they amounted to as much as one hundred thousand dollars a year.

"If I ever got as much as $6,000 out of Hot Springs and Garland County, I don't know it," he said. "They had the sorriest political organization of any group with an interest like they had to defend that I have ever seen in my life." He denied ever taking an outright bribe. He said he kept in his mind the image of the hard-working hill people who had put him into office. "I didn't want them to ever have to apologize for me or ever point the finger and say, 'Well, he sold out on us.'" He said he was once told that a certain official was the bag man whose job it was to deliver the gambling payoff to the governor. If so, he said, the man kept the money for himself because it never reached the governor.

Clay White, an FBI agent who investigated Hot Springs gambling and later became sheriff of Garland County, came to believe, based on his inside contacts, that the gamblers sent money to Faubus in two ways. First, the election-year contributions amounted to at least fifty thousand dollars, he said, and up to twenty-five thousand more if it was needed to pay for last-minute advertising. The routine pay-off month by month ran to about seventy-five thousand dollars a year, he said—a bargain, he noted, considering the huge revenues that the casinos took in. White's investigation showed that the money was picked up every Saturday night by a high state official, stowed in a black bag, and delivered to Little Rock. He didn't know whether it reached Faubus.

Late in his administration, Faubus began to feel pressure to stop the illegal enterprise. Rockefeller attacked him during the 1964 election campaign. Criticism came from ministers around the state, including Hot Springs, where some of the churches had always received generous donations from the gamblers—even from Owney Madden, the involuntarily retired mobster from New York who years before had settled peacefully in the town and bought an interest in a gaming establishment.

The federal government took an interest in Hot Springs after new laws gave it more power to intercede. A 1962 grand jury at Fort Smith came within one vote of indicting several public officials and other leaders of the town. The Justice Department reinforced its efforts and moved again in 1964. Two assistants to the attorney general toured the open casinos all one night in March and announced at a press conference the next morning that they would take their evidence to a new grand jury.

The state government, alerted to the threat ahead of time,

had already sprung into action. Introduced by a member who was a Baptist minister, a resolution was quickly passed in the state House of Representatives urging local officials to enforce the anti-gambling laws. Faubus seconded the motion, saying that he would send the state police to shut down the casinos if the local officers did not. The gamblers surrendered and turned out the lights. The state's voters ratified the closing a few months later. They resoundingly defeated a proposed constitutional amendment that would have legalized gambling.

Like a copperhead with its tail cut off, the vice took a long time to die. The casinos reopened furtively and repeatedly, operating under a new legal cloak as private clubs. They would operate until a new public outcry, then the state police would raid them and announce a new closure.

The raids were an inconvenience. Someone from Little Rock would telephone in the morning saying the operators should expect a raid during the afternoon—in time for the evening television newscasts. All hands would go to work rolling the expensive gambling equipment into storage rooms, leaving behind a few worn-out tables to be confiscated. By the next night, the dens would be humming again.

Faubus maintained a kind of amazed innocence. The *Washington Post* sent a reporter to Hot Springs one day in April 1965. He interviewed Faubus at the Arlington Hotel and was assured that no gambling was going on anywhere in town. The reporter walked across the street to the Southern Club and found its casino operating with a full house of players.

The Little Rock newspapers ran regular accounts of the illegal operations. Each time, raids were conducted and the casinos closed. Five months before the end of his tenure, Faubus was being accused by a Hot Springs correspondent of having accepted "a substantial donation" from the gamblers to let them reopen once again. After Rockefeller took office in 1967, the state police, under a new director, conducted a final raid. They hauled the gaming tables and slots into the street and burned them.

The seriousness of Arkansas's corruption during the Faubus years can be assessed in several ways. It was certainly more severe than in the succeeding administrations of Winthrop Rockefeller, Dale Bumpers, David Pryor, Frank White, and Bill Clinton. Any one of half a dozen adventures during Faubus's time was more genuinely corrupting than anything that came afterward, including the Whitewater affair, a picayune "scandal" that was artificially inflated to bedevil Clinton in his presidency. Reaching back, however, the twelve years of Faubus's administration were less tainted than many comparable periods of the state's earlier history. Systematic thievery was a hallmark of Arkansas's nineteenth-century politics, especially during the years immediately after statehood in 1836.

Against the record of other states, Arkansas under Faubus was not far from the norm. It was probably cleaner than Illinois but dirtier than Minnesota. For perspective, consider a decidedly atypical example: Huey P. Long's Louisiana. Faubus himself liked to think that he was a latter-day Huey. He had in mind the progress Long had brought to Louisiana, especially for the down-and-out country people. He assuredly did not have in mind the corruption and terror that Long imposed on his state.

The corruption started with Long himself. He organized a statewide system of graft and shakedowns with a share of the loot going to finance his own lavish style. Compared to the way Huey lived—expensive houses, decadent parties, extravagant travel—Faubus was spartan and tight-fisted. The Louisiana legislature in an ill-advised fit of reform once impeached Governor Long, charging him with nineteen counts of criminality ranging from misuse of state funds to carrying concealed weapons and even threatening the assassination of a legislator. He bought enough lawmakers to beat the rap. In Arkansas, not even the bitterest enemies of Faubus ever suggested any such lurid behavior on his part.

But the harshest consequence of the Long tyranny was the corruption he left behind him. During the five years after his murder, his political associates plundered the bicultural state with Catholic gaiety and Protestant efficiency, as the novelist Walker Percy once put it. Graft, fraud, and every form of theft went unchecked. The state university was used to build a private fortune for the president. Legislators, state officers, and parish politicians sold their influence and shook down contractors. Election goons went beyond anything seen in twentieth-century Arkansas. They not only stole ballots. They also beat up people, women as well as men, at the polling places.

A political newspaper started by Huey, the *Progress*, coerced businesses into buying advertisements and forced all state and local government employees to subscribe. His successors turned it into a cash cow and made hundreds of thousands of dollars. When Faubus got his own paper, the *Statesman,* he tried the same methods. His advertising manager started his telephone conversations with, "This is the governor's paper, and we would like to have your ad." State employees sold subscriptions. Bill Smith sold thirty-one. In spite of all that, the *Statesman* was losing money at the rate of four thousand dollars a year by 1963.

Millions of dollars were stolen—not just funneled into legitimate businesses with good connections, as with the Stephens companies—but flatly stolen during the Long administration and its aftermath. The only enterprises to rival that record in Arkansas were the insurance and securities swindles, and they mainly enriched not public officials but private hustlers who learned to manipulate the state's lax regulation.

President Roosevelt sent federal prosecutors to end the Louisiana hayride. Some 250 people were indicted. A large number went to prison, including one of Huey's successors in the governor's office, Richard W. Leche. The Faubus years in Arkansas, by contrast, produced a mere handful of criminal investigations and fewer prison sentences than Chicago might see in a single lush season.

CHAPTER

26

Faubus in his mid-fifties began to cultivate one last dream. He had surpassed the boldest of his boyhood expectations, and now he felt the advance of his years. What he wanted was a change of scenery, a renewal, a final gratification. Maybe he would go to the United States Senate. Fulbright would face reelection in 1968, and Faubus could take the seat easily. Washington would give him a new challenge and new friends.

Then he would find time to rest and reflect back home in the mountains. The friends of his youth would gather round. He would build a house there to fit the configuration of his achievement, a house suitable for entertaining the nobility of Washington and beyond. It would be a testimonial to his life—a monument, as it were—and when he tired of the Senate, or the governor's office if perchance he chose to return there, then he would live out his days in comfort and grace among the people of his beginnings, just down the road from the childhood frets, terrors, and embarrassments that he had overcome so satisfactorily.

Early in his sixth term as governor, he borrowed forty thousand dollars and started the house. He engaged the up-and-coming Fayetteville architect E. Fay Jones, who a generation later would be world-famous. They poured the foundation on a limestone bluff at the edge of Governor's Hill overlooking Huntsville. The hill had been the home of Isaac Murphy, the last lone holdout against secession in the state's convention of 1861 and governor of his state during the first difficult postwar years. Faubus had bought sixty acres of the Murphy homestead some years earlier and had looked forward to taking his place beside the spirit of his predecessor.

The house was begun in 1965 and took two years to finish. It was wood, glass, and native stone and stretched 214 feet along the bluff. Before the walls were up, it had become a political issue. Rockefeller's Republicans, expecting a Faubus-Rockefeller rematch in 1966, demanded to know how a public servant living on a salary of $10,000 a year could afford this palace. They estimated that it would cost at least $200,000, maybe as much as $280,000. Faubus pointed to his Scottish heritage and said he had saved his money.

Soon after the Republicans began raising questions, word went around that the governor would accept donations to help pay for the house. The money poured in. Department heads contributed, as did many of the men and women Faubus had appointed to boards and commissions. County political leaders sent from $25 to $250 each. And of course those who had done business with the state or who wanted to do so stepped up to prove their generosity. Thank-you notes went to 332 individuals and several business firms. Their donations totaled $59,549. They ranged from $1 to $1,000. Seventy-four donations were $10 or less. The larger sums came from the predictable crowd: the Stephens family, Bill Smith, Parkin, Darby, Raney, Baker, and other supporters and beneficiaries. Other

George Fisher's rural poll workers find it
unbelievable that Faubus, who has dominated
every Arkansas election since 1954, is not on
the ballot in 1966. Fisher in the North Little
Rock Times *July 31, 1966*.

donors pitched in later; the owner of Oaklawn, the race track, sent a $500 bill for Christmas 1966.

Others donated materials, equipment, and appliances. The state electrical cooperatives provided $11,000 worth of wiring, equipment, and labor. An east Arkansas friend gave a stove and refrigerator. Witt Stephens's gas company installed heating and air conditioning at no charge. The Winburn Tile Company of Little Rock gave the tile for the bathrooms and installed it. Someone sent along an expensive set of tools for the two imposing fireplaces. The final cost of the house was never made public. Jones's commission was based on $160,000, but that almost certainly did not include much of the donated material.

Newspaper editorialists were scandalized. The *Pine Bluff Commercial* said that in accepting money for his personal use, Faubus "might as well have announced that he was taking bids." His friends said the donations were not bribes; they were love offerings.

The Faubuses lived temporarily in rooms above the *Madison County Record* when they returned from Little Rock, then moved into the new house in July 1967. Alta was less impressed than Orval. She thought it was a man's house what with the massive fireplaces, the flagstone floors, the oversized rooms, and the bare expanses of glass. He thought it was perfect.

While waiting for the 1968 election, Faubus went back to work at his newspaper, answered letters and phone calls, visited with well-wishers, and started writing his first book, his wartime memoirs. Then one day in 1967 a dark-haired young woman entered his life, and the dream of his final fulfillment was suddenly and quite permanently shattered.

It was not that he had always been faithful. Alta had known and had accepted the bitter fact. But in earlier dalliances, he had been so discreet that not even the bloodhounds of the press had heard more than an occasional wisp of gossip. Politicians like John Kennedy, Lyndon Johnson, and Bill Clinton seemed to enjoy the very risk of being caught. Not Faubus. Rectitude in the hill people was no greater than elsewhere, but their code required that their amorous exertions, like their work and their exercise of religion, not be flaunted.

He was attracted at once to Elizabeth Drake Thompson Westmoreland, a New Englander with a proud family background, a divorce, two young children, and a taste for public attention. She came to his office at the *Record* to get advice on starting a statewide television program sponsored by the Democratic party. Other party supporters were willing to finance it. Faubus, just out of office and still the party's most knowledgeable member, was to help write the scripts. In a matter of months, they were spending too much time together. Alta began to wonder. He went to Fayetteville one day during the Christmas season of 1967 and did not come home until 5 A.M. She learned later that he had been with Beth.

He had already begun to think that he should forget about the Senate for a while and run for governor again. Rockefeller was having trouble in his first term and was vulnerable. Now with Faubus's love affair an increasingly open secret, Rockefeller's private investigators were soon on his trail.

Faubus became so besotted that for the first time he ignored the rules of adultery. He seemed not to care who knew. He would turn nonchalantly and wave at the Republican spies across the street before he entered the love nest in Little Rock. Alta tried to stop the affair, with no success.

It was out of character for him to surrender so completely to emotion. His posture toward Alta through the years had ranged from domineering to friendly and even affectionate, but, except in the earliest days of marriage, could hardly have been called romantic. He seems to have genuinely loved his mother, and he lavished warmth on his young son, Farrell, until he returned from World War II. The war apparently sapped him of any capacity for deep feeling toward other people. After the war, the only fellow creatures to infuse him with serious emotional commitment were dogs. He gave unfettered love to his dogs. Beth somehow broke through the emotional shell. He fell utterly and recklessly in love with her.

He especially liked their trysts in the woods. He took her to his favorite Ozarks haunts. He showed her the wildflowers and trees, naming them as his father had named them for him. He shared the springs, the creeks, and the limestone bluffs. It was as if the energy he had spent on the environment as governor, much of it

Orval and Beth chat with his old friend
Truman Baker (second from right)
during 1970 election campaign.

uncharacteristically out of the public eye, had been in unknowing preparation for these quiet, joyous days.

He never had been given much credit as an environmentalist, partly because that issue was in its infancy when he left office. His record was meager but interesting. He took pride in and got public credit for development of new state parks. Less known was his work to save patches of special lands. He had the state buy small remaining acreages of virgin prairie land in Prairie and Arkansas Counties. At his insistence, state money bought and preserved fields of wild azaleas on remote mountain slopes of the Ozarks. When he learned that loggers were starting to cut a stand of giant beech trees along a Newton County creek that drained into the Buffalo River, he interceded with friends who owned the logging company and persuaded them to leave the trees alone. The preserved area, Lost Valley, became part of the Buffalo National River.

Perhaps his proudest achievement for the environment was the Buffalo itself. Thousands of hill people including his old friend Rep. Jim Trimble had campaigned for years to have the Corps of Engineers dam the river and turn it into a recreational lake. Such lakes had brought prosperity to other parts of Arkansas. But another large group who loved the Ozarks opposed the dam, saying it would destroy one of the nation's finest wilderness streams. The controversy dragged on for years.

Then, just a year before he left office, Faubus stepped in. He had spent many hours on the river, and he credited it with saving his health and his sanity during periods of turmoil.

"In many places," he wrote to an acquaintance, "the giant power-driven machines of man are flattening the hedges, fence rows, and nooks, where the song birds nested, and the timid rabbits reared their young; draining the swamp where the wild ducks and raccoons once found refuge; leveling the forests where once roamed the wild deer; scarring the mountains and pushing down the lofty crags where perched the eagles; filling up the beautiful pools which furnished a home for the wary bass and the brilliant golden-hued sun fish."

He wrote to the corps and asked that the dam be abandoned. That letter put an end to the project. With his support, the federal government went on to preserve the river in its free state.

Now the aging man and his young lover explored the hills of his early vigor. One day, in a spot known only to them, they carved their initials on an old beech tree. They returned there every year for ten years to record the anniversary with another date carved into the bark.

Long before its tenth year, their love had turned dark. The first intimation came in 1968 before they were married. Orval drove to Little Rock one day to find out whether his old financial supporters would back him for one more run for governor. He came home that night crestfallen. Word of his affair with a young woman had gone ahead of him, and the hardheaded old tacticians knew that he could no longer sell himself to the small-town disciples who had thought of him as a kind of deity.

He divorced Alta in the winter of 1969. They had been married thirty-seven years. She had shared the anxieties and glories of office with him, had gone from wallflower to eager partner, and thought she had made him proud. She had even taken a few political intiatives that had proved valuable. Head Start, the program to help youngsters get ready for school, had been established in Arkansas because of her efforts. Through Senator Fulbright, and unknown to Orval, she wangled an invitation to a White House conference for project chiefs, then came home and called a similar meeting at the governor's mansion to get the program going. She had finally come to enjoy the role she had at first dreaded. Now, when they had both earned a comfortable retirement, she found herself discarded.

Orval married Beth three weeks after his divorce. He was fifty-nine. She was thirty. He moved out of the house he had longed for and dreamed of and, relying on romance to fill the gap, went with his new wife to live in middle-class obscurity in the northern Arkansas town of Harrison. He got a job managing Dogpatch USA, an early theme park based on Al Capp's comic strip "L'il Abner." Then he yielded to the pull of politics again.

Rockefeller was finishing a second tumultous term and announced that he would seek a third. The Democratic primary was crowded, but Faubus thought none of the candidates had the heft to unseat the wealthy Republican. Jim Malone Jr., who had taken the heat for Faubus during the angry campaign of 1956, was one of the first to enter. The others were Atty. Gen. Joe Purcell, a dull but competent man; Bob Compton, a lawyer; two men with experience in the legislature, Hayes McClerkin and Bill Wells; and an unknown figure named Dale Bumpers, who was given no chance of winning. Into the field marched the old warrior from Greasy Creek.

In a matter of weeks, the unknown Bumpers unhorsed two of the most famous men in Arkansas, first Faubus in the Democratic runoff, then Rockefeller in the general election. Faubus consoled himself by moving back into his big house at Huntsville. He had kept it and Alta had taken their commercial property, including the newspaper. But even the comforts of his monumental residence were not enough. Large as it was, the house was too small to accommodate a neurotic, ambitious wife, her two high-strung teenagers, and a cast-off chieftain with an aching ego. It was now clear that divorcing Alta and taking up with a woman half his age had not only cost him heavily among the old-fashioned voters of Arkansas; it had also savaged his peace of mind.

The rejection by the voters apparently hurt him deeply. He began to drink more than usual. He took on a persona that Elizabeth had not seen before. He became surly and uncommunicative. She feared to bring up even mundane topics in conversation because any subject might trigger anger.

There is evidence of violence. Her diary recorded the facts sketchily: "damaging head and neck blows . . ." "My back aches badly after the flip he yanked me through . . ." "Another argument. I escaped getting hit though." After her children got older, they joined the arguments. The Huntsville police were called to the house more than once to calm violent quarrels. The police chief came in one time to find Orval against the wall holding a fireplace poker, prepared to defend himself.

Pressure came from all sides, but now he had no loyal staff to help deal with it. Some of it was intensely personal. He and Beth wanted a baby. Time and again, her attempts to get pregnant ended in failure. The one time she conceived, she miscarried.

His income was too small to maintain the big house and his acquired family. He had a small pension from the state, and he sold his books. But there was never enough money to pay the bills,

Faubus and his second wife, Elizabeth,
get bad news on election night 1970.
His comeback failed partly because he had
offended voters by divorcing his first wife,
Alta, to marry the younger woman.

especially the increasingly frequent medical bills. He fell behind on the mortgage payments; with the house, he had acquired in the divorce the forty-thousand-dollar debt that he and Alta had taken on. The bank threatened to foreclose. Witt Stephens and John Cooper discussed various ways of bailing him out by taking over the property. Orval and Beth had become friends of Gerald L. K. Smith and his wife, and now the old bigot who had stirred the populist passions from Huey Long's Louisiana to the nutty precincts of California offered his own plan for taking over the house and getting Orval out of debt. Nothing came of it. Finally, Stephens helped him get a bank loan to get past the crisis. That debt and others plagued him for most of the rest of his life.

Then his son, Farrell, began to have problems. He had felt neglected by his father as he had come of age in Little Rock and Huntsville. Once when Orval was governor, the boy had tried for days to talk to him about a problem and had finally asked a secretary to make an appointment for him. Farrell became a lawyer, but his practice did not prosper. He tried teaching school at Huntsville. He made the first of several attempts to kill himself a few weeks after his father's divorce and remarriage in 1969.

His own marriage to his Huntsville sweetheart, Martha Jo Culwell, ended just as Orval and Beth began to have problems. Farrell learned that certain prescription drugs gave him solace, and he leaned on them ever more steadily. He began to have outbursts of violence. He threatened to kill his parents, his wife, and his two daughters. He attacked Orval, Alta, and an uncle one day at a downtown business and had to be restrained by the sheriff. In 1973, the family had him committed to the state hospital. He left but was apprehended in Kansas and returned to Little Rock. He wrote to his father in anger. "If you had been this interested 20 years ago, then this action would not have been necessary on your part." He had trouble keeping a job and ran up nine thousand dollars in debts.

Orval's sour moods grew worse. He got drunk several times on peach brandy. Then his wife began to show signs of instability. She had always been excitable and nervous. Now she decided, with some justification, that the people of Huntsville disliked her. More than one woman had seen Beth march to the front of the checkout line at the grocery store and demand special treatment as "the governor's wife." She in turn considered her neighbors to be uncouth and ignorant.

Her own thinking might have shocked the Massachusetts friends of her childhood if they had known. She watched the Democratic National Convention of 1972 on television and described it in her diary as a disgrace to America. "The hippies, queers, niggers— all disgusting. The nigger co-chairman sabotaged all of Wallace's planks in a most unfair, obvious manner . . . Niggers, such as that communist, immoral Abernathy and Jess Jackson full of hatred and vengeance."

Beth's right-wing tendencies were fed by her association with Gerald L. K. Smith, now living in Eureka Springs. The aging anti-Semite had built a Christian theme park on the edge of town. She proudly confided to her diary that she and Orval had been invited to the Smiths' fiftieth wedding anniversary party in 1972.

A few months later she took an interest in the school library at Huntsville. She wrote to the principal "suggesting strongly" that he remove *The Grapes of Wrath* from the shelves. That was about the extent of her civic involvement in the town.

Both husband and wife seemed to revive in 1974 when Orval decided once again to recapture the governor's office. Fulbright's Senate seat might have been his target, but the redoubtable Bumpers beat him to that, and he was left to oppose former representative David H. Pryor for his old job in Little Rock. Pryor jumped out front by acquiring the support of the Stephens combine. He would have been hard to beat, anyway. The Young Turk, as he had been labeled during his days as a legislative opponent of Faubus, was as formidable a campaigner as Faubus and had the advantage of youth and an unscarred reputation.

Beth joined Orval in the campaign. She worked in the headquarters plotting strategy, searching for weaknesses in the opposition, and trying to keep Farrell out of the public view. His drug addiction and an affair with a young woman he had met in a nightclub threatened to bring bad publicity. He was sent into hiding in Texas. That was a sad loss. Although he had shown little personal warmth, Orval had long valued his son's incisive political judgment.

Pryor won without a runoff, edging out Faubus and a third candidate, Bob Riley, by 1 percent. Faubus took the loss seriously.

Faubus and Gerald L. K. Smith, the right-wing founder of Eureka Springs's religious theme park. They became friends during the 1970s.

This time, he could not blame it primarily on his marital scandal, although that still swayed some voters. His home county went against him, probably out of loyalty to Alta. But he knew that he had lost in a fair fight to a young man who had outplayed him in the great game.

Faubus never forgot the betrayal by his old friends Stephens, Darby, Baker, Cooper, and the others. "I wanted to curse those who could have helped me but did not," he wrote later. "I thought of the many times I had helped many of these prominent men and at times when there was no great obligation, or none at all, to do so. Then in my hour of need they turned their backs to me and their hands against me." He understood that those practitioners of realpolitik had abandoned him for the soundest of political reasons. They wanted a winner and one with a future. Nevertheless, it took years to rid himself of the bitterness.

Faubus descended. His money problems grew worse, his debt larger. In desperation, he put the big house up for sale. Several people expressed interest, but no one bought it. He tried without success to start a radio station. He hawked his books at fairs. Pryor once encountered him at the War Eagle Fair in the Ozarks. He was selling his books and, if a buyer couldn't afford a book, he would autograph a slip of paper for a quarter.

He continued to dabble in politics, usually on behalf of conservatives. He had worked openly for George Wallace for president in 1968 and later, more quietly, had advised various functionaries of the Nixon administration. The state Republican party discreetly approached him about running for governor as a Republican in 1976. He considered it, then said no. However, he took far greater interest in the Republican presidential convention than in the Democratic. He and Beth pulled for Ronald Reagan. Beth confided to her diary that the Republicans had missed their chance by nominating Gerald Ford. She had nothing but contempt these days for Democrats, state or national. Orval had hoped that his old friend Wallace would go after the Democratic nomination in 1976. He had received confidential information in 1973, a year after the attempted assassination of Wallace, that his health was good and that he intended to seek the nomination in the next election. Faubus was eager to work for him. But that was not to be.

Politics was a diversion, even if a distant and evaporating one, from the progressive disintegration of their private lives. Beth became more emotionally unstable and Orval more morosely hostile. Her teenagers changed from childishly bothersome to unruly and troublesome. More urgently, Farrell's deterioration accelerated.

Farrell cashed in his meager resources and headed for Alaska during the early summer of 1976. He stopped in Seattle to stay a few days with one of Alta's sisters. He found that he needed a minimum of two hundred dollars to cross the border to Canada. On June 16, he tried by telephone to collect some money he thought was due him. Failing to get the money, and seeing himself in one more desperate situation, he emptied several bottles of drugs into his stomach. His aunt found him when she came home from work. The body was shipped home and buried in Huntsville.

Orval secluded himself in his office day after day with only his dog for company. Beth confided her unhappiness and disillusionment to her diary. On the prospect of a day at a reunion with "that Faubus tribe," she confessed that she resented them as much as they did her. They were prejudiced hillbillies. "They assume I'm a snob—so be it." She firmly cut all ties to friends and to his relatives. Then she picked quarrels with her own distant family. She refused to speak to her father for more than a year. She started wandering the countryside, driving to Fayetteville, Harrison, and other towns to drift unnoticed among the crowds, idling away the days.

As their debts piled up and creditors demanded payment, Orval finally admitted that he had to find more income. He wrenched loose from his pride and found a job. He became a bank teller. Every day in downtown Huntsville, he counted out money to people who had seen him walk to the courthouse in triumph on election night, who had seen him parley with presidents and defy the majesty of courts, who had seen him rise for thirty years and now were watching him fall. The bank paid him $125 a week.

His health went slack. An ulcer caused pain and he vomited blood. There were hurried trips to the hospital. In 1977 his heart caused trouble, and the doctors installed a pacemaker.

Farrell Faubus with his daughter, Fara,
and his wife's dog, Hercules.

Then in the fall of 1977 began a series of events that would sever his ties with the hills of home. Beth was arrested for speeding in October. A month later she was arrested again by the same state trooper for improper passing. She refused to get out of the car, and this time she was handcuffed—and manhandled by four strong officers, Orval insisted—and taken to the police station. She was convicted in municipal court three months later. She and her husband became so distraught that they created a scene after the trial. He knocked a camera from the hands of the editor of the *Madison County Record,* Carol Whittemore (who was Alta's niece), and Beth slapped her. The couple were hauled back into court on charges of assault, which were dropped after Orval wrote a letter of apology and paid for the broken camera.

He could take no more humiliation. He announced that they were leaving Huntsville. They again advertised the house for sale—asking $1.1 million—and drove away, leaving their whereabouts unknown to the public.

They surfaced in the fall of 1978 in Houston. Life there was no better except that the city had fewer prying eyes. Orval and Beth were sick constantly; they had surgery twice each. Her son Ric had an operation. The insurance company refused to pay for any of that, and Orval borrowed more money to pay the bills. He borrowed $35,000 in 1979 from the First National Bank of Huntsville where he already owed $66,000 on a real-estate note. In 1982 he borrowed almost $80,000 from the Union National Bank of Little Rock. With interest rates hovering around 20 percent, those loans quickly doubled his obligation. He was unable to lower the principal, and he borrowed more money to pay the interest. The Huntsville house continued to drain their finances. No buyers appeared.

He tried to get Governor Clinton to buy the Faubus-Murphy property, which included more than sixty acres of prime land, and turn it into a state park and museum. He made it clear in correspondence with several people that he would accept a price set by an independent appraiser. Clinton and various newspapers put it about that he was asking the state to cough up $1 million. He had in fact already lowered his asking price on the private market to $875,000. It became obvious that the young governor was using the phony higher figure to justify not doing business with his notorious predecessor.

Faubus had long wanted to write his own version of his years in the governor's office. He started research before leaving Huntsville. The resulting two volumes would include his narrative interspersed with newspaper clippings and cartoons. Relations with Beth continued to sour, making it easy for him to move temporarily to Little Rock to handle the publication of the first volume. He sold the books himself, wrapping and mailing them. All through 1980 he stayed in Arkansas, making occasional trips to Houston. The quarreling, whether in person or by telephone, was more or less continuous. He sent small amounts of money to help pay the bills. He wrote just before Christmas 1980 and enclosed a check for $300. He reminded her to be frugal. "I left home two and a half weeks ago with less than $100," he said. "I filled up my gas tank when I got here—$20—I've spent more than $25.00 for postage in my selling efforts, and I still have $5.00 left."

Then came a brief reprieve. Frank White, a Little Rock Republican, announced that he would oppose Clinton for governor. He was given little chance of defeating a popular young man seeking a second term. White asked Faubus for campaign advice, and Faubus, miffed over Clinton's rejection of his house deal, obliged with general suggestions on tactics and campaign strategy. To general amazement, White won. He promptly gave Faubus a job heading the state's Office of Veterans' Affairs. The salary was not large, but it was welcome.

He apparently found the job less than fulfilling. He was soon trying to see Jack Stephens to ask for a job with the investment company. He noted that he had tried to get an appointment five times without success. Finally on June 12, 1981, Stephens wrote him a one-paragraph letter saying he had no work for Faubus "at this time." It is not clear why Faubus approached the younger brother instead of Witt, but one thing is certain: the rejection deepened his resentment over the betrayal of his old associates.

The state job, however, improved his outlook on his marital problems. He became almost lighthearted in his contacts with Beth. He got a chilly response. He sent her a cartoon from the paper showing a husband saying to his wife, "You think we always have to keep up with the Joneses. Well, the Joneses are getting a divorce." She wrote in the margin, "Sent from OEF Feb 1982. Damn good

Faubus's fortunes so declined after leaving the governor's office that he was forced to take a job as a bank teller in Huntsville.

PHOTO BY CHARLES BICKFORD, COURTESY OF THE *SPRINGDALE NEWS*.

idea. EDF." Two months later, she scribbled on one of his envelopes, "TOTAL BASTARD" and "You miserable, wife, child beating louse."

About that time, her personal records—diaries on wall calendars, notes on paper scraps, comments in book margins and on letters and envelopes—became a pathetic, sometimes shocking reflection of the collapse of her life. She was apparently unable to make new friends or keep old ones. An angry confrontation with a nurse led her physician to refuse to treat her any longer. Her periodic efforts to earn money or to get her children established in careers were frustrated. Her regard for her husband declined steadily the longer he stayed in Little Rock.

In the fall of 1982, she filed for divorce. He learned of it when the papers were served on him in Little Rock October 27. He was still recovering from the shock when he was served with a court order prohibiting him from entering their Houston house.

He wrote a long letter to her November 3, 1982, saying how much he regretted the break-up. He mentioned places and events they had shared fondly and said, "And all my life I'll be constantly seeing things and having experiences, and thinking, 'Beth would have liked this' or 'She wouldn't like that.' My romance with you was my great hope, my great dream. How sad that we did not do enough to help each other, and so much to hurt each other . . . A proposed property settlement will be along soon. If you are determined on your course, you may accept and receive your divorce. The dream will have vanished."

Her scribblings and diary entries from that fall and winter recorded puzzling physical ailments and a rapidly deteriorating mental state.

Nov. 26:	"Fell last night—no muscle strength l. side."
Dec. 12:	"Shortness of breath. Ache like hell."
Dec. 28:	"Not hungry again—so depressed."
Dec. 31:	"Cold rainy"
Jan. 4:	"Made calls for jobs"
Jan. 10:	"Part time hostess in a rather mediocre place"
Feb. 12:	"Fighting migraine"

More disturbing were suggestions that she had come to fear her husband. She apparently decided that he intended to do her harm.

She covered almost the entire margin of a letter from him dated February 3, 1983, with comments. Referring to a highly publicized murder in Little Rock, she jotted, "McArthur killing a G.D. smoke screen." Then, "You're being too nice over phone. 'You're making a mistake, Beth.' Is there a hit on me again OE? Maybe you double-crossing S.O.B. has also been . . . ." In large printed capitals, she wrote, "BASTARD." Sometime during her last months, she wrote in the margin of one of her books, "Saw you Faubus in Little Rock with Jimmie Hoffa (I was shocked)."

Faubus dismissed all this as fantasy and irrationality. He said in later years that he had watched her become increasingly unstable long before she filed for divorce. He said he doubted that she was afraid of him. He portrayed the restraining order as her cautious effort to keep anyone from thinking that she was sharing her bed with him while the divorce was pending.

Her diary entry for February 28 said, "Told OEF he'd better NOT show up here—he thinks I'm kidding—I'm NOT—told him will have cops throw him out."

Orval was keeping his own diary. His entry for January 10, 1983, said, "Betty Faubus called at 5 A.M. this morning. My sister, June McGowen, is dead; heart attack at 3 A.M. this morning at home north of Combs." Five days later, Bill Clinton, who had decisively displaced White from the governor's office, fired Faubus from the veterans' office and put his own person in the job. Five weeks after that, Faubus made his first trip to Huntsville in more than four years to attend the funeral of one of his best friends, Freeman Shuster. On February 28, Beth called collect, and they talked fifty-three minutes.

March 1:

> 4:50 P.M. A rough day—making arrangements to move furniture from Houston, and conclude the paper work on the divorce decree. Last night 2-28-83 Beth seemed at the breaking point. I hope she gets the peace of mind she seeks with the conclusion. Beautiful spring day.

March 2:

> Called Beth during day (3-1-83). She's quite alright, and thanked me for calling.

And then, without warning, this on March 3:

> Beth found dead about 3 P.M. Betty and Doyle Faubus at
> Huntsville heard a news bulletin, and called me about 6:15.

Her nude body, bloodied, beaten, and strangled, had been found
in her bathtub. The Houston police first thought they detected the
pattern of a serial killer. Two other women's bodies had been found
in their bathtubs two days earlier. But in less than a week, they
arrested twenty-four-year-old David Scott Helfond, a Florida fugi-
tive with a criminal record, and determined that he had killed only
one woman: Elizabeth Faubus.

His confession related that he met her March 2 when she went
to inspect a vacant apartment at the apartment complex where he
and a girlfriend were living. Learning that Beth had some furnish-
ings for sale, he went to her house about 8 P.M. Two other people
were there looking at items Beth had advertised. When they left, he
told the police, Beth poured herself another drink and began
talking to him about her problems. He said she remarked that he
was "cute and good looking." He said he bought some of her
jewelry. He went outside to look at a bicycle. When he returned to
the kitchen, he said, she approached him closely and asked him to
stay a while longer.

"I pushed her away from me into the kitchen area, became
scared, and I hit her, I think just slapped her with my open hand to
scare her away from me." Then he struck her repeatedly in the head
with a large glass, undressed her, and put her into her bathtub. He
filled the tub with water, grabbed her bloody clothing, and left. He
put the clothing and the murder weapon in a dumpster outside his
apartment building.

Helfond's portrayal of Beth's behavior as sexually suggestive
should be discounted in light of his history. At the time of the
murder, he was wanted in Florida for sexual assault, burglary, and
kidnapping. He had been charged there in 1980 with sexual assault
of two women who had allowed him into their houses. In 1975, he
had been convicted of assault. In 1976, he had been convicted of
sexual battery. He had been sentenced each time to fifteen years on
probation. The Houston police said he had raped or tried to rape
Elizabeth Faubus.

Orval urged the state to seek the death penalty. But the prosecutor saw some technical difficulties in the case and agreed to a plea bargain. Helfond was sentenced to life imprisonment. Beth was buried in Memorial Oaks Cemetery at Houston.

Faubus returned from the funeral in time to start the death watch for his brother Elvin, who died April 12. A week later, Beth's son Ric tried to kill himself, and three weeks after Ric left the hospital he was arrested on suspicion of burning a business associate's car.

Faubus moved from his Little Rock apartment to his house at Huntsville. His debts lacerated him. His Huntsville bank loan, inflated by interest rates of near 20 percent, had grown to $200,000. He sold 980 acres of land for $171,000 and turned it over to the bank.

For a year, Orval became a hermit. His brother and his sister-in-law, Doyle and Betty Faubus, lived in the big house with him, but he saw few other people. One summer night in 1984, he stepped outside to smoke a cigarette. He studied the stars for a long time. He asked himself, "What the hell are we doing here?"

He started another book of memoirs, *Down from the Hills II*. It was only after he had finished it in 1984 that he began to appear in public again. He made a few speeches and moved back to Little Rock.

In 1986, still smarting from his treatment by Bill Clinton, he raised seventy thousand dollars and ran against him for governor. He knew he had no chance of winning, but no one else of consequence surfaced to oppose the popular young man. Faubus got 34 percent of the primary vote—a startling show of support for a man of seventy-six who had lost his power base twenty years earlier.

He was climbing out of despair. His personal life took a pleasing turn when he got acquainted with an attractive younger woman. Janice Hines Wittenburg, an elementary schoolteacher, had snapped his picture at a Parents Without Partners meeting on New Year's Eve of 1984. She was almost thirty-three years younger than he. One of her two children from an earlier marriage was still at home. She had red hair and a pleasing manner that said to fifth graders and old men alike, "Pay attention." They were married November 23, 1986. He moved into her modest house at Conway and settled into the longest period of quiet that he had known since he had left Madison County to go to war.

He continued dabbling in politics, sometimes quirkily. He endorsed the black activist Jesse Jackson for president in 1988, saying he was the only Democratic candidate who generated any enthusiasm. He said the others were dull and gray. "There are some good men but they have no color," he said, with no apparent intent at irony. He admired Jackson because "he speaks out for the underdogs of the nation."

He went out of his way to make up with his old enemy Daisy Bates. When hundreds of her friends gave a tribute dinner for her in 1989, Faubus made a speech praising her dedication. He said he had never held any personal animosity toward her and had never detected any from her in return—an assessment regarded as disingenuous, at the least. Like Lyndon Johnson and many other politicians, Faubus could not bear knowing that an old adversary might still oppose him.

He kept a wary eye on the despoilers of the Ozarks and attacked angrily when the U.S. Forest Service started clear-cutting the hardwoods there. In a letter to the service in 1988, he said, "I don't know who persuaded, directed or ordered you to begin this outrageous practice in the hardwoods region of the Ozarks, but you are wrong—dead wrong."

He finally sold his Huntsville house in 1989. It brought $318,000, enough to pay his remaining obligations. He was out of debt at age seventy-nine. Losing that house, the symbol of his days of fame and glory, was one of the last affronts to his pride. His eyes teared as he talked of not being able to live out his life there. He and Jan had bought a more agreeable house in a Conway subdivision, but it was a comedown from the Huntsville mansion.

Controversy still came easily. Friends raised money and had a bust sculpted of him. It was installed quietly in the capitol. The press learned of it in 1991, and an outcry followed. Black legislators objected. The *Gazette* commented that the special recognition was undeserved, saying, "He was the state's worst governor, and Arkansas still has not fully recovered from the wounds he inflicted on her in 1957." After Faubus made disparaging remarks about the quality of the sculpture, the artist, William Sapp, wrote to him angrily demanding an apology.

Faubus went to a funeral every few weeks. Witt Stephens died,

Janice Hines Wittenberg became Faubus's third wife and, in spite of problems, brought him some contentment during his last years.

PHOTO BY ALAN BUCK.

but not before Faubus got over his hard feelings. In a few years he had seen almost all of the old crowd die: Bill Darby, Harry Parkin, John Cooper, Pete Raney. The front porch of George Fisher's Old Guard Rest Home, a cartoon that had become a newspaper institution, was thinning out. Paul Van Dalsem died early. Wilbur D. Mills, Arkansas's most powerful congressman, died back home at Kensett.

Faubus's own health deteriorated. He learned that he had prostate cancer. The new marriage was not as happy as the couple had wished. He had fits of jealousy and threatened her with violence. He continued to worry about a shortage of money, and that worry was exacerbated when Jan learned in 1992 that she, too, had cancer. When she left her job to fight the disease, he complained about the loss of her income. She confided that she considered killing herself after that outburst. He went to her room later in the day and said, "I didn't intend to hurt you." That apparently was as close as he could come to apologizing. She noticed that he never spoke the words, "I'm sorry."

His physicians tried to eliminate his cancer with surgery. He had undergone surgery several times before, mainly for pacemakers and for angioplasty to improve circulation to his heart. He began radiation therapy for his prostate condition in the fall of 1991 at the age of eighty-one. A year later, the cancer had metastasized to the bone. He had been planning one more book, an account of his early life on Greasy Creek. When he got the doctor's ominous report, he turned to Jan and said, "I'd better get to work on that book."

He would not finish it. The cancer entered his spine. The radiation and the repeated trips to the hospital in Little Rock sapped his strength. The man who had always hated looking like a fool submitted to having nurses' aides clean his body and his soiled bedding. After surrendering his dignity, he gave up his grip on reality. One day, he ordered a relative to nail a hospital bedpan to the wall and was so insistent that the relative pretended to do so. Later, in a voice full of the old authority and speaking from some place that only he could see, he told a visitor, "If you break the vow of light, the whole plot will be ruined."

They took him home. Jan, herself barely ambulatory, held his hand and consoled him on the morning of December 14, 1994.

"You're going to see your mother in a few minutes," she said. "It's okay. You can let go." And he did. He was a month shy of eighty-five. They buried him at Combs a few paces from his parents and his stillborn babies. Many hundreds of people wound through the hills to see the spectacle and hear the preacher's last words. Alta and Jan, who had become friends and conspirators against pain, sat together.

Jan outlived him a little over a year. She was fifty-three.

CHAPTER

27

When Faubus's obituary went out on the wires, the forgetful world sat up, rubbed its eyes, and gave him one more kick to the groin. Editorialists from around the nation and even faraway continents were reminded of all they had against him and his ilk. The comment of the *New York Times* was typical: "These men wanted to be remembered for the many small things they did right. History has decreed, beyond argument and beyond appeal, that they will be remembered for the one big thing they got wrong."

That judgment looks fair on first reading. A little narrow, perhaps, in dismissing "the many small things" that citizens elect a governor to do—educate the young, worry about the poor, take care of the mentally incompetent, lure new industry, build parks and roads. Orval Faubus's record there was generally commendable, sometimes excellent. But where the editor's judgment falls short is in obliterating for all time the layers of context, nuance, and irony that lift a person's life from the mundane to the extraordinary and make it interesting.

The one big thing that Faubus got wrong was colossally, biblically wrong. But it was not simple. His explanation of why he blocked the desegregation of Central High with troops rested on five main arguments. Four of them were flawed in varying degrees. One was shockingly sound.

1. He wanted to preserve the peace and reduce the chance of injury and property damage. He pointed proudly to the small number of injuries during the crisis.

2. He wished to oppose the growing concentration of power in Washington and to demonstrate the importance of making decisions at the state and local levels when possible.

3. The Supreme Court's school desegregation ruling was illegal—morally correct, perhaps, but illegal.

4. The federal government should have enforced its own court orders, using marshals, not soldiers, instead of pushing the job onto a state governor.

5. An intimidating majority of the South's senators and representatives had signed the defiant Southern Manifesto declaring the 1954 decision essentially unconstitutional. That gesture cut the ground from under southern governors who might have wanted to go along with desegregation. For a governor to side with the federal courts in such an atmosphere would have been political suicide.

Take the arguments from the top:

ONE. Faubus's concern about violence was legitimate. Jim Johnson later took credit for creating an illusion of impending disaster—"there were no caravans"—but some of his followers apparently did not understand that their function was merely rhetorical. With tempers running high, killing was a real possibility.

"Look what happened to Medgar Evers," Faubus said to me one day. "Look what happened to the three civil rights workers in Neshoba or some place like that in Mississippi. Look what happened to President Kennedy. Look what happened to Martin Luther King. Now, you are the governor of Arkansas. Place yourself in my place. You want to be slack, slow, indecisive, afraid to act because of the reflection it might be on you, one way or the other as to prejudice, and let a bunch of people be killed?"

Almost certainly, there were hotheaded men in the outlying precincts who were eager to shed blood. Faubus believed that. So did his adversary Virgil Blossom, in spite of his public denials. But both overstated the dimensions of the threat—Faubus knowingly, I believe, and Blossom innocently. Blossom was the private coward trying secretly to persuade Faubus to come to his rescue. Faubus was the public alarm-spreader trying to force Blossom and the school board to postpone desegregation and keep the issue in the

courts a while longer. Court-sanctioned delay was at the heart of Faubus's strategy until the last moment. If he could have produced a semester's postponement, or just a couple of months, he might have avoided taking sides without looking like an integrationist. That was why he insisted on the fiction of impending wholesale violence. His state police concocted a hasty story that Negroes and whites in Little Rock were arming themselves with guns and knives. That yarn along with the hordes descending on Little Rock by caravan—cleverly overstated—was then used to construct a half credible threat that he could use to get a chancery-court injunction to delay integration. When that was swept away by higher authority, he had no alternative that he could perceive as rational except to call out the National Guard.

Aside from the fact that he might have used the National Guard not to block the Negro students but to protect them from the threatening men of violence—more on that later—what his claim of preserving the peace ignored was the very violence that his action inspired among people who saw him as the leader they had been waiting for, the man who would join them in using force against the hated integration that was being crammed down their throats. There was a direct link between his action and the subsequent mob violence in Little Rock. The injury there was minimal, as he pointed out. Less visible but more troubling was the indirect link between Faubus's heroic inspiration in Arkansas and the lynching and bombing that came later in the barbarous reaches of Alabama, Mississippi, and Louisiana. It is unfair to burden Faubus with the blame for all that because those states had their own political leaders who were more bluntly racist and irresponsible. There was no doubt, though, that he became a hero to many thousands of white supremacists beyond Arkansas, some of whom were killers.

Faubus, stricken by cancer and using a walker,
prepares for one of his last public appearances.
He eagerly accepted speaking engagements
until a few months before he died.
TRAVIS DOSTER, *MORNING NEWS OF NORTHWEST ARKANSAS.*

TWO.   Faubus came genuinely to believe in states' rights. When he entered the governor's office, he had no apparent core of belief beyond a few vague inclinations toward patriotism and improving the lot of the common man. He showed no evidence of zeal in religious matters. He had rejected the central teachings of his father's Marxism, keeping only a generalized sympathy for the down-and-out. When he finally developed a set of beliefs, they came from the crucible of 1957. His enemies blithely dismissed his utterances from that time as cynical, but that was probably unfair. Set upon by the superior force of the central government, he came to believe that the states should exercise rights and powers that are beyond the reach of the federal arm. All else in his quickly assembled vocabulary, from the spectre of too-powerful federal courts to the evils of "forcible integration," flowed from his belief in states' rights. Once forged, those beliefs stayed with him the rest of his life.

Replying to a student from Utah years after the Central High crisis, Faubus wrote that decisions made far from the source of the problem tend to be unwise.

> Time and time again, the people of the Southern states and others have voiced their sentiments through the democratic processes at election after election, only to have these sentiments completely disregarded and over-ridden by the use of federal force in attempting to enforce unwise and ill-timed court decisions that are contrary to the constitution by which we have been governed, and contrary to the democratic processes for which the people have come to have deep respect. To me, there is no difference between the imposition by force upon the South of an alien way of life, and the imposition of communism upon the Hungarian people by the Russian Communists, except in degree.

Hyperbole aside, that statement contains a grain of the Jeffersonian ideal. But his states' rights argument, in the context of Central High, ignored at least two developments of national consequence. First, the Supreme Court had long since settled the question of federal supremacy in matters of this sort. A number of governors had challenged the doctrine in earlier years. But in 1932, when the governor of Texas, in an attempt to control falling oil prices, defied a federal court order and sent his National Guard into the oil fields, the Supreme Court got tough. Chief Justice Charles Evans Hughes wrote the opinion. "If this extreme position could be deemed to be well taken," he wrote, "it is manifest that the fiat of the state governor, and not the Constitution of the United States, would be the supreme law of the land; that the restrictions of the federal Constitution upon the exercise of state power would be but impotent phrases, the futility of which the state may at any time disclose by the simple process of transferring powers of legislation to the governor to be exercised by him, beyond control, upon his assertion of necessity."

If there was any lingering doubt, the Supreme Court ended it when it got around to ruling on the actions of Faubus and the Little Rock School Board in 1958. In *Cooper v. Aaron,* the landmark case arising from the Little Rock problem, the court spoke resoundingly. In a conflict between state and federal law, it said, federal law prevails. And all state officials who take the oath to uphold the federal Constitution are bound to follow the rule. It was a governor's duty to uphold the constitutional rights of citizens—such as the right to an unsegregated education—and not to help people trying to obstruct those rights. To emphasize the point, the justices took the unusual course of signing the decision—all nine of them.

The second thing that flew in the face of states' rights in 1957 was the nation's growing disgust with southern politicians who used the doctrine to justify continued oppression of black citizens. Thanks to the genius of the federal system, the voice of the oppressed minority in the southern states was not finally silenced but was heard in Washington. A new national will emerged to correct the wrongs done to the minority. When public opinion coalesced into a critical mass, the central government could no longer ignore it. Only that concentration of federal power that states' righters so despised was capable of correcting the misdeeds of southern politicians who had abused the power of local decision making.

Even a strong states' rights president like Eisenhower could not refuse to act when a governor challenged the federal power so blatantly. "Eisenhower had to be pushed to the wall before he would act," Stephen Ambrose wrote, "but at the critical moment, he lived up to his oath of office. In the process, he convinced most white southerners that they could not use force to prevent integration."

THREE.   Faubus contended that the 1954 *Brown* decision was illegal because it allowed the federal courts to usurp control of schools from the states. Since the time of Jefferson and the Founding Fathers, he said, education had been a local concern, and the federal courts had no right to meddle in it. In later years, he repeatedly quoted James J. Kilpatrick, the conservative columnist who had revived John C. Calhoun's doctrine of interposition and . popularized it for the twentieth-century South. Some years after the desegregation fight was over, Kilpatrick acknowledged that life had become better for black people than it had been under the old separate-but-equal system. But he still held that the *Brown* decision was bad law, saying that changing a law is the business of Congress, not the courts. Faubus went so far as to say, years after the fact, that he would have supported congressional action to outlaw segregation. It was usurpation by the courts that he found distasteful.

That was perhaps the most unstable of the many arguments that he used, both at the time of the tumult and on through his declining years as he worked to polish and beautify the central episode of his life. Declaring the *Brown* decision illegal was an attempt to void a century or more of constitutional development that even a casual history buff like Faubus should have been aware of. The argument cast doubt on the legitimacy of the Fourteenth Amendment, which guarantees due process and equal protection under the law, a matter long since settled even if not to the satisfaction of the last Confederate holdouts. It suggested that the Supreme Court does not after all have the right to interpret the Constitution, a question that was answered, for better or worse but firmly, by John Marshall and his fellow justices during the first generation of the republic. It pretended that *Plessy v. Ferguson,* the 1896 Supreme Court decision that cravenly gave the stamp of approval to the statutory delusion of separate-but-equal, was still defensible in the mid-twentieth century in spite of every outrage that had been committed in Jim Crow's name. Faubus could not feign surprise when the *Brown* decision came down in 1954. It was not as if the Warren court's unanimous ruling was a sudden reversal of half a century of constitutional law. The court had steadily chipped away at the separate-but-equal doctrine for years. Decisions in 1938, 1948, and 1949 had made it clear that legal segregation was doomed. Arguing that the school decision was illegal was the sophistry of a man cornered by history.

FOUR.   His contention that the federal government should have enforced its own court orders, using marshals if necessary, is less easily disputed. The Eisenhower administration was divided over civil rights for blacks. The president himself, when he was finally driven to enforce the court order at Little Rock, did so with extreme reluctance. Almost certainly he was more of a segregationist than Orval Faubus while two of his main advisors were integrationists. Vice President Richard M. Nixon was at that time one of the main national leaders whom the black community considered friendly. He later prostituted his presidency for the votes of the South's uptown segregationists.

The other integrationist, Atty. Gen. Herbert Brownell, might have intervened to head off the Little Rock confrontation if he had believed that he had the legal authority to do so. One option would have been to persuade a federal judge to enjoin the agitators at Little Rock from interfering at Central High, as he and his lawyers had done at Hoxie. But there had not yet been any open violence at Little Rock. The segregationists had talked mightily, but they had not lifted a hand against anyone. Existing federal law did not allow the Justice Department to intervene until it had been asked to do so by a federal court or by a local school board when the board found its desegregation orders being obstructed. Violence like that at Hoxie was considered obstruction. The Little Rock School Board, anxious not to cause panic, declined to ask the department's help. The board did ask Judge Davies privately to provide marshals, and he declined. He eventually asked the department to enter the Little Rock case, but only after Faubus had defied the court's order by blocking integration with his guardsmen.

Most of Brownell's lawyers believed they would fail if they went to court without a local invitation. Efforts by Brownell and others to broaden the department's authority had recently been defeated in Congress. The foot-dragging in Washington was, of course, an accurate reflection of the national opinion. Millions of Americans wanted something done for the oppressed minority, but they had not yet summoned the persuasive anger to overrule the nineteenth-century southerners who ran Congress. The Eisenhower administration lost most of its backbone when Brownell resigned during the Little Rock crisis and turned the Justice Department over to his deputy, William P. Rogers. Far from advancing school policy to give the department more authority, Rogers retreated. He overruled a proposal to prosecute the Little Rock mob leaders. His civil rights advisors wanted to seek an injunction to thwart troublemakers after the federal troops left, and he rejected their advice. In fact, he decided to take no further action at all in Little Rock. The message to federal judges around the South was subtle but frightening: Don't count on Ike and his attorney general for help if you get stuck with an integration case.

FIVE.   In his last argument, Faubus was dead right. More than 85 percent of the members of Congress from the states of the Confederacy, including all eight members from Arkansas, had signed the Southern Manifesto. The document, even after it had been watered down by some of the more sensible men like Fulbright of Arkansas, was gratuitously inflammatory. It accused the Supreme Court of a "clear abuse of judicial power" and of using "naked judicial power." It said the *Brown* decision had no legal basis. It charged that the court had created an explosive condition that was being inflamed by "outside meddlers." It urged the southern states to "resist forced integration by any lawful means." The original language crafted by Senators Strom Thurmond of South Carolina and Harry F. Byrd of Virginia had called for interposition. Even diluted, the manifesto was still seen as legitimizing massive resistance, coming as it did from a significant part of the southern establishment.

But these members of the establishment spent their workdays in Washington. They were not back home to deal with the daily problems. Having signed their declaration of defiance, they retired from the battle and turned the problem over to the governors and school officials of their states. A few signers of the manifesto undoubtedly acted out of principle, wrong-headed though it was. The rest were unanimous in one of two intellectual convictions, hardheaded ignorance or cowardice. Granted that cowardice has its place in the pragmatic exercise of politics, the action of the congressmen was no more becoming than that of the hundreds of other officials from around the South who encouraged Arkansas and Faubus to fight the despised enemy while they cheered from the sidelines. Faubus was annoyed to see moderates like Fulbright and Representatives Jim Trimble and Brooks Hays buckle under and sign the manifesto even though it violated their principles. At the same time, he understood the pressure they were under. Faubus went with Brooks Hays to Trimble's hospital bed and the two of them advised Trimble to sign the document or risk being turned out of office. Southern moderates chided themselves for not trying to stop the manifesto earlier. But they figured they had no realistic choice except to clamber aboard once the juggernaut came barreling up out of the Black Belt, hell-bent and out of control.

Faubus saw his own political future imperiled in much the same way. He acted for the same reason they did: to save his political hide. He knew that he could have used the National Guard to protect the Negro children. He also knew that that would have been seen as enforcing integration, a stand that very likely would have ended his career. If avoiding political suicide was not admirable in Orval Faubus, it was no more so in the scores of senators and representatives who signed their names to a pandering public lie for the same reason. It should be noted also that, politically speaking, Dwight Eisenhower was no more eager to enforce integration than were Faubus and the southern congressmen. He at least had the solace of a national majority behind him.

Perhaps all that hand wringing and agony could have been avoided if the moderates had not persuaded the Supreme Court to approve their plea for ending segregation with "all deliberate speed." In hindsight, some have argued that the whole strategy of slow-motion integration was mistaken; that the change should have been made thoroughly and all at once so as not to give false hope to the segregationists. That might also have made the burden on blacks more tolerable. As John Egerton, the writer, put it: "The blacks were made to accept all the changes that were made: closed their schools, fired their principals, bused their children. And all the while, whites bitched about the inconvenience of it all to them."

While blame is being apportioned, most of Little Rock's power structure should not be overlooked. Using Virgil Blossom as their agent, the men at the top, those who ran the business establishment and selected the main members of the city council and the school board, insisted that Faubus take the heat by enforcing their desegregation plan. Blossom and the school board seemed not to care that asking Faubus to exercise his police powers to enforce desegregation was asking him to end his political career. They appeared to have morality on their side because they were aligned with the new national will. But Blossom and his masters were, with a few exceptions, no more committed to racial justice than Faubus was. The plantation bosses of Little Rock were mostly segregationists, and any concessions they made to the national will were intended as grudging bribes to maintain public order and keep the cash registers ringing.

Faubus said later, speaking of the school board, "They wanted me to pull their chestnuts out of the fire. They did not care what it did to me. It was life or death with me."

His final break with the board, the point at which his exasperation pushed him into the other camp, apparently came during the game-playing over the lawsuits that were filed in state courts to test Arkansas's anti-integration laws. He thought he had a deal with the school authorities. Some of the harshest language of his public life was used to describe their abandonment of him. "I had been doublecrossed and betrayed by those I had dealt with in good faith," he wrote in his memoirs.

The one justification for his Central High actions that Faubus never uttered out loud was class resentment. Nevertheless, he shared the anger of those social outsiders who watched the Little Rock establishment build a new school far away from the black neighborhoods so that their own children would not have to associate with blacks. The segregationists who shouted curses outside Central were just as angry at the high-collared white people who had deserted them as they were at the black children walking into their school. It was not by chance that Blossom and his friends tried to sell their plan not as right but as expedient. The white working classes knew that they were being sacrificed, not for a higher morality—which they didn't agree with, anyway—but for cynicism.

Some saw Faubus's calling out the guard as the only logical outcome of the policy laid out by the school board and endorsed by the establishment. The Little Rock minister Colbert Cartwright wrote of the board in *Christian Century*, "It had insisted all along that the only reason the schools were being integrated was that the federal government was forcing it to do so. It had consistently refused to seek the help of the community in gaining moral support for its reluctant step. Then the governor in shining armor came to the rescue. He said the school board did not need to integrate, that since the community was not prepared for integration there would be violence. He would call out the militia as the 'preservator of the peace.'"

At the slow pace that Blossom envisioned, it would have taken generations—maybe a century—for the schools to be fully integrated. The folly of the segregationists' rebellion was in not seeing that Blossom was the best friend they could ask for. By enlisting Faubus and the power of the governor's office in their cause, the radicals succeeded in torpedoing the strategy of delay that was their best hope.

Some of the more thoughtful among them would not agree with that. They came to believe that Faubus's action bought ten years to give the more impulsive of their number time to accommodate to the new reality. These men understood that they could not win an armed confrontation with the federal government. Faubus's intervention, as they saw it, headed off such a confrontation and probably saved lives.

Whatever the arguments taken in hindsight, one thing was certain at the time. Faubus's prodding of the federal giant finally stirred it to pay attention to the revolution brewing in the southern states. When the United States Army arrived in Little Rock, the troops brought a stark, reverberating message: The United States will not put up with any more of this defiance. The same message had to be sent a few more times, along with armed force, but it finally sank in.

Both radicals and moderates were left in disarray for some time after 1957. Jim Johnson and his people resembled one of those ragged bands of outlaws that roamed the South after the Civil War. They continued to assert their grievance, tired and increasingly frustrated but stubbornly refusing to surrender. A British writer once noted the same phenomenon elsewhere. "There are of course good logical reasons in history for this benign discrimination in favour of the defeated," said Colin Welch. "The defeated don't normally just go away; what they did is not normally obliterated in toto; they remain there below, muffled presences exerting a continuing influence on whoever conquered and oppresses them."

The moderates went through years of similar despondency. Walter Lippmann lamented that Faubus had set back moderation for a decade. Ralph McGill was more sanguine. He thought the moderates had simply been halted briefly, but would eventually win. He was right. By the mid-sixties, as race in its most virulent form lost its grip on the southern imagination, moderates and progressives began to be elected to southern offices in large numbers to replace the dying and retiring leaders of massive resistance. A generation later, only the occasional Strom Thurmond and Jesse Helms still lifted their plaintive voices for the lost and disappearing cause, and even they dared not call it white supremacy.

Much of the racial hostility that impelled the politics of the South in the 1950s was not pathological but merely unthinking. Most white southerners had been taught from birth nothing so vivid as hate but rather a quiet, unstated contempt for the black underclass, or if not contempt at least a kind of mild and mindless scorn. Many were otherwise well-mannered people who would never utter the word nigger but who failed to understand or even give a moment's thought to the harm caused by jokes and the other casual, habitual snubs designed to put black people in their place, just as they gave no thought to the racism behind much of the politics of the time. But there is no doubt that some southerners, troubling numbers of them, possessed a hatred that became a public threat.

Faubus's actions at Central High might have seemed to him simply a move in the Grand Game. He seemed never to recognize that the game of politics has consequences that go beyond winning or losing. While his 1957 moves played to something like applause among the ordinary unthinking white people, it found a more cruel sympathy in those who took their hatred seriously, the hard men who traveled by night. Among those who understood what was happening was Sam Faubus. He worried about the men of violence who had sprung up right across the country in the 1960s. He wrote to one of his other children, "They are trying to do the same thing in this country old Hitler did for Germany. It will be the Negroes here instead of the Jews."

Orval's detachment toward blacks puzzled some people who had admired his concern for poor whites. He never acknowledged a different attitude toward the two. He was certainly aware that blacks had been discriminated against. He readily admitted that the South had provided inferior schools and facilities for blacks. He argued strenuously that he had always attracted support from black voters, and that was true; black leaders understood pragmatism as keenly as whites. When Faubus spoke at a tribute for Daisy Bates in 1989, he proudly quoted an Associated Press story from 1966 reporting that more than two hundred Negroes had been employed in responsible jobs in state government during his tenure.

But Faubus had no appreciation of the ideal of integration that goes beyond political gain, the broadening of the spirit to include others, the enrichment of the whole that occurs when cultures are mixed. Neither did he understand the deep emotional wounds that pushed blacks into activism and caused them to pursue not just integration but healing. He did not understand the volcanic possibility of their "muffled presences" since the early days of statehood. He did not understand the sharecroppers' pain that had boiled into anger and touched off the racial slaughter at Elaine when he was a boy. He did not understand the childhood torment of Daisy Bates, who grew up knowing that her mother had been raped and killed by white men who had gone unpunished.

It is mildly surprising that some of the nine black youngsters who integrated Central High, those who felt the first direct consequence of his emotional distance, were more forgiving than many white liberals. Ernest Green, the first black graduate of Central High, who went on to stations of leadership in politics and commerce, said many years later, "I don't hate him. I don't have any malice toward him. But I do think that he was clearly misguided, and he could have been a real statesman during that period. He had the portfolio, he had the place, and I think he reduced himself to a mere politician."

Faubus did finally admit that he had underestimated the depth of prejudice among the more radical whites. Those people were suspicious of his commitment all along, and they broke with him after a short time. By the mid-1960s, the remaining organized segregationists were opposing him again quite openly. He then moved easily back to a position much like the one he had abandoned in 1957. He gradually stopped using the thinly veiled language of racism that had adorned his utterances during the early 1960s. He again associated freely with black political leaders, and some of them responded warmly.

But the acrimony of Central High and the years immediately afterward had dashed any hope he might have had of a national career in politics or of any sympathetic reputation among progressives. Some thought he could have had a sinecure with the national Democratic party if he had sacrificed the governorship for the cause of racial justice. Real success at the national level, however, was never a likely prospect. He had never had the breadth of vision to see beyond the possibilities in his own state and region, his early progressivism notwithstanding. He was limited in his awareness of the larger currents in society, the currents that any conscientious reader would have known about. Even a casual attention to the *New York Times* or the *Washington Post*—or a less hostile study of the *Arkansas Gazette*—would have told him that he was joining the losing side in the great national debate of his time. It was almost as if the limitations that blinded him were imposed willfully. He was held in check not just by his poor education but by something more, some inherent constraint against taking intellectual chances. He apparently received more of his mother's caution than his father's adventurousness. Limited though Sam Faubus was by birth and circumstance, there was a restlessness in his mind that would have saved him from the parochialism that crippled his son.

Even Orval's long-term prospects for making a living were uncertain because he had quite deliberately chosen not to fulfill the potential of his intellect. He sensed correctly that once he left the security of the governor's office he would face hard times again because he had not prepared adequately in his youth. After the war, when some of his peers were filling the gaps in their education, he had spurned college and Law School. Later, finding himself a little to his surprise in the governor's office, he realized that he had no career, no law practice, and no family business or fortune to go back to when it was all over.

Of all the calamity and tragedy of his last twenty years, the event that haunted him most was the death of a dog. Magreedy, an Australian terrier, had belonged to Farrell, and Orval had taken the pet into his new Huntsville house when his son had become too drug-addicted to care for it. Since childhood, Orval had shown more feeling for dogs than for people. The terrier won his heart as none other had. It went with him everywhere on Governor's Hill. But one summer day in 1974 when it wanted to get into the car and go with him, Orval reluctantly made it stay behind. He felt the car's wheels run over it as he pulled away.

He wrote a book when he was past eighty ostensibly about all the dogs he had owned. It turned out to be his most revealing memoir. He devoted several chapters to Magreedy. The chapter on the death of the little Australian is nine pages. Seven of those are a recording of his grief. In the artistry of his memory, he had never before suffered worse injury or more painful regret.

> The small form was now in the immutable, eternal grip of the everlasting stillness which finally claims all living creatures . . . the long, long sleep from which there was no earthly waking . . . my heart aching with unforgettable pain . . . I sat exhausted by the open grave and wept.

It would be easy to dismiss that as the unchecked bathos of an old man. But there is more to it. Those seven pages make up the longest sustained expression of emotion that he ever put on paper. He occasionally wrote reflections on grandchildren and other relatives. He wrote movingly about his comrades in battle during World War II. He sometimes set down lines of verse and a kind of awkward prose poetry, usually describing the hills, flowers, and trees of the Ozarks. In none of that did he approach the unrestrained feeling that he displayed over the death of his dog. Magreedy in the grave stood in for a lifetime of pain, sorrow, rejection, loss, and regret.

Faubus for all of his political life was at the beck and call not only of powerful interests but also of the multitudes who thought they owned him. No officeholder could possess more than the shallowest relationship with all those people. Telling the truth to them about his feelings was out of the question for a man of Faubus's dignity. As he practiced to deceive—or, more accurately, as he smiled and nodded to get through each day without injury—he so tightly protected himself that not even those closest to him could penetrate very often. Only his canine friends were privileged to see the real Faubus, unmasked. They obeyed him, they never crossed him, the favors they asked were trifles, and they loved him unconditionally.

Toward the end of his life, as we talked of all the things he had done, he said to me one day, "You know, you hear so many times people talking about, 'Well, if you had your life to live over, if there was some event that you could live over, something you could change, what would it be?' I know instantly what it would be. It would be that brief space of time when that little dog got killed. I'd change that."

The received wisdom of the thinking classes is that Faubus had much more than that to regret, that he inflicted permanent and irreparable harm on Arkansas. Such sweeping condemnation is hard to agree with. He certainly interrupted a centrist trend that the state had begun during the New Deal. But the most serious period of interruption lasted only a few years, and before the end of his administration the state was pottering along toward the American mainstream much as it had been before he entered the picture—and as it had been during the first two and a half years of his tenure. Industrial plants kept coming, although probably not in the numbers claimed by his public-relations force. Organized labor, to which he was mainly friendly, lost no more momentum in Arkansas than it did in other parts of the South during those anti-labor days. The state saw a shift in special interests so that the electricity lobby gave way to the powerhouses of natural gas and money handling. Business and urban interests, on the rise everywhere in Dixie, replaced the low-country planters as the dominant political force in the state. With black voters gaining new strength, the stage was set during Faubus's last years in office for a generation of progressive leadership in the state's Democratic party. The shifts in power that

Faubus presided over were similar to, if not as tumultuous as, those that occurred in Arkansas when the Civil War displaced the ruling class of that era. The movement was part of the rhythm of the time. Aside from the pause after 1957, it would have taken place whether Orval Faubus was governor or merely the editor of the *Madison County Record*.

Of course, there was one other possibility in the disruption of the rhythm. Imagine that Faubus had left office after two terms as almost all of his predecessors had done. He might have decided to stay out of the Little Rock school problem and let it take its course. He could have turned the governor's office over to someone else and gone on to another career. A governor who leaves office under honorable circumstances can usually find gratifying work even if he is not trained for a profession. He might have run for office again after an interval with good prospects for election. Or imagine a more extreme circumstance: that he had used the state police or the National Guard not to block the Negro students but to protect them from white rioters and as a result had been turned out of office at the next election. Voluntarily or otherwise, his leaving office would have meant that someone else would have become governor of Arkansas in January 1959.

The two strongest politicians waiting for Faubus to leave office were Bruce Bennett, the attorney general, and Jim Johnson, the Citizens Council candidate who had frightened Faubus in 1956. With his strong base of support, and with Faubus either politically crippled or retired, Johnson probably would have been elected in 1958.

Governor Johnson would have had little interest in day-to-day governing or in the compromises and negotiations required to push a program through the legislature. His interests were broader. He was dancing at the edge of revolution, and with the governorship of a state to propel and support him, he would have become overnight the commanding general of the southern resistance. George Wallace that year was still an obscure minor official in Alabama. He would not become governor until 1963. With four years' head start, Jim Johnson would have made George Wallace's southern leadership unnecessary. He was just as intelligent as Wallace and just as ruthless. He was better with words and better at

Faubus campaigning for the governor's office again in 1974.

speaking them. He was good-looking in a dark, menacing way; Wallace was merely pug-nosed and threatening. And one other thing: Wallace was held back from the precipice by some restraining hand, cowardice, perhaps, or just simple caution. Jim Johnson was not built for restraint. As governor of Arkansas, he would have carried the fight to the bitter and certain end. The feds might have had to take him by force, along with whatever fellows of fortune who had elected to go down with him. One could see him running for president from his prison cell in the manner of Eugene Debs, or some Guatemalan insurgent. And back home, Arkansas would have had to climb out of the abyss once again, much as it had done after the Civil War. Who knows: The reformer selected to clean up the mess might have been calm, reasonable Orval Faubus.

Faubus liked to hear himself compared to Huey P. Long. There were similarities, but their differences were more pronounced. Long built a dynasty that lasted for decades. He had a national following for his share-the-wealth scheme. He was a contender for the presidency. Even Huey's corruption was broader and deeper. What appealed to Faubus in Huey's reputation was the populism. He wanted to be remembered, like Long, as a friend of the poor.

Faubus was not much like any of the old southern demagogues. He was reminiscent of Tom Watson and James K. Vardaman in his populism, but they were more fervently committed to that cause. Vardaman had the makings of a liberal hero. He sacrificed his political career on the platform of pacifism when he stood in the Senate and opposed entering World War I. In some minds, Faubus is identified with the same sort of racism that Vardaman and Watson are remembered for. His stand on race, however, was far less offensive. Turn-of-the-century demagogues like Vardaman, Watson, and Arkansas's Jeff Davis blatantly used race hatred as a campaign tool. Faubus exploited the emotion, but far more subtly.

He was not even very like his wayward spawn George Wallace. The Alabamian was from the petty bourgeoisie, while Faubus was the genuinely poor hillbilly. Wallace, like the old-fashioned white supremacists, made the Ku Klux Klan virtually a part of his state government. Faubus always held himself aloof from the notoriously violent. While Wallace was clamorous and snarling in his defiance, Faubus was tentative and sometimes almost apologetic. When Faubus was moved to relieve the punishment of a segregationist bomber from Little Rock, he did so furtively. Wallace for his part was openly associated with the head of the Kluxers, and some of his main advisors were notorious racist rabble-rousers.

In instinct and style, Faubus was probably more like Richard M. Nixon than any other public figure of recent history. Nixon was insecure as a boy. He regarded his mother as a saint. He was not good at athletics. He admitted lying when he labeled an early California opponent a Communist, saying he did so because he desperately needed to win. His ideological convictions were lightly held. He despised the press and used it as a political foil. Nixon had a phony smile, Faubus a phony grimace of sincerity. Faubus, like Nixon, was capable of shrewd political thinking and sophisticated analysis and at the same time of sordid pettiness.

Faubus has been accused of betrayal—a charge that would have puzzled the white majorities that returned him to office time and again. There is no doubt that he betrayed the hopes, if not the expectations, of black people. His old liberal friends felt betrayed, and they never forgave him. There is some question as to whether he turned his back on his upbringing and betrayed the ideals he learned from his father. If Sam was really more populist than Marxist socialist—and he was more populist in his later years, if not in his youth—then Orval's gubernatorial career was more of a fulfillment than a betrayal of his father's politics. In accommodating to the men of wealth and power while making a place of substance for himself, Orval was living out the main tenet of the populist faith: that even a poor person can make it in America if he has half a chance. He did not betray his class. Americans, especially the have-nots, have always cheered those who rose from their class rather than with it. The Arkansawyers who applauded Orval's rise most enthusiastically were the white people of modest circumstances. The people who grieved hardest at his funeral were the hillbillies he grew up with.

The real betrayal by Orval Faubus was one that haunted him the last third of his life, all through the untiring revisionism, the endless pleading and explaining to justify the past to the future. It was the betrayal of his talent. He was a natural man of the middle. His gift was for compromise and consensus. When he was not distracted by race and intoxicated by ambition, he wielded that gift with uncommon skill. He had already achieved some of the more realistic goals of the political center when he was overtaken by the Central High crisis. He panicked. When his pollster told him that more than 80 percent of the state's voters opposed integration, and when he was unable to strike a deal for delay, he used the pollster's information not to calm anxieties but to create political mischief. As a man of the center, he knew that the vast majority of those 80 percent would never take up arms for the doomed cause. But he lost his nerve. He doubted that he could assuage their resentment and keep their support. Calculating for advantage and fighting for survival, he slipped from the center into the furious orbit of the never-enders and found himself, the born pragmatist, the man of practicality, leading the most hopelessly romantic lost cause since the Civil War.

He won four more elections because of the momentum that gave him. But the price was dear. His ties to the center were severed. He became a man of the right for the rest of his life; he had nowhere else to go. He finally, or so it seemed, came to believe in the austere doctrines of shalt-not and self-first. His pride and his fear of looking like a fool would not let him turn back once he joined that company. In a perversion of Sam's steadfast devotion, Orval never recanted. Even George Wallace finally apologized for the harm he had caused. Faubus never admitted that he had caused any.

CHAPTER ONE

3   "barely two": Joyce Gabbard interview,
    Aug. 18, 1990. Orval Eugene Faubus (OEF)
    letter to John Samuel Faubus, Jan. 11, 1960.
    OEF interviews, June 25, 1988; July 1, 1988;
    and Oct. 10, 1992.

5   "For years, he feared": OEF interview, June 22, 1988.

5   "Flux swept": Gabbard interview, Aug. 18, 1990.

5   "His grandmother": OEF interview, June 14, 1988. Orval E. Faubus, *In This Faraway Land: A Personal Journal of Infantry Combat in World War II* (Conway, Ark.: River Road Press, 1971), pp. 5, 6.

7   "Combs throve": OEF interviews, June 25, 1988, and Nov. 21, 1992.

8   "Thousands of Scotch-Irish": Charles Reagan Wilson and William Ferris, eds., *Encyclopedia of Southern Culture* (Chapel Hill and London: University of North Carolina Press, 1989), pp. 552–53; Gerald T. Hanson and Carl H. Moneyhon, *Historical Atlas of Arkansas* (Norman and London: University of Oklahoma Press, 1989), pp. 17, 18, 23.

10 "The first American": OEF interview, June 21, 1988.

10 "William was a Scot": *1969–1970 Faubus Book,* by Ada Anderson, privately printed, in author's possession. Size roll of Maj. Andrew Lewis, from the personal collection of OEF.

10 "Family records show": *Pineville* (Ky.) *Sun,* Aug. 7, 1958, reprinted in *Madison County Record,* Aug. 28, 1958.

10 "Further family lore": *Pineville Sun.* Family geneaology records provided to Roy Reed (RR) by OEF; OEF interview, Nov. 21, 1992.

CHAPTER TWO

13 "Addie Joslin Faubus told": Bonnie Salcido interview, May 17, 1990.

14 "Some of the young": Salcido interview, Aug. 18, 1990.

14 "He confessed late": Sam Faubus letter to Bonnie Salcido, Apr. 6, 1962, copy to RR.

14 "Even the poor": OEF interviews, Feb. 27, 1993, and July 1, 1988. Faubus, *In This Faraway Land,* p. 9.

15 "His friends called him": Salcido interview, May 17, 1990.

15 "Then one day": Connie Faubus Tucker interview, Mar. 28, 1990; OEF interview, June 21, 1988.

16 "Finding time": OEF interview, June 21, 1988.

16 "He had homesteaded": Department of the Interior, General Land Office, homestead documents, June 7, 1910, and Nov. 24, 1915, provided to RR by OEF; OEF interview, June 14, 1988.

16 "One night after": Orval E. Faubus, *Man's Best Friend: The Little Australian and Others* (Little Rock, Ark.: Democrat Printing & Litho Co., 1991), p. 14.

17 "After seeing its face": Faubus, *Man's Best Friend,* p. 19.

17 "Sam learned to sing": OEF interview, June 22, 1988.

17 "He circulated petitions": OEF letter to Harry Oswald, Feb. 1, 1966, Faubus Papers, Mullins Library, University of Arkansas, Fayetteville.

19 "Henry Faubus's religious": *Arkansas Gazette,* Feb. 16, 1964, p. 4E.

19 "In spite of": OEF interview, Sept. 12, 1988.

19 "Went to Huntsville": Sam Faubus diary, Mar. 5, 1938, provided to RR by OEF.

19 "You can prate": Several of Sam Faubus's poems are in the Sam Faubus file of the Faubus Papers.

20 "In one letter": Sam Faubus letters to Carl Doss, Oct. 15, 1965, and July 30, 1957, Sam Faubus file, Faubus Papers.

20 "If he was impatient": Bonnie Salcido letter to RR, May 1990, and interview, Aug. 21, 1990.

21 The essay "Man," Sam Faubus file, Faubus Papers.

21 "Orval believed": OEF interview, June 22, 1988.

22 "There was no doubt": Interviews with OEF, June 14 and June 21, 1988, and with his sister Connie Faubus Tucker, Mar. 28, 1990, and his brother Doyle Faubus, Mar. 27, 1990.

23 "Orval once fought": Salcido interview, May 17, 1990.

23 "Even family members": OEF interview, Dec. 23, 1992.

24 "Sam, in particular": Salcido letters to RR, Aug. 28, 1990, and Jan. 1, 1992, and interview, May 17, 1990.

24 "Bonnie softened": Letter published in the *Madison County Record* dated 1950s provided to RR by Salcido.

CHAPTER THREE

25 "One night during": OEF interview, June 14, 1988.

26 "In Marshall County": Garin Burbank, *When Farmers Voted Red* (Westport, Conn.: Greenwood Press, 1976), pp. 8–9.

26 "A radical farmers' organization": Randy Nenningson, "Upland Farmers and Agrarian Protest: Northwest Arkansas and the Brothers of Freedom" (master's thesis, University of Arkansas, 1973).

26 "The Socialists during this period": James R. Green, *Grass-Roots Socialism: Radical Movements in the Southwest, 1895–1943* (Baton Rouge: Louisiana State University Press, 1978), pp. 244–52; George Gregory Kiser, "The Socialist Party in Arkansas, 1900–1912" (master's thesis, University of Arkansas, 1980).

27 "Just how radical": Kiser, "The Socialist Party in Arkansas," p. 6. For an elaboration of that idea, see Roy Reed, "Orval Faubus: Out of Socialism, Into Realism," *Arkansas Historical Quarterly* 64 (spring 1995): 13.

27 "Kiser's description": Kiser, "The Socialist Party in Arkansas," p. 74; interview with OEF.

27 "The only vote Sam ever regretted": *Arkansas Gazette,* Feb. 16, 1964.

27 "Sam was so agitated": Sam Faubus letter to Bert Jackson, Jan. 24, 1964, Faubus Papers.

27 "Sam's children": "Sam Faubus," unpublished paper by Thomas McDonald made available to RR.

28 "When Sam and his friends": Socialist Charter, Mill Creek Local, provided to RR by OEF.

28 "Sam's family": OEF interview, Sept. 12, 1988; Curtis R. Swaim, "The Orval Faubus
    I Knew," paper provided to RR by OEF; and Salcido interview, May 17, 1990.

28 "For a while he subscribed": Salcido interview, May 17, 1990.

28 "The only conventional": *Arkansas Gazette*, Feb. 16, 1964, and Sam's letter to
    Carl Doss, Sept. 21, 1965, Faubus Papers.

28 "Orval believed": OEF interview, June 14, 1988.

28 "Green lived": Bonnie Pace interview, Nov. 9, 1990.

29 "When Green grew old": Sam Faubus diary, May 18, 1941, and June 7, 1941.

29 "One of the party's": J. S. Faubus article in the *Madison County Record*,
    Mar. 23, 1933.

30 "One late spring day": Faubus, *Man's Best Friend*, p. 30.

30 "The charter from the state": OEF private document provided to RR.

32 "Three years later": Sam Faubus file, Faubus Papers, and OEF interview,
    Feb. 27, 1993.

32 "As many as thirty": OEF speech to Young Democrats, University of Arkansas,
    Apr. 30, 1993; OEF letter to RR, Feb. 11, 1993.

32 "Altogether, the Socialist": Edgar Eugene Robinson, *The Presidential Vote,
    1896–1932* (Stanford University Press).

32 "A map": Kiser, "The Socialist Party in Arkansas," p. 95.

33 "Sam's letters": Combs news column, *Madison County Record*, Mar. 9, 1933.

33 "The platform of the Arkansas": Kiser, "The Socialist Party in Arkansas."

33 "But socialism, for all": Burbank, *When Farmers Voted Red*, pp. 108–28.

34 "In spite of the claims": Claude Williams letter to Billy and Viola Gilbert,
    Aug. 22, 1975, Claude C. Williams Collection, Archives of Labor and Urban
    Affairs, Reuther Library, Wayne State University, Detroit.

34 "Some university": Kiser, "The Socialist Party in Arkansas," p. 83.

34 "Then came the war": Wilson and Ferris, eds., *Encyclopedia of Southern Culture*,
    p. 672. Albert D. Kirwan, *Revolt of the Rednecks: Mississippi Politics, 1876–1925*
    (Lexington: University of Kentucky Press, 1951), pp. 279–80.

34 "In Arkansas and Oklahoma": Numerous articles in the *Arkansas Gazette*,
    Dec. 24, 1917, through Aug. 24, 1918.

35 "Sauer kraut may be eaten": *Arkansas Gazette*, May 31, 1918.

35 "Increasingly, the Socialist": H. Wayne Morgan, *Eugene V. Debs: Socialist for
    President* (Syracuse, N.Y.: Syracuse University Press, 1962), pp. 161–65, 177–80.

36 "There is some evidence": Carl Vanlandingham interview, June 28, 1989. Salcido
    interview, May 17, 1990. Swaim, "The Orval Faubus I Knew."

36 "Sam undoubtedly": OEF interview, Feb. 27, 1993.

36 "During one stay": *Wenatchie Daily World*, Aug. 25, 1938, editorial page.

36 "Sam probably had not": OEF letter to RR, Feb. 11, 1993.

37 "By 1920, socialism": Burbank, *When Farmers Voted Red*, p. 128.

37 "A favorite entertainment": OEF interview, June 21, 1988.

37 "Curtis R. Swaim, one": Swaim, "The Orval Faubus I Knew." OEF interviews,
    May 14, 1993, and June 20, 1993.

39 "Not much came": J. S. Faubus article, *Madison County Record*, Mar. 23, 1933.
    OEF speech to Young Democrats, Apr. 30, 1993. *Commonwealth College Fortnightly*,
    Nov. 1, 1932, p. 2, Reuther Library.

39 "Pronounced it Ruesevelt": Salcido letter to RR, Sept. 1991.

39 "Combs column of the *Record*": *Madison County Record,* Mar. 9, 1933.

39 "As late as 1941": Sam Faubus diary, May 10 and June 22, 1941.

40 "whispered about his politics": Vanlandingham interview, June 28, 1989.

40 "He had appendicitis": OEF interview, Sept. 12, 1988. Sam Faubus letter to Carl Doss, Sam Faubus file, Faubus Papers.

CHAPTER FOUR

40 "His parents praised": Faubus, *Man's Best Friend,* pp. 52–53.

40 "The boy became" through "Orval grew up": OEF interviews, June 22, 1988; July 1, 1988; Sept. 12, 1988; and Feb. 27, 1993.

43 "He was once sweet": Salcido interview, May 17, 1990.

43 "Sam and his oldest": Salcido interview, May 17, 1990.

43 "Orval's closest sibling": Tucker interview, Mar. 28, 1990.

44 "It took his parents": OEF interview, June 21, 1988; OEF letter to RR, Feb. 11, 1993.

46 "Addie's face became": OEF interview, June 21, 1988.

46 "'I got to be the boss'": OEF interview, June 14, 1988.

46 "'If he looked at me'": Salcido interview, May 17, 1990.

47 "Sam offered him a mortgage": OEF interview, June 14, 1988.

47 "His siblings learned': Owen Thornberry interview, Aug. 20, 1990. Salcido interview, May 17, 1990. *Mountain Air,* St. Paul, May 15, 1926.

47 "Orval was not": OEF speech, Pettigrew, Ark., reunion, Mar. 20, 1993, and OEF interview, Sept. 12, 1988.

48 "operated a still": OEF telephone interview, Jan. 6, 1992; Salcido interview, May 17, 1990.

48 "Zember Cornett got drunk": OEF interview, June 22, 1988.

49 "One day in March": OEF speech, Pettigrew, Ark., reunion, Mar. 20, 1993.

49 "'A fellow that ain't got'": Faubus, *Man's Best Friend,* p. 66.

49 "'I started back through'": OEF interview, June 22, 1988.

49 "'He was commonly fixed'": *Memphis Commercial Appeal,* Aug. 22, 1954.

50 "His first class": Faubus, *Man's Best Friend,* p. 69.

50 "He had paid the girls": Owen Thornberry interview, Aug. 20, 1990. OEF interview, June 22, 1988.

50 "Alta lived": Alta Faubus interview, June 1, 1989.

51 "Sam slowly got ahead": Faubus, *Man's Best Friend,* p. 59, and OEF interview, June 25, 1988.

51 "Improved as it was": OEF interview, Feb. 27, 1993. Salcido interview, Aug. 21, 1990.

52 "When it finally arrived": Salcido interview, Aug. 21, 1990.

52 "who rooted for the black man.": Salcido interview, May 17, 1990.

52 "Lye soap": Salcido interview, May 17, 1990.

52 "The family made do": Salcido interview, Aug. 21, 1990.

53 "hogs get into the cornfield": Faubus, *Man's Best Friend,* p. 72.

CHAPTER FIVE

53 "'In the autumn'": OEF interview, June 25, 1988.

54 "'The chiggers would nearly'": OEF interview, June 14, 1988.

55 "'When it was first clurred'": OEF interview, June 25, 1988.

55 "'I can remember him saying'" and "shade of a large white oak": OEF interview, Nov. 21, 1992.

55 "One day, Orval counted thirty-two": OEF speech, Pettigrew, Mar. 20, 1993.

56 "a good mule might be swapped": Thornberry interview, Aug. 20, 1990.

56 "'Here were all their ancestral'": OEF interview, Nov. 21, 1992.

56 "Sam, in middle age": OEF interview, June 21, 1988.

56 "'I read a book'": OEF interview, June 25, 1988.

57 "Alabam had more voters": OEF interview, June 22, 1988.

57 "two of them died violently": OEF interview, June 21, 1988.

57 "'your house is on fire'": OEF interview, June 25.

57 "There was the endless skein": OEF interview, June 21, 1988.

58 "The Socialist O. T. Green braved the risk": Pace interview, Nov. 9, 1990.

58 "'You come to an early'": OEF interview, June 21, 1988.

58 "The creatures of the woods": Salcido interview, Aug. 21, 1990.

58 "The war divided": OEF interview, Sept. 12, 1988.

59 "Orval's great-grandfather" and "Orval's great-grandfather Eli": OEF interviews, June 22, 1988, and Sept. 12, 1988.

59 "into the hills as slaves": Unpublished research by Theodore Smith, graduate student in history, University of Arkansas.

60 "One such community": OEF interview, July 1, 1988.

60 "Mrs. Ida Bevins Brashears": Pace interview, Nov. 9, 1990.

60 "'Dad, he was on the side'" and "Not surprisingly": OEF interview, July 1, 1988.

CHAPTER SIX

61 Riding the rails: OEF interviews, July 1, 1988, and June 20, 1993.

63 "continued his teaching career": OEF interview, Sept. 9, 1990.

63 "Most whippings were administered": Vanlandingham interview, June 28, 1989.

64 "He once switched his own wife": Salcido interview, May 17, 1990.

64 "He did not tell bawdy": Vanlandingham interview, June 28, 1989.

64 "His sister Bonnie" and "Orval enjoyed": Salcido interview, May 17, 1990.

65 "a fourth of the work force": According to *Historical Statistics of the United States Colonial Times to 1970*, pt. 1, p. 135, compiled by the Bureau of the Census, 24.9 percent of the American work force was unemployed in 1933.

65 "sky over Greasy Creek": OEF speech to Young Democrats, Apr. 20, 1993.

65 "Bonnie once wore a flour-sack": Salcido interview, May 17, 1990.

65 "Occasionally, the poverty": Faubus, *Man's Best Friend*, p. 77.

66 "He worked for the Biles-Coleman": Biles-Coleman letter to *Arkansas Gazette* reporter Dave Hacker, Sept. 22, 1954.

66 "In central Washington": Vanlandingham interview, June 28, 1989. OEF interview, July 1, 1988.

66 "'If we have to go down the road'": OEF speech to Young Democrats, Apr. 20, 1993.

66 "The migrants encountered": Ruth Neal interview, May 23, 1990.

67 "But at least two": Sam Faubus diary, June 5, 1938.

67 "The real mystery": Charles Dagnon interview, May 23, 1990.

68 "Back home" and "Sam understood": OEF interview, July 1, 1988.

68 "He refused to join": OEF letter to RR, Feb. 11, 1993.

68 "'I knew even then'": OEF interview, June 22, 1988.

69 "'I determined'": OEF interviews, July 1, 1988, and Sept. 12, 1988.

69 "Orval recalled one man": OEF interviews, June 21, 1988, and Nov. 21, 1992.

70 "Orval in later years": OEF interview, June 21, 1988.

70 "Addie Faubus came to weigh": OEF interview, June 22, 1988, and Salcido interview, May 17, 1990.

72 "Orval had been to Huntsville": Alta Faubus telephone interview, Aug. 22, 1994.

72 "The young marriage": Alta Faubus interview, Aug. 19, 1994.

73 "Failing to pass the state": Interviews, OEF and several ex-pupils at Greenwood School reunion, Sept. 9, 1990. OEF interview, May 14, 1993.

74 "They spoke the dreaded word": Alta Faubus interviews, Oct. 10, 1991; Aug. 19, 1994; and May 29, 1996.

74 "Alta needed the comfort": Alta Faubus interview, Aug. 19, 1994.

74 "The second baby": OEF interview, July 1, 1988.

CHAPTER SEVEN

77 "His career in public": OEF interview, June 20, 1993.

78 "Orval won a second term": Faubus, *In This Faraway Land,* p. 16.

78 "'I hope this is the beginning of the war'": Sam Faubus diary, June 22, 1941.

79 "He was the last person to speak": Faubus, *In This Faraway Land,* p. 347.

80 "Leading a ticket of Democratic": Faubus, *In This Faraway Land,* p. 677.

81 "Faubus and several acquaintances": E. J. Ball telephone interview, Aug. 8, 1995.

83 "'Yeah, he just out-slickered them.'": OEF interview, Aug. 5, 1988.

84 "Faubus hatched his plan.": Faubus, *Down from the Hills,* p. 15.

86 "the billboards of Clyde Ellis": OEF interview, June 14, 1988.

87 "The candidate knew how": OEF interview, Oct. 31, 1988.

87 "The first primary vote was": Faubus, *Down from the Hills,* p. 30.

87 McMillan put in race as stalking horse: William J. Smith telephone interview, Nov. 3, 1995.

87 "Both quickly lined up": William J. Smith and OEF joint interview, Oct. 13, 1989. OEF interview, Oct. 31, 1988.

CHAPTER EIGHT

88 "He established a fiscal code": Marcus Halbrook interview, June 14, 1989.

88 Crain and Adams on highway commission: *Historical Review: Arkansas State Highway Commission and Arkansas State Highway and Transportation Department*

1913–1992 (Little Rock, Ark.: Arkansas State Highway and Transportation Department, 1992), pp. 65–76.

90 "Adams was a personable": W. R. Stephens interview, Jan. 11, 1990. Sam Boyce interview, Jan. 9, 1990. Henry Woods interview, July 12, 1995.

90 "Political kingpins all over": Herman McCormick interview, Oct. 10, 1990. OEF interview, June 15, 1994.

91 Printing companies with official ties: Confidential source.

91 "'Cherry didn't have a damn lick'": Woods interview, July 11, 1995.

91 Paul Van Dalsem's manipulation of candidates: David H. Pryor interview, Aug. 2, 1991.

92 "It was Wells": Pryor interview, Aug. 2, 1991.

92 "William J. Smith, the ubiquitous": William J. Smith telephone interview, Nov. 3, 1995.

93 Baker and Crain two biggest contributors: Faubus, *Down from the Hills,* p. 22.

94 "'all he wanted to say at the present'": *Arkansas Gazette,* Aug. 1, 1954. Faubus, *Down from the Hills,* p. 33.

94 "One had approached Carl": Vanlandingham interview, June 28, 1989.

94 Faubus statement of Aug. 2: *Arkansas Gazette,* Aug. 3, 1954.

95 "He bore down": *Arkansas Gazette,* Aug. 3, 1954.

96 "vomited on the front porch": Pryor interview, Aug. 2, 1991.

96 "His confidence returned": Pryor interview, Aug. 2, 1991.

96 Veterans speak up for Faubus: Pryor interview, Aug. 2, 1991.

96 "told seven outright lies": *Arkansas Gazette* of July and Aug. 1954. OEF interviews, Oct. 31, 1988; June 15, 1994; July 19, 1993; and June 3, 1992.

96 "Through it all": OEF interview, July 19, 1993.

98 "Hidden behind all": Alta Faubus interview, June 15, 1989. OEF interview, June 20, 1989. OEF 1954 announcement statement, Albert King Papers, Arkansas Archives of Public Communication, University of Arkansas.

98 "He had also discussed": OEF interview, June 20, 1989, and Faubus, *Down from the Hills,* p. 34.

98 Faubus headquarters deserted next morning: Faubus, *Down from the Hills,* p. 36.

CHAPTER NINE

99 "One day a few years earlier": William Cobb interview with OEF, July 5, 1994; copy to RR.

99 "Statewide, the average income": *Arkansas Gazette,* Leland Duvall column, Mar. 26, 1989.

99 "Social Security would be inaugurated": *Madison County Record,* May 2, 1935.

100 "One night as the men": Bob Reed letters to RR, July 16, 1992; June 2, 1992; and Mar. 21, 1993. Salcido interview, May 17, 1990.

100 OEF found Socialist tracts at Sam's house: Unpublished memo by RR, Dec. 7, 1964. William Cobb interview with OEF, July 5, 1994.

100 "He finished his term": *Arkansas Gazette,* Mar. 9, 1935. Alta Faubus interviews, Aug. 19 and Aug. 21, 1994.

101 "Commonwealth had its roots": *Arkansas Gazette,* Nov. 28, 1954, p. 2F.

101 "Commonwealth's first 80 acres': Raymond Koch and Charlotte Moskowitz Koch, *Educational Commune* (New York: Schocken Books, 1972), pp. 12–21.

101 "The school turned out scores": Koch and Koch, *Educational Commune*, p. 89. *Arkansas Democrat-Gazette,* June 20, 1993.

102 "Others, less well known": Raymond Koch and Charlottte Moskowitz Koch letter to RR, June 28, 1992.

102 Mencken, Brandeis, Einstein, and others befriended the college: Koch and Koch, *Educational Commune,* pp. 79, 86, 146.

102 The legislature investigates Commonwealth: William H. Cobb, "The State Legislature and the 'Reds': Arkansas's General Assembly v. Commonwealth College, 1935–1937," *Arkansas Historical Quarterly,* 45 (1)(spring 1986): 3–18.

105 The article naming Faubus, with name misspelled, appeared under a one-column headline on page 7 of the *Arkansas Gazette,* Mar. 9, 1935.

105 The Finn, Carl Parker, Faubus's roommate: Cobb interview with OEF, July 5, 1994.

105 Dining at Zeni's cafe: OEF interview, June 15, 1994.

106 "The legislature's heavy-handed": Koch and Koch, *Educational Commune,* p. 166.

106 OEF remembered himself as "extreme liberal": RR private memo, "Faubus Remembering," Dec. 7, 1964.

106 OEF stood aloof from the organized left: Marion Noble letter to RR, Aug. 22, 1994.

107 Charlotte Koch made friends at Fayetteville: Charlotte Koch interview, May 13, 1992; Koch and Koch, *Educational Commune,* p. 169.

107 "the Communists had decided to move more aggressively": William Cobb interview with OEF, July 5, 1994.

107 OEF elected president and made May Day speech: *Fortnightly,* May Day issue, May 1, 1935. OEF interview, June 3, 1992.

108 The girls did not find him attractive: Charlotte Koch interview, May 13, 1992.

108 "the challenging range of coursework": *Fortnightly,* Sept. 1, 1934.

108 Commonwealth broadened OEF: OEF interview, June 3, 1992.

108 Speakers included Farrell, Conroy, and Bloor: *Fortnightly,* Apr. 1, 1935.

109 Expelled California students invited: *Fortnightly,* Jan. 1, 1935.

109 Commoners travel to Moscow: *Fortnightly,* Jan. 15, 1935, and Apr. 1, 1935.

109 Hike to Rich Mountain: OEF telephone interview, July 21, 1993.

109 OEF catches eels: *Fortnightly,* May 1, 1935.

110 Sharecroppers organizers jailed: H. L. Mitchell, *Mean Things Happening in This Land,* and Mitchell, *Roll the Union On* (Chicago: Charles H. Kerr Publishing Company, 1987).

111 Lucien Koch arrested: Koch and Koch, *Educational Commune,* p. 153.

112 Commonwealth farm hit by drought: *Fortnightly,* Sept. 1, 1934.

112 A fourth unemployed: *Historical Statistics of the United States Colonial Times to 1970,* pt. 1, p. 135.

112 "'I spent a night in a cell'": Koch and Koch, *Educational Commune,* p 159.

112 "Before the conference could begin": Raymond Koch interview, May 13, 1992; John Egerton, *Speak Now against the Day* (New York: Alfred A. Knopf, 1994), p. 161.

112 "Orval missed": *Fortnightly,* June 1 and June 15, 1935. OEF interview, June 3, 1992. Koch and Koch, *Educational Commune,* p. 42.

113 "That reluctance": Koch and Koch, *Educational Commune,* p. 22. Cobb interview, July 5, 1994.

113 "Orval was ambitious": Koch interviews, May 13–14, 1992.

113 "unless you join them in a church": OEF interview, June 3, 1992.

113 "His fellows also noticed": Koch interview.

114 "marriage was simply legalized prostitution": OEF interview, June 3, 1992.

115 Letter to Governor Bailey: OEF letter to Carl E. Bailey, Jan. 26, 1937, Carl Bailey Papers, Arkansas History Commission, Little Rock.

115 OEF worried about Commonwealth's ties to Communist party: Cobb interview, July 5 1994. OEF interview, June 3 1992.

115 "Locally, the fight": Cobb, "The State Legislature and the 'Reds': Arkansas's General Assembly v. Commonwealth College, 1935–1937," pp. 16, 18; *Arkansas Gazette,* Dec. 5, 1954, p. 2F. Koch and Koch, *Educational Commune,* pp. 190–92.

116 "That was not the end": Committee Report 1311 of Mar. 29, 1944, pp. 76, 167; cited in Committee report prepared for Rep. Wilbur D. Mills, D., Ark., Oct. 5, 1954.

CHAPTER TEN

116 "with a match stem in his mouth": Pryor interview, Aug. 2, 1991.

119 "you've got to get one story": Woods interview, July 12, 1995.

119 "to collect a box of damaging evidence": Confidential interview.

120 "the name Faubus was not on the list": Jim Malone interview, Oct. 8, 1990.

120 "that information would have been quite damaging": OEF interview, June 15, 1994.

121 "'this attempt at Communist indoctrination'": Knowles honors thesis.

122 "'in my further opinion you should be defeated'": Edwin E. Dunaway interview, Jan. 5, 1989.

122 *Gazette* refused attack ad: Harry S. Ashmore interview, June 20, 1992. Hugh Patterson interview, Nov. 17, 1990.

123 "He opted to help his other friend": Woods interview, Jan. 4, 1989.

123 "contradictions required 'pretty fancy footwork'": Ashmore interview, June 20, 1992; Woods interview, Jan. 4, 1989; and Malone interview, Oct. 8, 1990.

124 "The voters went to the polls": "Zero Hour for Arkansas: The 1954 Political Campaign," *Arkansas Recorder,* 1954, Scrapbook Section, p. 5. *Arkansas Gazette* Aug. 11, 1954.

126 Truman Baker handled the problem: Alta Faubus interview, June 15, 1989.

126 "By a second account": Malone interview, Oct. 8, 1990. Leland Leatherman interview, Nov. 28, 1990. Q. Byrum Hurst interview, Nov. 29, 1990.

126 Cherry's margin in Garland County reduced: *Zero Hour,* frontispiece.

127 "'Aw, just let it go.'": Robert R. Douglas, undated conversation.

CHAPTER ELEVEN

127 "'Judge, I brung it with me.'": W. R. Stephens interview, Jan. 11, 1990.

127 "At 8 o'clock the next morning": Edwin F. Jackson interview, Feb. 23, 1990.

128 OEF meets Stephens after election: Stephens interview, Jan. 11, 1990. *Faubus, Down from the Hills,* p. 52.

130 Adams was one of the first appointees: Faubus, *Down from the Hills*, p. 91.

130 Wallace Baker's box at Oaklawn: Baker interview, July 20, 1993.

131 Combs campaigned for OEF: Faubus, *Down from the Hills*, p. 62.

131 Made peace with money men: Faubus, *Down from the Hills*, p. 52.

131 Darby's Cadillac as peace offering: Faubus, *Down from the Hills*, p. 52.

131 Stephens helped pay OEF's campaign debt: Marcus Halbrook interview, June 14, 1989. Wallace Baker interview, July 20, 1993.

132 "under no illusion that he was popular in the capital": Faubus, *Down from the Hills*, p. 51.

132 booed at football game: Faubus, *Down from the Hills*, p. 51. Faubus interview, Dec. 19, 1988. Ben Allen interview, July 3, 1990. William P. Bowen interview, June 13, 1989.

132 "Davis delighted rural audiences": L. S. Dunaway, *Jeff Davis: Governor and U.S. Senator, His Life and Speeches* (Little Rock, Ark.: Democrat Print. & Litho. Co., 1913), pp. 35, 42.

132 "cultivated the merchants and their families": Salcido letter to OEF, August 1963.

133 OEF met Little Rock business leaders: OEF interview, June 15, 1994.

133 "loyalty oath to become an Army officer": *Zero Hour*, p. 38a.

133 "The interview ended with General Trudeau": Faubus, *Down from the Hills*, p. 68.

134 "More than 200 patients": Faubus, *Down from the Hills*, p. 83.

134 OEF's legislative session: Faubus, *Down from the Hills*, pp. 72, 80, 81.

135 Made peace with Charles Smith: Faubus, *Down from the Hills*, p. 54.

136 "executive secretary for eight years": Arnold Sikes interview, Sept. 4, 1990.

138 "take every opportunity to turn an enemy": Sikes interview, Sept. 4, 1990.

138 Cooper became a Faubus man: Joe Basore telephone interview, Aug. 21, 1995. OEF interview, Dec. 11, 1990.

141 Lloyd George becomes a local hero: Lloyd George interview, Mar. 14, 1990.

CHAPTER TWELVE

142 "John L. McClellan won that election": Undated conversation with Faubus.

144 "Harry Oswald . . . remembered it a little differently": Harry Oswald interview, Nov. 21, 1995.

145 "Wallace Baker was sitting in his office": Baker interview, July 20, 1993.

146 "The purchase price for a controlling interest": *Arkansas Gazette*, Feb. 3, 1957; *Arkansas Gazette*, June 28, 1977; *Arkansas Recorder*, Oct. 26, 1956.

146 "That further quickened Wall Street's interest": *Arkansas Recorder*, Nov. 23, 1956, p. 2.

146 State officials owned ARKLA stock: *Arkansas Recorder*, Oct. 19, 1956, p. 2; Hardy Croxton interview, Feb. 13, 1990.

147 "Hardy, I just had to change'": Croxton interview, Feb. 13, 1990.

148 "The aluminum interests threatened to fire Catlett": Faubus handwritten statement, undated, titled "controversy," Faubus Papers.

148 "he pushed ARKLA's earnings to more than 10 percent": *Arkansas Recorder*, Dec. 14, 1956.

148 Texas and Louisiana did not use fair field device: *Arkansas Recorder*, Mar. 1, 1957, p. 2.

149 Ark La stock rebounded: *Arkansas Recorder*, Mar. 1, 1957, p. 2.

149 "17 of the 35 state senators . . . on Stephens' payroll": Neal R. Peirce, *The Deep South States of America* (New York: W. W. Norton & Co., 1974), p. 131.

149 "'Faubus got his support from people like me'": Peirce, p. 131.

CHAPTER THIRTEEN

151 "Imagine then the amazement": OEF interview, Nov. 27, 1991. Faubus, *Down from the Hills,* p. 101. *Arkansas Gazette,* Nov. 18, 1955, and June 20, 1956.

153 "'Mr. Witt, let me borrow your shotgun.'": Baker interview, July 20, 1993.

155 "since J. M. Futrell had grudgingly acquiesced": C. Calvin Smith, "Junius Marion Futrell, 1933–1937," *The Governors of Arkansas,* edited by Timothy P. Donovan and Willard B. Gatewood Jr. (Fayetteville: University of Arkansas Press, 1981), pp. 180–81.

157 Kennedy cartoon: Faubus, *Down from the Hills,* p. 176.

157 Kolb stretched hospital's resources: Payton Kolb interview, Dec. 13, 1990.

158 "Van Dalsem forced the governor to relent": Kolb interview, Dec. 13, 1990.

CHAPTER FOURTEEN

161 Madison County election violence: OEF interviews, June 3 and June 4, 1992.

161 "Violence and quarreling were not confined": Harry S. Ashmore, *Arkansas: A History* (New York: W. W. Norton & Co., 1978), pp. 39–50. John Gould Fletcher, *Arkansas* (Fayetteville and London: University of Arkansas Press, 1989), pp. 196–219. Bob Lancaster, *The Jungles of Arkansas: A Personal History of the Wonder State* (Fayetteville and London: University of Arkansas Press, 1989), pp. 131–41.

161 "soldiers on both sides were mainly Negroes": Fletcher, *Arkansas,* p. 203.

162 "as many as 250 blacks had been murdered": Richard C. Cortner, *A Mob Intent on Death: The NAACP and the Arkansas Riot Cases* (Middletown, Conn.: Wesleyan University Press, 1988) p. 30.

162 "Young Jim Malone had expected": Malone interview, Oct. 8, 1990.

163 Arkansas Traveler certificate to Daisy Bates: Daisy Bates interview, Aug. 16, 1990.

164 "Most white supremacists": Tony Freyer, *The Little Rock Crisis: A Constitutional Interpretation* (Westport, Conn.: Greenwood Press, 1984), p. 31.

166 Signers of Southern Manifesto: Numan V. Bartley, *The Rise of Massive Resistance* (Baton Rouge: Louisiana State University Press, 1969), p. 116. Bartley footnotes Bickel's "The Least Dangerous Branch: The Supreme Court at the Bar of Politics," New York, 1962, p. 256.

168 "only six counties with black majorities": U.S. Bureau of the Census, *Seventeenth Census of the United States, 1950, Vol. 2: Characteristics of the Population* (Washington, D.C.: Government Printing Office, 1952), pt. 4, p. 65.

168 "The state was spending $102.25": Julianne Lewis Adams and Thomas A. DeBlack, eds., *Civil Obedience: An Oral History of School Desegregation in Fayetteville, Arkansas, 1954–1965* (Fayetteville: University of Arkansas Press, 1994).

169 "'I would have voted that way myself,'": Dunaway interview, Jan. 5, 1989.

169 "resented black servicemen's dating": Alta Faubus interview, June 15, 1989.

169 "desegregation the number-one issue": Virgil T. Blossom, *It Has Happened Here* (New York: Harper & Brothers, 1959), p. 25.

169 "'they'll never get me out of office.'": Leland Duvall telephone interview, Mar. 1, 1990. George Fisher interview, Feb. 20, 1990.

CHAPTER FIFTEEN

170 "'It took the balls'": James D. Johnson interview, Mar. 13, 1990.

170 "even stronger emotions than taxes": Wilbur D. Mills interview, Aug. 2, 1991.

170 "He had made valuable contacts": Johnson handwritten biographical notes in RR's possession.

172 "arrested in a counterfeiting scheme": OEF speech KARK-TV, July 16, 1956, Faubus Papers.

173 "firearms and grass ropes might have to be used": Freyer, *The Little Rock Crisis*, p. 65.

173 Outlining the Hoxie case: A. B. Caldwell, "The Hoxie Case: The Story of the First School in the Old South to Integrate in the Wake of the Brown Decision" (unpublished report, Caldwell Papers, Mullins Library, University of Arkansas, n.d.). John T. Elliff, *The United States Department of Justice and Individual Rights, 1937–1962* (New York and London: Garland Publishing, 1987). Elliff has an excellent analysis of the Hoxie case and its ramifications. See especially pp. 406–46.

174 "Johnson became Arkansas's point man": Francis M. Wilhoit, *The Politics of Massive Resistance* (New York: George Braziller, 1973), p. 178; Numan V. Bartley, *The Rise of Massive Resistance* (Baton Rouge: Louisiana State University Press, 1969), pp. 190, 258.

175 The nullification device: Bartley, *The Rise of Massive Resistance*, p. 128.

175 "'That amendment was damned near'": Johnson interview, Mar. 13, 1990.

176 Ben Laney's speech: *Arkansas Gazette*, May 1, 1956.

176 OEF poll on integration: Faubus, *Down from the Hills*, p. 120.

176 OEF's rationale in condemning Supreme Court: Faubus, *Down from the Hills*, p. 121.

177 "In Lincoln County, the sheriff": Bartley, *The Rise of Massive Resistance*, p. 101.

177 Members of the Bird Committee: Faubus, *Down from the Hills*, p. 122. Freyer, *The Little Rock Crisis*, p. 34.

178 "'No school district will be forced'": Faubus, *Down from the Hills*, pp. 134–35.

179 "'I don't have to jump up and down'": Robert Sherrill, *Gothic Politics in the Deep South* (New York: Grossman Publishers, 1968), p. 85.

181 "'You made me take positions'": Freyer, *The Little Rock Crisis*, pp. 87–88. Historical Report of the Secretary of State, Arkansas, Vol. I, p. 239. Wilson Record and Jane Cassels Record, *Little Rock U.S.A.* (San Francisco: Chandler Publishing Company, 1960). Johnson telephone interview, Nov. 3, 1991.

CHAPTER SIXTEEN

181 "a visitation of plague": Johnson interview, Mar. 15, 1990. *Arkansas Gazette*, Mar. 13, 1989.

181 Racial incidents in other states: Faubus, *Down from the Hills*, p. 146.

182 "He wanted to be governor of Arkansas.": Harold Engstrom interview, Jan. 11, 1990. Confidential interview.

184 "'The plan was developed to provide as little'": Corinne Silverman, *The Little Rock Story* (Tuscaloosa: University of Alabama Press, 1959), p. 262. Blossom, *It Has Happened Here*, p. 70.

185 "'Keep quiet'": Ken Parker letter to RR, Dec. 18, 1994. RR, unpublished manuscript, 1961.

185 Few whites had black contacts: RR, unpublished manuscript, 1961.

186 "'an Arkansas Gestapo'": Freyer, p. 89.

186 "more Negroes on the state Democratic party": *Arkansas Gazette,* May 8, 1957.

187 "One aspect was particularly offensive": Faubus, *Man's Best Friend,* p. 95. Vivion Brewer, unpublished autobiography, Sophia Smith Collection, Smith College, Amherst, Mass.

187 "It bought a full-page advertisement": *Arkansas Recorder,* July 5, 1957.

188 "'hell on the border'": Record and Record, *Little Rock U.S.A.,* pp. 31–32.

188 "Aside from all this": Blossom, *It Has Happened Here,* p. 36. Faubus, *Down from the Hills,* p. 185. Faubus correspondence files, Faubus Papers.

188 "He had told a couple of liberal friends": Irving J. Spitzberg Jr., *Racial Politics in Little Rock, 1954–1964* (New York and London: Garland Publishing, 1987), p. 62. Dunaway interview, Jan. 5, 1989.

189 "Faubus will fall for any story": Colbert S. Cartwright, "The Improbable Demagogue," *The Reporter,* Oct. 17, 1957.

189 McCulloch understood that minimal integration was necessary: *The Reporter,* Oct. 17, 1957.

189 "placate their enemies": Sikes interview, Aug. 16, 1990.

189 "supplement it with a second-hand furniture shop": Mamie Ruth Williams interview, June 25, 1996.

190 "85 percent of the state's white people": Faubus, *Down from the Hills,* p. 285.

190 Karam wanted OEF elected again: James T. Karam interview, August 19, 1971, Oral History Research Office, Columbia University, Eisenhower Library, Abilene, Kan.; RR interview with Karam, Oct. 9, 1990.

190 "Brown recalled that Faubus was agitated": Robert Ewing Brown interview, Aug. 30, 1990. Columbia interview with Guthridge.

190 "They came away . . . reassured": Columbia interview with Guthridge.

192 "'We were dedicated to hustling him.'": Johnson telephone interview, Feb. 3, 1994.

192 "'Your girls will not be alive'": Blossom, *It Has Happened Here,* p. 62.

193 "Johnson of course had already been": Phil Stratton interview, June 10, 1990.

193 "'And when he did this'": Stratton interview, June 10, 1990. James D. Johnson interviews, Mar. 13 and Mar. 15, 1990, and Feb. 3, 1994.

CHAPTER SEVENTEEN

194 "House and Caldwell gently inquired": Justice Department memorandum by Arthur B. Caldwell, Caldwell Papers, University of Arkansas Library.

194 "He and his clients felt even more isolated": A. F. House interview, July 28, 1990.

194 Caldwell pondered asking the FBI: Caldwell memo.

195 Upton's private meeting with Miller: FBI interviews with Wayne Upton, Sept. 5, 6, and 7, 1957, FBI collection, Mullins Library.

195 "Upton and Blossom joined Faubus": A. F. House letter to A. B. Caldwell, July 21, 1958, Caldwell Papers.

196 Upton, Blossom, and Engstrom to Fort Smith: FBI interviews with Upton.

197 "'If this happened in Georgia'": *New York Times,* Sept. 9, 1957, p. 18.

197 "'The situation was not that clear'": Faubus, *Down from the Hills,* pp. 193–95.

199 "Publicly, the state-court": Faubus, *Down from the Hills,* p. 201. Joint interview with OEF and Smith, Dec. 18, 1989. Blossom interview with FBI. Frankel, when he was interviewed by the FBI, admitted that he had taken the case at the urging of another lawyer but he refused to name him. When the FBI interviewed Wayne

Upton, a member of the school board, Upton said he had been told confidentially by Frankel that the unnamed lawyer was Smith. Years later, Smith denied having anything to do with the lawsuit. He did acknowledge that his law partner Pat Mehaffy had persuaded still another lawyer, Griffin Smith Jr., to get involved. Griffin Smith handled the courtroom work for Mrs. Thomason. Bill Smith said he upbraided his partner for his action.

202 OEF called Clinger and Lindsey: Memorandum from the director of the FBI to the attorney general, Sept. 9, 1957, FBI collection. FBI interview with Clinger, Sept. 6, 1957.

202 "He called them together again": Clarence Thornbrough interview, Sept. 6, 1990.

202 "Faubus decided to get": FBI interviews with DeLong and various members of Faubus's staff and cabinet.

203 "Very late, Faubus' liberal": Hugh B. Patterson interview, Nov. 26, 1990.

203 "Sid McMath tried": Patterson interview. Woods interview, Columbia University Oral History Collection, pt. 3, Dec. 8, 1972.

203 Adolphine Terry tried: Alta Faubus interview, June 15, 1989.

203 Rockefeller met with OEF: FBI director's memo to attorney general.

203 Blossom went to mansion late: Blossom, *It Has Happened Here*, pp. 65–66.

204 Ashmore meeting with Moses: Ashmore interview, Feb. 23, 1990.

205 "'I won't let people like that'": Ashmore interview, Feb. 23, 1990.

205 Bates quotation: Ashmore interview, Feb. 23, 1990.

CHAPTER EIGHTEEN

207 Blossom's telephone call to OEF: FBI interview with Blossom. FBI interview with Jackson. Faubus, *Down from the Hills*, p. 206. *It Has Happened Here*, p. 70.

208 "The telephone campaign": FBI interviews with crowd members, FBI collection.

209 "A tenth student, Jane Lee Hill": FBI interview with Jane Lee Hill, Sept. 1957.

212 Brownell hesitated: A. B. Caldwell letters to Archie F. House, June 19 and Aug. 12, 1958, Caldwell Papers. Engstrom interview, Aug. 21, 1991; *New York Times*, May 3, 1996, p. A29.

213 "Toward the end": Faubus interview, Oct. 18, 1991.

213 "As for caravans": FBI reports, FBI collection.

213 "In his old age": FBI reports. Summary of FBI reports by Warren Olney, assistant attorney general, Sept. 13, 1957; Johnson interview, Feb. 3, 1994.

213 "On September 6, the governor": OEF and Eisenhower telegrams, Faubus Papers.

213 "Little Rock had become": Hoyt Hughes Purvis, "Little Rock and the Press" (master's thesis, University of Texas, 1963); *London Times*, Sept. 11, 1957, p. 10.

214 *Time* and *Life* portrayed OEF as redneck: Purvis, "Little Rock and the Press"; Faubus letter to Mrs. Constance Loustalot, Oct. 16, 1957.

214 Industrialist disappointed: Harold S. Caplin letter to OEF, Faubus Papers.

214 "'I sat there'": Quoted in Brooks Hays, *A Southern Moderate Speaks* (Chapel Hill: University of North Carolina Press, 1959).

214 Atlanta football game: Alta Faubus interview, Oct. 25, 1991.

214 "Others offered": Faubus interviews, Nov. 24, 1991, and June 20, 1993. Claude Carpenter interview, Aug. 1, 1990.

215 "Not all . . . came from the South.": Faubus letter to Mrs. Connie Loustalot, Oct. 16, 1957, Faubus Papers.

215 "As tension rose": Faubus papers, state police files; letter, signature deleted, to Faubus, Dec. 27, 1993, Faubus Papers.

215 "'Here's a malignancy'": *Ozark Spectator,* Sept. 10, 1957.

215 "Now it was the turn": *State Press,* Sept. 6, 1957.

216 Thurgood Marshall arrived: *Arkansas Gazette,* Sept. 7, 1957.

216 "When Faubus blocked": Ozell Sutton interview, June 22, 1992.

217 "The Citizens Councilers": FBI interview with Hugh Lynn Adams, September 13, 1957, FBI collection.

219 "Eisenhower, for his part": Whitman memo, Eisenhower files on Newport meeting, Eisenhower Library. Marian Hays interview, June 22, 1992.

219 "Any Arkansas governor": Faubus interview, Oct. 3, 1990.

219 "The participants cobbled": Faubus interview, June 5, 1990; Faubus interview on CBS "Face the Nation," Aug. 31, 1958.

219 "Hays had miscalculated": Ashmore interview, Feb. 23, 1990.

219 "duty 'to suppress violence'": Hays, *A Southern Moderate Speaks,* p. 137.

220 Brownell foresaw "a clash of historic importance": Herbert Brownell speech at Abilene, Kan., conference on school desegregation, June 5, 1990. Warren Cikins interview, June 22, 1992.

220 "Faubus came to see": OEF interviews with RR. Hays, *A Southern Moderate Speaks.* Silverman, *The Little Rock Story.*

220 "Faubus gradually developed": Faubus speech at Abilene conference.

220 "'And the President told us'": Herbert Brownell interview, June 5, 1990, at Abilene, Kan.

221 Nixon opposed Newport meeting: Columbia University oral history interview with Woods, Dec. 8, 1972; *Arkansas Gazette,* Sept. 22, 1957, p. 1.

221 "'I can probe him'": Cikins interview, June 22, 1992.

221 "Hays did satisfy": Hays, *A Southern Moderate Speaks.* OEF interview, June 4, 1992.

222 Federal lawyers made a mistake: Freyer, *The Little Rock Crisis.* OEF broadcast speech, Sept. 20, 1957.

222 "'Now begins the crucifixion,'": *Arkansas Democrat,* Sept. 20, 1957, p. 1.

222 Joe Foster intercepted a caravan: OEF interview, Dec. 19, 1988; Dr. Bill Foster Jr. interview, Mar. 6, 1996.

223 "Wherever Faubus traveled": OEF interview, June 3, 1992.

223 Death threat against OEF: OEF interview, Oct. 18, 1991. Faubus Papers.

CHAPTER NINETEEN

224 Fire chief refused hoses: Woods interview, Jan. 4, 1989; state police investigation report, Sept. 23, 1957, Faubus Papers.

224 "At 11:30": Melba Patillo Beals, *Warriors Don't Cry* (New York: Pocket Books, 1994), p. 116.

224 "Back in front": *Washington Post* and *Times-Herald,* Sept. 23, 1957.

225 "not his fingerprints": Gay Talese, *The Kingdom and the Power* (New York and Cleveland: World Publishing Company, 1966), p. 45. The reference is to Turner Catledge, a Mississippian, the executive editor of the *New York Times.*

225 "If Faubus's fingerprints": Dunaway interview, Jan. 5, 1989.

225 "Claude Carpenter's sister": FBI interview with Mrs. Mary Anita Sedberry, Sept. 7, 1957.

225 "Many members": FBI interview with Capt. Alan Templeton of the Arkansas State Police, Sept. 8, 1957. *Arkansas Gazette,* Sept. 26, 1957.

226 "'Where's your manhood?'": FBI interview with Roderick MacLeish, chief of the Washington Bureau of Westinghouse Broadcasting Co., Sept. 1957.

226 "One Clarence Whitehead": FBI interview with Clarence Whitehead, Sept. 30, 1957.

227 Blossom conversation with Karam: FBI interview with Blossom.

227 "'The nigger started it.'": *New York Times,* Sept. 24, 1957. FBI interview with Roy Rowan of *Life* magazine.

227 "The crowd ran after another": FBI interview with Stan Opotowsky of the *New York Post.*

227 "keep an eye on Patrolman Tommy": Associated Press article in the *Gazette,* Sept. 27, 1957.

227 "Furthermore, Karam": Robert Troutt interview, Nov. 26, 1990.

227 "More ominously": *Arkansas Democrat,* Sept. 24, 1957. Daisy Bates, *The Long Shadow of Little Rock* (New York: David McKay Co., 1962), p. 96.

229 "He did so": Hugh B. Patterson Jr., publisher of the *Gazette,* picked up an interesting account of how Eisenhower signed the order sending troops to Little Rock. He said he was told by Philip L. Graham, publisher of the *Washington Post,* that word had reached the capital that Eisenhower planned to sign the historic order at his Newport vacation retreat. Graham was agitated over having so somber a matter handled from the golf course. Late in the evening, he went next door and shared his concern with his neighbor, Gen. Alfred M. Gruenther. The general, an old friend of Eisenhower's, was equally agitated. He went to the phone and called the president at Newport. "Ike," he said, "get your ass down to Washington." Ike did. RR interview with Hugh B. Patterson Jr., Jan. 6, 1997. Silverman, *The Little Rock Story,* p. 280. Kenneth McKee interview, July 17, 1990.

229 "a comic encounter with General Walker": Floyd Weaver's report to Herman Lindsey, Sept. 19, 1957, Faubus Papers.

230 "The *Gazette* led": *Northwest Arkansas Times,* Sept. 25, 1957.

231 "Rogers telephoned Ashmore": Patterson interview, Nov. 27, 1990.

231 Mann calls OEF action a hoax: *Arkansas Democrat,* Sept. 6, 1957, p. 1.

231 "Eisenhower might have avoided": John T. Elliff, *The United States Department of Justice and Individual Rights, 1937–1962* (New York: Garland Publishing, 1987), pp. 462–87. J. W. Anderson, *Eisenhower, Brownell, and the Congress* (Tuscaloosa: University of Alabama Press, 1964), pp. 40–43. Brownell letter to RR, Oct. 10, 1991.

232 "One who was not": OEF interviews, Oct. 3, 1990, and Sept. 30, 1994.

CHAPTER TWENTY

232 "Some days they assaulted": Beals, *Warriors Don't Cry.* Ernest Green interview, June 22, 1992.

233 "The soldiers": FBI reports. Jesse L. Long letter to OEF, Apr. 16, 1993.

233 "worth the suffering": Beals, *Warriors Don't Cry.*

233 "He was convinced that Faubus": Eisenhower press conference notes, Oct. 3, 1957, Whitman file, Eisenhower Library, Abilene, Kan. Ralph McGill letter to Eisenhower, Sept. 20, 1957, Eisenhower Library.

235 "The decision became": Interview with Supreme Court Justice-nominee Stephen G. Breyer in the *Los Angeles Times,* July 14, 1994. *New York Times,* Sept. 11, 1958.

235 "Rogers' Justice Department overruled him": Osro Cobb interview, Oct. 3, 1992.

235 "On May 25": Green interview, June 22, 1992.

235 "Boycott effect on *Gazette*": Patterson interview, Nov. 27, 1990. Leon Reed interview, July 13, 1992.

238 Columbus Day prayer: Ernest Q. Campbell and Thomas F. Pettigrew, *Christians in Racial Crisis* (Washington, D.C.: Public Affairs Press, 1959), p. 34.

239 Ogden son suicide: Bates, *The Long Shadow of Little Rock,* p. 195.

239 Mrs. Terry visit to Alta: Alta Faubus interview, Aug. 20, 1990.

239 "Other members": Salcido interview, May 17, 1990.

239 "The tension was taking": Alta Faubus interview, Aug. 19, 1994.

239 OEF told Alta not to leave: Alta Faubus interview, Oct. 15, 1991.

240 Rector accused OEF: *Arkansas Gazette,* Feb. 14–15, 1957.

240 "Johnson said later": Johnson interview, Mar. 15, 1990. OEF interview, Sept. 28, 1991.

242 "The governor took": *Arkansas Gazette,* July 2, 1958.

243 Dan Felton's gratitude: Faubus, *Down from the Hills,* p. 373.

243 Delta gave OEF over 80 percent: Patrick J. Owens, "Where Faubus Gets His Votes" (unpublished paper at Harvard University, 1963).

243 "Oddly enough": William F. Laman interview, Sept. 6, 1991.

244 Rogers memo to Ike: Letter and memorandum from William P. Rogers to the president, Aug. 18, 1958, Eisenhower Library, Abilene, Kan.

245 Bennett ordinances spread to other states: Bartley, *The Rise of Massive Resistance,* p. 221.

246 "Thurmond . . . wrote to praise": Strom Thurmond letter to OEF, Oct. 3, 1958, Faubus Papers.

247 "Some worked with stealth": Herman McCormick interview, Oct. 10, 1990. Steele Hays interview, Feb. 28, 1996. Marlin Hawkins interview, Aug. 2, 1990. Dale Alford interview, Aug. 6, 1990.

247 "Council leaders were working feverishly": Jim Johnson letter to Claude Carpenter, Feb. 17, 1959, Jim Johnson Collection, Arkansas History Commission, Little Rock.

248 "Faubus and Carpenter drove to Morrilton": OEF interview, Oct. 1, 1990.

248 "Carpenter delivered": Interviews with Claude Carpenter, Hawkins, and Dale Alford, Aug. 6, 1990. Brooks Hays, *Politics Is My Parish* (Baton Rouge: Louisiana State University Press, 1981), p. 182. Sikes interview, Aug. 16, 1990. OEF interview, Apr. 28, 1991.

249 "photograph of Hays": Carpenter interview, Aug. 1, 1990.

249 Coleman defeated after supported Hays: James P. Coleman letter to RR, Oct. 11, 1990.

249 Rayburn and Mills abandoned Hays: Cikins interview, June 22, 1992. Oren Harris letter to Joe K. Mahony, Nov. 11, 1958, Harris Papers, University of Arkansas Library.

251 "Hays declined": Hawkins interview, Aug. 2, 1990.

251 "Hays typically": James T. Baker, *Brooks Hays* (Macon, Ga.: Mercer University Press, 1989), pp. 95, 96. Cikins interview, June 22, 1992.

CHAPTER TWENTY-ONE

252 "During Eisenhower's last three": Richard Kluger, *Simple Justice: The History of Brown v. Board of Education and Black America's Struggle for Equality* (New York: Alfred A. Knopf, New York, 1976).

253 "Shortly after": Vivion Brewer unpublished memoir, p. 5.

253 Harlan S. Hobbs interview, Nov. 19, 1996.

254 WEC first meeting: Unpublished memoir by Adolphine Fletcher Terry, Terry Papers, University of Arkansas Library.

254 "It asked every principal": Lorraine Gates, "Power from the Pedestal: The Women's Emergency Committee and the Little Rock School Crisis," *Arkansas Historical Quarterly,* 51(1) (spring 1996): 48.

255 OEF criticizes Mrs. Terry: *Arkansas Gazette,* July 11, 1960.

255 "'get his wife out of nosing around'": Confidential interview, May 11, 1993.

256 "'I just turned around'": J. H. Cottrell interview, Mar. 27, 1996.

256 "traced to the state police": Confidential interview, July 2, 1990; Faubus, *Down from the Hills, II; Arkansas Gazette,* Aug. 11 and Sept. 18, 1959.

256 "That effectively ended": Osro Cobb, *Osro Cobb of Arkansas: Memoirs of Historical Significance* (Little Rock, Ark.: Rose Publishing Co., 1989); *Arkansas Gazette,* July 11, Sept. 14, and Sept. 15, 1961.

257 "Many years went by": Henry Woods and Beth Deere, "Reflections on the Little Rock School Case," *Arkansas Law Review,* 44:4 (1991): 971.

257 "The hero who stood": United Press International, Mar. 19, 1960; state police reports Feb. and Mar. 1960; Dunaway interview, Jan. 5, 1989; confidential interview, Mar. 1996.

257 "Arkansas's civil rights": Faubus, *Down from the Hills, II* (Little Rock, Ark.: Democrat Printing & Litho Co., 1985), p. 59. Memorandum from Herman Lindsey to OEF, Feb. 2, 1960, Faubus Papers.

261 OEF suspects Act 10 unconstitutional: Joint interview with OEF and William J. Smith, Dec. 18, 1989.

261 "a pleasure to cut the University's budget": United Press International article, undated, Faubus Papers.

261 "There was no longer": Dunaway interview, Jan. 5, 1989; Jean Woolfolk interview, Jan. 19, 1990; staff memorandum, Faubus Papers.

262 "For its part": Faubus, *Down from the Hills;* Bowen interview, June 13, 1989.

262 "Much of the state": *Arkansas Gazette,* Apr. 3 and Apr. 30, 1959.

263 "Most of the state's": Faubus, *Down from the Hills, II;* Parker Westbrook interview, Sept. 27, 1991.

CHAPTER TWENTY-TWO

263 "He encouraged the attention": *Arkansas Gazette,* Jan. 19, 1960; Faubus, *Down from the Hills, II;* Del Tyson memo to OEF, Feb. 12, 1960, Faubus Papers.

265 "His estimate": OEF letter to R. E. Duhnke, July 16, 1964, Faubus Papers.

265 "When young blacks": Purvis, "Little Rock and the Press"; *Arkansas Gazette,* Nov. 7, 1959; Jan. 7, 1960; and May 5, 1960; Faubus letter to Alford, May 10, 1960; J. L. Bland letter to C. G. Hall, July 6, 1960.

266 "He endorsed": *Arkansas Gazette,* Sept. 25, Oct. 29, and Nov. 9, 1960.

266 "This defeat": Robert M. Shelton letter to OEF, July 25, 1961; Memo to Bill
Smith, Oct. 16, 1963, and to OEF Aug. 27, 1963; Harold J. Morris letter to OEF,
Sept. 10, 1964, with undated article from *McGehee Times,* Faubus Papers,
University of Arkansas Library.

266 "As his racial": OEF letters to James F. Malone, Dec. 4, 1963; to David T. O'Riley,
Sept. 12, 1963; and to Lloyd D. Lawson, May 22, 1964; D. P. Raney letter to David
Mullins, May 18, 1964; Faubus Papers. Unpublished article written for *Arkansas
Gazette,* June 1979, made available to RR.

267 "His rancor": OEF letter to Raney, Catlett, and Young, Mar. 8, 1966, Faubus
Papers.

268 "Putnam's book": RR, televised interview with OEF, AETN, Nov. 29, 1993.

268 "Occasionally, he pulled": *Arkansas Gazette,* Nov. 17, 1960, Dec. 1, 1960, and
Apr. 13, 1961; OEF letter to Wade H. Scott, Apr. 25, 1963.

269 "'a place to spit'": R. E. Medlock memo to OEF, Oct. 11, 1963, Faubus Papers.

269 "pleased . . . to hear of the shooting": J. L. Crosser letter, Nov. 22, 1988,
Faubus Papers.

271 "'If that is true'": Orval Faubus to Sam Faubus, Aug. 6, 1964, Faubus Papers;
Arkansas Gazette, June 27, 1963.

271 "Perhaps under the goad": OEF letters to Mrs. Veit A. Hain, June 5, 1963; Walter J.
Berkowitz, Mar. 3, 1964; Sen. John L. McClellan, June 18, 1964; Ron S. Robinson,
June 24, 1965; Mrs. Cora Pinkley Call, Sept. 20, 1965; Richard F. Milwee, July 22,
1966; W. R. Stephens, Apr. 28, 1971, Faubus Papers.

272 "The lions": Clyde J. Moore letter, Sept. 21, 1960, Faubus Papers.

272 Mississippi Sovereignty Commission and M. L. King: *New York Times,* Jan. 30, 1990.

273 "Harding College, a Church of Christ": OEF correspondence with George S.
Benson, Aug. 15 and Aug. 17, 1961, Oct. 10, 1961, and Oct. 9, 1964, and with
W. P. Campbell, Sept. 11, 1962; John J. Johnston, May 16, 1966; and D. D. Fertig,
July 26, 1961; undated newspaper article quoting *Arkansas Gazette* letter, Faubus
Papers. Randall Bennett Woods, *Fulbright: A Biography* (Cambridge: Cambridge
University Press, 1995).

273 "Nearer home": A. W. Ford letter to Charles F. Smith, Aug. 27, 1959; Act 15 of 1961
Arkansas General Assembly; OEF letter to J. Paul Treen, Apr. 16, 1965, Faubus Papers.

274 "The governor and his employees": *Arkansas Statesman,* Feb. 24, 1961; OEF letters
to Rex Houston, Jan. 17, 1964, and W. E. Davis, Mar. 15, 1966, Faubus Papers.

CHAPTER TWENTY-THREE

275 "The conspiracy," "Then there was," and "An informant": State police files,
Faubus Papers, quoted in *Arkansas Gazette,* June 3, 1979.

276 "The same anxieties": *New York Times,* Jan. 30, 1990, and July 4, 1993.

282 "Faubus, in later years": *Pine Bluff Commercial,* May 7, 1986.

283 "A North Arkansas family": Confidential interview.

284 "The state police were used": Lindsey memos to OEF, Apr. to June, 1960,
Faubus Papers.

284 "Political use": OEF interview, Mar. 8, 1991.

284 Sources for this chapter include a confidential interview Apr. 23, 1996; a letter to RR from the Rev. Colbert S. Cartwright, Mar. 24, 1990; interviews with OEF, Apr. 28, 1991, and Nov. 21, 1992; a page-one article in the *Arkansas Gazette,* June 3, 1979; and state police memoranda and letters in Boxes 5, 57, 280, 281, 497, and 498 of the Faubus Papers.

CHAPTER TWENTY-FOUR

287 "They attacked": Faubus, *Down from the Hills II.*

287 "The opponents would have": OEF and Bland memos, Faubus Papers.

288 "He was nominated": *Historical Report of the Secretary of State, Arkansas, 1978, vol. I.* Faubus, *Down from the Hills II,* p. 39; OEF interview, Oct. 4, 1992.

288 "Faubus had only limited": OEF interview, Oct. 4, 1992; Faubus, *Down from the Hills,* p. 39.

288 "The Fulbright camp": OEF interview, May 14, 1993; Woods, *Fulbright: A Biography.*

289 "Faubus was only mildly": OEF letter to RR, May 15, 1993; Lee Williams interview, May 22, 1996.

290 "Mills and Fulbright cooked up": OEF interview, Oct. 4, 1992.

290 "'I have just left a meeting'": Alford interview, Aug. 23, 1990.

291 "Melton had enoucouraged McMath": Jim Lester, A Man for Arkansas (Little Rock, Ark.: Rose Publishing Co., 1976.)

291 "Less than a month": OEF interview, Apr. 28, 1991; Stephens interview, Apr. 29, 1991.

291 "Meanwhile, Alford began to understand": OEF interviews, Oct. 30, 1990, and Apr. 28, 1991; Faubus, *Down from the Hills II;* Alford interview, Aug. 23, 1990; Stephens interview, Apr. 29, 1991.

292 "Faubus denied it": Faubus-Stephens correspondence, May through Aug. 1962, Faubus Papers.

293 "He won without a runoff": Jim Ranchino, *Faubus to Bumpers: Arkansas Votes, 1960–1970* (Arkadelphia, Ark.: Action Research, 1972).

293 "an election judge at Pine Bluff": Owens, "Where Faubus Gets His Votes."

293 "There was growing sentiment": OEF interview, July 19, 1993.

295 "Smith and Ben Allen . . . were having lunch": Ben Allen interview, July 3, 1990; *Arkansas Gazette,* Nov. 8, 1962.

295 "During a trial at Morrilton": G. Thomas Eisele interview, Dec. 18, 1991.

296 "the state boards and commissions": Bob Lancaster, "The Pol and the Playboy," *Arkansas Times,* Nov. 1989.

296 "The governor's first chore": R. E. Medlock memo to Lee Tucker, Apr. 22, 1964; OEF memo to C. L. Denton Jr., Oct. 27, 1964; Fred H. Lang letter to Faubus, Sept. 30, 1964, Faubus Papers; OEF interview, Dec. 16, 1991.

296 "State employees contributed": Contributions list, Faubus Papers.

296 "Jobs were provided": OEF memo to Jim Bland, May 29, 1963; Stewart K. Prosser letters, Jan. 17, 1964, and Aug. 19, 1964; Herrn Northcutt memo to Faubus, Oct. 15, 1964, Faubus Papers.

297 "Some advisers": Jim McDougal memo to Faubus, undated.

297 "Before confronting": *Arkansas Gazette,* Feb. 13, 1964; Stewart K. Prosser letter
to OEF, Jan. 17, 1964, Faubus Papers; William J. Smith telephone interview,
Aug. 19, 1995.

297 "In the general election": Russell Wools memo to OEF, Sept. 24, 1964;
R. E. Medlock memo to OEF, Oct. 14, 1964; W. R. Stephens memo to ARKLA
department heads, Sept. 1, 1964, Faubus Papers.

298 "to stop wearing cowboy boots": John Ward, *The Arkansas Rockefeller* (Baton
Rouge: Louisiana State University Press, 1978.)

298 "The talk of jets": OEF letter to Mr. and Mrs. C. Joseph Huff, Oct. 29, 1964;
Bland memo to Faubus, Oct. 17, 1964; J. O. (Jake) Porter letter to Jim Bland,
Sept. 1, 1964, Faubus Papers.

298 "The high point of every speech": Roy Reed, *Arkansas Gazette,* Sept. 20, 1964.

299 "Rockefeller never understood": Ward, *The Arkansas Rockefeller;* Billy B. Hathorn,
"Friendly Rivalry: Winthrop Rockefeller Challenges Orval Faubus in 1964,"
Arkansas Historical Quarterly, 53(4) (winter 1994); Eisele interview, Dec. 18, 1991;
OEF letter to E. W. Hood, Oct. 2, 1964, Faubus Papers; OEF interview,
Dec. 23, 1991; RR, unsigned article for the *New York Times,* Oct. 8, 1964; RR,
Arkansas Gazette, Sept. 18, 1964.

299 "Faubus's polls had him worried": Alta Faubus interview, June 1, 1989; Alta Faubus
speech, 1964; OEF interview, Sept. 28, 1991; Robert Troutt interview, Nov. 26, 1990.

301 "Then Troutt heard": Troutt interview, Nov. 26, 1990.

301 "The next break": OEF interview, Sept. 28, 1991.

301 "Faubus had another": OEF interview, Sept. 28, 1991.

301 "There were dirty tricks": OEF interview, Sept. 28, 1991; OEF letter to Mrs. J. H.
Edmondson, Nov. 19, 1964; Ward, *The Arkansas Rockefeller;* Hathorn, "Friendly
Rivalry."

303 "The national Democratic": Ward, *The Arkansas Rockefeller;* Faubus, *Down from
the Hills II;* Hathorn, "Friendly Rivalry."; OEF letter to Mrs. A. H. Phillips,
Sept. 15, 1964; OEF letter to E. E. Barber Sr., Sept. 16, 1964, Faubus Papers.

303 "Rockefeller had his own": Hathorn, "Friendly Rivalry."

303 "Bates emerged from one session": RR, unpublished memo, Feb. 23, 1962.

303 "Faubus could not resist": Hathorn, "Friendly Rivalry."

304 "The election results": *Texarkana Gazette,* Nov. 5, 1964; OEF campaign memo,
Sept. 8, 1964; Carl Adams memo to OEF, June 13, 1962; OEF memo to Clarence
Thornbrough, May 6, 1963, Faubus Papers. Hathorn, "Friendly Rivalry."

304 "Faubus was able": Clarence Bell memo to J. L. Bland, Oct. 23, 1964; Faubus,
Down from the Hills II.

304 "Madison County managed": Dotson Collins letter to OEF, Jan. 28, 1965, Faubus
Papers; *Arkansas Democrat,* Nov. 4, 1964; *Arkansas Gazette,* Nov. 4, 1964, and
Jan. 24, 1965.

CHAPTER TWENTY-FIVE

305 "In the middle years": *Arkansas Gazette,* Mar. 2, 1961, and Mar. 12, 1961; Charles
Stewart interview, Sept. 1, 1990.

308 "Toward the end": Handwritten memo, OEF, undated, Faubus Papers.

308 "Many of the main": Faubus, *Down from the Hills,* p. 388.

308 "One of the worst": John Norman Harkey interview, Feb. 23, 1991.

309 "An Arizona man came": Leland Duvall interview, Mar. 1, 1990.

309 "The Arizonan's company": Duvall interview, Mar. 1, 1990.

309 "Companies were also allowed": Harkey interview, Feb. 23, 1991.

310 Background on AL and T came from a variety of sources, including interviews
     with William J. Smith on June 20, 1996; Ernest Dumas, June 20, 1996; John
     Norman Harkey, Feb. 23, 1991; and Gena Bradshaw, Sept. 27, 1991; and articles
     in the *Arkansas Gazette,* July 26, 1968, July 27, 1968, and Sept. 14, 1968.

312 "Pensions for Pals": Dumas interview, June 20, 1996.

312 "midnight pay raises": *Arkansas Gazette,* Apr. 6, 7, 8, 10, 12, and 14, and May 26
     and 28, 1966; numerous letters in correspondence files of Faubus Papers.

313 "Another scandal surfaced late": Waddy W. Moore, "George Washington
     Donaghey," *The Governors of Arkansas* (Fayetteville and London: University of
     Arkansas Press, 1981); C. Fred Williams, S. Charles Bolton, Carl H. Moneyhon,
     and Leroy T. Williams, *A Documentary History of Arkansas* (Fayetteville: University
     of Arkansas Press, 1984); Ward, *The Arkansas Rockefeller.*

313 "'to get a con to kill a con'": Sam Boyce interview, Jan. 10, 1990.

314 "One hapless prisoner with eye": *Arkansas Gazette,* Sept. 2, 1966.

314 "A Fort Smith minister": Correspondence between Faubus and the Rev. John F.
     Turner, Feb. 1966, Faubus Papers.

314 "What the investigators found": OEF letter to Austin MacCormick, Feb. 8, 1966;
     Eugene B. Hale Jr. memo to OEF, Dec. 1, 1966; Dan D. Stephens letter to the state
     penitentiary commission, Oct. 6, 1965; OEF letter to H. E. Murray, July 26, 1965,
     Faubus Papers; OEF letter to Jeff Wood, Nov. 3, 1965; *Arkansas Democrat,*
     Sept. 1, 1966; *Arkansas Gazette,* Sept. 2, 1966.

315 "He fired one member": Patsy Ellis interview, Oct. 16, 1990; Thornbrough inter-
     view, Sept. 6, 1990.

315 "There was unrelenting": Various OEF interviews with RR; OEF letter to Bonnie
     Pace, Jan. 8, 1964; George F. Edwardes (*sic*) letter to Arnold Sykes (*sic*), Nov. 21,
     1957; J. L. Bland letter to OEF, Mar. 25, 1958.

316 "In 1927, the city": *Arkansas Democrat,* Oct. 29, 1989, and Nov. 12, 1989; Roy
     Bosson interviews, Nov. 13, 1990, and June 28, 1996.

316 "The McLaughlin machine": *Arkansas Democrat,* Nov. 12, 1989.

318 Hastings became silent partner: Sam Anderson interview, Nov. 12, 1990.

318 "During the Faubus years": Anderson interview, Nov. 12, 1990; Owens, "Where
     Faubus Gets His Votes"; Clay White interview, Nov. 13, 1990.

318 "'If I ever got as much'": Faubus interview, Dec. 4, 1990.

319 "Clay White, an FBI": White interview, Nov. 13, 1990; Roy Bosson interview,
     Nov. 13, 1990; Anderson interview, Nov. 12, 1990; Troutt interview, Nov. 26, 1990;
     Hurst interview, Nov. 29, 1990.

319 "The state government, alerted": White interview; Faubus, *Down from the Hills II.*

320 "Faubus maintained": letter to OEF from James Patterson, Aug. 10, 1966;
     Washington Post, Apr. 11, 1965; interviews with Willie Lowe and Alphonso Logan
     conducted for Cranford Johnson Robinson Woods advertising agency, Aug. 10,
     1992; Faubus, *Down from the Hills II;* Faubus interview, Dec. 4, 1990.

321 "The corruption started": Harnett T. Kane, *Louisiana Hayride* (Gretna, La.: Pelican Publishing Co., 1970); Robert Sherrill, *Gothic Politics in the Deep South* (New York: Grossman Publishers, 1968); Western Union telegram to OEF, Apr. 7, 1964, and William J. Smith letter to OEF, Oct. 18, 1963, Faubus Papers.

CHAPTER TWENTY-SIX

322 "he would go to the Senate": Alta Faubus interview, July 3, 1966.

323 "Early in his sixth": Documents provided to RR by Faubus; confidential interview, Dec. 10, 1990; Bob Troutt interview, Nov. 28, 1990; *Arkansas Outlook*, Oct. 14, 1965; correspondence files, Faubus Papers. *Arkansas Gazette*, Oct. 29, 1965, Feb. 18, 1966, and Mar. 10, 1966; *Tulsa World*, Feb. 18, 1966; *Arkansas Democrat*, Dec. 24, 1965; OEF letter to RR, Nov. 21, 1988; Faubus, *Down from the Hills II*; Fay Jones interviews, Sept. 28, 1988, and July 2, 1996; OEF interviews, Aug. 5, 1988, Jan. 25, 1989, and Mar. 31, 1989; Alta Faubus interview, July 2, 1996.

325 "'that he was taking bids'": *Pine Bluff Commercial*, Mar. 9, 1966.

325 "It was not that": Confidential interview.

326 "He went to Fayetteville": Alta Faubus interview, June 15, 1989.

326 "He would turn nonchalantly": Ann Henry interview, n.d.

328 "'In many places'": Letter quoted in editorial in *Pine Bluff Commercial*, Dec. 21, 1965, and reprinted in Faubus, *Down from the Hills II*.

329 "home that night crestfallen": Alta Faubus interview, June 1, 1989.

329 "Orval married Beth": *Tulsa World*, Mar. 22, 1969.

330 "There is evidence": Confidential source; Elmer Cook interview, Jan. 12, 1991; Elizabeth Faubus diaries, unprocessed papers, Faubus Papers.

330 "His income was too small": OEF interview, Feb. 27, 1993.

332 "'If you had been this interested'": Farrell Faubus letter to OEF, Apr. 10, 1973; OEF letter to Farrell Faubus, Dec. 7, 1973, Faubus Papers.

333 "Her own thinking": Elizabeth Faubus diaries.

333 "Beth joined Orval": Letters and handwritten notes, including an undated memo from Farrell to his father analyzing the 1974 election, Faubus Papers.

335 "Faubus never forgot": Alta Faubus interview, Aug. 20, 1990; Faubus, *The Little Australian*, p. 189.

335 "Faubus descended.": Undated conversation with David H. Pryor; unprocessed documents and Elizabeth's diaries in Faubus Papers; OEF letter to William J. Smith June 27, 1973, unprocessed papers, Faubus Papers.

336 "Farrell cashed in": Faubus, *Down from the Hills II; The Little Australian;* Elizabeth Faubus diaries, Faubus Papers; Alta Faubus interview, Aug. 24, 1992; undated memo by OEF on events leading to his hospital commitment, Faubus Papers; OEF interviews, June 25, 1988, July 1, 1988, Nov. 24, 1991, and Nov. 27, 1991.

336 "Orval secluded": Elizabeth Faubus diaries, Faubus Papers; Faubus, *The Little Australian*.

336 "$125 a week": Faubus, *The Little Australian*, p. 202.

339 "Faubus had long wanted": Elizabeth Faubus diaries; correspondence between OEF and Beth, Faubus Papers.

339 "trying to see Jack Stephens": OEF letter to Jack Stephens, May 18, 1981; Stephens letter to Faubus, June 12, 1981; both in unprocessed Faubus Papers.

341 "He wrote a long": OEF letter to Beth, Nov. 3, 1982, unprocessed material in Faubus Papers.

341 "Her scribblings": Unprocessed material in Faubus Papers.

342 "Faubus dismissed": OEF interview, Oct. 4, 1992.

343 "Her nude body": *Houston Post,* Mar. 10, 11, and 19, 1983.

343 "His confession": Helfond confession, unprocessed papers, Faubus Papers.

344 "Faubus returned": Faubus diary; *Houston Post,* May 4, 1983.

344 "Huntsville bank loan": Personal documents in unprocessed Faubus Papers.

344 "'What the hell'": Handwritten note by OEF, Aug. 5, 1984, Faubus Papers.

344 "In 1986, still smarting": Faubus, *The Little Australian,* p. 233.

345 "He endorsed . . . Jesse Jackson": OEF letter to Bob Starr, undated, Faubus Papers.

345 Daisy Bates tribute: July 26 and 28, 1989; OEF prepared speech, July 27, 1989, provided to RR by OEF.

345 Complaint to forest service: OEF letter to U.S. Forest Service, Apr. 23, 1988, unprocessed material, Faubus Papers.

345 "He finally sold": OEF interview, Sept. 12, 1988.

345 Faubus bust: *Arkansas Gazette,* June 26 and 27, 1991; Sapp letter to OEF, July 7, 1991, unprocessed material, Faubus Papers.

347 "Faubus's own health": Jan Faubus telephone interviews, Jan. 8, 1993, and Feb. 7, 1995; Jan Faubus letter to RR, Jan. 3, 1993.

347 "His physicians tried": Jan Faubus telephone interviews, Dec. 5 and 14, 1994.

CHAPTER TWENTY-SEVEN

348 "'These men want'": *New York Times,* Dec. 17, 1994, editorial page.

349 "'Look what happened'": OEF interview, Dec. 19, 1988.

349 "and keep the issue in the courts": Nat R. Griswold, "The Second Reconstruction in Little Rock" (unpublished manuscript in RR's possession).

352 "Replying to a student": OEF letter to William Angus, Feb. 18, 1964, Faubus Papers.

352 "Hyperbole aside": Albert M. Witte, lecture, University of Arkansas, Sept. 14, 1988. For further discussion of the constitutional issue, see Freyer, *The Little Rock Crisis;* Bartley, *The Rise of Massive Resistance;* Elliff, *The United States Department of Justice,* etc.; Dan T. Carter, *The Politics of Rage* (New York: Simon & Schuster, 1995), and Harry S. Ashmore, *Civil Rights and Wrongs: A Memoir of Race and Politics, 1944–1994* (New York: Pantheon Books, 1994).

353 "'Eisenhower had to be pushed'": Stephen E. Ambrose, *Eisenhower* (New York: Simon & Schuster, 1983).

354 "Faubus contended": OEF interview, Dec. 22, 1988.

354 "That was perhaps": Witte lecture, Sept. 14, 1988, and Freyer, *The Little Rock Crisis.*

355 "Brownell . . . might have intervened": Elliff, *The United States Department of Justice,* p. 469.

355 "Most of Brownell's lawyers": Elliff, *The United States Department of Justice,* pp. 483–87; J. W. Anderson, *Eisenhower, Brownell, and Congress* (Tuscaloosa: University of Alabama Press, 1964).

357 "Perhaps all that": Egerton interview, Jan. 1, 1996.

358 "While blame": Griswold, "The Second Reconstruction in Little Rock."

358 "Faubus said later": Griswold, "The Second Reconstruction in Little Rock,"
pp. 10–27; Faubus, *Down from the Hills*, p. 202.

359 "Some saw": *Christian Century,* Oct. 9, 1957.

359 "Some of the more thoughtful": Phil Stratton interview, June 10, 1990.

360 "A British writer": Colin Welch, review of *The British Isles: A History of Four
Nations,* by Hugh Kearnedy, in the *Spectator,* Apr. 1, 1989.

360 "The moderates went": Lippmann quoted in Woods, *Fulbright: A Biography,*
p. 229; Ralph McGill, "The Southern Moderates Are Still There," *New York Times
Magazine,* Sept. 21, 1958.

360 "Among those . . . was Sam Faubus": Sam Faubus letter to Bonnie Salcido,
June 14, 1963, Faubus Papers.

361 "Orval's detachment": OEF interview, Jan. 19, 1990; OEF speech at Bates tribute,
May 11, 1989.

361 "'I don't hate him.'": Ernest Green interview, June 22, 1992.

362 "Faubus did finally": OEF interview, Dec. 19, 1988; Thornbrough memo to OEF,
Mar. 15, 1965, Faubus Papers.

362 "could have had a sinecure": Sidney McMath interview, Nov. 21, 1995.

362 "Even Orval's long-term": Ashmore interview, Feb. 23, 1990.

363 "'The small form was now'": Faubus, *The Little Australian,* pp. 174, 175.

364 "Toward the end": OEF interview, Jan. 25, 1989.

367 "Faubus liked to hear": Sam Boyce letter to RR, Dec. 6, 1994.

367 "his wayward spawn George Wallace": Carter, *The Politics of Rage.*

368 "rose from their class rather than with it": Shannon, *The Socialist Party of America,*
p. 266.

INDEX

Accident, Ark., 63, 72

Act 9, 260

Act 10, 261, 262

Adams, Carl, 91, 130

Adams, Charles, 90, 177

Adams, Sherman, 217, 220, 221

Adkins, Homer M., 90, 126, 136, 303

Advisory Committee on Education, 155

Agricultural Wheel, 26

Albert Pike Mansion, 254

Alcoholic Beverage Control, 146, 172, 308

Alford, Dale, 246–49, *250*, 265, 283, 290–93, 297

Algren, Nelson, 108

Alien and Sedition Act, 25

Allen, Ben, 295

Alma, Ark., 178

Altheimer, Ark., 226

Ambrose, Stephen, 353

American Association of University Professors (AAUP), 261

American Civil Liberties Union (ACLU), 101, 103

Appeal to Reason, 28

Arkadelphia, Ark., 140

Arkansas AFL-CIO, 304

Arkansas AM and N, 280

Arkansas Council on Human Relations, 253, 274, 277

Arkansas Democrat, 124, 156, 157, 189, 204–5; names Virgil Blossom "Man of the Year," 182

Arkansas Department of Education, 254, 274

Arkansas Department of Finance and Administration, 136

Arkansas Department of Parks and Tourism, 139

Arkansas Education Association, 155, 254, 262, 279, 304, 305

Arkansas Faith, 170, 174

Arkansas Game and Fish Commission, 287

Arkansas Gazette, 28, 35, 134, 136, 156, 161, 168, 169, 242, 263, 269, 273, 282, 294, 309; accused of Communist connections, 240, 274, 287; coverage of Central High School crisis, 225, 230, 235, 238; Commonwealth story, 95, 105, 119–22, 124, 127; Hugh B. Patterson Jr., publisher, 203; opposes Faubus's actions at Central High School, 230, 252; owned by J. N. Heiskell, 166, 204, 274; wins two Pulitzer Prizes, 230, 239, 241

Arkansas General Assembly, 103, 133, 138, 155–58

Arkansas Highway Commission, 84, 86, 117, 129, 141, 242, 288, 296

Arkansas Highway Department, 93, 139, 140, 142, 296, 312

Arkansas House Judiciary Committee, 104

Arkansas House of Representatives, 135, 141, 149

Arkansas Industrial Development Commission (AIDC), 140, 259, 266

Arkansas Loan and Thrift, 310, 311

Arkansas Louisiana Gas Company (ARKLA), 131, 134, 144–49, 297

Arkansas National Guard, 202–3, 208–10, 217, 219, 222–24, 233, 244, 351, 353, 357, 359, 365

Arkansas Power and Light Company (AP and L), 81, 86, 131, 146, 147, 149, 150, 156, 204; dispute with REA over territorial allocation, 141–42, 144

Arkansas Public Service Commission, 86, 134, 144, 146, 147, 148, 261

Arkansas Recorder, 75, 94, 133, 187, 268

Arkansas Senate, 135, 142, 149, 156

Arkansas state hospital, 134, 157–59, 243, 261, 288, 305

Arkansas State Police, 212, 257, 274, 276, 279, 284, 296

Arkansas State Press, 185, 215, 216, 259, 278

Arkansas Statesman, 268, 274, 322

Arlington Hotel (Hot Springs), 316, 320

Ashmore, Harry S., 121, 123, 124, 126, 166, 203–5, 208–9, 230, 231, 235, 242, 262, 282; Pulitzer Prize winner, 239, *241*

Associated Press, 361
Atkins, Ark., 32
Atlanta Constitution, 239

Bailey, Carl, 92, 115, 136, 140
Baker, Truman N., 93, 98, 126, 129, 130, 145,
    146, 151, 287, 323, *327*, 335
Baker, Wallace, 130, 145, 146, 151
Baldwin, Roger, 101, 103
Ball Creek (Madison County, Ark.), 50, 58,
    63, 70
Bartlett, Earnest J., Jr., 311
Bates, Daisy, 176, 205, 215, 216–17, 227, 229,
    234, 237, 257, 259, 277, 278, 287, 303,
    345, 361; state president of NAACP, 163,
    172, 185, *206*
Bates, L. C., 185, 215, 216–17, 227, 229, *234,*
    237, 257, 277, 278, 303
Batesville, Ark., 9, 124, 260
Battle of the Bulge, 79, 92
Bauxite, Ark., 35
Baxter, Elisha, 161
Bearden, Ark., 162
Bearden, J. Lee, 135, 157
Bell, Clarence E., 149
Bennett, Bruce, 196, 203, 245, 261–62, 285,
    287, 310, 312, 365
Berger, Victor, 34
Berryville, Ark., 32
Beston, John, 35
Bickel, Alexander M., 166
Bird, Marvin, 177
Black Mountain and Eastern Railroad, 7, 53
Blackwell, Lawrence, 242
Bland, J. L. (Jim), 135, 158, 287, 296, 303
Bloor, Ella Reeve (Mother), 108
Blossom, Virgil T., 182, *183,* 184–86, 192,
    195, 196, 200, 201, 203–4, 205, 207, 227,
    231, 246, 349, 358, 359
Blossom Plan, 182, 184–87, 217, 238, 247
Blytheville, Ark., 217
Bosch, Richard, 102
Brandeis, Louis, 102
Brandenburg, Arch, 32
Brashears, Ida Bevins, 28, 60
Brewer, Herbert, 176
Brewer, Vivion, 253
Bridges, Harry, 102

Britt, Henry M., 288
Brooks-Baxter War, 161
Brooks, Joseph, 161
Brothers of Freedom, 26
Brown, Minnijean, 232
Brown, Robert Ewing, 186, 190
Brown v. Board of Education, x, 60, 164,
    168–69, 181, 188, 216, 219, 354, 356–57
Brownell, Herbert, Jr., 212, 217, 219–22, 231,
    232, 269, 355–56
Buckingham, Cressye Faubus, *18, 41*
Buffalo National River, 151, 239, 328
Bumpers, Dale, 321, 330, 333
Burrow, Elizabeth, 215
Byrd, Harry F., 356
Byrnes, James F., 166

Caldwell, Arthur B., 194, 197–98
Caldwell, Erskine, 103
Caldwell, Eugene, 173
Calhoun, John C., 354
Camden, Ark., 92
Carpenter, Claude, Jr., 136, 146, 193, 225,
    247, 248–49, 311
Capital Citizens Council, 186–90, 194–95,
    197, 200, 213, 217, 257
Caraway, Hattie, 111, 112
Cartwright, Colbert S., 238, 261, 279, 359
Carver, George Washington, 265
Cash, Johnny, 299
Cash, W. J., 121, 166
Catlett, Leon, 145, 147, 148
Cella, John, 150
Central High Nine, 233, *236–37*
Central High School, Little Rock. See Little
    Rock Central High School
Chambers, Whittaker, 75
Chandler, Howard, 282, 283
Chappell, Winifred, 102
Cheney, Orville, 146
Cherokee Village, 138
Cherry, Francis A., 105, 140, 145, 158, 163,
    178, 284, 288, 293; addressing the
    Arkansas Democratic Party Convention,
    89; 1954 campaign for governor, 75,
    83–88, 91–99, 116–27, 131–32, 135, 136,
    138, 142, 150–51, 203, 284
Cherry, Margaret, 88, 138

Children's Colony, 243, 259, 288, 305
Christian Century, 359
Cities Service Company, 145
Citizens Council, 225, 244, 247, 249, 254, 256, 266, 276, 287, 292, 365. See also White Citizens Council of America, White Citizens Council of Arkansas, and Capital Citizens Council
Civil Military Training Camp (Kansas), 46, 62
Clarendon, Ark., 235
Clark, Tom C., 116
Clarksville, Ark., 32, 140
Clement, Frank, 182
Clinger, Sherman T., 202, 219
Clinton, William Jefferson (Bill), xi, 153, 155, 281, 297, 321, 325, 338, 339, 342, 344
Cobb, Osro, 235, 303
Coffelt, Kenneth, 118, 293
Coleman, James P., 165, 249
Collins, Elva, 50
Collins, LeRoy, ix
Combs, Ark., 11, 14, 19, 42, 44, 47, 64, 132, 168, 299, 342, 348; in early 1900s, 3, 5, 7–8, 53–56; school, 48, 60; and socialism, 29–30, 35, 38–39
Combs, Harvey G., 131, 308–9, 310
Committee to Retain Our Segregated Schools (CROSS), 255
Commonwealth College, 37, 38, 75, 77, 105–27, 133, 284, 315; and communism, 102, 104–7, 115–16; history of, 100–104; OEF's attendance at, 92–99, 103–15, *109,* 117–27, 133; and socialism, 101, 106
Communist party, 28, 75, 99, 245, 262
Compton, Bob, 330
Congress of Industrial Organizations, 158
Conroy, Jack, 108
convict leasing, 313
Conway, Ark., 87, 243, 259, 344, 345
Cook, Alice, 102
Cooper v. Aaron, 235, 353
Cooper, John, 138, 145, 332, 335, 347
Copeland, Curt, 170, 172–73, 178–79, 180
Cornett, Arch, 30, 32, 35, 36, 37, 69
Cornett, Zember, 48
Corning, Ark., 34
Cottrell, J. H., 255–56
Council on Foreign Relations, 282

Cousens, Frances Reissman, 102
Cox, David A., 293
Coy, Harold, 102
Coy, Mrs. Harold, 104
Crain, James H. (Jim), 88, 90, 93, 124, 129
Crank, Marion H., 135
Crawfis, Ewing, 158
Criminal Investigation Division (state police), 275, 277, 279, 280, 281, 283
Crossett, Ark., 170, 192
Croxton, Hardy, 147
Crow, Jim, 354
Culwell, Martha Jo, 332
Cummins Prison, 313
Cunningham, Agnes "Sis," 102
Cunningham, Bill, 102

Daily Worker, 28
Darby, W. E. (Bill), 131, 145, 323, 335, 347
Dardanelle, Ark., 283
Darrow, Clarence, 19
Davies, Ronald N., 200, *201,* 208, 212, 217, 222, 233, 355
Davis, Jeff, 132, 167, 189, 242, 268, 367
Debs, Eugene V., 7, 27, 33, 35, 101, 103, 263, 367
Decatur, Ark., 32
DeLong, Melvin, 202, 212, 213
Democratic Party Central Committee, 186
Department of Education, 254, 274
Dewey, Thomas E., 219
Dickey, Bert, 177
Dogpatch USA, 329
Donaghey, George W., 313
Douglas, Hal, 168
Douthit, George 189
Down from the Hills, 339, 344
Downie, Tom, 122
Dunaway, Edwin, 122, 123, 205, 261
Dunaway, Tommy, 227
Dungan, Rodney, 294
Dunlap, J. E., *152*

E. Haldeman-Julius Co., 28
E. Haldeman-Julius Weekly, 28
Earle, Ark., 177
East, Clay, 110

Eastland, James O., 174
Eckford, Elizabeth, 209, *210, 211*, 214, *236*, 238
Edens, Rev. S. P., 72
Egerton, John, 357
Eichmann, Adolf, 268
Einstein, Albert, 102
Eisele, Tom, 295
Eisenhower, Dwight D., 209, 212–13, 217,
    219–21, 229–33, 235, 252–53, 353, 355–57
Elaine, Ark., 162, 361
El Dorado, Ark., 249
Ellis, Clyde, 86, 142
Employment Security Division, 136, 267
Engstrom, Harold J., 196
Eureka Springs, Ark., 32, 333, 334

Fagan, Ellis M., 156, 157
Farrell, James T., 108
Faubous, William, 10
Faubus, Addie Joslin, 30, 32, 36, 43, 46, 47,
    48, 49, 52, 57, 65; death, 70; family life,
    23–24; family picture, *41*; house above
    Greasy Creek, *31*; OEF's mother, 5, 22;
    marriage to Sam Faubus, *12*, 13, 15; reli-
    gious beliefs, 19; at singing schools, 17
Faubus, Alta Haskins, 120, 188, 203, 239, 331,
    332, 335, 338; birth of son, Farrell, 78;
    death of first baby, 72; death of second
    baby, 74; death of son, Farrell, 332;
    marriage to OEF, 50–51, 63–64, 71–74,
    78–80, *82*, 100, *125*, 132, 286, 289, 290,
    291, 292, *317*, 325, 326, 329, 330; as pupil
    of OEF, 63–64
Faubus, Betty, 342, 344
Faubus, Bonnie. See Bonnie Faubus Salcido
Faubus, Cressye. See Cressye Faubus
    Buckingham
Faubus, Connie. See Connie Faubus Tucker
Faubus, Darrow Doyle, 17, 19, *41*, 304, 344
Faubus, Eli, 68
Faubus, Elizabeth (Beth) Westmoreland:
    marriage to OEF, 326, *327*, 329–30, *331*,
    332–33, 335–36, 338, 339, 341–44
Faubus, Ellis, 10–11
Faubus, Elvin, *18*, *41*, 42, 43, 344
Faubus, Fara, *317*, *337*
Faubus, Farrell, 80, *82*, 304, 326, 333, 336,
    337, 363; birth, 78; death, 332; at Little
    Rock Central High School, 187

Faubus, Janice Hines Wittenberg: marriage
    to OEF, 344–45, *346*, 347–48
Faubus, John Samuel (Sam), 43, 46, 47, 48,
    49, 51, 57, 64, 81, 93, 99–100, 129, 142,
    143, 271, 273, 362, 368, 369; birth, 11;
    childhood, 13–17; family picture, *41*; as
    farmer, 53–56; as Greasy Greek news-
    paper correspondent, 22; house above
    Greasy Creek, *31*; as "Jimmie Higgins,"
    21, 271; marriage to Addie Joslin, *12*, 13,
    15; poem by, 19; and the REA, 52; reli-
    gious beliefs, 19–20; as Socialist, 7, 25–40,
    67–70, 78
Faubus, John, 10
Faubus, June, 64; family picture, *41*
Faubus, Malinda (Lindy) Sparks, 11, 13–14,
    39, 79
Faubus, Orval Eugene, *18*, *41*, *45*, *152*, *264*,
    270, *286*, *294*, *300*, *306*, *327*, *334*, *340*,
    350; administrative assistant to Gov. Sid
    McMath, 84; advocate of improved
    education, 155–57, 178, 243, 259; advo-
    cate of industrialization, 139–40,
    155–56, 259–60, 364; ancestors of,
    9–11, 13–15, 59; appointed to state
    highway commission, 84; and
    Arkansas's prison system, 313–15; with
    Australian terrier, Magreedy, 365–66; as
    a baby, *4*; birth, 3, 6; birth of son,
    Farrell, 78; childhood, 5–7, 16–24, 25,
    29–30, 40–48, 53–60; at Civil Military
    Training Camp, 46, 62; and
    Commonwealth College, 92–98, 99,
    103–15, *109*, 117–27, 133; death of first
    baby boy, 72; death of second baby
    boy, 74; death of son, Farrell, 332; as
    environmentalist, 328, 345; governor of
    Arkansas, 131 passim; for improvement
    of state hospital, 157–59, 243; and inte-
    gration of blacks, 163–64, 168–69,
    172–78, 187–89, 217, 240, 268; and
    Little Rock Central High School
    crisis, 190–93, 195–204, 207–22,
    224–32, 233, 238–39, 263, 348–62, 369;
    mansion in Huntsville, Ark., 323, 325,
    330, 335, 338, 345; marriage to Alta
    Haskins, 50–51, 63–64, 71–74, 78–80,
    82, 100, *125*, 132, 289, 290, 291, 292,
    317, 325, 326, 329, 330; marriage to
    Elizabeth Westmoreland, 326, *327*,
    329–33, 335–36, 338, 339, 341–44;

marriage to Janice Wittenburg, 344–45, *346*, 347–48; and "midnight pay raise," 312–13; 1954 campaign for governor, 75, *76*, 83–85, 91–99, 116–27, 129–33; 1956 campaign for governor, 180; 1958 campaign for governor, 242–44; 1960 campaign for governor, 285–88; 1962 campaign for governor, 291–93; 1964 campaign for governor, 295–304; 1970 campaign for governor, *331*; 1974 campaign for governor, 33, *366*; 1986 campaign for governor, 344; opposition to Communist party, 271–74; position on gambling in Hot Springs, 318–20; proponent of property tax reform, 139, 146, 156–57, 169; publication of memoirs, 339, 344; pupil-assignment plan, 177–78, 180; relationship with son, Farrell, 79–80, *82*, 187, 326, 332; religious background, 17–21, 71; school-closing legislation, 245–47, 251, 253–56, 266; school-teacher, 48–53, 63–65, 70, 72, 73, 100, 110; and Socialist party, 37–38, 68–69, 113–14; and southern resistance to integration, x–xi; upgrade of state's roads, 308; and WWII, 78–80, 127, 168, 169, 326

Faubus, Sam. See John Samuel Faubus

Faubus, Thomas, 10

Faubus, William Henry, 11

Fayetteville, Ark., 9, 32, 34, 78, 99, 135, 140, 182, 233, 260, 266, 267, 280, 323, 336; *Northwest Arkansas Times,* 168; first southern town to integrate following *Brown,* 168, 230; University of Arkansas, 157, 168

Federal Bureau of Investigation (FBI), 178, 194, 198, 199, 208, 212, 213, 217, 222, 226, 235, 257, 271, 280, 281, 319

Felton, Dan, 243

Finger, Charles, 107

Finger, Helen, 107

Finkbeiner, Chris, 242

First National Bank of Huntsville, 338

First National City Bank (New York), 146

Fisher, George, 305, 306, 323, 324, 347

Fitch, Rolla, 85, 136, 146, 308

Fletcher, John Gould, 253

Fletcher, W. E. "Buck," 135

Flippin, Ark., 32

Folsom, James E., ix, 165

Ford, Gerald, 335

Ford, J. H., 30

Forrest City, Ark., 139, 177

Forrest Heights Junior High School, 277

Fort Smith, Ark., 34, 35, 112, 140, 187, 193, 194, 195, 196, 260, 292, 319

Fortnightly, 92, 95, 107

Foster, Bill, Jr., 223

Foster, Joe, 223

Fourteenth Amendment, 354

Frankel, Arthur G., 199

Freedom Riders, 269

Frisco Railroad, 47

Fulbright, J. W., 107, 122, *152,* 153, 168, 230, 235, 272, 273, 288, 289, 290, 322, 329, 333, 356, 357

Fulbright, Roberta, 168

Fulks, Clay, 39, 99

Fuller, Claude, 36

Futrell, J. M., 155

gambling, 126, 315–20

Garfield, Ark., 32

Garland Fund, 101

Garrett, Howard, 69

Gathings, E. C. (Took), 263

Gentry, Leffel, 92

George, Lloyd, 141

Goldwater, Barry, 303

Good Hope, Ark., 63

Gore, Al, 153

Governor's Advisory Committee on Education, 155

Grady, Ark., 285

Greasy Creek, 63, 65, 68, 70, 72, 73, 110, 347; birthplace of OEF, 3, 6; in early 1900s, 7, 14–23, 51–58; Faubus family home, *31;* and socialism, 25–40

Great Decisions, 282

Great Depression, 56, 57, 99, 111–12, 134, 155

Green, Ernest, 235, 261

Green, O. T., 28–29, 39, 58

Greenwood School, 6, 17, 32, 43, 51, 63, 64, 72

Greers Ferry Dam, 269, 271

Griffin, Marvin, 174, 196–97, 198, 214

Griswold, Nat, 277

Guardian, 28, 67
Guthridge, Amis, 172, 187–88, 189–90, 195,
    200, 203, 242, 243, 246, 262

Hall, C. G. (Crip), 120
Hall High School, 187, 225, 256
Hampton, Ark., 162
Hansen, William W., 280
Hardin, Joseph C., 284, 285, 287, 289
Harding College, 273
Hardy, Ark., 32
Harkey, John Norman, 310
Harriman, Job, 101
Harris, Dane, 318
Harris, Oren, 249, 263
Harris, Roy V., 174, 197, 214
Harrison, Ark., 32, 125, 329, 336
Haskins, Alta. See Alta Haskins Faubus
Haskins, J. C., 50
Hastings, Harry, Sr., 292, 318
Hawkins, Marlin, 130, 248, 249, 251, 295
Hays, Arthur Garfield, 106
Hays, Brooks, 217, *218,* 219, 220, 221, 231,
    242, 243, 246–49, 251, 357
Hays, Lee, 101–2, 107
Hazen, Ark., 268
Head Start program, 329
Helena, Ark., 223
Helfond, David Scott, 343, 344
Helms, Jesse, 360
Heiskell, J. N., 166, *167,* 204–5, 252
Hendrix College, 166
Hensley, Lee, 313
Herblock, 251
Highlander Folk School, 284
Hill, Jane Lee, 209
Hinkle, Carl, 266
Hinton, Walter L., Jr., 146
Hiss, Alger, 75
Hobson, O. J., 85
Hobbs, Harlan S., 253
Hoedemaker, Pete, 102
Hogan, Julian, 136
Hollensworth, Carroll C., 135
Hoover, J. Edgar, 221, 271
Hope, Ark., 281

Hot Springs, Ark., 34, 38, 84, 170, 274, 288,
    292, 295, 301, 315, 318, 319, 320; illegal
    gambling in, 126; Oaklawn horse track,
    130, 147, 150, 151
Hot Springs Rubdown, 170
Hot Town, 315. See Hot Springs
House, Archie F., 194, 198, 200
House Special Elections Committee, 249
How I Stole Elections, 130, 248
Hoxie, Ark., 35, 194, 198, 212, 233, 296, 355;
    school integration crisis, 172–74, 176,
    195, 231
Hughes, Ark., 177
Hughes, Charles Evan, 353
Humphrey, Hubert H., 303
Hunt, H. L., 272
Hunt, Will, 5
Huntsville, Ark., 32, 46, 49, 60, 71, 78, 80, 85,
    120, 132, 136, 161, 187, 332, 333, 336, 339,
    340, 342, 344; OEF's home on Governor's
    Hill, 323, 325, 330, 335, 338, 345
Huntsville State Vocation School, 73
Huttig, Ark., 216

Industrial Workers of the World, 33, 36
Ingram, W. B. "Bill," 150
Ink, Ark., 101
Internal Revenue Service, 262

Jackson, Carl, 205
Jackson, Jesse, 345
Jerome, Ark., 152
"Jimmie Higgins," 21, 33
Johnson, Anderson, 36
Johnson, Arthur, 48
Johnson, James (Jim), x, 188, 189, 192–93,
    196, 202, 203, 205, 207, 213, 222, 240,
    244, 247, 269, 291, 297, 349, 359, 365,
    367; 1956 campaign for governor,
    169–70, *171,* 172–73, 175–81
Johnson, Jess, 36
Johnson, Lyndon B., 153, 263, 303, 325, 345
Johnson, Minnie Joslin, 36, 42, 44, 63
Johnson, Tom, 36
Jones, Clint, 310
Jones, C. H., 185
Jones, E. Fay, 323, 325

Jones, Guy "Mutt," 87, 88, 118, 199, 136, 297
Jonesboro, Ark., 84, 88, 172, 173, 192, 260, 291
Joslin, Sarah Thornberry, 44
Joslin, Tom, 15

Kaplan, David, 102
Karam, Jimmy, 122, 123, 179–80, 190, *191*, 226–27
Kefauver, Estes, ix
Kennedy, John F., xi, 231, 249, 263, 269, *270*, 271, 325, 349
Kennedy, Jon, 157
Kennedy, Robert F., 269
Kensett, Ark., 347
Kilpatrick, James J., 174–75, 354
King, Martin Luther, Jr., 181, 182, 235, 266, 272, 349
Kingston, Ark., 32
Koch, Charlotte Moskowitz, 103, 107
Koch, Lucien, 102, 104, 107, 110–11, 112, 115
Kolb, A. C., 157–58
Kolb, Payton, 158–59
Ku Klux Klan, 157, 162, 182, 266, 281, 367–68

Ladd, Earl, 90
Lake Village, Ark., 190, 267
Laman, William F. (Casey), 243–44
Lamb, Ted, 127
Laney, Ben, 135, 158, 174, 176
Lauderdale, E. A., 257
Leflar, Robert A., 107
Leche, Richard W., 322
Leachville, Ark., 135, 157
League of Women Voters, 295
Ledford, Rev. Alonzo, 49
Lemaster, Bob, 57
Lemley, Harry J., 244
Lepanto, Ark., 140
Leslie, Ark., 32
Liberty Bond vigilantes, 34
Liberty Loan scheme, 34
Life-Line Foundation, Inc., 272
Life magazine, 172, 214
Lile, R. A., 203, 253
Lincoln, Ark., 74, 100
Lindsey, Herman, 202, 212, 215, 276, 283, 284

Lippmann, Walter, 360
Little Rock, Ark., 29, 75, 83–87, 91, 94, 104, 122, 123, 126–27, 130–33, 138, 141, 151, 159, 166, 172, 175, 176, 178, 242, 252, 253, 266–67, 268, 281, 282, 295, 304, 318–20, 332, 339, 341, 342, 344, 355, 365, 368; resistance to school integration, x–xi, 182–94, 196–239, 245–46, 257
Little Rock Central High School, x, 244, 252, 256–60, 275, 281, 303; resistance to integration, 182–94, 261; school crisis, 190–93, 195–204, 207–22, 224–32, 233, 238–39, 245, 263, 348–62, 369
Little Rock Fire Department, 224
Little Rock Police Department, 224–27
Little Rock School Board, 177, 187, 194, 200, 212, 246–47, 252, 254–55, 349, 353, 355, 358, 359
Livestock and Poultry Commission, 308
Livingston, Fred, Jr., 289
Llano Cooperative Colony, 101
Lodge, Henry Cabot, 219
Long, Earl K., 147, 152, *160*, 165
Long, Huey P., xi, 111, 153, 285, 321, 367
Longshoremen's Union, 102
Lonoke, Ark., 135
Lorch, Grace, 238
Lorch, Lee, 238
Lost Valley, Ark., 328
Lynn, Jack, 145

Machinists Union, 102
Mack-Blackwell Amendment, 242
Madison County, Ark., 15, 50, 63, 66–68, 77–78, 80, 84, 86, 124, 131, 161, 168, 304; birthplace of OEF, 6; economic conditions of, in 1900s, 14, 29, 31, 32, 37, 39, 56–60, 99; in 1800s, 9–11, 55
Madison County Election Committee, 304
Madison County Record, 33, 39, 69, 80, 325, 326, 338, 365; bought by OEF, 81; letter from Bonnie to Sam Faubus, published in, 24; and Sam Faubus's essays on socialism, 33
Madden, Owney, 319
Maddox, Lester, ix
Magnolia, Ark., 140
Magreedy, 363

Malone, Jim, Jr., 119–20, 123, 162, 163, 329
Malvern, Ark., 34, 266
Mann, Woodrow, 231, 235
Marianna, Ark., 178
Marion Hotel (Little Rock), 85, 169, 197, 222, 227, 239
Marked Tree, Ark., 110, 111
Marshall, John, 354
Marshall, Thurgood, 216
Marxism, 39
Matthews, K., 311
McCarthy, Joseph R., 77, 116, 117, 122, 133, 142, 272
McClellan, John L., 85, 88, 116, 122, 262, 269, 270, 288, 303
McClerkin, Hayes, 330
McCulloch, Richard B., 177, 189
McDougal, Jim, 297
McGehee, Ark., 217
McGill, Ralph, 239, 360
McGowen, June, 342
McLaughlin, Leo P., 126, 316
McMath, Sidney, 119, 121, 136, 150, 151, 156, 166, 176, 189, 203, 221, 231, 242, 261, 289, 291, 292, 293, 316, 318; and the highway commission, 129; 1948 campaign for governor, 81, 84; 1952 campaign for governor, 86–88; 1954 campaign for governor, 90–93, 122, 126, 127, 142
McMillan, Gus, 87
Meadors Hotel (Combs, Ark.), 44
Mehaffy, Smith, and Williams law firm, 150, 151
Melton, Marvin, 291
Mena, Ark., 100, 115, 139; home of Commonwealth college, 92, 93, 94, 99, 101, 103, 104, 105, 118, 121
Mencken, H. L., 102, 106
Methodist Federation for Social Service, 102
Mill Creek (Madison County, Ark.), 11, 100, 110
Mill Creek Local, 30, 32, 38
Miller, John E., 193–95, 196, 198, 199, 200, 311
Miller, Marcus, 104
Mills, Wilbur D., 249, 263, 288, 290, 347
Millsap, Hal, Jr., 285

Milum, Roy, 135
Milwee, Minor W., 240, 243
Missouri Pacific Railroad, 75
Mississippi River Fuel Company, 146
Mississippi Sovereignty Commission, 272
Mitchell, H. L., 110
Mix, Clyde, 38
Monticello, Ark., 178
Morrilton, Ark., 248, 295
Moses, C. Hamilton, 204
Mother Jones, 27
Mothers League, 188, 193, 199, 225, 226, 279
Mount Ida, Ark., 140
Mount Magazine State Park, 139, 141
Mountain Home, Ark., 180
Mountain View, Ark., 98
Mulberry, Ark., 32
Mullins, David, 266
Murphy, Isaac, 323

National Association for the Advancement of Colored People (NAACP), xi, 162, 163, 172, 177, 185, 194, 212, 216, 233, 245, 261, 277
National Guard. See Arkansas National Guard
Nelson, Howard, 58
Nelson, John, 14, 15
Nelson, Knox, 149
New Deal, 39, 99, 364
New York Times, 28, 108, 213, 281, 348, 362
Newell, Frank, 122
Newport, Ark., 93
Newsom, Eugene F., 176
Nixon, Richard M., 44, 75, 219, 221, 249, 335, 355, 368
Noe, James A., 298
North Little Rock, Ark., 140, 187, 226, 238, 243, 262, 265
North Little Rock Times, 305, 306, 324

Oaklawn, 130, 147, 150, 151, 325
Office of Veterans' Affairs, 339
Ogden, Dunbar, 238–39
O'Hare, Frank, 101
O'Hare, Kate, 101
Oklahoma City Daily Oklahoman, 28

Old Line Insurance Company, 131
101st Airborne, 229, 252
Oswald, Harry, 144
Ozark, Ark., 11, 32, 187, 215
Ozark Spectator, 215

Paragould, Ark., 34, 163, 242
Parker, Carl, 104, 105
Parker, T. D. "Tod," 49
Parkin, Ark., 149
Parkin, Harry, 145, 323
Patterson, Hugh B., Jr., 156, 203–5
Penix, Bill, 173
"Pension for Pals," 312
Petit Jean Mountain, 140, 279, 295, 298
Perez, Leander, ix
Perryville, Ark., 91
Percy, Walker, 321
Pine Bluff, Ark., 123, 140, 149, 178, 242, 243,
    293
Pine Bluff Citizen's Committee, 280
Pine Bluff Commercial, 282, 325
Pinnacle (Madison County, Ark.), 36, 50, 53,
    49, 50, 53, 63, 72, 94, 100, 110
Plessy v. Ferguson, 176, 354
Pocahontas, Ark., 180
Populist party, in late 1800s, 26–27
Pound, Ezra, 103
Powell, James O., 263
Powell, Velma, 253
Prairie Grove, Ark., 74
prison farm system, 313
Progress, 322
Pruden, Wesley, 187, 189, 190, 225
Pryor, David H., 92, 321, 333, 335
public service commission, 86, 134, 148, 261
Pulaski Heights, Little Rock, 185, 277, 279
Purcell, Joe, 311, 329
Putnam, Carlton, 268

Queen Wilhelmina State Park, 139

Race and Reason, 268
Rainach, Willie, 268
Randolph, Vance, 107
Raney, Dallas P. "Pete," 145, 266, 267, 323, 347

Raney High School, 245–46, 255–56
Rayburn, Sam, 153, 249, 263
Reagan, Ronald, 335
Rector, William F., 196, 240
Reed, Murray O., 198, 199
Reed, Robert M., 59
Remmel, Pratt, 131, 132
Reynolds Aluminum Co., 148
Reynolds, Newt, 49
Riley, Bob, 333
Richmond News-Leader, 174
Rison, Ark., 300
Rockefeller, Barbara (BoBo) Sears, 298
Rockefeller, Laurence, 301
Rockefeller, Nelson, 303
Rockefeller, Winthrop, 169, 172, 180, 186,
    203, 267, 278, 291, 295, 297–304, *302,*
    308, 310–11, 314, 319–21, 323, 326, 330;
    chairman of the AIDC, 139, 140, 214
Rogers, Ark., 32
Rogers, William P., 196, 197, 231, 235, 244, 356
Roosevelt, Franklin D., 33, 99, 214, 322;
    administration of, 39, 63, 111
Rorex, Sam, 247
Rose Firm, 194
Rosenberg, Edith, 77
Rosenberg, Julius, 77
Rozzell, Forrest, 279, 304
Rural Electrification Administration, 17,
    51–52, 86; dispute with AP and L over
    territorial allocations, 142, 144
Russell, Richard B., 153, 166, 174

Salcido, Bonnie Faubus, 17, *18,* 36, 46, 239;
    childhood, 23–24; family picture, *41;* as
    pupil of OEF, 63–64, 65
Sam Peck Hotel, Little Rock, 85
Sandberg, Sam, 37
Sapp, William, 345
Scopes, John T., 19
School on Wheels, 114
Seamprufe, Inc., 214
Searcy, Ark., 129, 140
Securities and Exchange Commission, 127,
    128, 310
Sedberry, Anita, 225
seed and feed tax, 135

Seeger, Pete, 102
Shaver, James L. "Bex," 135, 138, 177
Sheridan, Ark., 87
Sherman, Harold, 98
Sherman, O. L., 243, 304
Shivers, Allan, 181, 186
Shuster, Freeman, 342
Sikes, Arnold, 136, 138, 146
Siloam Springs, Ark., 285
Simmons, James, 32
Sin City, 315. See Hot Springs
Sinclair, Upton, 103, 108
Smith, Don, 310
Smith, Charles "Rip," 135
Smith, Gene, 224, 256–57, *258, 259*
Smith, Gerald L. K., 265, 332, 333, *334*
Smith, Maurice Sr., 90, 91
Smith, Will, 190
Smith, William J., 88, 92, 136, *137,* 138, 196,
    199, 200, 240, 260, 261, 295, 297, 311,
    322–23
Snoddy, Jim, 178
socialism, in Arkansas, 25–40
Socialist party, 99, 106; and Commonwealth
    College, 100–102; and Sam Faubus, 7,
    25–40, 67–70
Southern Baptist College, 285
Southern Club, 320
Southern Manifesto, 166, 263, 349, 356, 357
Southern Mediator Journal, 185
Southern Regional Council, 274, 277
Southern Tenant Farmers Union, 110–11, 162
Spa, the, 315. See Hot Springs
Sparks, Eli, 11, 27–28, 59
Sparks, Malinda (Lindy). See Malinda Sparks
    Faubus
Special Committee on Un-American
    Activities, 116
Sprick, Dan, 283
Springdale, Ark., 34, 281
St. Joe, Ark., 32
St. Paul, Ark., 35, 36, 37, 59, 73, 293, 295;
    early settlers of, 10–11
St. Paul Mountain Air, 35
Standard Oil, 299
state audit commission, 142
state labor commission, 136, 202

state racing commission, 150–51
state sovereignty commission, 186, 188
state supreme court, 240; fair field pricing
    ruling of oil and gas interests, 148–49
States' Rights party, 265, 268
Stephens, Dan, 313
Stephens, Jack, 305, 339
Stephens, W. R "Witt," 83, 85, 127, *128,* 129,
    130, 145–49, 153, 189, 242, 271, 285, 290,
    291, 292, 297, 305, 322, 323, 325, 332,
    333, 335, 345; purchase of ARKLA, 131,
    134, 144
Stevenson, Adlai, 121, *152*
Stop This Outrageous Purge (STOP), 255, 262
Story, Frank A., 136
Stranahan, Kneeland, 102
Stranahan, Lois, 102
Student Non-Violent Coordinating
    Committee, 280, 282
Sturgis, Mack, 247, 255, 308, 312
Sulphur Springs, Ark., 32
Summers, Luther D., 115, 116
Sutton, Ozell, 216
Swaim, Curtis R., 37, 38

T. J. Raney High School, 245–46, 255–56
Tackett, Boyd, 92, 118, 119
Terry, Adolphine Fletcher, 203, 239, 247,
    253–55
Terry, David D., 247
Texarkana, Ark., 92, 122
Thomas, Herbert L., Sr., 253
Thomas, Norman, 106
Thomason, Mrs. Clyde A., 199, 226
Thompson, J. C., 29, 38, 68
Thornberry, Minerva (Minnie) Cornett, 59
Thornberry, Owen, 59
Thornberry, Sarah, 15
Thornberry, Sherman, 57–58
Thornbrough, Clarence T., 136, 202
Thurmond, Strom, ix, 170, 246, 289, 356, 360
Time magazine, 214
Times (of London), 214
Trimble, James W. (Jim), 80, 84, 328, 357
Troutt, Robert, 301
Trudeau, Arthur G., 133
Truman, Harry S., x, 116, 166, 203, 212

Tucker, Connie Faubus, *18, 41,* 44, 45
Tucker Prison, 313, 314
"Tucker telephone," 314
Tuckerman, Ark., 75, 93
Typographical Union, 136
Tyronza, Ark., 110

Union National Bank of Little Rock, 338
United Klans of America, 266
United Radio and Electrical Workers
 Union, 102
University Medical Center, 138
University of Arkansas, 34, 166, 168, 261, 266
University of Arkansas at Pine Bluff, 280
University of Arkansas College of Medicine,
 277
Upton, Wayne, 195, 196, 199
Urban League, 190, 227, 277
U.S. Court of Appeals for the Eighth
 Circuit, 193, 235
U.S. Department of Justice, 173, 194, 196,
 197–98, 212, 217, 220, 231, 235, 244, 269,
 319, 355–56
U.S. Forest Service, 345
U.S. Supreme Court, 77, 102, 194, 209, 271,
 349, 352–53; Act 10, 261–62; and *Brown
 v. Board of Education,* x, 60, 164, 168–69,
 181, 188, 216, 219, 354, 356–57; *Cooper v.
 Aaron,* 235, 353; enforcement of desegregation ruling, 193–96, 204; fair field
 pricing ruling of oil and gas interests,
 148; massive resistance to desegregation
 ruling, 164–66, 170, 172–73, 175–78, 179,
 181–82, 184
U.S. Treasury Department, 281

Van Buren, Ark., 32
Van Dalsem, Paul, 91, 130, 135, 157, 158, 159,
 247, 310, 311, 347
Vanlandingham, Carl, 36, 94
Vardaman, James K., 34, 153, 367
Veterans' Hospital, 265
Voting Rights Bill of 1965, 273

Wade, Clifton "Deacon," 135
Waldron, Ark., 140
Walker, Edwin A., 229
Walker, Wyatt Tee, 266–67

Wallace, George C., xi, *264,* 335, 365–69
Walnut Ridge, Ark., 135, 285
Walls, Carlotta, 259
Walther, Glenn F., 135
Ward, Lee, 242
War Memorial Stadium, 132
Warren, Ark., 179, 223
Warren, Earl, 215, 219, 354
Washington Post, 251, 320, 362
Watkins, David, 281
Watson, Tom, 367
Ways and Means Committee, 249
Weaver, Floyd, 229
Welch, Colin, 360
Wells, Bill, 330
Wells, John A., 75, 91–95, 105, 118, 122, 133,
 252, 268
Wenatchie Daily World, 36
West Helena, Ark., 34, 223
West Memphis, Ark., 135, 138, 150, 217
Westbrook, Parker, 263
Westmoreland, Elizabeth Drake Thompson.
 See Elizabeth Westmoreland Faubus
Westmoreland, Ric, 338, 344
Whelchel, Y. W., 312
White Citizens Council of America, 165,
 170, 174, 177
White Citizens Council of Arkansas, 170
White, Clay, 319
White, Frank, 339, 342
Whitehead, Clarence, 226
Whitewater, 321
Whittemore, Carol, 338
Whitten, Vernon H., 293
Williams, H. E., 285, 287
Wilson, Alex, *228*
Wilson, Woodrow, 34
Winburn Tile Company of Little Rock, 325
Winslow, Ark., 32
Wittenburg, Janice Hines. See Janice Hines
 Wittenberg Faubus
Witter, Ark., 32
Wobblies, 36, 40
Women's Emergency Committee to Open
 Our Schools, 254, 278
Woods, Henry, 119, 122–23, 189, 231
Woodward, C. Vann, 121

Works Progress Administration, 63
World Peace League, 34
Wynne, Ark., 177

Yale Lock Company, 139
Yellerhammer, Ark., 63
Yellville, Ark., 32
Young Democrats, 267

Zeuch, William E., 101